KV-637-819

# Human Development in the Life Course

Drawing on philosophy, the history of psychology and the natural sciences, this book proposes a new theoretical foundation for the psychology of the life course. It features the study of unique individual life courses in their social and cultural environment, combining the perspectives of developmental and sociocultural psychology, psychotherapy, learning sciences and geronto-psychology. In particular, the book highlights semiotic processes, specific to human development, that allow us to draw upon past experiences, to choose among alternatives and to plan our futures. Imagination is an important outcome of semiotic processes and enables us to deal with daily constraints and transitions, and promotes the transformation of social representation and symbolic systems – giving each person a unique style, or 'melody', of living. The book concludes by questioning the methodology and epistemology of current life course studies.

TANIA ZITTOUN is a Professor of Psychology and Education at the University of Neuchâtel, Switzerland.

JAAN VALSINER is a Professor of Psychology at Clark University.

DANKERT VEDELER is Associate Professor Emeritus at the Norwegian University of Science and Technology (NTNU).

JOÃO SALGADO is Assistant Professor and the Head of the Department of Social and Behavioural Sciences at the Maia Institute of Higher Education (ISMAI), Portugal.

MIGUEL M. GONÇALVES is a Professor of Psychology at the School of Psychology in the University of Minho, Portugal.

DIETER FERRING is Professor of Developmental Psychology and Psychogerontology at the University of Luxembourg.

# Human Development in the Life Course

*Melodies of Living*

---

Tania Zittoun

*(Université de Neuchâtel, Switzerland)*

Jaan Valsiner

*(Clark University, USA)*

Dankert Vedeler

*(NTNU-Norway)*

João Salgado

*(ISMAI-Portugal)*

Miguel M. Gonçalves

*(Universidade do Minho, Portugal)*

Dieter Ferring

*(University of Luxembourg)*

CAMBRIDGE
UNIVERSITY PRESS

**CAMBRIDGE**
**UNIVERSITY PRESS**

University Printing House, Cambridge CB2 8BS, United Kingdom

Published in the United States of America by Cambridge University Press, New York

Cambridge University Press is part of the University of Cambridge.

It furthers the University's mission by disseminating knowledge in the pursuit of education, learning, and research at the highest international levels of excellence.

www.cambridge.org
Information on this title: www.cambridge.org/9780521769389



First published 2013

Printed in the United Kingdom by T. J. International Ltd, Padstow

*A catalogue record for this publication is available from the British Library*

*Library of Congress Cataloguing in Publication data*
Zittoun, Tania.
Human development in the life course : melodies of living / Tania Zittoun (Universite de Neuchatel, Switzerland) [and five others].
pages cm
Includes bibliographical references and index.
ISBN 978-0-521-76938-9
1. Developmental psychology. I. Title.
BF713.Z58 2013
155–dc23 2013007949

ISBN 978-0-521-76938-9 Hardback

# Contents

# Figures

# Tables

# Boxes

# Preface: from dispute to collaboration

This book is the result of twelve hands writing. One of us (JV) invited the others to take part in an interesting experience of collective writing. Having a dinner together is a delicious starting point for collaboration. As with most interesting new projects, the writing of this book had its very beginning in the middle of a confusion of interactions during a Portuguese dinner in Porto in 2006, where one of the present authors (MG) denied that his current research work on psychotherapy had any direct links with developmental science, while another (JS) replied that it might have some, but they were not as explicit and full blown as a dynamic systems approach would probably imply – 'how is it possible to know if our perspective is developmental if we know so little about developmental science?' 'But you should know something about it', argued a third (DV), who started propagating dynamic systems approaches for elaborating on development within dialogical self theory. As the risk-taking opportunist that he always has been JV then solved the problem by suggesting that we find out in practice by writing a joint book on the developmental science of the human life course. For him, it seemed unreal that people who study adult psychotherapy processes – the very difficult processes that are to lead to further personal development – have anything other than a developmental approach. The others – somewhat disbelievingly – accepted the challenge. Soon the first quartet of adventurers to this new field of the study of adult development understood that they could not truly cover the human life course because of their lack of perspective on the dynamics of ruptures and the use of cultural resources in coping with these (which is the focus of TZ who then joined the team), and all of us were feeling totally lost when it came to understanding the very end of the life course (and DF joined to assist on this theme).

The process of the collective writing of one book was a developmental adventure in itself. Academics in any country are busy people, as they are increasingly dragged into administrative tasks and need to sit through many boring and inconclusive committee meetings that make them want to be elsewhere and have the freedom to do their work. That desire is usually frustrated by the unavoidable demand to be present at the next committee meeting. If one succumbs to such a mundane way of playing academic 'leadership roles', the senility of the mind is likely to arrive long before the senility of the body. This is why deservedly famous scientists often fail to produce new ideas after gaining prominent social positions. The tension between creative work and the obligations of social roles is a perennial problem for the academic life course. For the six of us, joint writing of this book was a 'window of opportunity' to at least temporarily resolve that tension in favour of creative effort.

Of course it was no easy task. Some of us were lucky enough to have the time and concentration to work quickly, others more slowly – and then the others became quick and the first ones slow. This somewhat un-coordinated heterochrony – at times leading to apologetic e-mails to one another for not getting promised parts finished on time – retained our understanding of one another's roles as constantly multi-tasking human beings. Understanding the Busy Other by being a Busy Self comes easily. In a sense, the writing of the book was itself a process of developmental emergence.

Most of the initial work was done at a distance. We decided the structure of the book through a series of 'pairs' meetings. We then distributed each chapter to those who were 'in charge' of it; we also decided, through a collective meeting, how each of us could contribute to chapters written by others. The inclusion of different voices often led us to substantially rewrite the chapters, or even to transform our understanding of what we were doing (if not of what development might be). Eventually, the book as a whole evolved through these dialogues, discussions, resolutions and questions left open.

Aside from dinners and e-mails, it is also productive to come together in the framework of workshops dedicated to a common goal. In the writing of this book this happened when almost all the separate pieces were prepared – in March 2010 – and in a place most fitting for such collective endeavour – the quiet campus of the University of Luxembourg at Walferdange.[1] What had been discovered in the course of working on the book at a distance – namely, that we could write it and that it was interesting to do so – was corroborated at the meeting of its authors. We felt good working on the joint goal – and our very different perspectives became mutually complementary. Collaboration entails mutual enrichment with ideas – many insights about elderly people began to fit the

[1] Our gratitude goes to the University of Luxembourg, and its INSIDE Programme, for making this meeting possible, and to Dieter Ferring and Lea Feltgen for setting it up in ways that worked very well for our task.

perspective of the dialogical self of mid-age psychotherapy patients, and even of infants.

During the meeting at Walferdange we discovered that *basic ideas of development are one* rather than many, divided artificially between different sub-areas of developmental psychology. Of course that idea has been put forward by others before – but rhetorical declarations cannot replace the immediate joint experience of feeling the beauty of working together, even while disagreeing on many issues. The disagreements are the resource for further development of ideas, while the emerging feeling of joint endeavour in the team of the authors is the condition that makes further development possible.

To summarize, this book is the result of a truly collaborative enquiry. It is based on the very deep assumption that thinking does not occur in a void, and that there is no such thing as a lonely thinker. Creation of new ideas always occurs in a specific context, through dialogues with present and absent others and, in the case of scientific writing, through dialogue with other texts and theories, as well with empirical facts and mundane observations.[2] A collectively written book is simply fully exploiting this observation, and trying to catalyse processes of emergence, by purposefully choosing the real others of the dialogue in which one engages.[3] Such a book is, in itself, a demonstration of what a sociocultural understanding of creativity may actually lead to do.

[2] Glaveanu (2010).

[3] On the dimension along which one can try to modulate the generation of collective work, see for instance Cornish, Zittoun and Gillespie (2007); Zittoun, Baucal, Cornish and Gillespie (2007).

# Introduction: melodies of living

Music is one of the main creations of human beings – they create it and live with it. Hence selecting the metaphor of a melody to be the core of our story of the human life course is not an accidental choice. Our lives are filled with melodies of various kinds and functions – ranging from the lullabies mothers sing to their babies to get them to sleep to the never-ending flow of Christmas carols played in pre-New Year shopping places, to our own individual humming of favourite melodies when involved in some mundane activity. The melodies of church bells, calls to prayer from the minarets of the mosques or marching bands leading public events are all examples of how deeply music saturates our lives.

Melodies have permanence. If you know the music of Elvis Presley, Bach, Robert Smith or Ray Charles, then you will recognize immediately, after a few notes, a new or unknown version of one of their pieces. If, on the other hand, you are familiar with visual art, you will recognize in any museum, and at first sight, a piece as a Matisse, a Rembrandt or a Bruce Neumann. We live in a world of patterns – musical or visual – that we have created out of the need to live our human lives.

Why is this so? Let us propose that it is a matter of *style* and of *motives*.[1] In the musical creations by Shostakovich, for example, there is a certain atmosphere, coming from the composer's time, his life in central Europe, his familiarity with traditional Moravian music as well as emerging jazz. Yet there are also, like a signature, little motives or musical phrases that appear, with all kinds of variation, in most of his pieces – a specific melody. Similarly, we identify people's writing, or we recognize old friends from afar because of their general silhouette or their way of moving. If there is something so unique in each person's externalization – their movements, paintings, expressions – than there is probably something unique, too, about their lives. And indeed, there is a unique way in which each of us lives through our life: how we understand it, what sorts of question we

[1] This idea is developed on the basis of Hans Thomae's work (1968).

face, how we interpret it, how we make our decisions. Of course, each of us changes through time: we move from one place to another, our body strength changes, we learn from experience and sometimes we decide never to act in the same way again. Yet – even so – there is a style to each life, and so there are motives that appear regularly, with more or less variation. This uniqueness, this property of each person as a whole, manifested in her ways of thinking or acting, speaking or moving – living – we propose to call her *melody*. *Human Development in the Life course: Melodies of Living* thus has the ambitious goal of giving one possible account of what makes people's life trajectories so unique, yet human in a shared world.

## Meaning-making and imagination in the centre

This book is written by a group of psychologists. Our goal is to describe the human life course: how people develop and change, and how their life trajectories come to be what they are. We are not the first to address this issue. Yet we have at heart to account for the uniqueness of human life – each person's melody.

We believe that to account for uniqueness, we have to show how people make sense of what happens to them. The specificity of our approach will thus be a strong emphasis on people's experiences of the world, and of their inner lives – of course, as might be understood on the basis of their externalization. In particular, we will be interested in how people come to understand their present and make sense of their actions and trajectories. Such understanding includes both real and unreal parts – people understand their current state of being, yet they selectively borrow from their past life experiences, and create imaginary scenarios for the future. Humans are 'social animals'– with the very special gift of giving their meaning-making a symbolic, or – as we shall subsequently write in this book – *semiotic*[2] expression, through which humans may communicate between themselves, sharing experiences and ideas and coordinating actions. Even though sharing direct experiences and coordinating actions are not dependent on semiosis, they are still considerably enhanced by semiotic communication. For example, sharing the experience of watching a soccer match does not entail the immediate semiotic creativity of the fan-filled stadium cheering for their teams – yet the whole meaningful context where such sharing of experience happens – the game, the symbolic honouring of 'key' players, game rules, etc. – are all semiotic

[2] Semiotics, the science of signs and symbols (from the Greek word σημειῶ, to mark).

constructs. This implies that the experience of watching a soccer game is always already given as social; yet, and this is our emphasis, how each person experiences that soccer game, what she may feel, think, or say or whether she decides to stay until the end of the match, clap her hands or leave the crowd, just depends on her own unique free choice or agentic power – and her ability to imagine what is beyond the immediately given.

Other animals are, of course, also able to coordinate themselves, but only the phylogenetic development of semiotic abilities allowed humans to develop culture (art and science), representations of the future or elaborated forms of coordination that can occur even in the absence of real people (e.g. through the internet).[3] Such complex semiotic abilites, coupled with the existence of cultural artefacts and semiotic systems inherited through generations, have enabled humans to develop a unique capacity for imagination. In effect, the internalization of signs will allow for inner dialogues, among which are dialogues with self, recall of memories and planning for the future and even constructing a mental reality: impossibilities in the outer world become possible and lived experiences. This inner life, synthesized through constructive *imagination*, plays an important role in our making meaning of our lives. It will receive particular attention in this book.

A person who imagines some future event is not doing something useless. Just the contrary – imagining potential future events makes it possible to strive towards them, or – in the case of adverse imaginary events – to try to avoid them. When imagination is orientated towards the future it becomes a project or an intention. In a similar vein, imagination can also be turned towards the past – and it is a memory. Memory is a reconstructive process – using imagination oriented towards the past to create meanings for the present. Hence imagination can be turned towards alternative experiences and life-worlds, real (happening in other social frames) or possible or impossible ones (as in fiction and daydreaming), and so it enriches the present and opens up new possibilities. Imagination in life is thus a constant process of expansion of the present, along three dimensions – time, space and degrees of reality.

How imagination expands the present and enhances life trajectories is also dependent on the life lived so far, and how much of it one assumes to be left. Hence, imagining the past or the future, moving through spheres of experience, does not have the same implications at ages seven and at seventy-seven. Accounting for this is our task as we propose to follow imagination over life-course trajectories.

[3] See the difference proposed by G. H. Mead (1934) between communication by gestures and communication through significant symbols.

## Traditional lifespan psychology and our proposition

There have been numerous accounts of people's life development. Many of them have started by describing typical life trajectories, and have then identified the processes that shaped them. Very often, the processes that were highlighted reflected current agendas in science – in education, health or well-being. Hence, to take the example of two important works, Erik Erikson's study of ruptures and stages proposed to identify people who 'failed' to become adults, or, on the other hand, people who were 'greater' than others;[4] Paul Baltes's proposition to study the core processes of the lifespan also distils the view that old age is an 'illness' in which one has to compensate for biological and functional losses to remain high functioning.[5] Baltes could see the realities of old age – while there may be a decline in physical functioning, there can simultaneously be an increase in general understanding of human life or wisdom. Many societies are known to rely upon the wisdom of elderly people – frail though they may be physically – in resolving local conflicts and granting justice to local communities.

Of course, there is an inherent moral dimension in any scientific project, and we cannot do without it. Our proposition is both very ambitious and – simultaneously – rather modest.

First, *we do not wish to describe typical trajectories*; we rather wish to convey an idea of how various ingredients that enable us to account for the incredible diversity of ways of life, in combination, and over time, make each life course a unique trajectory that requires to be understood on its own premises. Yet we are not naïve, and so we want to highlight the social and cultural, very often invisible constraints, that guide the ways in which people creatively unfold their lives.

Secondly, we wish to *identify core processes, along specific dimensions, which offer an entry into people's life trajectories in complex societies.*

Thirdly – if we have to make explicit our normative beliefs of what constitutes 'good development' or a 'good life'– we would probably say that this is a *life in which playfulness is experienced, and remains possible.*

History – especially recent European history – has seen politically driven, massive attempts to prevent people from developing their 'own melodies'; without similar repression, and beyond a discourse of 'everything is possible', our ultraliberal society exerts other pressures on how people carry on their lives. Understanding the interplay between social guidance – as enabling, yet constraining – and playful adaptation is one of

[4] For instance Erikson (1968, 1993b). [5] For instance Baltes (1997).

our goals. We will, furthermore, suggest that play is not only fun, but a serious principle for how we face the challenges of daily life, as well as the important crossroads in life. One important stance is that any event in the external world, including social guidance, will be experienced and understood against the background of personal history and how earlier experiences are made sense of. Therefore, any intentions of social others to guide a person are 'played with' and so modified; what is important is to examine how social guidance is received and dealt with.

## On what this enquiry is based

This book is the result of a shared activity of writing. It hopes to be an accessible theoretical exploration, offering an original perspective on developmental processes in the life course. Yet it has not grown out of nowhere; it implies a constant dialogue between four sources of knowledge. First, we draw on 'classic' authors – authors who are often considered as part of the 'history' of psychology and disregarded before the actual implications of their propositions have been fully understood. Here, we reread these authors and extract and expand important theoretical ideas, some of which have been overlooked, which can enrich and support our current exploration. Second, we draw on the theoretical reflection that each of the authors has developed in his or her field of expertise and we attempt to integrate these propositions. Third, we have been very attentive to daily experiences, people's accounts of their life choices, usual and surprising forms of life – and so we draw on many journalistic, literary or artistic accounts of people's lives as 'data' to exemplify and expand our reflections. And fourth, we also include current studies in various fields of psychology, for example, developmental, learning or social psychology, providing us with further, up-to-date factual or theoretical information. Yet to this needs to be added a fifth dimension – which is precisely given by the dialogical nature of this book, bringing each author to include his or her reflections on the expertise of the others or the material they have contributed. Within the framework given by the book, each author has quickly expanded his or her understanding and reflection, and so this book's fifth dimension is the added creativity triggered by its very making.

## Structure of the book

The book is organized by the very idea that human beings' life courses expand through sense-making along three dimensions – time, from the present to our past into the future, space, including the social, material and institutional framing of our experiences, and degrees of reality – or the gradual variations between what is experienced as real, imaginary or anything in between (what could be, what might perhaps happen, what will never happen). These three dimensions confer on the book its three-part structure. The first part of the book defines a theory of time to capture life courses. The second part theorizes the social spaces in which life courses unfold. The third part of the book considers the many ways in which humans can overcome the constraints of time and space, of temporality and social worlds.

The first part of the book emphasizes time. Chapter 1 brings to the fore a few basic theoretical ideas for a life-course psychology. It distinguishes between a view on development from the 'outside' – from a 'neutral' observer – which enables us to identify epigenetic processes as well as the dynamic, systemic nature of the life course, and an internal view, which accounts for semiotic processes – what enables human beings to make sense of what happens. Chapter 2 gives a phenomenological grounding to the first exploration and introduces the next chapters by giving various 'inside' accounts of what imagining one's life is, at various ages. Hence it appears that a five-year-old, a young adult or an older person all enter in a certain way in to a dialogue between what is and what could be, and was once and what might be. On this basis, Chapter 3 explores theoretically imagination and its link to memory. It also attempts to show how the expansion or the direction of memory and imagination may vary according to one's location in the life journey. Chapter 4 then proposes a theoretical model of time that might underlie our assumptions – the irreversibility of time – and findings – its flexibility.

The second part of the book then adds the spaces in which development occurs. Chapter 5 theoretically explores the nature of the 'social frames', or settings, in which people move over time. Chapter 6 explores the therapeutic framework as one type of social setting designed for change to happen. Learning sites are explored in Chapter 7 as another socially designed change-setting. Both settings have been the occasion of quite specialized analysis; bringing them together, as two variations of socially situated change, makes it possible to highlight processes of development and to expand our understanding of them.

This leads us to the third part of the book, which now considers time and space in combination with a third dimension: imagination. Chapter 8 indeed observes that as people move through a plurality of settings over time, they have to develop ways to maintain a sense of continuity, and also use the experience acquired in one framework in another. As imagination is what enables us to take distance and engage in transformation, it may thus play a key role in people's 'migrant' lives. Chapter 9 then explores the fundamental playfulness of life as a core process of change. Yet in Chapter 10 we are reminded that it is also through these imaginative processes that people are most likely to be guided, unknowingly, by the discourse and values available in a society. Finally, Chapter 11 concentrates these reflections around a specific aspect of life – that of getting older.

The idea running through the book is that, beyond the constraints of time and social worlds, people develop a unique life melody; and so the book invites us to consider the processes by which these melodies are created. This book, which opens a new enquiry, still remains without conclusion. However, in the epilogue, we highlight the results of our theoretical exploration; we also take a reflective stance, which leads us to say more about the method used in this book and the epistemological status of the knowledge produced, inviting us, it is hoped, to another way of doing science.

*Part I*

# Time for development

# 1 Solidity of science and fullness of living: a theoretical exposé

> Many years later, as he faced the firing squad, Colonel Aureliano Buendia was to remember that distant afternoon when his father took him to discover ice.
>
> Gabriel Garcia Marquez, *One Hundred Years of Solitude*, p. 11

Our lives are unique. There are no two persons in the world who can claim to have 'the same' life course – even twins are different as they proceed through life. The human life course consists of relative stability that is always related to change. Throughout life – experiencing new fascinating, upsetting, demanding or any other kinds of life event until the last day of life – be it on a sickbed or battlefield – we are in a sense the same while constantly changing in a changing world. And – by our being and acting in that world – we are agents who participate in its changing. We imagine the future – and selectively bring back the past. We often reconstruct the past in a way that ends up changing our future. Nostalgic – or happy, or heroic, or shameful – memories of the past, combined with desires for the future, come together in a kind of personal feeling of immersion in *life-as-it-flows-on*. This feeling overwhelms us – the grand melody of living. We may worry, complain, criticize others (and ourselves), be depressed or flow in ecstasy, act morally or become involved in all kinds of acts that others find indecent – yet we live, we create poetry and writings, we dedicate ourselves to important causes and so on. WE LIVE.

Our melodies flow out of all that we have experienced. They make us who we are, here and now, and let us face our futures. Our individual melody of living defines – and is defined by – our identity, lifestyle, ambitions and hopes for the future under more or less stable circumstances. Even when altered, such a melody mostly persists even through radical changes in life situation and even when I state 'that nothing will ever be the same' – there is still a core that recognizes myself as myself.

This uniqueness of our lives, captured by the poet Phillip Larkin[1] as 'the blind impress/All our behavings bear', will remain unique and distinctive.

How can we approach these obvious facts of our lives in a way that helps us understand the human condition? Novelists do it through creating fictional characters that remain with us as our life melodies encounter them. But how can science handle such a unique and subjective world of human living? How can we have a science – characterized by the abstract generalization of principles across inter-individual uniqueness – in the wide field of human habitat where the myriad of personal life melodies unfold?

Our enquiry is based on two assumptions that are necessary starting points for understanding human lives – the *irreversibility of time* and the *semiotic nature of making sense of our human experiences* – which have been systematically explored by two developing theoretical traditions: a developmental science and a sociocultural psychology. The challenge will be to define a science that accounts for the uniqueness of the individual person through a dialogue between these two traditions.

*The imperative for developmental science:* our first assumption is that any scientific account of the human life course needs to be developmental. *Development is the property of open systems to undergo transformations in qualitative forms, under constant relating to the environment, and within irreversible time.* This general definition fits all sciences – biology, psychology, anthropology, sociology – that deal with developmental phenomena.

*Developmental science* is a general perspective that is orientated towards the study of developmental processes. As was stated in the mid-1990s, it:

> refers to a fresh synthesis that has been generated to guide research in the social, psychological, and bio-behavioral disciplines. It describes a general orientation for linking concepts and findings of hitherto disparate areas of developmental inquiry, and it emphasizes the dynamic interplay of processes across time frames, levels of analysis, and contexts. Time and timing are central to this perspective. The time frames employed are relative to the lifetime of the phenomena to be understood. Units of focus can be as short as milliseconds, seconds, and minutes, or as long as years, decades, and millennia. In this perspective, the phenomena of individual functioning are viewed at multiple levels – from the subsystems of genetics, neurobiology, and hormones to those of families, social networks, communities, and cultures.[2]

This general developmental orientation is applicable to all systems that can be considered to develop – biological, social and even some physical[3]

[1] In the poem 'Continuing to Live', Larkin (1953).

[2] Carolina Consortium on Human Development (1996, p. 1).

[3] Astrophysics, for example, deals with the development of celestial objects – like stars and galaxies – which all are developing systems, that emerge, exist and decay.

systems. Undoubtedly, everything, from DNA and the order of each cell, to cultural experiences and global cultures, participates in the organization of human development. Thus general developmental principles also apply to human functioning.

*Human development as regulated by signs:* however, what makes the difference between the human species and other species is a condition that mediates everything from personal experiences to culture, through social communication: *the semiotic function.* Human beings create signs through which they organize and make sense of their subjective worlds all through their lives – and this is our second assumption.

Human beings are remarkable in turning their adaptation *to* the world into a form of pre-adaptation *of* the world to their expectations and needs – by constructing tools of different kinds. The tools to self-regulate the human mind are signs – we use them at every moment in our living, not even noticing their richness.

The use of signs – the *semiotic function*, by which we *substitute* 'things' by verbal symbols or other semiotic forms – enables us to manipulate the world beyond what *it is* at any given moment. We not only eat – as all animals do – we can refuse to eat if the nutrient offered to us is deemed to be inedible, or we can refuse to eat anything as a form of political protest – which would be nonsensical from a biological perspective. There may be a piece of meat in front of you – but we create multiple meanings of the nutrient ('a delicious *entrecôte*' – 'a part of a massacred animal') and of the very act of eating ('dinner in a French restaurant' or 'binge eating' or refusal to eat because of 'being vegetarian'). The implications of the semiotic function will be discussed throughout this book as we examine personal and social experiences, imagination, communication and narratives throughout the life course.

*Inside vs. outside views:* engaging in a scientific enquiry aiming at developing a theoretical view enabling a generalized understanding of human development, one quickly realizes a major epistemological problem. In effect, most of the social and natural sciences currently available to account for development and the social world, in search of 'objectivity', have proposed theories that consider individuals – as organisms, as social entities within a social field – so to say 'from the outside'. On the other hand, most attempts to capture people's work of sense-making have tried to capture subjectivity and people's perspective 'from the inside'. This divergence of perspectives is mainly due to theoretical traditions, methodological choices and the inertia of disciplinary boundaries. However, and without reopening classic debates, we will start from a third assumption: it is clear that we need to take into account social and biological processes usually described 'from the outside', as well as semiotic ones, usually described 'from the inside'. We thus will have to integrate these 'outside' and 'inside' views into one consistent conceptualization of the human life course.

## The outside view

The outside view on development is the external – 'objective'[4] – perspective of the natural scientist on the trajectories of human lives. It is a way of thinking about development abstractly, and it aims to conceptualize the many determining features that turn organisms into unique human beings. It is our ambition here to make it less abstract.

### *Epigenetics and epigenesis*

In the recent development of biological sciences the concept of *epigenetics* has become increasingly prominent. The concept was originally proposed by Conrad Hal Waddington[5] to account for cell differentiation that could not be accounted for by DNA regulation alone. 'Epigenetics' – since the 1930s – has been understood as the study of environmental influences on gene expression in the formation of cells. In recent years technical advances in molecular genetics research have revealed the existence of components of genes that are, on the one hand, determined by the gene, but on the other hand are modifiable by environmental influences. Such components are called *epigenetic marks* or markers.

Thus, genes are responsible for the properties and function of the cell – but not alone. They operate (gene expression) through the conditions of their immediate environmental settings – cellular environments. Whether or not a particular gene will be active in cell division will depend on the epigenetic marks of that gene in that cell. Thus the properties and function of the cell will depend on environmental influences. Consider that all cells in an organism carry the same genome, that is, the same set of DNA. Nevertheless, different groups of cells are highly specialized in the functioning of the organism. This specialization depends on different types of cells having different *epigenomes*, that is,

[4] The division we propose here does not strictly cover the classical division between what has been called an *etic* perspective in contrast to an *emic* perspective, after the proposition by Pike (1967) taken on by anthropologists.

[5] Waddington is known as the major promoter of the epigenetic theoretical framework (Waddington, 1975), see Figure 1.2 below. For a contemporary coverage of the perspective see Jablonka and Lamb (1995).

different sets of epigenetic markers, depending on different cellular environments.[6]

Research in epigenetics has furthermore evidenced that epigenetic markers may be inherited not only from parent to offspring cells in cell division, but also over generations, from parent to offspring organism. The discovery of epigenetic markers as regulators of gene expression, and the fact that they may be inherited, has not invalidated natural selection as a principle of evolution. However, it has become clear that genetic diversity is not random. Randomness can be a transitory state in the making – or breaking – of an organizational form. This has important consequences for understanding the relationship between nature and nurture. Even the genes are nurtured, that is, genes cannot function without an environment, which is, first and foremost, intracellular. But this intracellular environment is, in turn, dependent on the extracellular environment, and so on up in a hierarchy – as we will see.[7]

*Challenges to evolutionary theory:* this poses a challenge to mainstream evolutionary theory, for which genetic diversity is based on, in principle, random recombinations of genomes (e.g. through reproduction or through mutations). The theoretical basis for evolutionary theory – the 'modern evolutionary synthesis' – combined Darwin's principle of natural selection with Mendelian genetics, thus firmly denying any influence of individual adaptation on population genetics, and thereby also opposing Darwin to his contemporary, Jean-Baptiste Lamarck,[8] who proposed the idea of inheritance of acquired characteristics.[9] Since the 1960s genetics

[6] Stem cells, on the other hand, are undifferentiated, and able to constitute different epigenomes, depending on the environment in which they develop. For an up-to-date view on contemporary epigenetics, see special section in *Science*, 2010, vol. 330, pp. 611–30 (29 October).

[7] As Günter Wagner (2004, p. 1405) has succinctly summarized: 'The only proper word we have for what is going on in biology is interaction. Interaction means that the effect of a factor depends on many other so-called factors, and the dependency on context ensures that the explanatory currency drawn from measuring the effects of causal factors is very limited.'

[8] Lamarck (1809).

[9] However, Darwin, whom evolutionary theory claims as its originator, was himself not opposed to Lamarck's ideas. It was in the later disputes about issues of development that the contrast between Darwin and Lamarck crystallized. In fact, our contemporary protein genetics since the 1960s (emphasizing the role of different kinds of RNA in both protein synthesis and in limited reverse transcription of DNA) prove Lamarck's basic premises to be quite adequate. The dynamic system of folding (and unfolding) of protein structures demonstrates selective openness to environmental guidance. The focus on cell membrane as a productive boundary illustrates such a conditional-environmental role in organism function (Wickner and Scheckman, 2005). The new focus on prions in biology makes the study of the inheriting of environmentally modified characteristics a new frontier of science (Halfmann and Lindquist, 2010).

has undergone major changes discovering, among other things, the principles of gene-protein reconstruction that transcend the axioms of population genetics. The epigenetic perspective, as well as a new look at Lamarck's ideas from two centuries back, is the result of these new findings.

This consideration makes us turn from epigenetics to *epigenesis*. *Epigenesis* is an older concept, which in the eighteenth century opposed the then predominant idea of *preformation*, according to which the egg or the foetus consisted of a fully formed organism, only minuscule, that simply needed to become bigger in order to be grown up. Opposed to this conception, *epigenesis* then meant the development of the organism through successive cell differentiation. With the discovery of DNA the epigenesis of an organism was understood as the implementation of a 'program' for its construction. Hence, epigenesis was first understood as the relationship between genes and the organism as a predetermination that had its origin in the genes.[10]

*Probabilistic epigenesis:* while 'traditional' epigenesis implied that development was preprogammed, or predetermined, Gilbert Gottlieb (see Box 1.1) proposed *probabilistic epigenesis*, thus advocating the view that ontogenesis is not determined solely by the genes, or by a weighted combination of gene and environment.[11] He refers to a vast array of recent research supporting well-established theory and concludes that development is a result of gene–environment interaction on all levels of organism functioning:

> in developmental biology the ubiquitousness of interaction is taken for granted and extends to the activation of genetic activity by nongenetic influences, not just the formative influences of cell–cell, tissue–tissue, and organ–organ interactions. It makes good sense to extend this point of view to developmental psychobiology and, with some added refinements, that is what the author has been attempting to do with the metatheoretical model called *probabilistic epigenesis*.[12]

Gottlieb proposed a hierarchical model for levels of mutual influences on the functioning of a human organism, from chemical processes at the genetic level to culture, in which it appears that genetic processes are

[10] This relationship – in traditional terms – is that between the genotype and the phenotype. The genotype is the genetic set up of an organism, that is, the same DNA assembly (=genome) that can be found in all the cells of an individual organism. The phenotype was considered to be the necessary result of the expression of the particular genotype, that is, the whole living organism, with all the characteristics that have emanated from the genotype.

[11] Gottlieb (2003, 2007). For an overview of research findings see Lickliter and Honeycutt (2010).

[12] Gottlieb (2007, p. 1).

### Box 1.1 Gilbert Gottlieb – the originator of the idea of *probabilistic epigenesis*

Gilbert Gottlieb (1929–2006) was the leading researcher of developmental science in USA in the second half of the twentieth century. His main work was accomplished in the study of epigenetic processes in the ontogeny of duck embryos and new hatchlings – demonstrating experimentally how the usually assumed phenomena of *imprinting* in birds are actually created by a step-by-step epigenetic process.[13] Here the behaviour – of the vocal communication between the mother duck and the not yet hatched offspring – constrains the behaviour of the young hatchlings as they leave the nest and start to follow the mother duck in the natural environment. Later in his life, Gottlieb took particular interest in the ways in which the genome is regulated by the conditions of the environment – developing the theory of behavioural neophenogenesis.[14] He was one of the key scholars who established developmental science in the 1990s at the Center for Developmental Science of the University of North Carolina at Chapel Hill.[15]

[13] Gottlieb (1971, 1999). [14] Gottlieb (2002).
[15] Carolina Consortium of Human Development (1996).

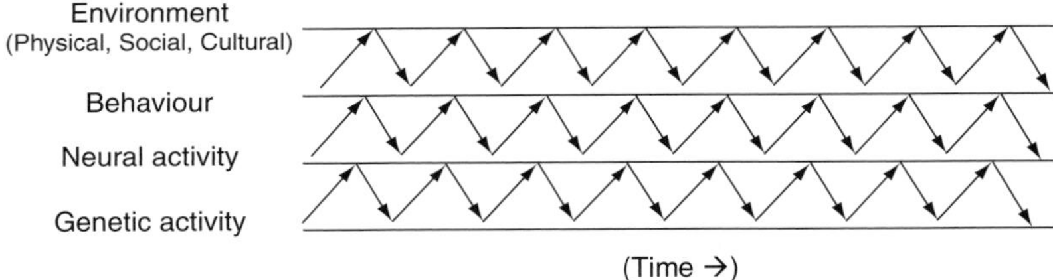


Figure 1.1 Hierarchical model of influences in epigenesis.

dependent on meaning-making and social processes – and vice versa. They are illustrated in Figure 1.1.

The key idea in Figure 1.1 is the *interdependence* of all levels of human functioning over time. This will be at the centre of our understanding of the life course. All the levels of organization – genetic activity, neural activity, behaviour and the environment in all of its forms (physical, social, cultural) are continuous through the whole life course of an organism. At different times over the life course the different organizational levels relate to one another in different ways. At the arrival of sexual maturity it is genetic and neural activity levels that trigger the emergence of new behaviours – which are immediately regulated by the physical, social and cultural conditions of their expression. After the establishment of regular sexual functions the latter – environmental – influences will take precedence over genetic and neural regulation.

All relationships between the levels in Gottlieb's scheme are probabilistic – they are determined under the local conditions of the organism in its life course. The scheme requires bidirectional structure–function relations in development:

GENETIC ACTIVITY ←→ STRUCTURAL MATURATION ←→ FUNCTION/ACTIVITY/EXPERIENCE

or in terms of epigenetics:

DNA←→ RNA ←→ PROTEIN

The probabilistic nature of relations between levels guarantees both the continuity of the life of the organism and its flexibility. This feature makes probabilistic epigenesis a suitable perspective to start from in the study of life-course development.

Gottlieb's understanding has its roots in biology. With a groundbreaking insight he proposed that the environment, through the influence of gene expression, would have an impact also at higher levels, such as on neural activity, behaviour, up to extra-organism influences, such as the physical, social and cultural environment.[16]

Gottlieb's research and perspective of probabilistic *epigenesis* (depicted in Figure 1.1) forecast – and was later substantiated by – the recent findings in modern *epigenetics*, some of which are referred to above, although Gottlieb himself did not use this concept. Thus, Gottlieb's perspective is supported by an increasing amount of empirical evidence, both from modern epigenetic research and from other sources,[17] although the path of influences from the social environment to gene expression is still poorly understood.[18] We are thus in the position to restate the relationship between *probabilistic epigenesis* and *modern epigenetics* as a relationship between a general perspective on development and a branch of microbiological research lending support to this perspective.

### *Previous epigenetic thinking in the history of psychology*

Before Gottlieb, other developmental researchers sowed the seeds of an epigenetic view of development. Thus in including psychological development in a biological account, Gottlieb continues along the lines of theories such as those of Kurt Goldstein,[19] Jean Piaget (Box 3.5) and Heinz Werner (Box 1.2).

Common to these theories is the assumption of an inner driving force striving for *equilibrium* between organism and environment. Yet this equilibrium never actually happens as the striving organism constantly creates a new disequilibrium in relation to its environment. This happens

[16] This proposal has found support in empirical findings. For example, Caspi *et al.* (Caspi, McClay *et al.* 2002; Caspi, Sugden *et al.* 2003) found that maltreatment in early childhood increased the likelihood of aggressive or anti-social behaviour in adult males. Not an unexpected observation *per se*. An epigenetic investigation, however, suggested that the early maltreatment might permanently alter the gene expression responsible for a chemical compound needed for dopamine and serotonin neurotransmission. This effect was permanent, so that adults with a low level of the compound in question (i.e. who were maltreated as children) were more likely to be violent and/or anti-social. These findings also provide an example of the interdependence of biological and social factors in life-course development.

[17] See more examples in Shanahan and Hofer (2005); Lickliter (in press). A probable candidate would be neural processes (Johnston and Edwards, 2002) but Shanahan and Hofer (2005, p. 72) hypothesize that the immune and endocrine systems may also be involved.

[18] This is not surprising since probabilistic epigenesis as a general principle is already constructed as a major framework to give an interpretational framework for empirical findings. It is an axiomatic standpoint that opens the door to new empirical projects for discovering the specifics of development. In itself it does not need further empirical support – like the notions of gravity and relativity in physics.

[19] Goldstein (1934/2000).

### Box 1.2 Heinz Werner – developmental perspective from Goethe to our time

Heinz Werner (1890–1964) was an Austrian developmental scientist who united the *Naturphilosophie*, the perspective of Johann Wolfgang von Goethe, the philosophy of Ernst Cassirer, the personology of William Stern and the ecological theoretical biology of Jakob von Uexküll into a coherent theory of development as a process of constant differentiation, hierarchical integration and de-differentiation. His theoretical credo – emphasizing the role of cultural means in human development – was a close parallel to that of Lev Vygotsky.

Werner studied at the University of Vienna (1909–15) – first history of music, then philosophy, psychology, biology and Germanic languages. His primary focus on human psychology placed him close to the traditions of *Ganzheitspsychologie* and the introspective psychology of the 'Würzburg school' of Oswald Külpe and Karl Bühler (whose assistant at the University of Munich he was in 1915–17). In 1917 he moved to Hamburg as assistant to William Stern, and gained a professorship at Hamburg University from 1926. Werner was forced to leave his position in 1933 and emigrated to the United States where he found temporary research and teaching appointments, until Clark University offered him a permanent position in 1947.

The central focus of Werner's developmental analysis was that of finding the process mechanisms that lead to outcomes. In the most general terms, that process is the unity of *differentiation* and *hierarchization* (increasing subordination) within the structure of human mental and affective processes. Developmental processes are open ended in their constant movement between quasi-differentiated and quasi-hierarchical states towards other states – lower or higher in the depth of hierarchical subordination. Werner's orientation is best outlined in his own book *Comparative Psychology of Mental Development*. Werner's interests stemmed from his own musical education – but transcended it in the direction of the study of perception and construction of melodies, speech utterances and graphic symbols. He looked at the holistic perception processes involving both the environment and the perceiver (*physiognomic* perception). The person is involved in relating to the environment through the whole of the body (the sensori-tonic theory of Werner and Seymour Wapner).

through progressive mutual adaptation by a refinement of the structural organization – or reorganization – of the whole organism and/or its environment. Development always remains open ended – while equilibrium is being sought, it is either never reached or it may be a dynamic equilibrium implying further changes. Thus, for example, Goldstein concluded from studies of war-injured soldiers that it was inherent in human nature for people to make the best out of their actual capacities, and always move ahead in life, whatever war damages they may have sustained. This can be understood as a basic teleological assumption that is also inherent in the notion of epigenesis. All organisms, including humans, have an inherent tendency to strive for as adaptive a relationship as possible between self and environment.[20] Note that Gottlieb's probabilistic epigenesis stresses genuine mutuality between activity at different levels of the organism, between levels and between the organism as a whole and the external environment.

### *Epigenesis and the changing of the change*

Genesis is about 'coming into being'[21] – or even, 'becoming', as opposed to 'being'. *Epigenesis* would then mean 'becoming as an unfolding process', if we were to be faithful to tradition. The word originally designated the successive differentiation and specialization of cells in an organism, from a single fertilized ovum to an adult organism, which has been described as the 'orthogenetic principle'.[22]

However, the notion of epigenesis being probabilistic has an implication other than the idea of development from the simplest to most complex structure of an organism. It indeed suggests that *any developmental change in the structure of an individual organism has as its point of departure the structure this organism has achieved up to then.* From the first cell division of the fertilized egg to a full-fledged individual, pursuing his or her life course, every developmental change this individual goes through is based on his or her previous changes and, of course, also on the environmental circumstances he or she faces at that particular moment.[23]

This means that at each point in time past changes will be the prerequisite for future changes. Consider the chain of changes an individual goes through during a life course as crossroads, where alternative routes will continually be deselected in favour of others. The total number of routes selected will then be a very small compared to all the possible alternative routes that have been deselected along the trajectory.[24] In the long run this means that it would be absurd to consider the life course as

[20] However, later in this chapter we will, in the section on dynamic systems approaches, suggest another view on the issue of equilibrium and organization of behaviour relative to capacities and situation.

[21] Merriam-Webster's dictionary. [22] Werner (1957).

[23] For an easy to understand explication of this point, see van Geert (2003).

[24] See Kauffman (2000, pp. 142ff.) on the actual and the adjacent possible, something that will reinforce the argument below on the non-ergodicity of a life course.

predetermined. The 'choices' along the trajectory may only be evaluated in terms of probabilities.

It would be tempting to say that at any particular moment along the life course the individual is in this or that particular 'state'. Yet, as living organisms are in constant change, on the move, all states are transitory. Even when the organism is apparently stable in behaviour and mood, metabolism and cell division never stop. The body moves, the heart beats, the brain emits and receives electrical impulses and so on. Assume, for example, a person in sleep. She wakes up feeling hungry, or she wakes up with a nauseous feeling, either feeling being a result of bodily processes that have taken place during sleep. One or the other sets the stage for what she will do next, in combination with other internal and external influences, such as the urge to go to work, to take care of children, the weather, etc.

In addition, living organisms are dependent on other living organisms. For example, humans are dependent on bacteria in their body that support digestion of food, and are threatened by noxious bacteria and viruses (the latter should perhaps not be considered as organisms). Humans are also dependent on other organisms as food, and may (albeit rarely nowadays) also be food for other organisms. We are dependent on other human beings for our coming into the world and for developing social, cognitive, emotional and cultural qualities. All these interdependencies highly contribute both to the stability and to the constant change of the individual life course. How can we model this vast and ever-changing array of influences on a life course?

### *How epigenesis works: the epigenetic landscape metaphor*

Still pursuing our 'outside view' of human development in the life course, we propose a model for thinking about development as probabilistic epigenesis unfolding in time. Imagine the life course of a person as a path down a very, very long hillside. Think of the unfolding of the life course as a ball rolling down the hill along the path. The path sometimes passes through deep valleys, sometime over a flater landscape. However, the path is nowhere on the hillside completely traced beforehand. Rather, think of the topography of the landscape as shaped continuously along with the rolling of the ball. Notably, the individual's own present actions, as well as those of other organisms – of the same or some different species – will also be part of the landscape. Thus, humps may suddenly pop up in front of the ball preventing it from rolling straight ahead. In a very deep and narrow valley, that will not make much of a difference. The ball may be hit, but return to the stable course it had before. In a more open landscape, however, such a bump may have a decisive influence on the ensuing path of the ball. Depending on some minor differences in where on the hump the ball hits it, the ball may continue either to the left, or to the right of the hump, or even straight ahead over the hump. Different humps can also cancel each other out.

The difference between a deep valley and a flat landscape should not be conceived of as an either or. There may, of course, be an infinite number of possible different topographies between a deep valley and a flat landscape. Furthermore, the path, more often than not, is tortuous, constantly putting more pressure on either the right or the left side of the ball, by gravity striving for the straightest possible line of direction.

The spatial metaphor of a ball rolling down a hillside is borrowed from Conrad H. Waddington.[25] He used this metaphor to describe the relationship between the genome of an organism and its environment (Figure 1.2). He used the term 'creode' to describe this kind of developmental change – a term derived from the Greek root *chre-* (as in *chreia*, necessity; *chreôn*, necessary; *chre*, it must be) and the word *he-* (as in *hodos*, the path).[26] Creode literally signifies a necessary path; and it designates both the specific morphology and also the inherent functionality of this interaction. We, on the other hand, use the metaphor here to give a

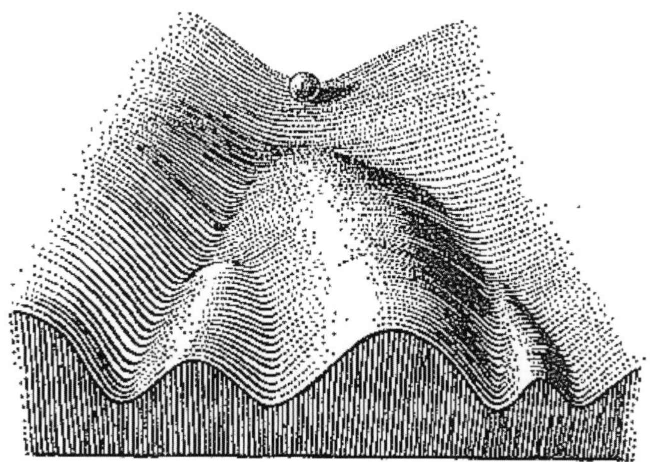

Figure 1.2 Waddington's epigenetic landscape.

[25] Waddington (1975). [26] We thank Jean-Jacques Aubert for this etymology.

topological-spatial representation of the temporal life course of an individual and all the circumstances that at each moment in time influence this course.

In such a metaphorical reading of the life course, neither external nor internal causality will therefore explain the trajectory of the ball. Rather, constraints will reinforce or neutralize each other. Indeed, the trajectory of the ball – individual development – can be seen as constrained by a combination of all possible influences, from DNA to culture, which are all to be represented in the topography of the landscape.[27] All these organism interdependencies also imply change, that is, movement. Taken together, *intra*organism as well as *inter*organism and other environmental influences are represented in the topography of the landscape, constraining, in combination, the rolling of the ball.

### *Unity in diversity*

So far we have discussed the concepts of *epigenetics* and *probabilistic epigenesis*. Genetics is about heredity and diversity. We are all different from each other, and at the same time we resemble each other in different ways, in particular our parents. Consider that we share 97 per cent of our genes with a closely related species, the chimpanzee. How come that we are still so different from chimpanzees? Epigenetics may explain. The genes are the same, but *how they work* is different. The overlap in the genomes can explain the similarities in chimpanzee and human body structures – but not their dissimilar psychologies. Besides, the vast majority of our genes are passive and do not contribute to our lives. Genes are turned on and off; and this is done under the influence of environment, at all levels in Gottlieb's model (Figure 1.1). However, the epigenetic perspective challenges the traditions of statistical inference in psychology – and in population genetics, as we shall see below.

## Why population statistics cannot illuminate the studies of life course development: where ergodicity fails

Traditional academic psychology has a number of limitations that do not fit developmental science. First, it would have us think of the relationship between organism and environment as a simple linear *causal relationship*: the more there is 'strength' in the cause, the greater the 'extent' of the effect. The quality of a relationship between assumed 'cause' and 'effect' is translated into quantitative terms – as it can thus be statistically evaluated.

[27] A similar concept – *restraint* – borrowed from Bateson (1972/1999), will be used in Chapter 6 to explain the development of narratives of life and change in psychotherapy.

Modern academic psychology has recognized the complexity of psychological influences, and solves the problem by inventing sophisticated statistical tools, such as advanced methods of regression analysis, which are used to study life-course development.[28] However, much of this research is based on accepting *the ergodicity axiom*.[29] 'Ergodicity' in the context of psychology entails the axiomatic belief that data collected over the life course of an individual will fit the same conditions as data collected at only one point of time from a population or a sample of a population. For example, you get to know the official statistics about crimes last year in your home country, and find that *x* per cent, of crimes are committed by immigrants of different ages, say, with most crimes among immigrants mostly committed by teenagers. This does not imply that you can predict the probability of a particular teenager immigrant committing a crime. You may not extrapolate from the statistics on the population of immigrants to the probable behaviour of any particular immigrant individual or vice versa.

As mentioned above, probabilistic epigenesis implies an enormous number of possible life-course trajectories over time, making each individual trajectory unique, even from the perspective of the lifetime of our universe. The time it would take to visit all the possible life trajectories of a single individual would be longer than the lifetime of the universe.[30] The probability that any individual life-course trajectory would recur within a given population at any given time period is therefore so infinitesimally small that for all practical reasons it has to be considered as non-ergodic. Averaging the crime rate in a particular immigrant population may tell us something about the population, but nothing about the individual members of this population.[31]

[28] For example, 'structural equation modelling', LISREL (Jöreskog and Goldberger 1975).

[29] A central aspect of ergodic theory is the behaviour of a dynamic system (see here below) when it is allowed to run for a long time. One of its consequences is the Poincaré recurrence theorem, which claims that almost all points in any subset of the phase space eventually revisit the set. More precise information is provided by various ergodic theorems which assert that, under certain conditions, the time average of a function along the trajectories exists almost everywhere and is related to the space average. Two of the most important examples are the ergodic theorems of Birkhoff and von Neumann. For the special class of ergodic systems, the time average is the same for almost all initial points: statistically speaking, the system that evolves for a long time 'forgets' its initial state. Stronger properties, such as mixing and equidistribution, have also been extensively studied. (We are grateful to Razi Naqvi, Professor of Physics at NTNU, Trondheim, Norway, for explaining the concept of ergodicity.) Now it is clear that developing systems do not fit these properties – they do not 'forget' the initial states, and the inter-individual variability cannot be equated with the intra-individual, across-time, changes.

[30] Kauffman (2000).

[31] To use another metaphor, let us imagine a weather station on a remote island in the middle of an ocean. Data are collected on wind direction, speed, temperature from the

It is clear, then, that despite the popularity of sample-based studies that build developmental accounts without longitudinal evidence – as follows from the assumption of ergodicity – this approach cannot be maintained in the life sciences.[32] *Human development – and all other developmental phenomena – is to be viewed as non-ergodic.*[33] Hence the study of *inter*individual variability – as it is present in samples and populations – cannot represent adequately the *intra*individual variability reflected in the life course of any particular individual in the population. For example, if you draw a sample from a population of toddlers, to measure in one and the same session aggressive behaviour in each toddler after having watched violence on a video, you cannot, from a statistical conclusion on this population, predict how video violence will influence the aggressive behaviour of any individual child over his or her toddlerhood. This may seem quite obvious or commonsensical. However, such statistical conclusions are common in life-course and lifespan psychology, where longitudinal statistics are consensually assumed to work in the same way as cross-sectional statistics.[34]

*Why does ergodicity fail?* The reasons for the ergodicity hypothesis not holding for human life courses may be summarized in three notions: *heterogeneity of developmental trajectories*, *equifinality* and *multifinality*.

The idea of the *heterogeneity of trajectories* describes the fact that humans are all different and that each life course is unique. As we have seen, epigenesis implies constant change as well as permanent mutual interdependencies. Thus, not only do human beings all have different DNA

weather station. The data collected over time are analysed statistically in order to categorize weather conditions in the region. In order to make statistical predictions, indices such as mean value and variance are used. Such indices are usually obtained by observing a sufficiently large sample, or an entire population. Hence, ideally, the statistical calculations on weather conditions would assume a large number of planets, similar to our earth, with the same island in the same ocean. Because such conditions are impossible, the calculations have to assume that it would be theoretically possible for the same weather conditions to recur on the same island. The ergodicity hypothesis authorizes the assumption that valid estimations on the island can be obtained by sampling from the same weather station over time instead of trying to collect data from similar islands on similar planets in the universe. Weather is an extremely complex issue; a huge number of variables are taken into consideration. Furthermore, initial conditions are crucial – hence the often quoted example of the butterfly flapping its wings in Tahiti and initiating a tornado in Texas. Still, the ergodicity hypothesis is assumed to hold, at least in principle. *It does not hold for human life courses.* A human being is capable of learning and responding to inputs and impulses; he or she accumulates experiences, changing the conditions for further development. All life courses are non-ergodic. However, 'the inner dimension' of human experiences adds considerable complexity to the epigenetic landscape, with an enormous increase in the number of possible life trajectories.

32 The previous example also shows how categorization of human beings matched with the biased use of statistical tools can generate unsupported social prejudices.

33 I.e. including all life sciences that take epigenesis into account.

34 Molenaar, Huizinga and Nesselroade (2003).

(except for identical twins), but they also, all live in different environments: no two persons occupy the same space at the same time. There are certainly similarities between people; however, humans within the same outer environment also constitute environments for each other (as we will see) thus making the environment different for each other. Consequently, the trajectory will be unique for every single member of the human species, from the time of its emergence, and until the species, possibly, is extinct.

In contrast, *equifinality* designates the fact that different developmental paths may lead different individuals to arrive at the same or similar points in the life course. The notion of equifinality derives from the notion of *equipotentiality* in embryology[35] – the same form of a state of organization of an embryo can be achieved through various pathways of biological growth.

Finally, besides and complementary to the concept of equifinality one may also add the notion of *multifinality* describing the notion that one and the same behaviour may serve different goals at the same time. Within the context of human development this indicates that one developmental path may serve several developmental goals. This adds further to the uniqueness of individual development since the multifunctional potential of given behaviour changes across the life course.[36]

### *Beyond ergodicity and linear causality*

The problems raised by the ergodocity hypothesis have been recognized,[37] and various attempts have been made to overcome the limitations of simple predictions or simplified causalities. On the one hand, several alternatives to generalization from population statistics have been proposed. Many approaches, though, are quantitative, and it is unclear whether they assume ergodicity.[38]

On the other hand, authors aiming at a better understanding of epigenetic processes have proposed models of *systemic causalities. Developmental causality is systemic* – in the sense that the causal factors consist of a set of elements that are bound together by mutually interdependent relations. These relations are *catalysed* – in the sense that a causal linkage occurs only

35 Introduced by Hans Driesch (1899, pp. 67–77).

36 'Use of language' is clearly multifinal since it serves the need to communicate with oneself and with others, it raises awareness of the self, it serves intra-psychic regulation . . . Once achieved the exchange of signs via language will serve several other individual goals across the life course.

37 See for instance Magnusson, Bergman, Rudinger and Torestad (1994).

38 Bergman and El-Khouri (2003).

when certain conditions are present. Catalysis has been a well-accepted principle in chemistry since the 1830s, but in psychology it has barely arrived at its beginnings.[39]

Similarly, Gottlieb and other researchers working in his framework propose a development systems theory, where causality is distributed and relational, according to Figure 1.1 (see above). Their stance is succinctly expressed by Robert Lickliter:

> The process of development is thus inherently historical and situated and the causes of developmental outcomes are to be found in the dynamic relations among the complex array of internal and external resources occurring across the organism–environment system.[40]

Here, as much as in ergodic models, there is a causal model, which specifies the conditions under which causal linkages occur. The views on causality are in both cases subsumed under the ergodicity hypothesis, that is, it is assumed that, whenever the specified conditions and relations hold, a causal relationship may be identified. That means that it is assumed that *the same* conditions and relationships may hold at different points of time. However, that is never the case for living, epigenetic systems, so the ergodicity hypothesis has to be rejected. *The conclusion, as we see it, is that the linear version of causality (A causes B) is an inappropriate concept for describing influences on biological, psychological or even social development.* It may be used for delimited issues, but then at the cost of disregarding the systemic organization, and the relationship with the context.[41] Mainly, this reflection will lead us to replace the notion of *causality* with that of *constraint*, as illustrated in the epigenetic landscape metaphor, where constraints are represented as the shape of the landscape along the trajectory of the ball.

## The inside view: the organismic perspective

While the 'outside view' considered life trajectories from a perspective in which each individual life could be contemplated as unfolding in a multi-dimensional space, the inside view aims at capturing the human *experience* of development, and how we make sense of our experiences.

We first need to raise a fundamental question: how can humans have a sense of what is within them, and how can we have access to what other humans experience 'in themselves'? First, we need to consider that persons are bodies, organisms present in the world, which are able to feel the world and themselves as they move, act and meet its resistance. In

[39] Valsiner and Cabell (2011). [40] Lickliter (in press, p. 49). [41] Toomela (2011).

addition, they interact with others, with things, in specific situations, whether in a street in New York or a location in the Gobi desert (even the desert has been imagined as an uncivilized place). Second, the person can capture, reflect upon and interpret her being in and feeling the world. In the perspective proposed here, the core means by which human experience becomes detectable by one person or by another is given by its semiotic nature – the fact that is is constituted in and through *signs*. In their most simple forms, past experiences of our contact with the world leave mental traces – signs, which *stand for something beyond themselves*. To have a mind means not only to have contact with the world here and now, but also always to have the ability to make present past encounters thanks to such sign-traces. Such 'present-making' is commonly called 're-presentation'. Sign uses create a holistic field that we generally call 'experience', in the sense of 'experiencing'[42] – a sense of being in contact with the surrounding world beyond the here and now. In more complex forms, experiences become designated by signs which are socially acknowledged, such as words, and organized into systems, such as language. They then transform the nature of human experience, and become the stuff that constitutes the flow of consciousness as well as dreams, memories and desires.

### *The origin of semiotic function*

The huge variety of emotional expressions that the human body is capable of is the basis for sharing experiences between humans. Through its expression we recognize emotion in the other and can relate it to the same emotion in ourselves. When a person understands that someone else has the same emotion as her, and that second person has the same emotion as the first person, it can be said that both 'share' the same emotion, the same experience.[43] In reality experiences are never 'the same' – although similar[44] – yet through intersubjectivity we create the basis of mutual understanding by considering them 'the same'.

[42] Experience can have three main meanings: (1) experience as experienc*ing*, or feeling-in the world, the meaning we privilege in this book; (2) experience understood as encounter, such as in a 'shared experience'; and (3) finally experience as in 'life-experience' – as a synthetic knowledge coming from a long history of learning from experience*s* (see Chapter 7). When there is a risk of confusion we clarify the meaning.

[43] Some authors have called the impression of achieved shared experience 'intersubjectivity' (Trevarthen, 1977, Trevarthen and Hubley, 1978); however, others have expanded the notion of intersubjectivity to the mere *process* of trying to establish a form of relative understanding (Grossen, 1998, 2010).

[44] See Sovran (1992) on the similarity/sameness difference. When in everyday discourse we say 'this is the same as that' we actually mean 'this is *similar to* that'.

Furthermore, such *shared experiences*[45] being linked to particular conventionalized expressions have made it possible for *semiotic systems* to emerge, thanks to which earlier shared experiences are shared with third parties within the human species.

One way to present the origins and the functioning of signs as means for communication and self-regulation particular to humans can be borrowed from Jean Piaget.[46] As part of his attempt to define the semiotic function, Piaget describes his daughter, Jacqueline (J.) imitating the temper tantrum of a visiting boy the day before:

> At I ; 4 (3) J. had a visit from a little boy of I ; 6, whom she used to see from time to time, and who, in the course of the afternoon got into a terrible temper. He screamed as he tried to get out of a play-pen and pushed it backwards, stamping his feet. J. stood watching him in amazement, never having witnessed such a scene before. The next day, she herself screamed in her play-pen and tried to move it, stamping her foot lightly several times in succession. The imitation of the whole scene was most striking. Had it been immediate, it would naturally not have involved representation, but coming as it did after an interval of more than twelve hours, it must have involved some representative or pre-representative element.

In Piaget's view, this is simply an example of *deferred imitation*, and thus an emergent faculty of internalization, and 'storage' of an imitation that could, at the outset, have been executed directly after the model the day before. In Piaget's view, such internalized and deferred imitations are the precursors of representations.

This interpretation can be complemented. We can also say that this incident carries with it the germ for communicating to a third party the behaviour of the boy from yesterday. This act of communication need not be intended by the girl herself. Piaget's daughter might just have recalled for herself what has happened the day before. However, this imitation took place in a specific social situation – which is not mentioned in the texts. We may presume that Jacqueline was able to register the reaction of people around her: perhaps some smiling faces and nods, accompanying verbal comments that Jacqueline does not understand, are enough for her to have confirmed their understanding of the relationship between the boy's temper and Jacqueline's imitation. This form of social recognition might have made Jacqueline aware of other people's shared experience both of the temper, and of the imitation. The social recognition of the incident from the day before makes the imitation emerge as a

[45] The concept of *shared experiences* will be central to our argument for the development of self and settings (frames) as based on interpersonal relationships and contexts over time.

[46] Piaget (1945/1951, p. 63, obs. 52). In the quote I. is for the place and 4(3) means four years and three months.

communicative tool, as a symbol for Jacqueline. Also, not only does she happen to 'invent' symbols in this way, she quickly recognizes that her social environment is full of symbols, notably the words of the language spoken in this environment, and that she can learn to use them and obtain some results.

Hence, such 'symbolic imitations' are not simply internalized to become mental representations in the child. Internalization – constructive transformation of the meanings from the social environment into the subjective world – leads to innovation of personal meanings – through the social embedding of the imitation act and its implied functionality of sharing experiences. In that sense, internalization has a social origin and a 'dialogical' nature. We 'feel in' to others' socially presented selves. Through internalization such intersubjectivity then becomes the means of sharing experiences with oneself, eventually constituting a complete realm of thought and imagination.[47] More generally,[48] thanks to signs people can think for themselves – take distance from their experiences, reflect about them. Signs thus originate in shared experiences instigating social recognition of symbolic representations, eventually forming a semiotic system, which, internalized, becomes a basis for the 'inner' mental life characteristic of the human species. We have an inner consciousness, because we are social. The signs make it possible to re-present ('make present again') earlier experiences from the past[49] that enter into social communication – making the future through it.

### *From shared experiences to imagination*

We have thus established *shared experiences* as a central component of the semiotic function. This has huge consequences for the nature of human life and experience, and will thoroughly be discussed in the following chapters. Here we will only outline some basic ideas about the mental dimension of our lives.

First, modern infant research shows that the human infant is a social being right from birth and may show advanced communicative skills at two months of age.[50] Also, the arm and finger movements of newborn babies are different in a social context, from when interacting with an

[47] For the idea of being in dialogue with oneself, see Chapter 6.

[48] For other, congruent accounts of the origin of the semiotic function see Vygotsky (1934/1986); Nelson (2007); Fonagy, Gergely, Jurist and Target (2005), etc. The notion of semiotics goes back to John Locke's *Essay on Human Understanding* (Deely, 2010, p. 25).

[49] In German *Vorstellung*.

[50] This direction of thought has been prominent in infant psychology since Trevarthen (1977).

object.[51] As the child manages to co-ordinate social interaction and interaction with an object, the stage is set for the development of the semiotic function.[52] When child and adult both recognize and are able to signal to each other the mutual recognition that their individual experiences are similar, being about the same thing in their common outer environment, then a structure is in place that allows the child to learn that he or she can perform acts of meaning.

Therefore, these *acts of meaning are social at the outset*. Eventually, though, they may become internalized, where the child, so to say, is in dialogue with him- or herself. That lays the ground for imagination, thinking and planning. The child is ready for a cognitive development that is unmatched in the animal world. In due time, the child is also capable of distinguishing between an inner and an outer world.[53] Also, thanks to this semiotic capacity, we may thus gain access to human 'inner experience', or experiencing, as we will explore through the rest of the book.

## Inside and outside mutualities

For the sake of clarity, we have until now separated two epistemological perspectives on human development: one that considers human trajectories from the outside, emerging as part of a complex set of constraints, and one that sees them 'from the inside', in the stream of lived experience. However, both of these epistemological perspectives come to the same statement: human development unfolds as 'inside' phenomena (genetic, psychological, emotional), interact with their 'outside' (environmental conditions, social others, language). The principle of progressive movement between the inside (mind, soul, or self) and the outside (*Umwelt*, environment, context) domains has been the core of William Stern's personalism (Figure 1.3). The two infinities – of the inside of the self, and of the environment – are in constant forward-orientated movement into each other.

Going beyond Stern's scheme – which merely reflects the structural unity of person and environment – developmental science accepts the dynamic unity of the two. What is happening in the PRESENT (see Figure 1.3. centre) is the two-way movement from the INNER INFINITY of the depth of the human psyche towards the OUTER INFINITY of the environment that the person tries to relate with. That OUTER INFINITY is

[51] Rönnqvist and VonHofsten (1994). [52] Trevarthen and Hubley (1978).
[53] For instance Winnicott (1971/1991) on the progressive creation of the inner/outer distinction.

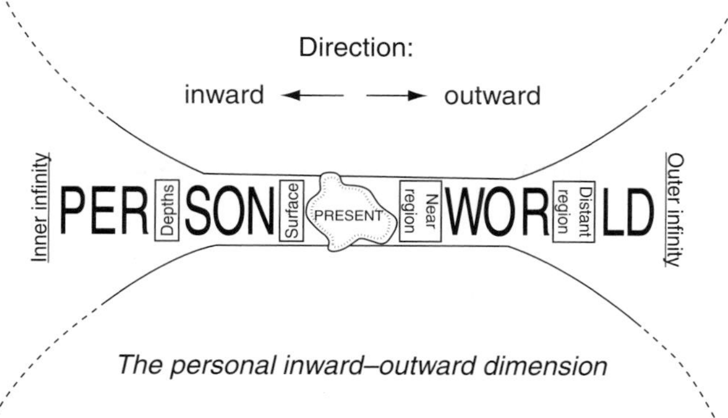


Figure 1.3 William Stern's view of person<>environment relations.

a kind of horizon – tempting, yet never reachable – as moving towards it entails the horizon constantly moving with the person. Likewise, the 'inputs' from the *NEAR* and *DISTANT* regions of the environment – eventually stemming from OUTER INFINITY – are on the move into the intrapsychic world. In that process of coordination, maintenance of the status quo and ruptures happen. A dramatic event in the outside world – observing a war scene – can feed into the 'inner infinity' and catalyse its dramatic transformation.

*An examples, from peace to war:* an adolescent volunteer soldier (later to become a writer) has the experience of being on his first battlefield and is paralysed under the shock of his impressions – just images:

> And then I see my first bodies. Soldiers young and old, in Wehrmacht uniforms. Hanging from trees still bare along the road, from linden trees in the marketplace. With cardboard signs on their chests branding them as cowards and subversive elements. A boy my age – his hair, like mine, parted on the left – dangling next to a middle-aged officer of indeterminate rank or, rather, stripped of his rank by a court-martial. A procession of corpses we ride past with our deafening tank-track rattle. No thoughts, only images.[54]

Yet once reflected upon, as this first-person monologue suggests, the strong impressions – dead bodies that could be the narrator's – can start to be read as signs, which refer to the whole imagery and symbolic system of war – jackets without indications of rank, indications of non-respect for the soldiers' bravery, martial courts and tanks. Altogether these signs of destruction are intended to keep him committed to destroying

[54] Grass (2007, p. 121).

'the enemy', rather than creating peace and understanding. Hence in this short meeting between the narrator and his warscene, two infinities meet: his inner, whole life experience so far, and the infinite historically anchored material and symbolic machinery of war. This meeting allows the political project to penetrate the narrator's inner life and guide his beliefs and actions in the next future.

Likewise, a rupture in the 'inner infinity' can lead to radical transformation of its outer counterpart – as we can observe (from aside) in our world filled with suicide bombers. Thus – in contrast to William Stern – development is in the most general terms the process of reconstituting a new steady state after a rupture, resembling but never the same as the status quo ante. The 'inside of the self' thus has always an origin in the 'outside of the self', and notably in social relations to other humans. There is no notion of self at the outset, except for the social skills that the infant has from birth. The experience of self is primarily constituted in interaction with others[55] and in our experiences of the world; in that sense, self is dialogical.[56]

Thus we may say that the outside and the inside continuously constitute each other in an ongoing mutual relationship. What happens in our external world is important to what we experience, but our experiences are also selective and coloured by our internal world. The same 'objective' event may – depending on the inner state – not be registered if, for some reason or another, a person considers it irrelevant, or it may be the object of different evaluations.[57] Moreover, the same person may respond differently to the same 'objective' event at different times and in different places.

### *The landscape metaphor revisited: the inside and the outside.*

How can we integrate these ideas on the inner – lived-through experience – into the version of the epigenetic landscape metaphor proposed above?

We suggest *the movement of the ball*, that is, the rolling of the ball down the hillside, as the central aspect of the metaphor (see Figure 1.2). Not only is the ball rolling, but another essential aspect of the metaphor is that *the constantly evolving topography of the landscape arises with the rolling of the*

55 Stern (1985).
56 The 'dialogical', or social nature of the experience of 'self' in the world has been identified by many authors, ranging from James to Mead, passing via Freud and Janet. It has received recent theorizations in the work of Marková (2005) or Hermans (2001); see also Garvey and Fogel (2007). See also Chapter 6.
57 Research on human stress has some intriguing examples for this (Lazarus, 1993).

*ball*. The ball is a kind of mole – an animal who digs out a path under the constraints of the environment. Therefore, ahead of the ball there certainly is topography with a structure; however, the structure may be modified by the rolling of the ball.[58] The preconditions for what is going to happen next are continuously modified by the preceding movement, change, processes, activity and outside events. Thus, events or actions need not be finished and delimited to influence the topography of the landscape deploying itself along with the rolling of the ball.

Similarly, in a life course, an adult might imagine the future of a child from a younger generation, and would like to give her advice as to how to handle future challenges. What the adult cannot imagine is what will have been the child's past experiences (in her future) when she meets these challenges. The way she faces her challenges may benefit from *the adult's* experiences, but, *her own* experiences, and, by implication, her values and preferences, will be for more important.

The landscape evolves due to the junction of processes usually described either from 'the outside' or from 'the inside'. First, as mentioned above, human interactions play a fundamental role: through social-communicative interactions, each person is always 'in the landscape' of the other, mutually affecting each other's landscapes. Second, because of the semiotic nature of experience, these engage in meaning-making and transformations of personal sense-making. Third, the ongoing activities of an individual have an impact on his or her environment. The impact may be of varying strengths, and works at different levels: what people eat affects their capacity to experience the world; their sensori-motor actions change their physical and symbolic environment, etc. All of this is included in every person's epigenetic landscape, as well in everyone else's. All the influences are related in a complicated network.

*The realities of the developmental landscape:* considering the trajectory of the ball in the topography of the landscape, we have to examine what is 'behind' the ball – what happened before the present moment: what has happened, has happened. It is impossible to return to a past state of the topography – the status quo ante can never be achieved again. Development is *irreversible*. In terms of the life course, this means that

[58] In that sense, the static image picture given in Figure 1.2 is misleading: a film would be more adequate. Even so, what would be necessary would be a software program in which the very movement of the ball constrains its trajectory by changing the topography of the landscape (Almås, Hajduk *et al.* 2003). Even more: in order for the program to generate a topography and a trajectory, it is necessary to define specific parameters, and obviously these have to be limited in number. In real life, these parameters are innumerable, with complicated and ever-changing interactions between them.

*we accumulate experiences*. Yet such accumulation is not a simple 'piling up' of our life-course events. Notably, it is part of epigenesis:[59] in the context of experiences, this means that we are situated at the present moment through a *history* of past experiences which implies a selective, reconstructive and deeply affective operation, *taking the form of building up dynamic representations of the generic ways of living a life*. This is the precise sense in which the past is present for us. These *re*presentations are included in the dynamic scheme of moving to the future – they become *pre*sentations that are crucial in the making of the next relative state of stability in the life course. The past and present function to move us towards the future by determining what and how we experience what is happening outside.

Such transformative accumulation of experiences can be described in two ways. From the outside view, as in the epigenetic landscape, the past history remains and cannot be changed. People have acquired habits, routines, opinions, preferences, etc.; especially important is the invention of ideologies. Not only have these historically conditioned parts of themselves led them to where they are, they also constitute part of the outline of the landscape ahead of them, in the sense that they will constrain what happens to them.[60] Both animals and humans recognize similarities between past and present events. Yet humans also have the ability to recall memories of past events – and to transform them.

Hence, from the inner perspective, it is not *what* we experience, but *how* we experience it that matters. And in particular, from that perspective, the past can be transformed or reinvented and the future can be constantly created.

### *Moving toward a dynamic understanding of the life course*

As we have seen, there is a constant interplay between the different levels of organization of an organism and its environment. This relationship can be understood by taking into consideration that organisms are *open systems*[61] dependent on a continuous exchange relationship with their environments that can maintain or enhance their organization. In addition, organisms and their environment are mutually dependent. The

[59] See above, under the heading 'Epigenesis and the changing of the change', where, in terms of our epigenetic landscape metaphor, epigenesis means that the further trajectory of the ball first and foremost depends on the place in the landscape to which the past trajectory has brought it at the present moment.

[60] We will come back to the notion of *environment* later in this chapter and of *frame* in Chapter 4.

[61] Bertalanffy (1968).

landscape metaphor covers both organism and environment: hence, internal dynamics within the organism (from DNA to past experiences) and external influences (external environment, from chemical to cultural environment) can be seen as *one single system*. In that metaphor, the environment is thus *included in the system* – there is no outside to the system. Yet if we consider life-course development, we need to take into consideration the fact that human beings have an *inner environment*. Well-being depends not only on comfortable (outer) surroundings, but also on a smooth functioning of the body. More generally, there needs to be an 'inner' environment to account for human beings' experience of duration, moods or ideas. How can we handle the system–environment dichotomy?

The solution is actually simple. Consider the simple figure (Figure 1.4) – a circle. When we draw a circle on an 'empty' surface, how many objects appear on that surface?

Our common sense says – one (i.e., the circle), yet this is not so. What has emerged as a result of our drawing of this simple circle is a mutually linked triplet (*OUTSIDE/BORDER/INSIDE*). The space bound in by the contour acquires the quality of *INSIDE* (simply by the act of being 'bounded in' by the contour), qualitatively different from the *OUTSIDE* (which is 'bound out' by the very same contour). If this circle is sketched with a chalk on a black board, and wiped off, all parts of the triplet (*INSIDE/BORDER/OUTSIDE*) disappear in unison. This is the central idea of *co-genetic logic*.[62] This logic makes it possible to study development as an open system – concentrating the focus on the key issue of *how the border*

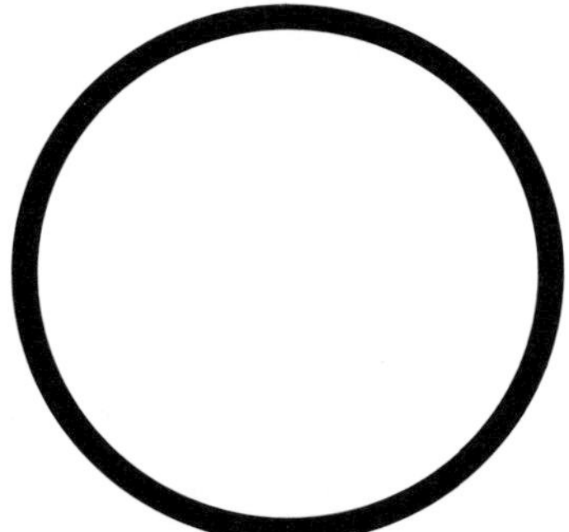

Figure 1.4 A circle.

[62] Herbst (1995).

*functions.*[63] All dynamic systems models are models of the functional dynamics of that border.[64]

Above we have implied that the topography of the epigenetic landscape has a structure, yet is ever changing. Also, we have found a way to handle the time dimension, and the irreversibility of time through the rolling of the ball downhill, a movement that never stops along the life course. The spatial representation of time is not the slope, but the movement of the ball. However, movement implies continuous change. Coming back to the life course, is change so ubiquitous in development? What about the fact that humans actually experience stability?

## Dynamic systems theory (DST)

How can we study the human life course as a historical phenomenon of experienced duration, as situated in complex environments yet enabled by multiple internal dynamics, as observed and experienced? *Dynamic systems theory* (DST) may offer solutions to these issues.[65]

Let us start with general principles. For example, there is much speculation on the origins of life on earth. Life implies the incredibly complicated structure of matter, which develops over time to be more and more complex. This is as true for simple organisms such as bacteria and amoebae as for humans, when compared to non-organic matter. However, the *second law of thermodynamics* states that *entropy* in the universe increases. Simply put, this means that the same is true for the universe as for a cup of hot tea in a chilly room. The cup of tea will, practically, cool down to the temperature of the room, while the room may be very slightly heated by the cup. The end result is that there will be no difference between the temperature of the tea and the temperature of the room. That is entropy. It implies an evening out of differences, a loss of structure.

63 From that point of view, all developmental sciences are *sciences of membranes* (Valsiner, 2007b, 2009a) – functional borders in between parts of the system, and between the system and its environment. What is designated as 'an environment' is so only in relation to the system (the OUTSIDE of the INSIDE as it becomes defined by the BORDER and our focus of interest: for a psychologist the person is the 'inside' and the geography of the environment an 'outside', for a geographer, the geography of the place is the 'inside' and the persons inhabiting it are the 'outside'.

64 For a dynamic systems view on the relationship between system and environment, see the sections below.

65 For an insightful introduction to DST see Sundarasaradula and Hasan (2005). Dynamic systems theories have much in common with *chaos theory*. Similarities and differences between these two paradigmatic approaches will, however, not be discussed here. The reader interested in chaos theory can examine Prigogine and Stengers (1984), as well as Wikipedia on chaos. More specifically here, van Geert (2003) and Kauffman (1993) are the most relevant sources.

How then comes it, in the universe, that there can also be *increase in structure*, at least locally (e.g. epigenesis), which means a *decrease* of entropy rather than an increase? The answer is in the question: it happens locally. Although the universe develops towards total entropy, there may be, here and there, a decrease of entropy. In effect, as far as we can know, the universe as such is a *closed system*. This means that there is no environment for the universe as a system. Also, and therefore, there is – again as far as we know – no exchange of energy between the universe and (the non-existent) outside of the universe. The increase of entropy of the universe implies a tendency toward thermodynamic equilibrium between its components. This is true also when the properties of the component may change – for example, when the weather temperature sinks below 0° C, water freezes to ice. This is entropy regulated and thus considered as an equilibrium freezing point.

However, under certain conditions water may stay liquid far below 0°C, for example, when it is divided into very small droplets. In such cases there will be a non-equilibrium relationship between these droplets and their environment (normally cold air, down to −25°C). It may then happen that the molecules of each droplet start to organize themselves, clustering, first in an unstable way (i.e. clusters dissolve) then becoming stable. Then the clusters grow and form amazing patterns that can be admired as snowflakes. What gives form to the individual snowflake? The answer to that question is crucial to what follows. Under the particular conditions in which the snowflake was formed, the molecules of the water droplet organized themselves into the structure the snowflake ended up with. This is a ubiquitous phenomenon of nature: *self-organization*, that is, *under particular conditions of non-equilibrium relations with the environment, systems may self-organize into specific structures*. This can be found in systems of non-organic matter and, notably, in systems of organic matter and, in particular, in organisms. As a result of such self-organization, snowflakes may acquire a certain structure – for instance, it may turn them in to powder snow ideal for skiing. This structure is said to be an *emergent property* of the particular self-organization of molecules within each droplet of water. Simply summarized, *emergence* means that the whole is more than the sum of its parts:

> Emergence . . . refers to the arising of novel and coherent structures, patterns, and properties during the process of self-organization in complex systems.[66]

[66] Goldstein (1999, p. 49). Note that the concept of *emergence* is a very old concept in psychology (see Lewes, 1875).

Thanks to emergence, lower levels of self-organization produce higher-level properties, which may, in turn be elements in higher-level systems. Thus, to come back to our question, it may be conjectured that life has emerged on earth through the self-organization of particular combinations of non-living matter under specific circumstances.[67] This implies that the environment is structured – notably *dynamically structured* – that is, it is a continuously changing structure.[68] What do these assumptions imply in terms of the relationship between system and environment as open?

The answer is threefold. First, open systems emerge and exist far from thermodynamic equilibrium. They may do so only through a constant exchange relationship with the environment, and this is what makes them open. Second, self-organization means that the exchange between system and environment is *unspecific* regarding structure. Structure from the environment is not transferred to the system; only unspecific influences, such as energy, are fed into and out of the system. This means, among other things, that there is no external creator or designer of the system, and nor is there a blueprint – the system is not a piece of engineering. Third, dynamic systems are interdependent. Notably, the concept of emergence allows for hierarchical analyses of levels of systems, where higher-level emergent properties depend on lower-level self-organization. In their consequences, the levels of systems correspond to Gottlieb's idea of interdependence of levels of functioning depicted in Figure 1.1.

### *Open systems that operate far from equilibrium*

In contrast to closed systems, *open systems* are defined by *continuous* exchange relationships with their environment – notably exchange of energy. Increase in, or maintenance of, the structure is dependent on the continuity of this exchange. For example, living organisms are systems far from thermodynamic equilibrium maintaining themselves through constant input of energy and matter (e.g. food and drink) and output of waste products. They are *far from equilibrium* in the sense that they are far from the evening out of entropy implied by the second law and that they are highly structured. This structure is sustained or enhanced by the open system's continuous exchange relationships with the environment – what

[67] For a very elaborate view on this point, see Kauffman (1993).

[68] The principle of emergence of higher levels of organization has been identified in the natural sciences. This principle has also been applied to social sciences, where open systems may exchange not only energy, but also matter, people, capital and/or information with their environments (Wikipedia (last modified 2009), entry 'Open systems').

Ilya Prigogine has called a 'dissipative system' of energy between the system and its environment.[69] Without such exchanges, the system loses structure (according to the second law), for example, a living organism will die. In other words, the essence of DST is that development of structure is not a striving *for* equilibrium, but *self-organization far away from thermo-dynamic equilibrium*, far away from entropy. *It is in these far from equilibrium states that novel structures emerge*. All developmental processes break the previous *equilibria* in their move towards new structural states.

## DST and life-course development

DST has been developed to account for natural, inanimate phenomena, and has been extended to describe all types of organism. It has inspired psychologists as well. Yet in order to apply DST to psychological development, a few specifications have to be made.

*What is a system and what is an environment?* Approaching psychological phenomena in terms of DST – in terms of self-organization and emergence – demands the identification, in each case, of what is the system and what is the environment. For Paul van Geert:[70]

> a system is basically any collection of phenomena, components, variables or whatever that we take from our universe of discourse that we are interested in. This collection is a system in as much as its components relate to one another. It is a dynamic system if its components affect and change one another in the course of time.

In this definition, a 'universe of discourse'[71] roughly designates the area of research in which we are interested. Hence, as psychologists, we might define as a 'universe of discourse' a situation such as a mother interacting with her infant, and define as a system either the child's language-learning abilities or the child–adult dyad.

[69] The relationship with the environment means both input from and output to the environment. Both are needed: if there were only input, the system would sooner or later be saturated, which would imply closure (no more input is possible) and the system would start losing both what has been fed into it and its structure, that is, entropy would occur, until equilibrium was reached. The structure is maintained – or enhanced – by active output of energy (to the difference of losing energy). Imagine a (very unlikely) 'active cup of tea' – hot, but placed in an even hotter room – managing to increase the temperature in the already hot room. This unlikely cup will get rid of its entropy problem with the environment by exporting it to the room, which will have to deal with it in relation to the other rooms in the building, etc. Thus this 'active cup of tea' keeps its distance from equilibrium. It is thus necessary to imagine that this very special cup of tea is also drawing energy from somewhere else – it is thus an open system.

[70] Van Geert (2003, p. 655). [71] Van Geert (2003, p. 654).

According to van Geert, the *environment* is 'everything in the universe of discourse that does not belong to the system but nevertheless interacts with it'.[72] If we limit the system to our language-learning toddler, the adult will obviously be the environment for her. If we choose to describe the child and adult dyad, then the room in which the child–adult interaction takes place as well as the broader cultural context might be considered as the environment.

### *Attractors in the life course*

In DST terminology, periods of stability are labelled 'attractor states', or simply *attractors*.[73] However, beyond stability the open system is in continuous interaction with its environment and there is therefore constant movement in the system. That also means that dynamic systems are time dependent. The structure of the system is achieved and maintained through self-organization and the environment only supplies energy and other resources to the system, while the system dissipates energy, thus also enriching the environment with new resources.

Let us apply this to the life course, and consider the system constituted by a man, a husband in a family, with wife and children, being a dedicated partner in a company. If a person does his or her regular business from day to day, we may say that the person (i.e. the system) is *in an attractor*. In the attractor, the system is continuously disturbed by various fluctuations in the conditions for its existence. Normally such disturbances will not make it deviate from the actual attractor. They may, however, become so strong that the stability of the attractor will be put in danger. For example, our man may be daily nagged by customers. With a stable family life, the attractor we may label 'his emotional stability' is not disturbed by demanding customers. At some point in his life, however, his relationship with his wife deteriorates. He makes an extra effort not to let this problem affect his relationship to his children. However, at work he becomes irritable, and, in particular his patience with customers falters, so that he loses customers. His company questions his skills, and he is eventually made redundant. Thus, the conditions for a stable attractor have changed;

[72] Van Geert (2003, p. 656).

[73] The words 'attractor state' might give the impression that the system is inactive, static. This impression is highly relevant to the discussion of dynamic systems. The word 'state' is a received concept in the area, and mathematically the time dimension is defined as changes over a series of states, where the transition from one state to the next is defined by a differential equation. In this respect, therefore, DST is an eloquent example of the intellectual conception of time that Bergson criticizes (see Chapter 2.) More on stability and change below.

initially minor disturbances have put the poor husband/worker system in a state of instability – that is, *out of the attractor*.

This DST description does not take in to account the history of the system, or the memory of the past – which our earlier landscape metaphor would. From an epigenetic landscape point of view, we may trace the life history of our gentleman back to the point where his relationship with his wife started to deteriorate. This history may have gone through ups and downs, and transition points where life could have taken different directions,[74] depending on the presence of specific attractors. In between, there have been periods of stability, where routines and habits have been allowed to be formed. In DST terminology, such 'stable' developmental processes would be considered as attractors, which may be 'deepened' at both a cognitive and an emotional level. This is true for different areas of our man's life, such as home and work, and for particular activities within each of these areas.[75]

In the landscape metaphor, a relatively deep valley with a broad bottom, allowing for parallel 'sub-valleys' in between which daily life may switch, would represent the stable periods in the life of our man. These sub-valleys would represent, for example, home and workplace. The deeper these valleys are, the more stable would be the corresponding life situation. In DST terminology, stability here means resistance to disturbances. For instance, arguments between wife and husband will not have any impact on their shared life before the deterioration of their relationship. However, as the atmosphere of the home changes, single arguments will be less tolerated by the couple as a system. This will threaten the attractor, pushing the system into instability and possibly also resulting in a far more noxious attractor, where the wife–husband life has a stable pattern of nagging, arguments and reciprocal hurting. Such a stable attractor will, in turn, change the whole life-course attractor of our man, making the valley considerably shallower, thus also threatening the stability of the work attractor and of the whole family system.

### *Attractors vs. equilibrium*

Earlier in this chapter we have seen that psychologists interested in epigenesis were suggesting that development tended towards equilibrium – equilibrium thus being a teleological notion. On the other

[74] Bifurcation points in the landscape metaphor, maybe points with trifurcation or even more than three possible alternative trajectories. These are also important concepts for DST.

[75] Later in this book these stable attractors will be referred to as *frames*: see Chapter 5.

hand, in DST, *thermodynamic equilibrium* is understood as the state of entropy. From that perspective, complex dynamic and open systems like organisms are striving to get away from that entropy; they achieve attractor states *far from thermodynamic equilibrium*.[76] Hence, what corresponds to the commonly used notion of 'equilibrium' in epigenetic approaches is actually the notion of 'attractor': when the system is in an attractor, it has found a form of structure that enables regular exchanges with its environment.[77] In the context of life-course development, we therefore propose to associate the concept of attractor with *stability*, rather than with thermodynamic equilibrium. While equilibrium is a global concept associated with the relationship between an organism and its (external) environment, attractors are defined relative to the level of analysis chosen for the dynamic system in question. Thus in some theoretical contexts a 'personality trait' (such as 'ambitious') may be considered as an attractor, likely – but not necessarily, in DST terms – to last a lifetime. At a microgenetic level, a sudden cognitive insight that lasts a fraction of a second may also be considered an attractor.[78]

Furthermore, attractors may take different forms. The simplest ones to be considered here are *fixed point attractors* – for example being consistently ambitious over all situations and in all phases of life would be a fixed-point attractor. In contrast, consistently oscillating between being ambitious and being self-satisfied would be a '*limit cycle*' *attractor*.[79] However, these types of attractors are periodic, and there are also (non-periodic) chaotic[80] attractors, called *strange attractors*, of which the famous fractals, that is, complicated patterns that can be broken in to parts which replicate the structure of the whole, are the best examples. At a biological,

[76] For an easy presentation see Thelen and Smith (1994, pp. 52ff.).

[77] In that respect, Piaget's view evolved over the years: although the notion of equilibrium was from the beginning at the heart of his idea of the striving force of genesis, his later work included recent developments in cybernetics and his conception evolved accordingly (see for instance Ducret & Céllerier, 2007).

[78] See Richardson (2008).

[79] See Chapter 6 for an example of a cyclic attractor between two opposite self-positions, called mutual in-feeding (Valsiner, 2002).

[80] The word 'chaos' has taken on a particular, and paradoxical meaning in DST. The behaviour of a dynamic system may appear chaotic, as it is virtually unpredictable. From a strictly mathematical point of view, however, the system is deterministic: it only appears chaotic because it is very sensitive to initial conditions. In reality, however, the definition of initial conditions must be a choice of the researcher (who also defines what is to be considered as system and what is to be considered as environment, see above). This discussion is interesting relative to the ergodicity hypothesis above and Valsiner's (1997) proposals on indeterministic determinism.

not to mention a human and semiotic level, the complexity of attractors may be huge.[81]

### *Resources in the life course*

Dynamic systems are dependent on continuous supplies of energy, or, depending on their complexity, matter (e.g. food) or information in order to feed the (self-organized) structure of the system. The notion of *resource* can thus designate these sources of various 'fuel' that the system needs and uses to maintain its stability or to develop.[82] Thus, a complex dynamic system will depend on the resources it can obtain to sustain stability.

However, the structure of used resources or of the environment *is not transferred to the system in a one-to-one relation*. Consequently, living organisms, like any self-organized system, cannot be designed or instructed from the outside. They function according to their own parameters, and resources from the environment are to be used by a system according to its own design. The system can be disturbed (or even destroyed) by the environment, but the environment has no power to determine how the system will respond and reorganize to take account of the perturbation. It can sometimes function out of a self-referential logic, which turns it into an *autopoietic* system (see below).[83] Hence, in a human life course, taking advantage of the semiotic function, information – as well as semiotic resources – may be said to have an *unspecific* impact on a person. This is a property of *meanacting – human beings act in meaningful ways within any specific environmental context, changing that context into a new form, resulting in environmental input into their own subsequent actions.*

This provides a nice example of the principle derived from epigenesis, that any future situation[84] of the system will depend on previous ones, and that epigenesis, as depicted in the epigenetic landscape metaphor, also includes changes in the environment that constrain further development of the system. For instance, when a child learns to speak, there is no structure fully implemented in her environment that will pass on to her; the environment only contains utterances derived from the language. Furthermore, at the level of the child (ontogenesis), developing the ability to speak is only partially about learning the 'structure' of language (semantics and syntax); rather, learning includes perceiving, thinking, feeling, experiencing the world and other things, all of which constitute

[81] For an accessible overview of the different types of attractor, visit Wikipedia on 'Attractor'.

[82] Van Geert (2003, p. 656). [83] Maturana and Varela (1987).

[84] We thus avoid the problematic concept of 'state'; see note 73 above.

a dynamic, open, self-organized system. From this self-organization emerges a child capable of telling what she wants, what she thinks, what she dislikes in the world. Each act of communication will, in this understanding, change the environmental context and act as an input into the developing system.

### *Levels of change*

In a dynamic system, change may occur at various levels, implying either the stability of an attractor, resisting or assimilating influences from outside, or change from one attractor to another. In developmental models inspired by DST, such levels have been described as follows.[85]

In a system such as mother–child interaction, some patterns become attractors: hence, the mother and child playing together develop 'typical' sequences of goodnight routines, with more or less variations – a different story is read, sometimes the child asks for a song before the story or not after. For the observer, even typical sequences have some flexibility: the games of routines can be considered functionally 'the same' – without being strictly similar.[86] Such changes, occurring *within an attractor*, can be called level 1 changes.

In contrast, level 2 changes occur when there is a change in the pattern of changes, that is, a shift from one attractor to another: for example, a couple dating for a long time, meeting in different places – level 1 changes – might suddenly start considering a marriage. This may bring in new patterns of exchanges, as new options are considered, new actions conducted, and the meaning of the situation may be reconsidered.

Finally, if the couple got married, this would lead to a level 3 change, demanding a radical reorganization of the system, which is developmental at the level of the whole life course. Being married is a very different 'attractor' from dating. Failing to understand this may hence put a couple at risk of separation, as the transformations required by marriage (level 3 change) are seen as a kind of betrayal of the former rituals. Thus:

> Developmental change is the creation of new attractor patterns and the loss of others. Development is the destabilization, re-organization, and re-stabilization of the collective system of historical attractors.[87]

[85] Fogel (2006, p. 15).

[86] This is a reverse condition to the usual SIMILAR→ 'SAME' cognitive transformation of heterogeneous classes into homogeneous ones (Sovran, 1992). This reverse condition is based on the notion of equifinality that is present in all open systems – the same (similar) outcome can be reached by qualitatively different ('not even similar') pathways.

[87] Fogel (2006, p. 15).

### *Stability and change*

From a DST perspective, thus, development in the life course alternates between relative stability – as maintained by attractors – and more intense changes that can be understood as a move out of one attractor towards a new one. Some attractors might be more stable than others. Hence, within the epigenetic landscape metaphor, a stronger attractor would correspond to a deeper valley – the system resists perturbations better. Conversely, a shallow valley means that the system is very sensitive and may be disturbed by small perturbations. For instance, someone who from an outside perspective is commonly called a 'resilient' child is a child who can tolerate perturbations from deleterious living conditions, such as parental alcohol abuse, bullying in school and non-consequential corrections from teachers, and end up as a self-confident and diligent person. A sensitive child, on the other hand, in spite of very supportive parents and teachers, might end up having serious personal problems due to small perturbations, such as relatively mild bullying from some classmates. The deep valley of the resilient child would represent a strong attractor, while the shallow valley of the sensitive child would represent a weak attractor. Of course, as life courses are unique, resilience and sensitivity will imply different conditions for different children in different situations (which would appear very clearly from an inside perspective) and the outcome will always be individual.

### *Self-organization, autopoiesis and* bricolage *in the life course*

Any dynamic system that is exposed to a perturbation that cannot be absorbed in such a way that the present attractor state can be maintained faces the task of reorganizing itself to move into a new attractor state. This is done through *soft assembly*[88] finely tuned to the specificities of the situation, without planning, without design, using the structures and resources that are available at that particular moment in that particular situation. In contrast, *hard assembly*[89] would be a more engineering- like change, disregarding the situational context in favour of a generalized solution based on a preconceived design, a blueprint or a plan. Thus *hard assembly* implies implementation of an organization conceived outside of the system, while *soft assembly* implies that the system organizes itself according to the demands of the situation. It also implies a more

[88] Thelen and Smith (1994). We are grateful to Beatrix Vereijken for pointing out this important idea to us.

[89] See the consequences for learning in Clark (1997) and Thelen and Smith (1994).

flexible relationship with its environment as well as a more flexible solution to the task facing the system.

Development may be for better or for worse.[90] It is true that the system through self-organization 'strives for' stability through one attractor state or another. However, the system never 'looks beyond' the present stability, and changes it into another attractor state if the conditions for its stability change. The implicit differentiation of epigenesis is not a goal for a dynamic system, it is only the emergent result of the processes of self-organization.

At the level of organism, the concept of *autopoiesis* suggests stability across changing conditions, and thus some purposefulness. The best example of an autopoietic system is a living, self-maintaining organism, be it a cell or a human being. The authors of this concept,[91] however, deny any external purposefulness for autopoietic systems, that is, among other things, the system is not future orientated. Nor are self-organized dynamic systems. However, autopoiesis adds to self-organization the maintenance of the system under changing conditions, and thus offers a clearer distinction between system and environment than in DST, as well as relative independence of the environment.

Our dilemma with this discussion is that the time dimension is left out. We have denied to self-organization and autopoiesis the history and future orientation essential to epigenesis. We may find, however, a bridging term, where future orientation may be conceived without planning and design, thus linking together the atemporality of dynamic systems and the temporality of epigenesis. This term is *bricolage*, a French term originally designating the process of producing an amateur handmade object, with the material available and stored 'just in case', which can eventually have its own temporary consistency (it can range from making a table using a door and piles of books, to constructing a real car from this and that). The French anthropologist Claude Lévi-Strauss[92] used the word metaphorically to qualify the *pensée sauvage*, 'wild thinking' as opposed to 'engineering'.[93] Thus it is akin to soft assembly, that is, absence of design, at the same time as the term applies to the relationship between

[90] In this book the reader will find statements that emphasize the inherently teleological nature of human development, that is, development is purposefully oriented towards making the best possible adaptation between the individual and her environment. However, a contrasting view is also advocated in this book, namely that development is blind to adaptability. The argument is based on the absence of a design in self-organization.

[91] Maturana and Varela (1987). [92] Lévi-Strauss (1962/1966, pp. 16–19).

[93] François Jacob (1981), a Nobel prizewinner in medicine, used this distinction to characterize natural evolution as a form of bricolage.

an *autopoietic* system (in this case, a human being) and his or her environment.

Let us imagine the observation of a *bricoleur* in action. In her present situation, she is in an empty and dilapidated apartment without money. She is tired from standing and from sitting on the floor. She needs to do some writing (perhaps writing a paper by which she could earn some money, she is a scholarly person, piles of books are spread around in the apartment). She has tried on the floor, as well as standing, holding the papers against the wall. She sorely misses a table and a chair. A box in the apartment seems strong enough to afford sitting. But there is nothing that could serve as table. *She has no idea*. This is an important point: she is not able to figure out how to get a table, thus the total absence of design. However, moving around the books, she encounters the affordance of the relationships between a loosely hanging door (not too heavy) and the piles of books around it. This was empirically observed in Wolfgang Köhler's studies on Teneriffe of apes in a cage with a banana hanging from the top of the cage and some boxes around. Her perceptual field has self-organized into a new attractor from which the approximate non-verbal notion of 'tableness' emerges. From this perceptual organization she may act purposefully to construct a table as a category – and a tool for guiding her further experiencing the affordances within new environments. This soft assembly of elements in her perceptual field was achieved in a task as *autopoietic* system, striving for maintaining integrity (providing her with more comfortable working conditions). From our outside perspective, as observers of this *bricoleur*, her actions are understood as purposeful. However, from an inside view, if she were able to provide a phenomenologically honest narrative of her experiences during the process, she would not describe herself as purposefully constructing a table. Rather, the table emerged for her eyes and also for her hands in a way that is elsewhere in this book described as playfulness, the deeper meaning of which is more serious than it sounds, namely, it is a crucial aspect of *autopoietic* self-sustaining, in which we propose soft assembly based self-organization to be crucial.

Applied to life-course development this view means, among other things, that the way in which development – over the whole life course – works can be compared to a permanent *bricolage*. Processes of change are constrained by the limits of the present situation, the resources being used, and each step enables and constrains the next one (epigenesis). Humans are intentional beings and humans build their life paths through interactions, more often than not unplanned; they mostly learn in situations not intended to be educational (the cinema, the post office, etc.); many of the most significant persons we meet may have crossed our path in unexpected ways. Each of these opportunities closes down some options, and yet creates some possible futures. Life is not designed, not 'engineered' – life is *playful*.[94]

Human invention meets limits as well. Through their life course, people live in a world where some aspects of their lives are socially highlighted, others defocused from and still others tabooed. At any moment of time the environment of humans is perceived as having boundaries – even if these can be renegotiated; these offer a *zone of freedom of movement*.[95] What precisely happens within these boundaries is not determined by the boundaries – hence *indeterminacy* and the notion of 'freedom'. Yet as these outer boundaries exist, the whole set of events within the borders of the field is completely constrained by the boundaries (*determinacy*). Hence human activities are *self-organized*, though socially guided through the general *principle of bounded indeterminacy*.

## Summary: developmental science of the human life course

In this chapter we have covered the basics of a developmental perspective to the whole human life course. It becomes clear that the developmental perspective – shared by developmental biology, psychology, sociology and anthropology – is built on foundations that are different from their non-developmental counterparts. This entails a look at mutual relations between various levels of the organism – from genes to society – as they operate over the whole life course. Both the stability of the organism over its life course, and its dynamic flexibility are generated through the general process of *probabilistic epigenesis*.

The premises of sample-based inferential techniques – statistical inference – are not appropriate for the study of development. Human development is non-ergodic – we cannot extrapolate from the study of interindividual variability in a population to the intraindividual analysis of the life-course dynamics. Instead of statistical models, new formal systems, like DST, replace the traditional methodologies.

Finally, we have introduced the notion of the human life course as semiotically organized – human beings make meanings as they move along the landscapes of their lives. Our use of Waddington's epigenetic landscape metaphor may help to view our human life courses as trajectories constrained by what the environment at any time affords, in combination with the history the person carries with her, including earlier

[94] See in particular Chapter 9 and 10.
[95] Valsiner (1987, 1997); see also below, Chapter 7.

experiences and actions made meaningful through her own earlier meaningful actions.

This theoretical foundation therefore brings us to see human development as an ever-renewed adventure, based on a constant and mutual adjustment between a person and her human and non-human environment. As these proesses unfold, some patterns of conduct, or some ways of interacting, some capacities or habits, some ways of using resources and engaging in *bricolage*, seem to stabilize – but all of them are only temporary attractors. This view opens up space for thinking about the inherent creativity of human life: what, from the outside, may appear as random and undeterminated adjustments, may provide for a person a space for permanent *bricolage* and reinvention. Hence, patterns of adjustment, dynamic changes and stabilities, are part of the consituents of a person's unique 'melody'- what makes her unique, and enables others to recognize her as such. The perspective proposed here thus invites us to consider seriously the fundamentally evolving nature of human existence – where obstacles, troubles and ruptures might be seen as calls for new attractors, and as challenges for people to use whatever resources they find in their environment and their imagination to support this process of permanent transformation. In particular, as humans are meaning-makers (the semiotic species), imagination provides them with unique and potent resources to meet challenges that call for reinvention.

# 2 Imagination and the life course

> Many of us feel like we're young even when we aren't. And, of course, the other way around. (Becker, 2008, p. 261)

> There is no single reality, Corporal. There are many realities. There's no single world. There are many worlds, and they all run parallel to one another, worlds and anti-worlds, worlds and shadow-worlds, and each world is dreamed or imagined or written by someone in another world. Each world is the creation of a mind. (Auster, 2008, p. 69)

It takes wisdom – and also much energy – to attempt to live in only the present moment. If we pay attention to the flow of consciousness, we soon realize how much we keep travelling in time – think about what was, what will be and what could be otherwise. In this chapter, we propose to listen to various people's perspectives on what they think and how they examine events. We will soon realize that their ability to deal with daily or existential issues is made possible through these constant moves. We will also see that they use various semiotic resources. Our proposition is here that these processes are mainly *processes of imagination*.

*Imagination* is a derivation from the Latin word *imaginari* (to 'imagine') which means 'to create a mental picture to oneself'. It is by virtue of our semiotic function that we create these images, becoming able not only to experience the present world (by virtue of sign-mediated operations, such as perceiving and acting upon the material world, expressing and observing feeling states, by talking to other people, or by thinking with symbols) but also progressively to go beyond the present. Creating such pictures within oneself makes it possible to create further contrasts both within the subjective realm and in actual dealings with the environment. The imaginary leads the movement to the new real.

Hence most of us (humans) can remember what came before the moment we call *right now*, and can imagine – often in a blurred way – what might come next. Sometimes we are all too sure that something that *perhaps may* happen – restoration of justice or the end of the world – certainly will. We go into an examination thinking that we will succeed, and sometimes, to make it easier, we imagine that 'the experts' – deities, parent, or psychologists – will be there to help us in an absurd situation. We rely on our imagination for *what is about to* happen. Singers and musicians imagine the shape, colours and direction of the communicated feeling before blowing a horn or launching into the singing of a song. The lover imagines, full of delight, what will happen when meeting the object of her longing. The person up late at night imagines creatures in the dark, or robbers, when he hears the creaks of the wooden beams or of the furniture. Sometimes we create elaborate scenarios to counter the imagined horrors with equally imagined counter-measures. As a child, a woman reports later,

> [I] had a strange idea of safety when I was alone in the dark; I always imagined that at each corner of my bed there was a lion, who was always on the alert to fight with the ceaseless number of tigers and snakes which I fancied were prowling up stairs all night; *so long as the lions were there I felt safe, but if I thought one disappeared* I would lie awake in dreadful fear that the others would not be enough to struggle with the tigers [added emphasis].[1]

Facing the unknown darkness of her room, the child calls upon images of lions – probably as they can be described in children's books, with all the values and emotions attached to them in a given culture – and she creates the imaginary presence of lions with specific attributes around her bed. These have the power to transform her expectation of the future from a frightening one to one in which she is safe.

Imagination is possible thanks to semiotic processes: we work with representations of the past, as well as images and representations shared in our social and cultural environments; we decompose and transform them, and reinvent new ones. Thanks to semiotic mediation, we imagine tastes before cooking, an argument with the addressee before writing a letter, or the gaze of others before buying an orange suit. And after we have written the letter or bought the suit – we decide not to send the letter, or we return the orange suit to the shop as if it had some 'defect'.

Our orientations towards the past and the future are not epiphenomena: they are both the very basic conditions of our survival as organisms (they enable us to anticipate dangers) and the roots of our achievements as members of human civilizations (they enable the transmission of human experience and thus progress). In addition, each of us humans has only one life (or so we believe in our society)

[1] Hall (1897, p. 185).

and we feel it is a very special one. What renders us different from our cat, or from our neighbours, is in great part our memories of the past (which tell us who we are, where we come from, what happened to us, who we love and who shouldn't be trusted, how to open a can of tuna and how to apply for a better job), and how we imagine our future (which tells us who we want to become and where we want to be, and thus makes it worth engaging in new relationships, travelling to foreign countries, not taking one more slice of cake, slowing down before our car enters a bend, etc.).

We travel through time in our imaginative activities, but we also travel throughout time in a very specific or material sense. The central characteristic of humans as living organisms is that we live for a limited time that never stops flowing. We enter the world, small and with very little experience of our environment, we experience events and we die, after having gathered some memories of these experiences, and having anticipated, or not, that death. In between, we keep moving. Therefore, the internal imaginative travelling and the external physical flowing of time are interconnected, giving form to the future a person faces. So let us imagine a person moving on the imaginary line of her life course: as a child, there is a very short past, and the future seems infinite; as an adult, one sees clearly the immediate past and the next moments, but childhood and old age seem far away; as an old person, there is much more to remember and much less to expect. Not only is there a change of perspective, but also a change of capacity to imagine: as the child progressively becomes proficient in manipulating symbols in a socially articulated way, past and future will no longer only be anticipated in organic ways (such as bodily reactions based on previous learning), but can also be symbolically re-presented – pre-constituted or re-constituted. Adult capacities are enriched by all further skills, competences and knowledge, and these capacities evolve until old age. Imagining – including remembering, planning and examining alternatives – plays a key role in terms of adaptation. When exceptions occur, for example when neurological disorders emerge, difficulties of maintaining regular adaptation to the social and material world become quite dramatic, and people then need social support in order to sustain their human lives.

In other words, a person is not a series of snapshots in time, but a constantly evolving organism, his or her past and his or her future are also constantly transformed – extended, reduced, reorganized, revised. *The development of a person during her life course is also the development of her imagination of her past, future, and alternative lives*. And such imagination has a fundamental role to play in the actual shape that a person's life course will take.

## Childhood memories, pretend-play and futures

Childhood is a time of very intense memory and infinite openness. As a child has not yet lived through many experiences, and as he or she has not yet developed some of the modes of thinking that later adults will have, his or her experiences seem to have a great emotional and perceptual intensity.

It is difficult, if not impossible, to ask young children about their first autobiographical memories; however, daily conversations with parents reveal the slow and progressive genesis of memory, together with the construction and maturation of children's thinking abilities. Katherine Nelson, a child psychologist, and her colleagues have recorded the monologues of young Emily around her second birthday. Everyday, before her nap and before bedtime, her parents would briefly interact with her; once they left her alone, she would usually engage in a monologue (sometimes on the themes just discussed, sometimes not). Nelson's hypothesis is that 'Emily's monologues were motivated at least in part by the effort to construct a coherent representation of her experience'.[2] In effect, elements that need intensive elaboration appear in these monologues. In contrast, daily events that occur on a regular basis disappear from these monologues when Emily is about 2½, suggesting that these do not need further elaboration once they become generalized patterns; rather, it is mainly the exceptional and the future that needs such elaboration. The psychological means to understand these new events seem to be lacking. These means, which Nelson calls representations, have also been called schemes by Piaget, or categories by others – and can be called, as we propose here, internalized semiotic hierarchies. Such semiotic capacities result from the synthesis of a plurality of traces of repeated experience, together with socially shared signs. Nelson similarly suggests that these representations are greatly dependent on Emily's linguistic acquisitions (pronouns, indicators of time).

Here is an example of personal memory of an unusual event during which the family car broke down, which occurred two months before it actually was mentioned in a monologue, as such (words in brackets are uncertain transcriptions):

> (21 months 7 days)
> What do my,
> Emmy get (tooky)
> The the booty,
> The broke, car broke, the... Emmy can't go in the car.
> Go in green car.

[2] Nelson (2006, p. 34).

No.
Broken. Broken,
Their car broken,
So Mommy Daddy go in their their car,
Emmy Daddy go in the car,
Emmy Daddy Mommy go in the car,
Broke,
Da . . . da, the car . . .
Their, their car broken.
So go in the green car,
Fix the car broke,
So their car broke . . .
So my daddy went in the meeting in c- in the, in the car.
So Emmy out the (circles) in the, (w-) in the way.
Daddy stop it, in the (circles) over there. . .
Emmy put over there,
So car broke, Car B[last name],
Car broken, So have to go in the green car,
Then then green car broken, so my go to nap. (Nelson, 2006, pp. 63–4)

In this sequence, Emily seems to try to grasp the components of the event – the green car, the fact that it is broken and its consequences – and to try to relate them one to another. She just seems to try various combinations, which allow her to distinguish sorts of car (broken car vs. green car), people that can go in a green car (daddy, mommy, Emmy), actions that can be engaged in about the car (break, be fixed, be driven to a meeting, be stopped), and eventually the consequence of having all cars broken – go to nap! Hence, Emily seems to decompose the reality in components, some of which are grouped as part of sets, some others become superordinate (signs that can act upon signs), and some are linked in chains of successive actions. This progressive hierarchic organization of semiotic means is greatly facilitated through her now mastered language. Note, however, that these traces of experience and their organization are presented in a pure present.

In order to turn them into memories located in the past, Emily needs to master specific temporal terms and ideas of succession. Hence, a few weeks later, the same memory is recalled after the possibility that a tow truck might take another car was discussed with her mother. This time, 'then' is used to designate successive events in the past; the idea of 'different time' is used to distinguish a comparable yet separate instance of an experience:

(24 months 1 day)
Maybe the tow truck come back,
And then tow truck nother car (?)..

Maybe my tand by the tow truck with the (ho-)..
May be tow, the tow, tow (woo-) h-,
Go back and then yellow car come (back).
And then leave the blue car.
The it's broken. Now the (big) tow-tow truck back with the blue car...
And then my Tanta get Mormor,
And, and maybe Tanta saw the tow truck, and Mormor.
Maybe the broken my . . . and then we go back to tanta.
And then we go back Tan-..
May be Daddy come back here..
We go back my..
And then..
The tow truck come back and tow nother car...
And then come back tow different kind..car
But then we,
This go to my house,
And we come back.
And then . . . different time . . .
Somebody come and get..
The little.
No one with, keep the (whether anyone) like the (with) and out (with)
And come in the house..
And then the truck come back...
For little car...
But then... (Nelson, 2006, p. 65)

In this example, additional elements come into the monologue: other actors, green and yellow cars; and these are disposed in a hypothetical mode ('may be') as well as what seems to be a ludic one (play on syllables and sounds). Hence, aged a little more than two years, Emily already expands her memory of events that have taken place, and with the aid of the adequate vocabulary, turns them into events that could be (or not), and that might eventually be.

Our example suggests that a child elaborates memories, very early on and also transforms them into possible futures. These verbal explorations of the past and the future are limited by their author's representational capacity – the words she has mastered and their related ideas. Here, as these semiotic tools enable the designatation of objects, persons and attributes such as colour, and their basic relations – this is what seems to be represented. Their personal emotional quality for Emily is not expressed in words; however, the very fact that these events are mentioned (there are five occurrences of the broken car episode in five months), and the length of their evocation might represent their subjective relevance.

Paradoxically, thus, the child's progressive mastery of socially given semiotic means, together with her experiences in the world and with others, enables her to develop her thinking and remembering capacities, and together with this, her ability to create her unique version of her life.

More usual are "first memories", as recalled by adults. As genre, these memories often consist in some moment of specific emotional quality. They might be recorded in terms actually quite close to those of a young child, as in the autobiographical recollection of the elderly, former Czechoslovak president and pedagogue Tomas G. Masaryk (1850–1937), written down by Karel Čapek:

> My oldest memories . . . These are so loose memories. Once – I was may be three years old – I saw in Hodonin a bolted horse. He was rushing in the street, people were escaping from all sides. Only a child fall under his feet, but the horse jumped over it. And the child was not harmed. This remained like this, in my head.[3]

However, adolescents and adults have access to a wider vocabulary; they can use words to describe emotions. On a blog called 'What's your first memory of?',[4] Norski reports an earlier memory on the 15 August 2007:[5]

> My earliest memory, probably, is that of the view from the bottom of a stairway leading up to the 2nd floor of the house I grew up in. Judging from the angle, I'd say I was crawling at the time. I remember the sense of wonder and curiosity.

This memory might date back to an age similar to that of Emily; however, the description of a 'sense of wonder and curiosity' could only be given many years later. In the same style, an online user called 'mawkish' writes the following on 15 August 2007:

> My earliest memory is my fourth birthday. I was the first awake and very excitedly woke up my parents, who told me to go play until they got up so we could celebrate. I remember being upset that they didn't bound out of bed like I did and they seemed to take forever before they came out to join me.

Here as well, the event is reported with terms describing quite accurately emotional states. Such examples, randomly chosen, suggest that we may actually remember experiences about which we might not have been able to speak at the age at which they occurred. The question is therefore, whether the emotional quality of these events is 'in' the memory, waiting to be named a few years later, or whether it is provided by a later interpretation of these early memories, or even whether it is a socially guided interpretation and narration imposed on earlier events. As we have seen

[3] Čapek (1991, p. 3), our translation from French.
[4] www.blogcatalog.com/discuss/entry/whats-your-first-memory-of.
[5] www.blogcatalog.com/discuss/entry/whats-your-first-memory-of.

from Emily, early memory telling and its transformation into playful explorations of the future are only a few steps from each other . . .

The close relationship between reality and imagination, what is and could be, is also expressed in the first page of a novel by Howard Buten, a child psychologist expressing the perspective of an eight-year-old child:[6]

When I was five I killed myself.

I was waiting for Popeye who comes after the News. He has large wrists for a person and he is strong to the finish. But the News wouldn't end.

My dad was watching it. I had my hands over my ears because I am afraid of the News. I don't enjoy it as television. It has Russians on who will bury us. It has the President of the United States who is bald. It has highlights from this year's fabulous Autorama where I have been once, it was quite enjoyable as an activity.

A man came on the News. He had something in his hand, a doll, and he held it up. (You could see it wasn't real because of the sewing.) I took my hands off.

'This was a little girl's favorite toy,' the man said. 'And tonight, because of a senseless accident, she is dead.'

I ran up to my room.

I jumped on my bed.

I stuffed my face into my pillow and pushed it harder and harder until I couldn't hear anything anymore. I held my breath.

Then my dad came in and took my pillow away and put his hand on me and said my name. I was crying. He bent over and put his hands under me and lifted me up. He did this to the back of my hair and I put my head on him. He is very strong.

He whispered, 'It's ok, Son, don't cry.'

'I'm not,' I said. 'I'm a big boy.'

But I was crying. Then Dad told me that every day somebody gets dead and nobody knows why. It's just the rules. Then he went downstairs.

I sat on my bed for a long time. I sat and sat. Something was wrong inside me, I felt it inside my stomach and I didn't know what to do.

So I layed down on the floor. I stuck out my pointer finger and pointed it at my head. And I pushed down my thumb. And killed myself.

In this section, the child runs from the present to the past, explores the boundary between present and distant reality (what is here and what is further and needs to be imagined) and what is real and what is fictional (the doll being sewn); what is clear is that these events all emotionally touch the young boy – they scare him, make him rejoice, but also bring him to deep despair and wishing that time or his life would stop.

[6] Buten (2000, p. 9).

Each of these childhood memories presented us with emotionally moved young persons, dealing with an unexpected situation. Each with their own story, people with whom they share experiences, semiotic and material means at their disposal, they engage in unique actions and thoughts: playing with the ideas of different cars and trucks, feeling the whole excitement of seeing one's staircase, wanting to hide in a pillow. These children all discover the world of houses, parents and stories people tell; each interprets it in a unique way. And this uniqueness of one's style of living – one's melody – is largely defined, these examples suggest, by a person's imaginary life, which gives to daily experience all its depth and richness.

*Such changeability and accuracy of real-imaginary emotional experiences, deeply felt by a unique person – this is what as developmental psychologists we want to account for.*

## Imagination in adolescence

Adolescence and youth are supposed to be the ages when everything seems possible. Yet these are also periods of many ruptures and changes. In societies marked by numerous recent crises – the end of communism in the late 1980s, a climate of general insecurity following September 2001, the economic crises of 2008 – more and more young people find themselves facing a society with no clearly marked future pathways. In contrast, such as in communist times in the former Soviet countries, the school careers of young people would clearly train them to occupy specific professional positions in the labour market.[7] Once a track was chosen (or offered), there were no hesitations and insecurities.[8] Today, at the other extreme, more and more educators and parents have to confess that they are preparing the next generation for a future that they cannot anticipate. The older generation fears the future and regrets the lack of orientation marks; yet the younger may actually be much more ready to deal with uncertainty, ambivalence and the need to create new options as these occur.

Imagination here plays a crucial role – be it the capacity to make projects based on the past, or the ability to imagine options in a field of ambivalence. Culture provides people with many means to trigger and mediate

[7] Of course, starting one's adult life facing multiple choices or being chanelled into one life path has deep consequences for the very definition of selfhood. See Baumeister (1987) and Danziger (1990) for an account of the evolution of the concept of 'self'.

[8] Roberts (2008).

their work of imagination. These means may appear as extensions of Emily's goodnight dialogues and monologues: talking with friends or writing a diary are means to give oneself the space to deploy one's imagination. However, the problems of a young adult are more complex and arise in a heavily constraining environment. Here is the first entry of an online diary of an anonymous young student:

Friday, 1 May 2009 – 2:55 am

Right now I'm kind of sad and don't really know what to do with my life. I've decided to start a new diary because I need a place where I can just let it all out.

The reason why I'm sad right now is because we've (me and my fiancé) been trying to make it out on our own with the house and the bills but not really working. I'm glad we have his parents to help us out but I feel so bad of always taking their money to make it. I'm starting to regret the day we decided to buy this house. I can't wait for him to finish college and get a job that pays enough so we don't need to ask them for help. I'm just so scared that he doesn't get a well paid job. I guess the only thing I can do for now is wait and hope for the best. Another thing I'm scared of is not getting into my Bachelor next year. I'm very happy I did pass the class I needed for it, but now I need to wait to see if they'll accept me. This is killing me! I'm also scared that I won't get a loan for next year so I'll have to figure a way to get the money to continue my studies. Again, I tell myself, wait and hope for the best. One day at the time! But really, I don't want to lose another year or have to go to college. I've wasted enough of my time already and one year off is too much. I'll have to start with people I don't know and it's kind of bugging me. If I do get in (which I really hope) I'm a year behind my friends and it's really making me sad. They'll have a job in two years and I'll still be in university. Oh well, hopefully I'll make new friends. I guess I'm not really there to make friends, but to get my degree so I'll be ok, I think. (AngelCurl)[9]

AngelCurl explains her need for a diary as the search for a place where she can let her sadness out. However, what follows is not so much the exposure of a sad event, as anxieties about a series of issues whose outcome is uncertain. Her anguish is that of someone who can consider possibilities and engage with some (buy a house; study for a bachelor's degree; or get a well-paid job), but who has no mean to verify that her choices were the 'right' ones and that the expected outcome will happen.

Her diary appears as a place in which her imagination can open its wings, and so she imagines – what happens if I have a well-paid job? What will happen if I do not have a well-paid job? One way to interpret her anxiety comes from a discrepancy between a fiction promoted by her social environment, the actual situation and her own imagination. Indeed, we may think that she was exposed, through her education, the

[9] www.my-diary.org/read/?read=383673.

media and daily encounters, to a certain social representation of the 'good life' as defined by the North American and British economies at the turn of the millennium. She seems to have internalized certain value-laden discourses or images, such as the one encouraging settling down early, buying a house with a mortgage, taking a loan to study, etc., as part of the promises of happiness. Once internalized, these social semiotic means seem thus to have strongly guided the young woman's choices, rendering certain choices more appealing than others at various life bifurcations. However, after the economic crises, it is no longer certain that the choices made will actually lead to the expected outcomes. Hence we might say that AngelCurl is anxious because she has too much imagination about the future (after all, she would be less worried if she were sure that she would get the job she expects) or, on the other hand, because she has not enough imagination. In effect, had she not been so guided by the values she has internalized, she might realize that there were other possible trajectories than the one in which she was engaged.

Culture offers us further catalysts or techniques to expand our imagination. People can use other people's experiences (as when one discusses similar life experiences with a close friend) or fiction as symbolic resources in order to do so. Hence, Lily is in a situation close to that of AngelCurl; her difficulty is to decide what to do after college. In an interview on the role of culture in young people's lives, she mentioned the importance that the film *After Life*[10] has taken on for her.

*After Life* describes a group of recently deceased people staying in a remote building where they are asked to reflect about their lives and to identify their best memories. The clerks that work in that place then construct that memory in a studio, and film them. At the end of the week in which people live in these limbos, a projection of all the films thus made is organized: each person who watches her own memory on screen vanishes, rejoining it for eternity. People who cannot identify their best memory become clerks. Here is the version Lily gives of that film:

> It is a Japanese movie . . . They end up . . . it is like an immigration office, and they have to pick up a memory – and it is all about the selection process . . . So you have young people, you have old people, and all kind of people. And it is all about this process, you know, about going, choosing, and being able or not able to choose, and these people who are unable to choose . . . so they are stuck there, for centuries. I always think of that – I think about that often for a reason or another. I've thought about it the other day, just a couple of days ago – but I can't remember. It is interesting, because when I watched that movie, I didn't think automatically what

[10] *After Life*, a film by director Hirokazu Koreeda (1998).

would I choose. But the people I was watching the movie with, just asked me – what would I choose, I really don't know – it would be sort of logical, but I didn't ask myself . . . I think about it because – when death comes in memory. I think about it when I think about sorts of life . . . about relative happiness, and the difference between being content, and not, or having lots of energy, or not much energy. I mean all these things I have been thinking for a long time, it is a schedule for life. So every time these things come out, and because I am thinking about the future quite a lot right now, and about people, whether they are staying in my life or not staying in my life. Because how people choose their memories, has a lot to do with how people choose their lives.

In this short interview sequence, Lily actually tells how a discussion with friends first brought her to reflect about the memory she would choose, were she in that situation; she then says that every time that she has a decision to make, she thinks about that film. The film indeed provides her with a strategy to guide her decision-making: she imagines possible futures, imagines herself at the end of her life, and from there, imagines herself remembering these potential events and examining whether they would be possible candidates for a good 'best memory'. Such complex semiotic guidance, offered by the film and the subsequent discussion Lily had with her friends, is an example of the use of a film as a symbolic resource.[11] It shows how works of fiction available in our culture can become techniques to increase our imagination and thereby our understanding of present, past and future events.

## The many ways of adulthood

In Western societies, so-called 'adulthood' is actually the longest part of most people's lives. Contrary to what this general term suggests, this period is usually not uniform. Life constantly exposes most people to options and decisions, changes, discoveries, renunciations and losses. And, as earlier in life, each opportunity demands the examination of possible outcomes, links to past events and alternatives. And so imagination is constantly at work. See, for example, the very common experience of having one's children leaving home, as described by an online diarist:

There was a deafening silence as I stood in my daughter's bedroom. I looked around at all of her belongings that were still in place. I turned my attention to the many pictures that were hanging on the walls and especially to the ones that were sitting on the dresser. I looked at each one slowly and methodically. As I did, a lump began to swell in my throat. Without warning, my eyes filled with tears and I stood there, crying like a baby. We had taken her to college three days before, but

[11] See Zittoun (2008b) for a further analysis of that case.

now, for the first time, as I stood in her bedroom, reality finally started to sink in. Thoughts began to race through my head, thoughts that I did not like. Is she gone for good? Will she come back and live with us again? Will we still have that special father/daughter relationship that we had before?[12]

If looking at pictures and objects can make present an absent other, it is thanks to the symbolic power of these objects – they stand there, but looking at them unlocks a chain of memories – imaginations of the past – as when one rubs the genie's lamp. These memories are generated, and become significant, in relation to events in the future: the daughter will no longer be there. This movement generates possible alternatives, one being that the daughter will come back, so that the future will be like a projection of the past in to the time ahead, the other being that the daughter will not, so that the future will be the negation of this past.

Memories are traces of past experiences, elaborated through various ways, organized psychologically into hierarchical sets. If, as with Lily, external artefacts can trigger these experiences, these can also be deliberately more externalized, or projected on to objects. In this case, this father's traces of experiences are, so to say, 'in' the objects, or carried by them. And thus, as much as we can play with past memories – imagine how things were, could have been – we can also play with things that get 'outsourced' traces of experiences. And again, it is with this play with one's memories, or reorganization of traces of past experiences, that a person creates her own life trajectories and style.

Such style, which becomes one's melody of living, can become much more definite in adulthood. As in youth, the use of symbolic resources may help to generate specific imaginings in daily situations and at turning points. However, adults start to have many experiences, and can develop generalized understandings not only from actual situations and experiences, but also, from past imagining themselves. In the following sequence, a man in his seventies had been asked to reflect about transitions in his life. In his accounts, specific texts, songs and discussions seem to have supported his imagination in his youth. However, presenting professional decisions he had to make in his adult years, he mentions 'images' that orientated his fantasy about the sort of psychologist he wanted to be:

At this time [of my life, at around 35] I had as a student of psychology three ambitions . . . Images:

(i) (mastery of clinical diagnosis): the magician, the intellectual acrobat, the trapeze in his little circus with curtains;

[12] www.my-diary.org/read/?read=293249.

(ii) (learning and developmental psychologist): the good mother and her baby (concave); self-realization – as conquest of space and time – better, of time–space (convex); the moving spiral, re-creation starting always from the centre;
(iii) (psychoanalysis): earth–sky, red and green in the blue; to know and recognize myself (feel my animal, know (my) life in the intimacy of my heart, in my becoming and under the sky full of stars); mirror, passage and transference (how much can I be another, how much the other can be me); saving (me? My patient?).[13]

Hence, in this sequence, fictional images used as resources are not referring to one specific cultural element (e.g. a particular film, an album of Pink Floyd); rather, they seem to be hypergeneralized images. They probably result from the traces of different yet similar cultural experiences: under (i), stories of magicians, perhaps like in Thomas Mann's *Mario and the Magician*,[14] or of acrobats, like the hero of *Till Eulenspiegel*,[15] both of which he had read, and which evoke 'circus life', and suggest mystery, dexterity, excitation, glamour, etc. Hence, an image like the 'magician' becomes a very personal creative synthesis, crystallizing the stories and representations available in this person's sociocultural environment, and finding a unique resonance in his personal experiences, dreams and fantasies. In turn, this new image becomes itself a symbolic resource that can be used to regulate a trajectory: to imagine better ways of acting, to guide personal or professional decisions, or as points to facilitate self-reflection. One might thus decide not to go on with diagnosis, as the image of the magician suggests the wish to impress the public, rather than to counsel a person in need. In that sense, one's melody of living will be shaped by the resources carved by the person herself – already resulting from a long story, yet still open to change.

As people get older, their experiences multiply. Many events become routine, and fail to become significant memories. In turn, the resources to handle them may also have become so generalized that they usually evade deliberate reflection. Such apparent routines give people the impression that time runs without leaving traces; this is also why, retrospectively, events that differ from daily ones become such significant memories. In time of relative continuity, ruptures become salient, as they demand more work of imagination[16] – the unexpected is the basis of sense-making and narrative building; in hectic times, it may be precisely times of unexpected peace that make it possible to free one's imagination.

[13] Private notes; however, the life trajectory of this man has been partly analysed in Zittoun (2007a).
[14] Mann (2000). [15] Oppenheimer (1995).
[16] In adult lives it is the unexpected that needs more elaboration – we will come back to the importance of ruptures, conflict and the possibility of innovative moments in the life course (Chapter 6).

Life continues under all possible environmental conditions – peace or war. For example, during the Second World War in Britain, people experienced a highly unpredictable period; however, on a daily basis, young women who were forced to work on the home-front (supporting the country's war effort) lived short periods of a relatively regular life (which could be disturbed at any time). Hence June, a young woman who had to work in the fields, which substantially questioned the sense of who she was or the plans she had for herself before the war, answers as follows the question asked by Mass Observation, doing a survey in October 1942:

Q: (a) How do you think you have come to hold your present beliefs or forebodings about what things *will* be like after the war?, and (b) How have you formed your own plans and desires about what you *want* after the war?
A: (a) Imagination, what I have read, heard and what it was like [overwrites 'life'] after the last war. (b) Imagination again, personal experience & other peoples experiences books.[17]

In a similar vein, people locked up in concentration camps in communist Czechoslovakia for a long-term sentence had been victims of random arrests or denunciation; none would consider their actions as criminal. After this radical rupture of their life course, prisoners lived an extremely routinized daily life, only likely to be arbitrarily disrupted by a transfer to another camp, an interrogation, etc. How then to survive on a daily basis, if one's life has been radically disrupted, in a situation which is personally meaningless? Interviewed by two historians,[18] Hana Truncová, arrested when she was twenty-seven, sentenced to thirteen years and released after nine, says:

I was thinking about my future life, I planned a family and was also thinking about things that happened. In my imagination I walked on trips, travelled and remembered my life. *I would say that a prisoner lives again the life he has already lived.* You remember everything from childhood, you remember people who were important to you. It is not that you would judge your life because you cannot change anything but in prison you appreciate the fact that you were able to live and that you enjoyed it.[19]

Other prisoners – as means of resisting this life – indulged in thoughts, imagining being back home, ruminating their faith, or their hatreds – all activities demanding active work from the imagination.[20]

[17] Example taken from Zittoun (2008d).
[18] Bouška and Pinerová (2009) collected 'oral histories' to document the lives of political prisoners.
[19] Bouška and Pinerová (2009, p. 91).
[20] It is also to be noted that, in complement, all these prisoners mentioned the extreme importance of the strong relationships they established with each other, as if the anchorage of their lives in time and space (as in free life) was replaced by an anchorage within a tight relational network.

Observations in extreme cases usually highlight phenomena which appear in a weaker form otherwise. These examples suggest two complementary observations: one is that isolation from the 'normal' flow of life may open more space for imagination of the past and the future. This may be partly why people have always been tempted by temporary or long-term retreats to escape from daily demands and develop a richer imaginative life. The other fact to highlight is the vital strength of imagination – what one imagines can actually feed one's capacity to live (or one's death).

## Getting older – the many faces of ageing

One fact, however, is clear: if a child has infinity open before her; if a young adult is starting to have significant memories of childhood, but is exploring new avenues, getting older presents people with the more and more palpable promise of their own end. This does not mean that they stop imagining, on the contrary – more time and fewer daily demands can allow the mind to range more freely.

When looking at age and ageing we may hold as a first point (again) that 'ageing is universal but not uniform'. Thomae has pointed out that depending on the dimension under consideration one may observe differing 'ageing styles' (*Alternsstile*) and 'ageing fates' (*Altersschicksale*).[21] In this sense people age differentially – one person may have many physical impairments but retain a high sense of morale and well-being; another may have excellent physical status but suffer from cognitive impairments induced by early neurodegenerative disease. Getting older thus has more than one face – and the many faces of ageing manifest at the phenomenological level the dynamic of its underlying bio-sociocultural co-construction.

It is a well-documented phenomenon that reminiscence increases with age. More than young people, elderly people seem to think about the past: as the temporal space for living is getting narrower one may thus escape into the past. Moreover, if physical and functional impairment prevent an elderly person from staying mobile and active that person may use imaginary space to engage in virtual activities and experience him- or herself as actor. Imagination in old age is fed by a larger thesaurus of memories than in former periods of the lifecycle and it may be used to construct and reconstruct realities. On the other hand, growing older also means that one has acquired more and more experiences leading to the impression that nothing new ever happens and that a lot of things happening in life are already known. Days are guided by routines which

[21] Thomae (1983).

may give security and predictability on the one hand, but which may on the other hand also foster a uniform life where one day resembles another and where no significant events or changes occur. As was the case in early childhood and throughout life, in old age memory does not react to these kinds of everyday experiences – the perception, reflection and the memorizing of life events is guided by events that ask for our active attention. Attention is selective and it is triggered by those events that are personally significant. But what becomes significant in old age? Is it the inevitable, genetically programmed physical and functional changes, or do we learn to integrate these into our view of the world and the self and thus 'normalize' them? Significance of what happens in one's life is constructed against the background of one's personal history. In this view, ageing is not a circumscribed stretch of time but there is continuity or discontinuity in our self-view: 'I still see myself wearing this leather jacket and having this long hair, being 20 years old – I am not old' is the answer of a 75-year-old man to a question about his view of himself. We certainly do not give up our self-view and we do not wait to obtain a new identity when reaching the officially claimed date for starting to age which is in most countries associated with the withdrawal from work life – be it the classic age of sixty five, be it other age markers still to be constructed in a changing society where becoming old has to be newly defined. We continue and we construct our self-view using our biographical memory – and here we are selective as well. It is one of the most interesting findings concerning autobiographical memory in old age that we remember things that have been forgotten. While we are busy with life issues during the so-called productive phase of our lives the mind is busy with processing what is happening in work and family life. Age implies another 'speed' of life as well as other content. We may not have the 'bottom-up' data input but we now use the top-down input, that is, we take a walk down (and backwards) the memory lane.

In doing so we may emphasize certain of our most diagnostic self-aspects. Some aspects of life lived up to now are personally salient. These become semiotic organizers of the life course, as the person looks back at the life lived so far. This may be illustrated by the following, certainly not daily, experience of a ninety-five-year-old lady, accidentally found in a newspaper:[22]

> 'I'm calling it my flight down memory lane,' said X, who will turn 95 Jan. 30. 'My first flight was in a biplane, and I think this will be my last ride.'

[22] *Charlotte Sun-Herald*, Florida, 19 January 2003.

Mrs X first took to the sky in 1930, when her brother . . . bought her a trip in an open-cockpit biplane as a college graduation present. The pilot flew her through an open field in a rural town outside Philadelphia.

'The only thing that would have made it any better was if I was flying the plane,' she said.

A love of flying stuck with her throughout her life. She often flew with another brother in his Piper Cubs.

The example also shows the significance of certain traits, or traces of experience, that have become generalized, and have acquired a value as higher-level signs, guiding other signs. Linked to a long series of comparable personal experiences, rather than to existing cultural figures as in the example of the psychologist above, these generalized themes can also be seen as varieties of unique creative synthesis, which then become 'what defines us', and continue and stay with us across the lifespan. Here, the experience of flying – first encountered in youth – becomes the organizing core for all life account. What happens if one is no longer capable of being active or of selectively choosing satisfying social interactions that may serve to consolidate our view of the self and the world? Imagination in old age may help to preserve one's personal view of the self and the life – as a person wants it to be. Such self-presentation thus involves memories of the past, and using these to reconstruct one's life and/or to construct alternative life routes.

We know from theory building on reminiscence processes that several forms and functions may be differentiated here, ranging from obsessive, escapist forms of narratives, to transmissive forms of reminiscence.[23] As we have seen, imagination may be used as an escape from a reality which may be hard to bear, it may be used in an obsessive way, ruminating about past events that can no longer be changed, and it may be used as a wish-fulfilling fantasy helping to construct a counterfactual reality. Especially, when being confronted with losses that cannot be compensated for and that do not allow for a re-establishment of a status quo ante, imagination will become more and more important for the regulation of well-being. Furthermore, depending on what is salient in the motivational system of the ageing person, different forms and functions of imagination may be observed.

The finiteness of life – the inevitability of its ending – becomes more and more salient in old age, especially when a person is increasingly confronted with functional and physical impairments. The meaning-making system of the developing person enters into the process of living under the threat of impending end. Implicitly this induces specific future orientations concerning the end of life and even the 'afterlife'. 'Non-existence' may represent a significant content of imagination, not only, but

[23] Wong and Watt (1991).

especially in old age. How do we use imagination with respect to 'something' that cannot be imagined? There may be hopes concerning a possible life after death fed by theological and/or philosophical eschatology. There may also be imagination and planning of one's inheritance, burial ceremony or tombstone – such as a decision about one's epitaph, ultimate externalization or trace of one's memory for the future. Still, uncertainty remains. Further scenarios may deal with the way we might die. 'I am not afraid of death but I am afraid of dying' – is a sentence that is often heard when people talk about the end of their life. Several fears – such as fear of pain, fear of the uncertain and of the unknown and fear about those we will leave behind – may characterize these imaginations that may not be easy to bear. Non-existence, though inevitable, is not easily accepted. Finally, obituaries follow a rather standard script – they spell out that the person who no longer exists *still lives on in the memories of those who keep on living*. Death is a form of 'going away' – to some other place – while continuing to live. It is a prime example of the unity of the AS–IS and AS–IF modes of thinking.

There are poems, songs, paintings, movies elaborating the experience of meeting death as a person – as anthropomorphism. Emily Dickinson's 'The Chariot' may serve here as an example:[24]

> Because I could not stop for Death,
> He kindly stopped for me;
> The carriage held but just ourselves
> And Immortality.
> We slowly drove, he knew no haste,
> And I had put away
> My labor, and my leisure too,
> For his civility.
> We passed the school where children played,
> Their lessons scarcely done;
> We passed the fields of gazing grain,
> We passed the setting sun.
> We paused before a house that seemed
> A swelling of the ground;
> The roof was scarcely visible,
> The cornice but a mound.
> Since then tis centuries; but each
> Feels shorter than the day
> I first surmised the horses' heads
> Were toward eternity.

[24] Dickinson (2004).

We use these socioculturally shared resources – created fictions – to construct our imagination about the end of life. And so we may also approach the cliff that separates life and non-existence in our mind. Moving between reality and imagination in old age thus does always imply going back, as well as going forward – using all the symbols and meanings one has collected throughout life.

## Summary: from personal stories to a psychology of the life course

People are complex organisms, which can be seen as systems adjusting to their environment and adjusting their environment to their needs. People develop specific abilities – including that of using signs – and have access to all kinds of resources. Instead of simply reproducing what is around them, or following constraints, they actually have a unique capacity to alter their relationship to the world – which we have called imagination – a process central in the making of unique life melodies.

In this chapter, drawing on various phenomenological materials, we have suggested that the process of imagination varies along one's life, as life challenges vary, and one's skills, experiences and knowledge – traces of experiences systematically organized, in a personal way or through institutional guidance, and that are mobilizable as resources in further situations – expand. We have shown that imaginative productions may be more or less adaptative, and that they can be orientated in various directions. They can be oriented towards the past, the future or hypothetical alternatives; and they vary according to age, expectation and experiences. Especially, but not only in times of rupture, imagination replaces the unknown with representations, transforms obscure fears into actionable ideas, and thus makes new actions possible. Is imagination boundless? What material and social constraints can be transformed by imagination – how much can the epigenetic landscape be shaped by it? One of the most constant human constraints is time – we live, time passes and we die; and so imagination is transformed through time. But in turn, imagination may transform our whole experience of time . . . How then can we theoretically conceive time, if it can be transformed through the games of imagination?

# 3 Moving through time: imagination and memory as semiotic processes

Human lives proceed in irreversible time. We cannot return to our previous moments of living – other than through imagination. Our capacity for imagination creates a realm of objects in the vicinity of our real lives – what we imagine does not exist (as 'real' objects) *yet it also does <u>not</u> not-exist* (as these non-real objects can be imagined as if they existed). By virtue of the semiotic function imagination may play an important role in human development. Instead of the strict classical logic that deals with the either/or designation of TRUE and FALSE (either true or false, both cannot coexist), our capacity for imagination creates a third class of objects in between (FALSE – yet IMAGINATIVELY TRUE).[1] The crucial feature of the human mind is the capacity to imagine itself in other times – in childhood, or in the future (or even in the 'afterlife') – yet all these imaginary scenarios are created in the present. Through such imaginary scenarios we move forward to ever-new experiences in our unique personal life courses, and these participate in the making of our melodies of living. Even our understanding of what we call 'identity' is a result of our imagination: we need indeed to imagine, in the middle of our ever-changing 'stream of consciousness', that we are in a stable state – and we say that we 'have an identity' (of self, of gender, etc.). We need such illusions of stability to live in our in principle non-stable relations with our environments. We are active in our lives, changing both ourselves and our environments – and operate as open systems – although some pretend not to be active in their self-reflection. In our common language, and even in psychology, we present ourselves not as systems but stable, unchanging persons, as if we consisted of conglomerates of static traits![2]

[1] Of course, logic in the twentieth century has moved beyond the classical Aristotelian-Boolean two-valent version into multi-valued varieties.

[2] This is most prominently visible both in commonsense self-presentations of the kind 'I am X' ('sociable', 'intelligent', etc.) as well as in personality psychology where a certain number of 'factors' (usually five) or 'traits' (over 16,000 – Allport and Odbert, 1936) are believed to be *stable entities within a person.*

As we are proceeding towards the future at every moment in our life courses, the imagination – based on our past – may set up expected and desired scenarios for what may happen. From that perspective, the pretend play of young children, the professional and personal aspirations of adults, and psychological adaptations in later years are all generated by the same basic system: the constructive capacity to imagine the AS-IF state of objects that are accessible in the AS-IS form or, in other words, the capacity to imagine that what is the case could be different, or that what is not could be for real.

AS-IF thinking can be orientated towards the future (as when we imagine what will or what could be), towards the past (when we remember what was or what could have been), as well as towards alternative presents (when we imagine what were if certain things were different).

Our proposition is that the basic human capacity that enables imagination, moving through the 'real' and the likely, and that coordinates past and future in the present, is the semiotic function – the capacity to use signs. This perspective borrows from the theory of semiotics founded by Charles Sanders Peirce (see Box 3.1).

### Box 3.1 Charles Sanders Peirce

Charles Sanders Peirce was an American mathematician and logician, and the founder of semiotics. He is known for his work on signs, out of which grew *semiotics*, the study of signs.

Peirce invented a new terminology – including the notions of representamen, interpretant, 'thirdness', etc. – which have established themselves in the contemporary philosophy of semiotics. His primary classification of signs into *icon*, *index* and *symbol* has been the most widely used, even though these are only three of the twenty-seven classes of signs that Peirce's classification entailed.[3]

More important from a developmental perspective are his attempts to analyse the logics of thinking. For instance, to capture semiotic processes, Peirce described the ever-renewed relationship between a *representamen* (*e.g.* a material sign), an *object* (an object of thought) and an *interpretant* (the mental representation of the relationship between representant and object). Hence for Peirce, a sign represents something, for a given mind, in some particular respect; and in this process, an interpretant might become an object, or an interpretant might become a sign and so on.

Another crucial notion from Peirce for our purposes is his notion of abduction – as a third alternative to induction and deduction. *Abduction*

[3] Rosa (2007).

**Box 3.1 (cont.)**

(Peirce also called it *retroduction*) makes its start from the facts, without, at the outset, having any particular theory in view, though it is motivated by the feeling that a theory is needed to explain surprising facts. Induction makes its start from a hypothesis which seems to recommend itself, without at the outset having any particular facts in view, though it feels the need of facts to support the theory. Abduction seeks a theory. Induction seeks facts. In abduction the consideration of the facts suggests the hypothesis.

Peirce's example:

we encounter a surprising fact X
and think
if Y were the case, the fact X would be explained

Thus, abduction entails a 'jump' to explanation after the fact. In induction the study of the hypothesis suggests the experiments that bring to light the very facts to which the hypothesis had pointed. The mode of suggestion by which, in abduction, the facts suggest the hypothesis is by *resemblance* – the resemblance of the facts to the consequences of the hypothesis. In induction, the hypothesis suggests the facts by *contiguity* – familiar knowledge that the conditions of the hypothesis can be realized in certain experimental ways.[4]

## Reality and imagination

What is real, and what is imaginary? How we can differentiate these experiences is a very old philosophical question. From an outside perspective, it can be answered in very different ways, depending on one's ontological and epistemological beliefs. Here, for now, we are located at the level of a person's experience. From that perspective, imagination is part of our realities as humans. Yet our experiences of real entities differ in some respects from our imaginary experiences.

Intuitively we consider as real things in the world that we experience here and now, and that have a material structure, and on which other people can agree – these things are AS IS. We thus may see the world as real – even if doing so entails a perceptual illusion (see Figure 3.1). A table, the wind or the sound of a clarinet all belong to what we consider as reality. Yet this is reality only thanks to our relating to the environment – seeing and

[4] Peirce (1901).

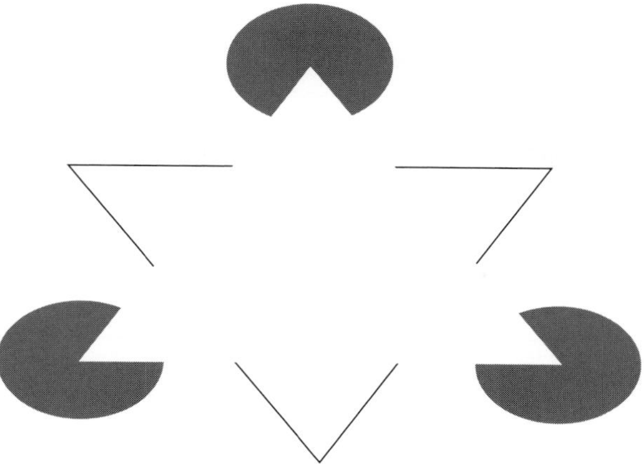

Figure 3.1. Kanisza's triangles – an example of a visual illusion where we perceive non-existing objects (triangles) through the co-constructive functions of our perceptual systems.

feeling the shape, receiving the sound waves and recognizing '*it is a clarinet*', and attributing the agency to the wind ('*the wind is blowing*').

As Von Foerster[5] once beautifully said:

> 'Out there' there is no light and no color, there are only electromagnetic waves; 'out there' there is no sound and no music, there are only periodic variations of the air pressure; 'out there' there is no heat and no cold, there are only moving molecules with more or less kinetic energy, and so on. Finally, for sure, 'out there', there is no pain.

Psychological phenomena exist only due to the dynamic relating of the perceiver/actor to the environment. Yet these phenomena entail reflexivity with agency – we say '*I perceive THIS*' rather than accept that whatever the given *THIS* may be is in constant relation to my body. The latter is the basic reality – the former – a personal construction *made possible* by the basic reality. In Figure 3.1, the perception of triangles is made possible by the graphic patterns in the field – but actualized by the synthesizing perceptual system.

In contrast, people's dreams, their fantasies, their memories of childhood and their wishful thinking, are created by the generative processes of the mind and are not shared; they are part of imaginary experiences. Yet they look as real to us as others – we may wake up from a dream and wonder whether it is 'real' (and find out that it is not). Or we may believe in the love our fiancé, spouse or a deity directs towards us. These mind

[5] Von Foerster (1984, p. 46).

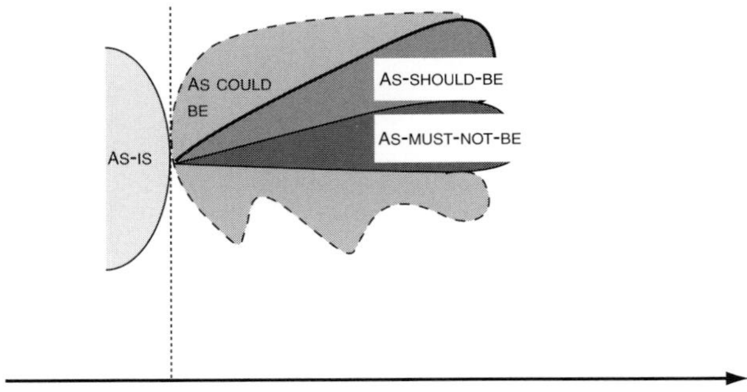


Figure 3.2 Differentiation of the AS-IF domain.

constructions are crucial for living (and dying) in reality – yet they are our meaning constructions in the AS-IF domain.

More fundamentally, the very basic fact that we live in an irreversible time implies that our experience is for the most part beyond what is given to us as real, AS IS. In Figure 3.2, the perpendicular line represents the ever moving here-and-now present; only at this moment can we have the experience of what is AS IS – it is what is the case for us until that precise moment. What will immediately follow is necessarily given in a subjunctive mode: it implies what we expect will happen, what we hope, what we should not make happen and so on; we therefore reason in an imaginary mode, belonging to the WHAT IF range of experiences.

Hence we do not live *either* in the real *or* in an imaginary mode: there are a whole range of phenomena *in between*. In addition, we can be watching a film, reading a poem and, in some cases, participating in a religious ceremony. These are all activities which require objects and material things (the film roll, the text, the temple and its objects) and the mastery of shared languages and conventions; yet these experiences occur because each participant 'invents' a world: he or she can imagine WHAT IF they were travelling in time, living like Mme Bovary or talking to angels – a world beyond the visible and what is here and now. The 'real' objects give rise to new flows of imagination – that may lead to the construction of other 'real' objects.

*'Higher' and 'lower' objects:* most contemporary psychology has – unfortunately – lost a touch with unreality, although it was a part of the agenda of psychologists such as Lev Vygotsky (see Box 3.2). However, the world of meanings of objects that are not perceivable is part of our daily life: we can think about these objects, and use them in our thinking and discussions. For example, *infinity* cannot in principle be perceived. Yet as a concept in mathematics it can be used in consensually acceptable ways.

### Box 3.2 Lev Vygotsky

Vygotsky (1896–1934) was a literary scholar who became a psychologist in the context of the Soviet Union in the 1920s. His reliance on the phenomena of complex psychological kinds – such as Shakespeare's *Hamlet* and Russian literature and theatre – made him interested in the construction of meaning in the flow of human experience. His look at the instrumental use of signs in human higher (volitional) psychological functions amounts to bringing semiotics and psychology together. Being closely intertwined with Continental European thought of his time, Vygotsky focused on the issues of making sense of art[6] and the role of speech in human mental functions.[7] Vygotsky's work was largely forgotten in both the Soviet Union and in international psychology between the 1930s and 1950s. It was brought back to the attention of new cohorts of social scientists by the active propagation of his ideas by Alexander Luria in the USSR and Michael Cole in the United States. Since the 1970s Vygotsky has become popular in European and North American educational contexts where his heritage is interpreted as prioritizing the role of the social environment in human development. While undoubtedly that focus was central for Vygotsky, at the same time he accepted the notion of hierarchical organization of psychological functions ('higher' – volitional – versus 'lower' – automatic – functions) and the central role of dialectical synthesis in meaning-making. Vygotsky – alongside James Mark Baldwin and Jean Piaget – was a consistent promoter of the ideas of development as open-ended process in the first decades of the twentieth century.

Our cognitive capacity to relate the AS-IS and AS-IF domains makes it possible to free our thinking from the straightjacket of the present moment. We can think of objects that we cannot perceive. Some such objects are in principle impossible – a *round triangle*, for instance.[8] Yet, the most remarkable feature of human thinking is that – despite recognizing an impossible object in reality – we *still can think about it.* The same applies to the famous impossible drawings of Escher, like infinite stairs that go up at the same time as they go down and vice versa. Our capacity to create signs, and use them, bridges the gap between the real, the possible and impossible unreal and the imaginary.

6 See Vygotsky's *Psychology of Art*, in English (Vygotsky, 1971).

7 For in-depth overview see Van der Veer and Valsiner (1991).

8 The issue of the psychological roles of impossible objects such as *round triangles* or *golden mountains* was the crucial theme for the discussions in the Graz School of psychology, led by Alexius Meinong (1853–1920). Meinong's object theory (*Gegenstandstheorie* – Meinong, 1904) and Stefan Witasek's (1901) theory of aesthetic cognition as well as Vittorio Benussi's work on object and time perception (Benussi, 1913/2002) are productive results from that tradition which by now is seen only as a philosophical one (Griffin and Jacquette, 2009; Grossmann, 1974).

For example, astronomers who observe exo-planets (planets out of the solar system) or psychologists who analyse the 'social representation'[9] of nature that brings people to buy organic salads are not describing what is 'real'; these scientists observe facts and make hypotheses about invisible entities – and these created facts are considered as 'real' only by these happy few scientists. In that sense, the situation of scientists seeing these constructs may seem similar to people believing that some creatures from another planet will soon invade the earth.[10] All these observations are meant to be about what is the case in the social and material world; yet, in some sense, all these cases require the imagination of invisible entities. These entities can be unreal – yet functional. The main difference between scientific and mythological non-real objects is that in the former, the observers have a methodology that would enable other people to make sense of similar entities if they wished to.

These examples suggest that imagination is not incompatible with knowledge or science; it is often one of its components.[11] Science – if we consider its bold hypotheses rather than mundane data collection routines – operates in the realm of imagination. It is crucial for the development of ideas. Likewise, such thinking ahead into the imaginary world out there – beyond the horizon – drives all exploration efforts. The invention of vessels floating on water and the tools to move them over the water has been the basis for exploration of our planet. As Michel Foucault has remarked, 'In civilizations without boats, dreams dry up, espionage takes the place of adventure, and the police take the place of pirates.'[12]

Of course there is no reason to fear the end of human creativity – that continues in the enquiry into microscopic worlds as well to outer space.

*Imagination defined by modality:* hence, from a psychological (as well as philosophical) perspective, *imagination is not defined by its object, but by the modality by which a person relates to* it. Imagination can be characterized by a specific *mode* of producing ideas or experiences. Classically, authors

[9] For the study of social representations – conglomerations of ideas, beliefs and affects, socially shared, that guide identities, practices and communications – see Marková (2005); Moscovici (2008).

[10] Festinger, Riecken and Schachter (1956/1964) thus studied how a group creates the means to maintain its imagination of such a vision although it has been refuted as an actual perceptible fact.

[11] Studies on 'mirror neurons' suggest that *imagining* doing certain actions or having certain perceptions activates the same neuronal circuits as *actual* actions or perceptions (Gallese, Fadiga, Fogassi and Rizzolatti, 1996; Iacoboni *et al.*, 2005). But, as psychoanalysts pointed out a century ago, young infants can hallucinate the absent breast as much as they want – it won't feed them (Winnicott, 1971).

[12] Foucault (2006, p. 100).

have distinguished information coming from our *perception* – we perceive the sun through our vision of the illuminated landscape, the heat on our skin, the thirst in our throat – and those that come from inner images – our 'mind's eye' – imagination. We can thus imagine buying a red Ferrari, without actually perceiving it. In that sense, what is real is a perception actually caused by an external stimulus; imagining the smell of the leather of the seats is not caused by such an actual stimulus.

Imagination can be defined as the dynamic process of imagining, orientated towards specific objects.[13] Imagination may be very closely linked to memory and experience – as when a person who usually buys his bread at the corner, imagines going to his baker to buy bread tomorrow. Yet imagination can also be free to operate by transforming rich realities into abstract schemata. Hence, a child can generalize out of her total experience with her parents that adults should not be trusted; or most people generalize from their experience that any object with a sharp side can cut. What we most commonly call 'imagination' requires a combination of memory, or the internalization of some experience, and generalization (see Box 3.3). For example, it is easy to imagine 'a flying, blue elephant with a tiger-tail': in order to do so, we have to draw on a general idea of elephant*ness*, abstracted from all the elephants we know; a general idea of blueness; a general idea of tiger-tail; and these various general schema are recomposed in a new manner. Some modes of imagination proceed at such a distance from actual examples that they may appear as authentic creations. Yet overall, imagination is very mundane: in daily life, people imagine how it would be to have a ham sandwich, what would happen if they were to study psychology, or how nice it would be to be on the beach.

### Living through AS-IS and AS-IF

Imagination is the core of development – it merges the AS-IF world – something that is not – or not yet – there, with the AS-IS world. Hans Vaihinger was the key philosopher of the end of the nineteenth and beginning of the twentieth centuries who developed the ideas of the unity of AS-IF – 'useful fictions' – into a coherent philosophical system (see Box 3.4). Over the twentieth century, psychology has at times recognized Vaihinger's contribution, but only partially. It has been proposed that a consistently developmental perspective makes it necessary to build all new methodology and theoretical systems on the axiom of AS-IS ⟷

[13] Sartre (1936/1989) defines imagination on the basis of Husserl's phenomenology, and sees it as an intentional, active synthesis. More recent definitions are still quite close to this, as for instance in Singer and Singer (2005, p. 16). See also Harris (2000).

**Box 3.3 Internalization, externalization and the definition of personal culture**

The idea of memory and imagination presented here suppose that interactions with the world lead to the construction of an internal model of personal culture, based on all the 'traces' of the encounters with the external world that have some social meaning – encoded by signs. The psychology we propose here is based on an analysis of *semiotic processes* – processes in which these signs emerge, are used to guide immediate actions as well as long-term goal orientations, and which can be abandoned or preserved, given the demands of a person's life situation. The basic idea is that signs present in the world (in language, images, melodies) find some sort of reconstruction in the intra-psychological plane of subjective meanings. *Internalization* is the term used to designate this process by which signs or experiences in the world are reconstructed on that mental plane. This internalization is never mechanistic; it demands an active reorganization and appropriation of experience. The internalized meaningful 'picture' of the external world is not a 'mirror image' of the latter, but a new version that anticipates the possible change in the external world.

Conversely, the notion of *externalization* designates the processes by which humans are able to produce signs in the world – through language, movements, colours, singing, etc. Again, externalization is not a pure translation of pre-existing thoughts in the mind.[14] Rather the very fact of using signs to give a visible form to the flow of thinking participates in its formulation.[15]

It is through these processes of internalization and externalization that people define their own version of collective culture – their personal culture – which will, in turn, and through externalization, contribute to modifying the collective culture. Hence melodies of living are not isolated, they are part of a more general concert of lives...

AS-IF mutual coordination.[16] We exist – act, feel, think – in our present here-and-now situation in ways we can be aware of if (and only if) we can create a scenario of there-and-then. Since the latter has to happen concurrently with the former – in the present – then imagination is a necessary condition for any distinction we make – 'this is THIS' we know because we simultaneously find out 'THIS is not THAT'. But for such discovery we need to be able to construct THAT. As we have seen such construction may happen through imagination, which is systemically linked with abstract generalization.[17] We all are involved in two constructive subjective

[14] Lawrence and Valsiner (1993), Valsiner (1997). [15] Vygotsky (1934/1986).
[16] See Josephs (1998).
[17] Vaihinger explained: 'This generalization breaks up the very constituents of existence and puts them together again in a far more general manner, in the process discovering the

### Box 3.4 Hans Vaihinger

Hans Vaihinger (born 1852, died 1933) was the key philosopher of the end of the nineteenth and beginning of the twentieth centuries who developed the ideas of the unity of AS-IF – 'useful fictions' – into a coherent philosophical system (Vaihinger (1911) – *Philosophie Als Ob* – which is mostly his thesis from 1876).[18] His own explanation: 'I wanted to say ... that As If, i.e. appearance, the consciously-false, plays an enormous part in science, in world-philosophies and in life' (1935, p. xli). He labelled his philosophy *positivistic idealism* or *idealistic positivism*.

meaning-making processes in our dynamic flow of living at the same time – while imagining a particular future scenario we are generating some – approximate – generalized semiotic means that would frame that flow of imagination.

*Fictions as stabilized imagination:* imagination – the process of engaging in thinking AS-IF something were the case – enables the creation of *fiction*. The notion of fiction thus designates experiences lived through AS-IF modes. Yet fictions can be differentiated on various dimensions. First, some fictions are very temporary – we have them once and they disappear, such as the content of a dream, or a story told to a friend, while others last – such as those that are written down or recorded.

This is linked to a second point, the fact that some fictions are private, such as when a person has a fantasy of becoming rich and famous; others are socially shared, as when an audience are watching a film together, or a group engages in a ritual celebration, or when readers of a bestseller have a common experience of a fictional world. Shared fictions are often 'crystallized', or fixed, in some semiotic form – a text, a film, a song, a mathematical theorem – and can be transmitted through time and space (we can read fictions and philosophical texts written two thousand years ago).

Third, fictions can be about events or situations located in different time and space relative to the person who experiences them: if one says 'I wish I could go to the swimming pool and not stay at work'; the fiction opens a parallel reality to the present; a fiction can be located in the past – 'I wish I hadn't been hiking when it started to rain yesterday', or in the future 'Next year I will go to Japan', or in an unlocalizable time ('once

many possibilities which might still have been possible. Then the laws of *compossibilitas* (in the sense of Leibniz) are studied and the particular is thus more profoundly understood' (1935, p. 55).

18 In English Vaihinger (1935).

upon a time'). In everyday public communication one can hear promises: 'We will get X done for you *as soon as possible.*' Such completely vague statements about time may indeed be calming for time-anxious recipients of these messages – despite the message being completely indeterminate. Such 'there-and-then' fictions can occur in places that are close to real ones, or with a very strong degree of similarity to places that their authors or audience know. But they can also occur in places that do not exist, with a very low degree of similarity to places people know or could know (places in which objects speak, trees grow from the sky and so on).

Fourth, fictions have different forms, and social and psychological functions. There have been numerous studies on the psychic forms and functions of personal fictions,[19] about the genres and social functions of cultural production;[20] there have been many fewer about the developmental function of fiction, as these are located at the border between mind and the social world.[21]

### *Productive nature of fictions*

Human lives entail the constant creation of fictions that – sometimes very successfully – are treated as if they were real. Vaihinger distinguished different types of fictions. Contrary to commonsense nuances of the meaning of fiction as something untrue, unreal and not trustable,[22] Vaihinger emphasized *the productive nature of fictions* in the human mind. Fictions are mental structures – aids to making sense:

> The psyche weaves this aid to thought out of itself; for the mind is inventive; under the compulsion of necessity, stimulated by the outer world, it discovers the store of contrivances that lie hidden within itself. The organism finds itself in a world full of contradictory sensations, it is exposed to the assaults of a hostile external world, and in order to preserve itself, it is forced to seek every possible means of assistance, external as well as internal. In necessity and pain mental evolution is begun, in contradiction and opposition consciousness awakes, and man owes his mental development more to his enemies than to his friends.[23]

[19] Freud (1900/1953), Segal (1991). [20] Bakhtin (1996), Bourdieu (1996).

[21] Baldwin (1915/2009), Benson (2001), Vygotsky (1971).

[22] The very same common sense gives us a reversal of this distrust in practice – we trust some fictions (e.g. that Anna Karenina committed suicide by throwing herself under a train) *because the fictions are really created by the writer* (Tolstoy) and are hence trustable as fictional characters in the world of the real. Yet we are never quite sure about real-world assertions that Hitler committed suicide (Eco, 2009). Furthermore, we use the whole universe of created fictions – films, novels, paintings – as relevant symbolic resources for our personal lives – we sometimes trust the fiction (film character X suggested Y in film B) rather than a nextdoor neighbour who said the same.

[23] Vaihinger (1935, p. 12).

Fictions are means to an end – and are necessary to adapt to an irreversible time. This becomes particularly visible in situations in which people experience ruptures of what they know. For example, being at war, having to change country, losing a close friend are all situations that present people with 'hostile' situations for which they seek assistance. They are then likely to use all the information, knowledge, gossip available to make plans for the next action – these become semiotic resources. In these situations, shared fictions can play a particular developmental role.

A woman forced to work in the fields during the Second World War in England as part of the national war effort thus read the novel *How Green was My Valley* and used it as means to see the beauty of her environment, so as to adjust herself to its new demands.[24] In turn, a young man just migrated to an unknown country could use *Till Eulenspiegel*, an epic novel about a wandering trickster, as a way of giving consistency to his own trajectory.[25] Hence, other people's imaginations, as well as various forms of social discourse, can be used as semiotic resources. When it is an already stabilized fiction that is used as a personal resource, it can usefully be called 'symbolic resource' – a semiotic discourse that has become personally invested and used. Such personal, symbolic resources, guide people's processes of redefining their identity, of elaborating affects, their identification of values, or the acquisition of specific ways of doing or understanding the world.[26]

*Purposefulness of living – without purpose*: what we can take from Vaihinger's philosophy is a necessarily teleological look at the phenomena. However, teleology – future goal-orientatedness – is not deterministic. Its teleology is a result of a negotiated result of the AS-IS <> AS-IF relations in time. The psyche:

> is an *organic formative force*, which independently changes what has been appropriated, and can adapt foreign elements to its own requirements as easily as it adapts itself to what is new. The mind is not merely appropriative, it is also assimilative and constructive. In the course of its growth, it *creates its organs* of its own accord in virtue of its adaptable constitution, but only when stimulated from without, and *adapts them to external circumstances*.[27]

The core psychological concepts of Jean Piaget (unity of assimilation and accommodation) (see Box 3.5) and Lev Vygotsky (semiotic mediation) (see Box 3.2) carry forward this same constructive notion of adaptation to the future. Since the future is not (yet) in the present, constructive

[24] Zittoun, Cornish, Gillespie and Aveling (2008). [25] Zittoun (2007a).

[26] For the study of symbolic resources see Zittoun, Duveen, Gillespie, Ivinson and Psaltis (2003); Zittoun (2006b, 2007b).

[27] Vaihinger (1935, p. 2).

## Box 3.5 Jean Piaget

Jean Piaget (1896–1980) was a Swiss psychologist mostly known for his work on the development of intelligence. Interested in the genesis of cognitive capacities (mainly, rational reasoning) his work as philosopher and entomologist provided a double inspiration. His patient collection of thousands of observations of children brought him to propose a series of simple developmental dynamics, his central focus being the *genesis* of cognitive

**Box 3.5 (cont.)**

structures. Basically, the child is engaged in a permanent movement of mutual *adaptation* between itself and its environment, under the double demands of maturation and actual circumstances. The structure of understanding of the child (his behavioural and cognitive *schemes*) permanently *assimilates* new events or information to his understanding, and conversely, *accommodates* the structure of understanding to situations – that is, transforming its responses to better suit the situations at hand. Assimilation and accommodation should thus be smoothly balanced processes. Yet states of disequilibrium are regularly reached: when assimilation dominates, the child turns the world into his own – such as in play or what Piaget called autism; in excess of accommodation, the structure of understanding meets another limit. *Equilibratio*n is thus the process of reorganization of the scheme or structure to a more complex form, more stable, more adjusted to the demands of reality or of tasks.

For Piaget, thus, epigenesis is a dynamic process, a 'march toward equilibrium' – always attempting to gain a balance which can never be achieved.[28] Jean Piaget also designated typical phases within this movement towards adaptation – and unfortunately, generations of textbooks have chosen to emphasize these stages rather than the processes, turning Piaget's dynamic psychology into a static description.[29] However, some of Piaget's students – particularly Juan Pascual-Leone (see www.yorku.ca/tcolab) have preserved the dynamic focus and have developed Piaget's ideas further into a dialectical theory of cognitive development.

adaptation creates imagination and uses fictions. This guarantees the *general purposefulness* of living – striving towards adaptation to the future through the construction of its organs. Yet the actual purposes of the created fictions may remain vague – they emerge within a dynamic system that is moving in some direction – yet their emergence is local.

Much of Vaihinger's concern was with the role of fictions in scientific discoveries. It could be argued that he focused on the crucial aspect of all enquiry – the capacity to construct hypotheses based on imagination – in parallel[30] to Charles Sanders Peirce's painstaking work on abductive (retroductive) reasoning in the 1860s to 1900s.[31] Hypotheses come

[28] This view constrasts with the DST perspective, where complexity of structure is achieved in attractors *far* from thermodynamic equilibrium (Chapter 1).
[29] For instance Piaget (1952, 1955, 1980); see also Perret-Clermont and Barrelet (2008) on the evolution of Piaget's ideas.
[30] Fiction points to indirect byways – Vaihinger (1935, p. 79).
[31] Pizzarroso and Valsiner (2009).

from the coordination of the perception of the object with the cultural-historical knowhow and with the goals of the future in sight. For Vaihinger, fiction was the 'third member' of the logical science – the other two being induction and deduction.

*Social guidance of fiction:* fictions make a considerable contribution to human life trajectories, and are also an important component of the progress of science. Yet the construction of fictions themselves is socially guided. Social guidance renders some of the AS-IF options more likely to be actualized, or on the other hand renders them impossible for practical or normative reasons. In other words, the AS-IS<>AS-IF opposition is further differentiated – the AS-IF of the present becomes structured into AS-COULD-BE (contrast between an imaginary wish and potential action), and the latter further divides into AS-SHOULD-BE and AS-MUST NOT-BE – giving a socio-moral imperative to the adaptation process. The lively imagination about the future (AS-COULD-BE) becomes socially guided in the present through the AS-SHOULD-BE <> AS-MUST NOT BE opposition.

As an example, consider the feelings of a person on Dobu Island (Papua New Guinea) reflecting upon the newly introduced Christian church services. The man – in his sixties he claimed to be an active sorcerer – did not reject the functions of church services (as social-institutional guidance for conduct), yet he did not attend the services, countering the institutional guidance by his own meaningful explanation:

> When we are fine, why waste time singing hymns? Better to go and do your work. As for me, I do not like going to Church, *but it is good that we are Christians now*. For when we get sick and die, that is when the Church is good. *We can say sorry* (*ta'ona*) to God and go to heaven.[32]

The social guidance of fictions takes the form of different zones of acting, feeling, and thinking – differentiated into the domains of what is socially allowed and promoted.[33]

## Memorizing – and forgetting – as tools for the future

Memories are a particular kind of fictions. In psychology, they are usually viewed as fictions orientated towards past events.[34] Psychology's treatment of memory has largely been determined by the special interest of social institutions to maintain relevant social information. So the capacity

[32] Kuehling (2005, p. 150; added emphasis). [33] Valsiner (1997).

[34] Historically, memory and imagination were closely related; Aristotle, however, proposed seeing memories as imaginings located in time – imaginings orientated towards the past (Danziger, 2008, p. 189).

to remember and the accuracy of recall are crucial features in social institutional lives – in delivery of oral messages, in legal negotiations where 'what really happened' matters.

The other side of memory – that of forgetting – is rarely emphasized as a positive function in psychology. Yet it is important in human lives – together remembering and forgetting form the constructive sieve through which people build future efforts, and move ahead on their life course.[35] Memories – modified by forgetting – become fictions that pave the way to the future.

A person's remembering can refer to past experience – whether the experience of learning specific contents or having an actual interaction with the others and the world. Memories are traces of experiences; some of them seem to be quite simple registrations of perceptions, while others are more complex semiotic traces of events. When the memory is about one's own past experiences, it is usually called 'autobiographical memory'. This can be deliberate recollection or an involuntary irruption of the past into the present.[36] It differs from memories of grammatical rules or the date of the creation of a nation. We will here focus on autobiographical memories. Given their semiotic nature, what people remember and how they remember depends, like all aspects of the imagination, on their overall knowledge and semiotic capacities – which is, to some extent, dependent on their location in their life course and on its sociocultural context.

*First memories, earliest memories:* memory plays an essential role in the life of very young children – or so we (adults) think. It is entirely possible that in early ontogeny it is the forgetting part of the memorizing process that leads to development – through that, different adjustment difficulties can be conveniently downplayed, thus giving priority to memories of those aspects of development that lead to the later life course. Human development starts with elementary embodied forms, such as imitation,[37] and progressively develops into the memory of specific patterns of interactions with their emotional values, the objects they include and their emotional tone. The memory of such events is the condition for the emergence of the use of symbols and then words – which designate the same sets of events in

35 See Schachter, Eich and Tulving (1978) on how memory research in psychology has resisted the hypothesis of the reconstructive growth of memory. From a sociocultural psychology perspective on the last two decades the reconstructive nature of memory – emphasized by Frederick Bartlett in the 1920s and 1930s – has again become an accepted perspective (Wagoner, 2011).

36 On involuntary autobiographical memories see Berntsen (2009).

37 Here the central role is that of play – or persistent imitation, as James Mark Baldwin (1915/2009) labelled the basic process of *trying and trying again* (in a slightly new way).

different conditions.[38] Study of the talk of children under the age of three suggests that they may remember specific and recurrent situations of things that happened; yet they do not incorporate these into an explicit sense of self. Only children at school age seem to start remembering things as things that happened *to them*, that is, as episodic, autobiographical memories.[39] It seems indeed that younger children have not yet mastered fully the sense of self and the sense of time required for such autobiographical memories.[40] Their discourse suggests that they live in a here-and-now experience (they speak in present time), which progressively extends to the immediate before and after ('we'll do this').

Through their participation in interactions with adults, children are progressively exposed to linguistic terms – semiotic mediators – that organize time, discriminating between what is NOW and what is NOT NOW, and who is who – what is ME and what is NOT ME. Once a child can relate an event as being ME in the past – as NOT NOW – she can give it an autobiographical account.

Various studies suggest that children remember stories (or exhibitions, or tasks) better if they have discussed them with adults before they happen, and if they discuss them with adults afterwards. Furthermore, these memories differ in kind according to the discursive style of the parent, for instance, more canonical narratives, with a common temporal organization (past–present–future) are more easily remembered than narratives that have the temporal dimensions organized in a different manner (e.g. future, present, past).[41] Similarly, the kind of questions and elaborations a mother addresses as she remembers recent events guides the construction of the autobiographical memories of young children.[42]

In terms of psychology's traditional look at memory – as a relationship between *episodic* and *semantic* memory systems[43] – we can here think of a culturally guided relationship between the two. The adult (or a peer) – in interaction with the child – addresses specific questions about the episodic memory experience of the child. Through that interaction the semantic memory system – which operates through meaningful categorization (or the construction of semiotic sets) – is guided to organize the experiences encoded into the episodic memory system. The development of such guidance of the memory from episodic to semantic may lead to embedded and higher level forms of organized traces of experiences.

[38] For instance Nelson (2007).
[39] Nelson (2007) reports observation based on parents' diaries and parent–children interactions; the memories in question are therefore fairly recent (pp. 179–208).
[40] Fivush (2009); Howe, Courage and Rooksby (2009); Nelson (2007).
[41] Nelson (2007, p. 196). [42] Fivush (2009).
[43] This distinction has been brought into psychology by Endel Tulving (1972).

These experiences which are referred to relate to one's 'identity' or one's presentational self[44] can also, with the mastery of the appropriate cultural semiotic mediators, become identified as autobiographical memory – life narratives. Furthermore, it is the processes of cultural guidance by newly established meanings that may lead to the reconstruction of episodic memory experiences from times long past.[45]

However, the developing person – child or adult or 'the elder' – is the reconstructor of his or her memories. The social guidance of the direction of such reconstructions is an enabling condition, rather than a cause, of the flow of memories. Many accounts given by adults of memories dating before their second birthday seem to be memories of simple visions, smells or colours, and sometimes general feelings, as we have seen above.[46] This seems to suggest that these experiences are remembered, although they may not have been discussed with an adult. These experiences would probably not have been captured by a study of mother–infant talk.[47] In ontogeny, episodic memory systems prevail – and only with the development of semiotic systems of self-regulation start to provide the semantic memory system with its leading role. Most accounts also suggest that later first autobiographical memories, at ages four or five, are more complex – they occurred at a time when children had already mastered language, and became real narratives. *With the mastery of language, the structure of remembered experiences changes*. In addition, they are transformed by actual recall, narration or complemented by other persons (to the point where many people do not know whether they are remembering the event or the memory of the event).

[44] The notion of presentational self has been introduced by Komatsu (2010) as a way to capture the roots of self-referential discourses of children interacting with others about the life events of their own, of the others, and of the world jointly observed.

[45] Such as the sudden emergence of sexual *abuse* narratives in our time – 1961 in the USA: the physical abuse category was created, followed from 1975 onwards by the sexual abuse notion (Hacking, 1999, Chapter 5). These social constructions enable referencing back to episodic encounters of sexual kinds in early childhoods.

[46] 'Childhood amnesia' or 'infantile amnesia' covers the space between birth and the onset of first memories – the term thus depicts the period of life where no memories exist. Usher and Neisser (1993) asked college students about events that had occurred when they were one two three four and five years old; students' reports were validated and confirmed by their mothers. The study showed that there is a link between the nature of the event being remembered and the age at which events were recalled. The earliest age of recall was age two for birth of a sibling and hospitalization; move and death of a family member were recalled at the age of three. The authors conclude that it is 'a mistake to think of childhood amnesia as a unitary phenomenom that terminates at a specific age. Our results show that the offset of amnesia varies with the kind of experience in question.' (Usher and Neisser, 1993, p. 164). The offset of childhood amnesia is thus the age of two for some events – those events that have a high emotional significance to the child and/or those events having an early and well-structured narrative. See also Draaisma (2004).

[47] However other techniques gather evidences of memories over two to three months in children under two: Fivush (2009, p. 265).

*Evolution of memories in the life course:* as people move through the life course, memories and their relative importance evolve. In general, it seems that memory of surprising events or non-routine events remains stronger than memories which become quickly general: one might remember a unique attempt to play the violin, but a person who cooks everyday probably does not remember what he cooked on 27 January. Indeed, like any other form of imagination, memories tend to generalize, and specific events tend to fade out.[48] One explanation for this is that the function of memories is to prepare for the future. Events that are routine have been generalized and do not need to remain in the awareness. The memory of exceptional events, or events with a particular emotional significance, seems more easy to retain; the memories become points of reference, events or experiences, to which one may come back, which may be used as semiotic resources if comparable events happen again.

Clinical studies, as well as common experience, suggest that adults cannot remember early childhood years (the so-called period of latency). Also, as people become older, some memories of their childhood or their youth that were very vivid a few years earlier seem to fade. In general, during adulthood, the years around youth – the so-called 'formative years' – seem to provide important memories and offer permanent resources. In apparent contradiction to the preparatory function of memories, it seems that older people have strong reminiscences of their early childhood memories. As there is not much to anticipate, why is that so? Memories that had a stronger inscription, because of their emotional impact, or because they were recorded before a person had had many experiences, may be the only surviving ones. Indeed such experiences – the first time that I did *x* – also become important time-markers in people's own sense of their life trajectories.[49] However, it may also be that older people have more time to think about their life course, to create links between events and thus build up a sense of a personal and consistent narrative.[50]

[48] Unlike the case of persons who have an exceptional memory for details but seem unable to see general case or abstract principle and continuities (Draaisma, 2004, pp. 61–72; Luria, 1987).

[49] Draaisma (2004, p. 218); Zittoun (2008d) on time markers.

[50] Analysing the results of a questionnaire submitted to elderly educated people, Hall (1922) noted that some of them seemed to be reducing their interest to the here and now, others to worrying much more about history and the future of humankind. However, most of the interrogated persons seemed to stop imagining alternative lives: to the question whether they would live their lives differently if they had the opportunity to live them again, most seemed to conceive their own trajectory as the only possible life. However, Hall (1922, pp. 344–5) himself mentioned wanting to explore all the alternative lives once considered but not lived in his past.

Altogether, memories are traces of past experiences, shaped by the semiotic means to which a person has access, guided by social norms and expectations, and transformed by any later recall – that is, when they are used as possible fictions to guide the present or the future.

*The future lies in the past:* the main way of orientating present actions is to define an orientation for the future. To understand this we need to remind ourselves about the irreversibility of time – our ways of acting and reflecting in the present inevitably bring us to specify the not-yet-known immediate future.[51] The need for such future orientation becomes more salient when people experience ruptures that question their routine and self-evident actions. Hence, deciding to improve one's language skills after having lost a job gives some organization to one's daily life. However, these future orientations need to have a meaning for a person; and such meaning is often to be found in the past. Research on school-to-work transitions suggests that students are more likely to commit themselves to specific 'projects' if these can be interpreted as rooted in their memories.[52] For example, a young woman confers sense on her training as a hotel receptionist (a second choice) by linking it to her childhood dream – recollected now in her adulthood – of living a luxurious lifestyle.[53] In such cases, memories of the past are often slightly transformed so as to fit in the future (as when one says 'actually, when I think of it, I always wanted to do X'). Hence, past memories become the ground for defining a range of possible futures; and the present rereading of our past in the light of the future transforms our memories of the past.

However, the need to explicitly ground the present in the future, and the future in the past, is culturally defined. At one level, it is our school systems and the life patterns of our societies that require individuals to have plans, or to be able to present their curriculum as consistently leading to the specific job which is being applied for. The planning of our actions is a result of the social structuring of our lives. All through our life course there exist social suggestions for planning – and non-planning – of our actions to face different possible events. Planning to avoid earthquakes (leading to constructing fortified homes) or health problems during an upcoming trip (promoted by insurance companies) is suggested by social institutions – evoking collective memories of adverse events in the past.

[51] A new theoretical framework that captures that aspect of meaningful making of the new present is the trajectory equifinality model (TEM) developed by Tatsuya Sato (Sato, Hidaka and Fukuda, 2009, 2011), see below.

[52] These transitions are covered by a system of ritualistic relationships between the school and the home (Marsico, Komatsu and Iannaccone, 2011).

[53] Zittoun (2006a).

Thus, expectations about what kinds of plans are suited to what 'stage' of our life courses are socially guided – with boundaries inserted and defended by socio-moral imperatives. Thus, a woman personally deciding to bear a child at age fifteen may be reproached, similarly for one at the age of sixty-five. Likewise, a newly married young couple who opt not to have children may be reproached for this decision. Young adolescents in any society are guided towards fulfilling their 'patriotic duty' by enlisting in armies, or as suicide bombers follow a particular social suggestion – precisely similar to the opposite suggestion (reproaching other institutions for recruiting 'child soldiers' or using child labour).

More deeply, our attempts to tell stories about our lives, futures and past, cannot escape general cultural patterns. Research on autobiographical accounts suggests that people tend to organize accounts of their life-course story according to the narrative patterns classically available in their culture (salvation, drama, etc.), themselves reflecting some state of the culture.[54] However, in contemporary times, as the future seems less and less predictable, other narrative patterns seem more appropriate; they appear in fictions focused on a present open towards an unpredictable future,[55] and in the narratives of the generation of young people in countries in transition.[56] This may in turn transform the role of memories in defining the present. Finally, in situations where the future is seriously interrupted – for example when people have to spend the next ten or twenty years in detention[57] – the role of memories can also change; for such people, as not much that is now happens, exploring their memories becomes their main present.

*Atemporal memories:* memory dynamics can, like any dynamics, be disrupted. Events which have a very strong emotional impact may become memories punctuating the past (and many first memories are of that kind); yet events which have a too strong emotional load can be 'frozen' out of time and seem not to evolve with later experiences.

*Trauma* involves a form of fixing an experience with a particular form of vividness, partly because the person who suffered the trauma cannot turn it into a semiotic form, either because she does not yet have access to

[54] Bruner (1991); Gergen and Gergen (1988); McAdams (2001).

[55] In films such as *Matrix*, or the TV serial *Fringe*, which show that alternative futures can co-exist; in a so-called postmodern literature such as that of Houellebecq (2001).

[56] Roberts (2008).

[57] Bouška and Pinerová (2009) report how people survived arbitrary detention in so-called 'concentration camps' in communist Czechoslovakia; one woman reports that she did so, because the internees locked themselves into their pasts – she was there, but her mind was AS-IF she was at home and pursuing her past life; many others report having revised and explored at length their memories. See also example in Chapter 2.

adequate language, or because she perceives a strong social disapproval of the event. Trauma research shows that some events perceived as shameful or dangerous – early abuse, a humiliation during wartime, a car crash – may be felt as being not speakable; as they are not told, they remain non-assimilated.[58] These memories are highly painful, leading the person to avoid them and this avoidance prevents the possibility of semiotic elaboration of that experience. The memories do not develop into a narrative, and they tend to remain vivid, but fragmented, as dispersed flashes. The stories they generate become dispersed, broken and, given the human tendency to avoid pain, the experience remains disintegrated or dissociated from the rest of the life story. In such fragmentation we can observe the limiting of the transition between episodic and semantic memory systems by persons – even if the social environment encourages them to bring these experiences to a narrated state. The response is silence – and forgetting. Such events may be apparently forgotten during daily life, yet can come to mind in dreams or in flashback with a great vividness, AS IF they were present. The clinical treatment of traumatic events suggest that it is by gradually approaching the memories around such experiences and by translating them into semiotic form that people can progressively generate new possibilities of meaning for such events and bring them back into the flow of time.[59]

A special type of atemporal memory is *flashbulb memory*, occurring usually when a socially and personally significant event occurs – many of us can remember where we were and what we were doing when we heard that two planes crashed into the twin towers in September 2001. It may be that such experiences become oversaturated with meaning, which leads to a mini-shortcut that 'freezes' the memory of the particular event.[60]

*Screen memories* as identified by Freud[61] are at the meeting of these two types of autobiographical memory. Some memories may have some shameful content, yet lack the intensity of trauma; they become AS-IF they were forgotten. Instead, other apparently innocuous memories seem to overwrite them and acquire some particular emotional significance. In

58 Leiman and Stiles (2001). 59 Foa and Kozak (1986); Tisseron (2006).

60 It may also be that, at such a moment, a person who hears about that event also immediately imagines the reactions of many, known and unknown others, and it is the gaze of others that saturates the event. This has been documented in the case of the proliferation of the fight against 'child abuse' in the USA:

> By 1985 there were cities – Portland, Oregon, for example – in which anti-abuse activists had been so successful that men were advised never to touch a child in public, if a child not in the family is hurt, be sure there is a friendly witness before helping in any physical way. [Hacking, 1999, p. 160]

61 Freud (1899).

that case, recent memories receive some of the values of older memories, which are in turn transformed – and are no longer accessible. In other cases, however, events of the past seem to become significantly charged memories; these are *screen memories* when they were anodyne events, yet charged with the emotional charge of later experiences, which are either shameful, or socially disapproved. The content, or the emotional charge of some memories is thus as if displaced onto others.[62]

The paradox revealed by such atemporal dynamics is that it is precisely because these memories are accurate that they are dysfunctional – *memories prepare the future only if they can be used as fictions.* Indeed, because during the process of remembering we reread under new perspectives, or recombine autobiographical events, memories appear as imaginations of the past. As Freud emphasized:

> It may indeed be questioned whether we have any memories at all *from* our childhood: memories of *relating to* our childhood may be all that we possess.[63]

One implication of these observations is that an authentic developmental science cannot consider memories as 'truth'; rather, it should be able to capture the *development of memories* – as these are components of the constant invention of our future. The important 'take home' message here is that it is not the 'truth of the past' that matters when people bring to their consciousness long-forgotten memories, but the 'truth of the impending future' for which these memories become relevant building resources.

## Summary: processes of imagination in the life course

In this chapter we have seen that our senses of 'reality' and 'imagination' are two modalities of our permanently changing experience of the world and ourselves. Both are made possible thanks to semiotic processes. Imagination is the process of engaging in AS IF thinking, in contrast to AS IS; turning the present and the actual into the possible or the subjunctive actually creates options for the future. In turn, because we can only imagine on the basis of past experiences, AS IF relies on and transforms

[62] Note that controversies on child abuse come from these types of observations. Is a memory of abuse real, or a recent fantasy confused with a memory? Or is the memory not confused with later suggestions, and in particular, with adults' suggestion which leads memory to be transformed? Years of investigation brought specialists to identify signs of real abuse in children's discourse and behaviour, and to interview techniques which enable, to some extent, avoiding participating in the transformation of memories (for instance, Jensen 2005).

[63] Freud (1899/2001, p. 322).

memories. These processes are essential both in the construction of autobiographic memory and the sense of self, and conversely these processes are also the conditions for people and communities to move forward into their futures.

If imagination and sense-making have such power to reshape our experiences of time, then how can we theorize time itself? This is what we examine next.

# 4 Models of time for the life course

In everyday life, people have both the illusion that things have a certain stability – that after every day will come another day – and the sense that time is very variable – some minutes are endless, while some months disappear in a second. People hope for a brighter future, and regret the past. People's sense of time, imagination and memories mutually shape each other; and time appears as a variable reality, if not an illusion.

However, a theory of life-course development needs to go beyond this illusion. *Psychological science works through generalized concepts* – abstract tools for our minds to make sense of the ever-changing character of development.[1] A psychology of the life course thus needs a theoretical foundation for the very notion of *time* that enables us to articulate an 'objective' perspective on time and people's subjective sense of it.

One initial difficulty in any attempt to describe time is that we cannot capture time 'as such'; we always apprehend it through semiotic means – language, schemas or numbers.[2] Hence we cannot speak of time 'in itself' – although we assume that there is such a thing as time, which makes us mortal. So theorizing time implies examining existing models of time, and their theoretical and pragmatic implications. We will thus examine the very experience of time, in the social world, as well as models of the life course and the necessary time markers. Hence our goal in this chapter is to propose a satisfactory way to represent *time* which enables us to respect the dynamic nature of the human life course.

[1] For an alternative way of making sense of development, see our use of the epigenetic landscape metaphor in Chapter 1.

[2] For example, in our use of the epigenetic landscape metaphor (Chapter 1), the time dimension is represented by the movement of the ball, not by the spatial dimension of the slope.

## Models of time

The question – what time is – was of course a puzzle for philosophers long before psychology entered on to the scene of the sciences.[3] Time has been the basis for all doubt – 'here I seem to exist . . . but . . . will I exist at the next moment?' – or of identity worries – 'here I am now X, but I was not it last autumn . . . am I *still the same* person?'[4] Philosophical models of time differ between different cultural-historical traditions, and formal models of time can take many forms.[5]

The basic starting point is the detection of a changing sequence of events (Figure 4.1). The two rectangles in Figure 4.1 are spatial extensions – yet the event of their production entails an unfolding act (of drawing). That act creates duration of itself, and its direction. The two rectangles could have equally well have been drawn from left to right or vice versa.[6] Yet the duration of the act in and by itself does not make time detectable – for that there has to be the measure[7] that delimits the given quality – the 'stop signal' for the event. The first contrast that allows us to detect time is the start/stop system of an event. Time cannot be detected if an event is infinitely extended – the event exists, but its duration is not determinable (imagine either of the rectangles extending spatially infinitely to both left and right).

In the case of the start/stop system (the 'measure' – which determines the quality of the event) it is the duration of the whole that makes it possible to specify any sub-units of the quality. Thus, retroactively we can 'unit-ize' the extension in terms of its unfolding (e.g. the notion of 'half-time'

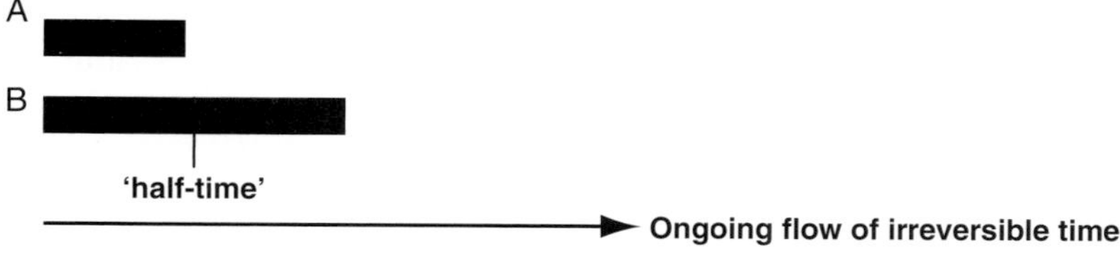


Figure 4.1 Detection of time.

[3] The first time this question of self-identity was raised, in Western philosophy, was by John Locke, in the seventeenth century. Until then the permanence of the soul was so taken for granted that it prevented this question being asked at all.

[4] As Zittoun (2008d) has described, a person may change his or her name over the life course as a cultural marker of identity change, yet over the life course remain the same person.

[5] A mathematically sophisticated account of these is in Rudolph (2006).

[6] Although it seems that people have a general tendency to represent time from left to right (Draaisma, 2004, p. 211).

[7] In Georg Friedrich Hegel's terms (1986, 2001, 2008) – *measure* is the marker on the field of similar quality – the maximum of it is the border at which new quality emerges.

in B – possible by contrasting B with A – if A is contrasted with B we get 'double time'). This first division is equal for the two directions of unfolding (right to left, left to right) – for both the 'half time' is the same. Yet every next division would separate the directions (e.g., 'one quarter' time in B moving left to right equals 'three-quarters' time while moving right to left).

*What 'measuring time' does:* by specifying a marker on the quality of duration – 'half-time', 'quarter-time', 'three-quarters-time' – we create an account of time by turning the unfolding event into an already static existing dimension similar to space. Time here does not 'flow' – a metaphor that implies movement – but is crystallized as it already exists ('real time'). We can locate some happenings on that 'real time scale' – event P happened at 'half time', event Q happened 'half-of-the-halftime' (='one quarter' or 'three quarters' – depending on the direction) after P (or before). Happenings have their *specific locational address on the objective timescale* of history – it would be impossible to make statements like 'Jesus Christ was born five years BC' as the Occidental Christianity-based marking of history uses the presumed event of Christ's birth as the starting point for time marking.

*'Real time' that is not real: getting rid of time, turning it into a commodity:* In this objective timescale the contrast between past → present → future is irrelevant (since the timescale is already given (crystallized in the past)). Based on past time the future is assumed to be given – although we do not know yet what will happen in the future, we can be fully certain that whatever happens will have its appropriate location on the time line exactly as events of the past have theirs. Given such symmetry, it is possible to turn the directional flow of time into measurable units that can be taken out of their context and contents by using the cyclical nature of events (sunrise, sunset) to translate the directional nature of time into its repetitive nature – thus downplaying the uniqueness of the event ('every sunset is just another sunset' rather than 'every sunset is unique'). This kind of *translation of 'similarity' into 'sameness'* is a cognitive move that is characteristic of all human meaning-making[8] – resulting in prioritizing stability over change.

Getting rid of the directionality of time – and turning time into 'measurement units' that are treated as reversible and transposable – happens through elimination of the repetitive cycles:

Among the physical quantities that are considered extensive, several are basically periodic. The two most familiar examples are clock time, which has a period of

[8] See Sovran (1992) on how cognitive categorization makes the shift from similarity (fuzzy set) to sameness (crisp set) descriptions.

> either 12 or 24 hours, and angle. [Other familiar examples include both finer-grained versions ('watch time'?) of clock time with periods of either 60 minutes or 60 seconds, and coarser-grained versions with periods of 7 or 365 days.] . . . [T]he periodic measure relates simply to an ordinary extensive measure. For example, the time duration of 76:35 hours is the same as 3 days and 4:35 hours, and so in terms of clock time it is simply equivalent to 4:35 hours, *because the complete cycles (days) drop out*.[9]

Such a 'drop out' is an act of cognitive convenience – allowing us to specify recurring new events as if they were the same. Thus the '8.45 Geneva–Paris express' is considered to be the same in an interval of 24 hours, even though the railway cars, the locomotive, and the personnel working in the train may be different;[10] it also remains 'on time' if it departs between 8.45 and 8.59. If it departs later, it is the '*delayed* 8.45 Geneva–Paris express'[11] – yet it retains its basic identity. Even if it were to make its final stop on the way (for technical reasons) it would still maintain its identity as the '*broken down* 8.45 Geneva–Paris express'. In all cases of the qualified identity, the time marker is an anchor point within the implied 24-hour cycle of the given day.[12]

From creating such markers on the 'real-time' scale time is made measurable as units. So, the measurable difference between the '8.45 Geneva–Paris express' and the '10.45 Geneva–Paris express' is two hours – the difference between markers is turned into a unit of time. This unit is assumed to be the same if found in another location of the cycle (e.g. the '18.45 Geneva–Paris express' – '20.45 Geneva–Paris express'). The result is complete elimination of irreversibility from time – 'measured' time ('two hours') is cognitively transposable as if it were free of any context. So we get common-language expressions about 'saving time' – up to administrative rearrangements like 'daylight saving time' twice a year. The management of 'objective time' is of major importance for social administrative systems.[13]

To summarize: *the 'objective time scale' is an axiomatic* 'AS-IF' *position that considers time to be symmetric* – the past is like the future – hence there is no past and future. No development – the emergence of a new quality of

9 Rudolph (2006, p. 176). Mathematically, this is captured by the notion of integers modulo $n$ – the complete cycles that 'drop out' of use allow the particular natural number $n$ to be manipulated separately from its time-flow context.

10 Example given by the linguist Ferdinand de Saussure to present the notion of identity (de Saussure, 2005, p. 151).

11 Tsuji (2006, p. 178) provides information about what 'delay' means in different railway systems: France 14 minutes, Italy 15, Japan 1 minute.

12 Yesterday's '8.45 express' would probably be cancelled, rather than depart today at 8.45 *as yesterday's*.

13 Edensor (2006) reviews how time management becomes linked to national identity.

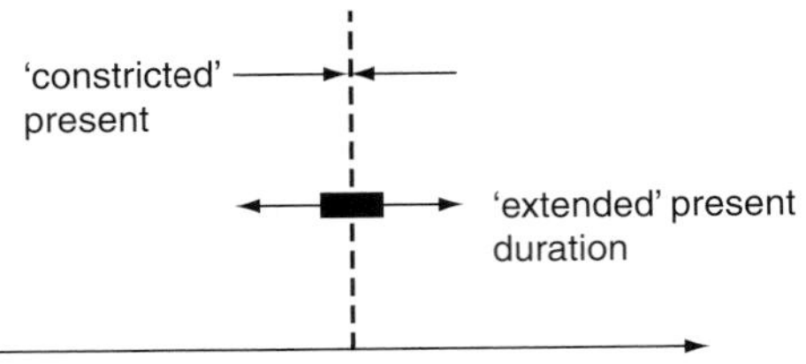


Figure 4.2 Models of the present moment: constricted (*à la* Peirce) vs. extended (*à la* Bergson).

time – is possible.[14] Furthermore, denial of the asymmetry of time between past and future contradicts the temporal logic that has been developed in the latter half of the twentieth century.

*Subjective time:* subjective time behaves differently. There have been two contrasting ways to capture experienced time. In one conception, held by Peirce among others, the *present constitutes an infinitesimally short, point-like moment* of time. The other assumes *the present to endure* and to be delimited by activity, and is inspired by Bergson[15] (Figure 4.2).

*The constricted present:* from the first perspective, assuming that the present is an infinitesimally short moment implies that it is essentially a meeting point of the past and the future. In that version, held by Peirce,[16] it is impossible to capture, not to say describe, the here-and-now, as it will immediately be passed on to the past. Instead the here-and-now is created by reflection about 'past before past' and 'past' (that is, two pasts) as the time flow is already ahead of both these pasts.

*Subjective time of duration and immediate future:* the alternative subjective conception of time focuses on an extended *present* and was developed by Henri Bergson (1859–1941). His proposition is that the core of a human's experience of time is *duration* – an ongoing present. Opposing spatial descriptions of time, Bergson saw duration as *process*, or movement:

> Inside of me, *a process of organization*, or mutual penetration of facts of consciousness is occurring, which constitutes the true duration.[17]

[14] In the philosophical and anthropological language this time frame is labelled the 'B-series' (Gell, 1992; Mellor, 1981 – after McTaggart, 1908). As Hodges (2008, p. 404) explains, in the B-series 'events have definite and unchanging temporal relationships to each other ... [it is] a metaphysical statement about the objective, autonomous nature of real time: events exist, have definite relationships to each other'. In contrast, the 'A-series' entails the subjective movement from past through present towards the future.

[15] Bergson (1888/1970). [16] For example Peirce (1892).

[17] Our translation from the original: 'Au-dedans de moi, un processus d'organisation ou de pénétration mutuelle des faits de conscience se poursuit, qui constitue la durée vraie' (Bergson, 1888/1970, Chapter 2).

Duration is only *presence* – to the present time. Yet this present is extended – duration implies both the past (the present past, that is, a recent past that has actuality) and the immediate future. Consequently, from the perspective of duration it does not make sense to distinguish between past, present and future. For Bergson such experience of time is captured only by *intuition*[18] – not intellectual reasoning.

If Bergson makes the *continuity of change* the essence of duration,[19] how can different 'presents' be distinguished one from the other? Bergson specifies what qualifies the current 'present':

> What is present for me, at this moment, is what occupies me here and now, what I do, what I say, what I experience, or what I want. [Il s'agit d'un présent qui dure.] (It concerns a present that endures.)[20]

Hence, the unit of duration seems defined by its content – the *experienced ongoing activity*. A subjectively defined *unit of duration* is thus given by the *activity* in which the person is engaged. In terms of clock time, it may be very short, as when one asks for the salt at the dinner table, or it may be longer, as when it stretches over a symphony. The past is present in this duration as the 'before' that matters for the 'now'. As soon as it loses interest for the 'now', it is no longer part of the duration, which, presumably, has shifted to another duration.

Bergson's view of duration and the blending from past in the present leads him to propose an original representation of the future as constantly emerging:

> By the sole fact of being accomplished, reality casts its shadow behind it into the indefinitely distant past: it thus seems to have been pre-existent to its own realization, in the form of a possible. From this results an error which vitiates our conception of the past; from this arises our claim to anticipate the future on every occasion.[21]

Our inclination to anticipate the future is based on past possibilities having been actualized. However, the future is fundamentally indeterminate, as the possibilities of the future are not solely dependent on possibilities and actualities from the past. *Possibilities are constantly in the making during the flow of time.* In other words, what is possible at time $t_{t+1}$ need not be the same as what was possible at time $t_t$. Anticipation, based on past experiences, is ubiquitous in the animal world. As such, it is part of our duration. However, the field of possibilities ahead can never be defined in advance, as the continuous changes in the flow of time will

[18] Bergson (1946/2007, p. 907). [19] Bergson (1972, p. 906).
[20] Bergson (1972, p. 909; see also p. 152). [21] Bergson (1946/2007, p. 22).

continuously change this field. Bergson labelled this 'blending into the future' *creativity*: 'in duration, considered as a creative evolution, there is perpetual creation of possibility and not only of reality'.[22] *Thus the immediate future is implied in the flow of the duration.*

*The subjective time that is real – but ungraspable:* both views on subjective time – as constricted present or as extended present – come to the same point: the present cannot be grasped directly.[23] For our purposes of developmental science the axioms of temporal logic – the asymmetry of time – need to be accepted, given the nature of developmental phenomena. The key terms in the developmental look at time are PAST, PRESENT and FUTURE, and prediction of the latter is not possible on the basis of the past. In this sense, time, which is always of the immediate future (as it is turning into the present), is not graspable. We do not know – only assume – what is going to happen. And, of course, we act in anticipation of different possible future scenarios.

Is this kind of subjective time 'real'? As long as we look at human development as construction of the human world, all the results of the construction are 'real' as they are actualized versions of imagination. From that point of view, a building, a feeling of love for music and a conceptual system used to look at the world – even a very transitory one – are all real.[24]

By contemporary notions of temporal logic, time has eight characteristics:[25]

1 It has the capacity to order events (a world without time would be chaos, if one were unable to make statements about 'earlier' and 'later' kind).
2 It turns unique events into relationships ('X was earlier/later than Y').
3 Past, present and future states differ in terms of the number of available features (predicates).
4 Time flows.[26]
5 Time is universal.
6 Time is irreversible.
7 The future is not pre-fixed.
8 Time has a meta-structure (usually likened to an arrow).

[22] Bergson (1946, p. 21).

[23] In Greek mythology there were two representations of time: *chronos* and *kairos*. Chronos is time on the move in its sequence between past, present, and future – time which can be quantitatively depicted. Kairos is the experience of the moment – the quality of time. Kairos was allegorized as a man with a tuft at his forehead – you have to grasp the hair – to hold and experience 'the right moment'.

[24] Developmental science – building on the axiom of the open systems – treats all results of organism–environment transaction as real (as long as that interaction takes place).

[25] Anisov (2001).

[26] Takiura (1978, p. 81) corrects that claim: 'Only either we or things can flow in time, it is contradictory to say that time itself flows in time . . . For time cannot act upon material bodies to make them move.'

These eight characteristics fit – in different combinations – both subjective and objective times. Yet characteristics 3, 6, 7 and 8 are central for representing subjective time.

*From the 'arrow of time' to the 'broom of time':* the asymmetry of the future and the past (feature 3) creates a situation where the traditional 'objective time' models (based on the notion of 'arrow of time') do not fit. The future is rich in potential courses of events, while the past is characterized by unilinearity – in our 'objective' retrospect. Aleksander Anisov has suggested the use of a new metaphor – 'the broom of time' (Figure 4.3).

Since the future is constantly in the process of becoming past, movement towards the 'new present' (to become past) entails losing the features of possible future trajectories (loss of predicates in terms of logic). In terms of Figure 4.3 this amounts to ignoring 'branches' of the possible future as the singular present course is being created. Once this has happened the (by now) present becomes the immediate past – with the loss of the 'branches' crystallized. According to Anisov:

> The mentioned removal of ignored branches is of great importance for an adequate understanding of the phenomenon of the past. Earnest historians come to a conclusion that *history does not allow the subjunctive mood.* Any argument about what would have happened if dinosaurs did not exist, if Napoleon was killed in his youth, or if Lenin was arrested in 1917 by the czar's authorities, contain no scientific meaning and may not have any. The offered axioms of time order precisely express this specific aspect. The past has no valid alternatives even given that sometime back certain past meta-moments contained the listed events in the zone of real possible future. The essence of the issue is in the impossibility to return back to such meta-moments.[27]

Thus, the branches f and g in Figure 4.3 would be inaccessible from the point of view of temporal logic. A century before Anisov (1906), his predecessor in the effort to build a logic of development, James Mark Baldwin, commented on the issue of how to study development:

> that series of events is truly genetic [developmental] which cannot be constructed before it has happened, and which cannot be exhausted backwards, after it has happened.[28]

This claim anticipated the future development of temporal logic – any developmental science needs to be clear about the nature of time.[29]

What would have seemed an agnostic or nihilistic statement a hundred years ago makes sense in conjunction with temporal logic as it developed

[27] Anisov (2005, p. 81). [28] Baldwin (1906, p. 21).

[29] Anisov's and Baldwin's points in this respect are in perfect agreement with our version of the epigenetic landscape metaphor (as described in Chapter 1), where the movement of the ball will always be downward, and where the bifurcation points in the landscape

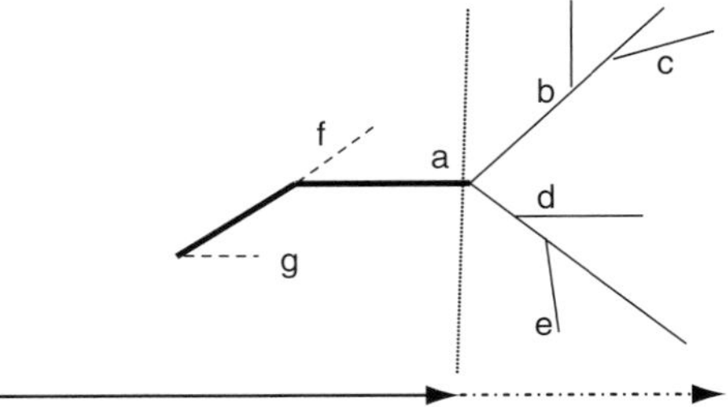


Figure 4.3 The broom of time (after Anisov, 2001).

in the second half of the twentieth century. The overcoming of 'mainstream' psychology's institutional habits of 'predicting' different separated 'variables' over time as a 'study of development' becomes obvious when one moves away from an axiomatic system of time as a moving event-organizer between past and future to empirical investigations. *Developmental science requires the establishment of its own concise theoretically elaborated and phenomenologically situated research methodology. The methodology used in 'mainstream' psychology is incapable of producing adequate knowledge about development.*[30]

## Constructing the life course

Common sense is the reservoir of knowledge for all sciences at the outset. Yet it is the practice of scientists to make the best use of it while creating conceptual systems that transcend any culture-specific worldview and aim at human universal models – across societies and, in our case, in this book – capturing the life course.

The traditional occidental model of human life course is that of the 'staircase of life' (Figure 4.4). It entails the notion of a linear stepwise progression from the 'naïve and innocent' state of the infant, to that of the fully functional mid-life adult, followed by similar stepwise regressing into the oblivion of death – and possible entrance into eternal afterlife either in hell or heaven (the latter being indicated with the open door with celebrating doorpersons). Images of such staircases of life have been visible in European environments since the middle ages. In our contemporary terms these images were normative life-course advertisements – messages

illustrate Anisov's point with the broom of time. It is assumed that it is impossible for the ball to 'change its mind' and return (uphill) to a passed-by bifurcation point. This also illustrates the irreversibility of time.

30 For elaboration of this point see Smedslund (1995), Toomela (2007, 2008, 2009), Valsiner and Rosa (2007).

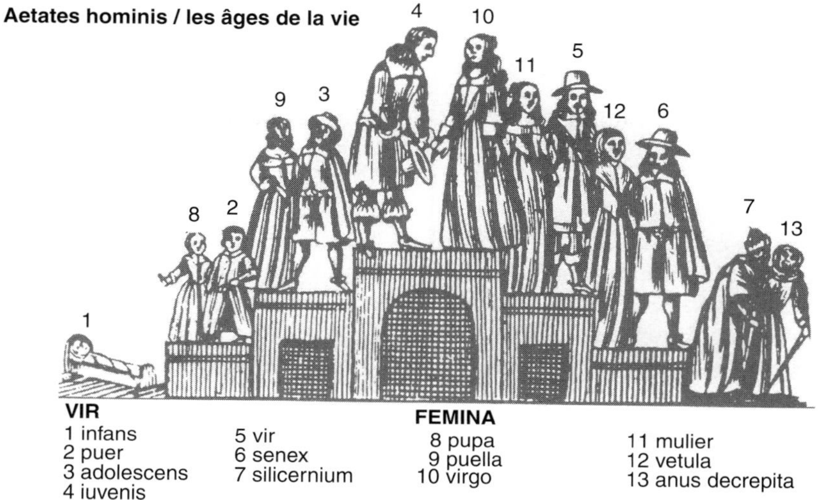


Figure 4.4 Prototypical depiction of life course in Europe ('staircase of life').

that guide the conduct of people of different ages: one reaches the final destination through orderly progress through the appropriate stages of the human life course.

Psychology has been largely eurocentric, and hence the different life-course models that have been created for the life course have been based on the 'staircase of life' folk model.

With its focus on identity development, the model proposed by Erik Erikson is often used as a reference in life-course developmental psychology. Although the interest of Erikson was in 'the unity of the human life cycle', he actually proposed to examine 'the specific dynamics of each of its stages, as prescribed by the laws of individual development and of social organization'.[31] The processes described by Erikson – that of the individual's need for continuity and sameness, while he is submitted to the changes of his organism and the specific demands of his social and historical environment – are dynamic in nature. However, the staircase model is so powerful in our culture that it led Erikson to propose a model of the life course organized in eight stages, and represented by a staircase, this time going from the bottom to the top of a page, from left to right. The

[31] Erikson (1959a, p. 1). Erikson also explains that he intended to develop further the Freudian model of the four stages of psychosexual development.

simplicity of this model certainly helped the diffusion of Erikson's work (it can be found in any textbook) but unfortunately led the reader to forget the dynamic aspects of Erikson's account of development.[32]

A later attempt to identify the core processes of development in the life course comes from lifespan psychology, as developed by Paul Baltes.[33] It has the elegance to explain development with a set of very simple principles. One of them is the idea that, as humans get older, the importance of their genetic capital progressively declines; the importance of culture grows to compensate for biological losses, and eventually, even the importance of culture does not compensate any longer for these losses. This idea is represented by an ascending, then descending curve that follows the general shape of the staircase model. Hence, an apparently complex idea simply seems to reproduce this basic model. This idea is supported by another principle: the *SOC principle* – the idea that development proceeded by *selection* (of only one behaviour among possible ones), *optimization* (of our efficiency to achieve that behaviour) and *compensation* (of the losses of excellence caused by age by other means). For example, a person who is a good swimmer (and a less good student) would concentrate on swimming, develop his crawl and compensate for his later loss of speed with the help of new swimming equipment. Note that under such apparent scientificity, another commonsense idea is turned into theory: the principle of optimization (the idea that choices are made so that losses are limited and gains maximized).

*Bounded rationality as inevitable in the life course:* the principle of *bounded rationality* – introduced by Herbert Simon – shows the limits of such a model. Most of the tasks and problems people have to solve are extremely complex. Defining the optimal solution would require an absolute thinking power that our finite minds do not possess. Indeed, rationality is bounded. Consequently, suggests Simon, 'we must find techniques for solving our problems approximately – not precisely – and we arrive at different solutions depending on what approximation we hit upon'.[34] The idea of *bricolage*, or soft assembly, introduced above (Chapter 1), precisely designates the creativity of such approximation as humans use available resources to reach a good enough solution to

[32] The same problems happened to the work of Freud and Piaget – the general public retained the stages, not the dynamic processes that were at the heart of the demonstration of the genesis and the evolution of functions. Hence Jean Piaget's theory of equilibration (see Chapter 3, box 3.5) is essentially an account of dynamic processes; however, his work is usually presented – especially in textbooks – as if it were reducing the dynamic process of development to a sequence of stages.

[33] Baltes (1997); Baltes, Staudinger and Lindenberger (1999).

[34] Simon (1990, p. 6).

situated environmental challenges. If, on the contrary, we had an unbounded rationality, people would perfectly fit to their environmental demands, and it would be sufficient to analyse these to describe human action.[35]

Yet the European folk model – especially what it meant for still living people who are guided towards the Otherworld – misses the other side of the transformation. Most other societies adhere to a cyclical model of the life (and death) course, promoting the idea of a complementary cycle with the return of the departed 'soul' in a new reincarnation. Hence the organization of both the exit point (death) and entrance point (birth) are symbolically overdetermined in all human societies. The notions of the cyclical rebirth of souls can be found both in oriental (Figure 4.5a) and occidental (Figure 4.5b) subjects in the twentieth century. The souls of the deceased are believed to 'move through' the 'other place' and return in the new generation.

*The marking of souls for the future–naming:* traces of the conception of framing the future can be seen in naming practices. Giving a name is indeed marking the entrance of a child into a world of culture, and attributing to him or her a specific place on the social map and in the order of generations. Hence, among traditional East European Jews, the custom was *not* to name a child after a living relative, in order to avoid reducing the relative's life duration, but usually after a dead grandparent. In the group of Yoruba, from present-day Nigeria, names are found by specialists who have to recognize which person the child is. Such practices seem to follow the implicit idea that names designate an entity which is at one time dead, at another alive, and thus reflect a cyclical conception of time. Such practices differ from Russian ones, where it is normal to name a first child after the first name of his living parent. In that case, the continuation seems linear, people being distinct from each other although they are named similarly.[36]

Most current practices thus reflect mixed conceptions of time, where people 'don't believe' in cyclical time, while calling their child after a grandparent 'to keep his/her memory alive' or to honour him/her – as if the person could thus be present in the child. Interestingly, as the child becomes older and gets a life of her own, the name usually changes meaning – as if the new existence came to overwrite the memory or the presence of the other person who carried that name. With the advance of

[35] Given the fact that most economic models are still based on this optimization model, the recent crisis can be seen as a proof of its inadequacy.

[36] Slavic languages, among others, allow members of three generations of the same family to be distinguished. In Czech, if a man in his sixties is called Pavel, his son in his thirties would be Pavlík, and his grandson aged five would be Pavliček.

(a)

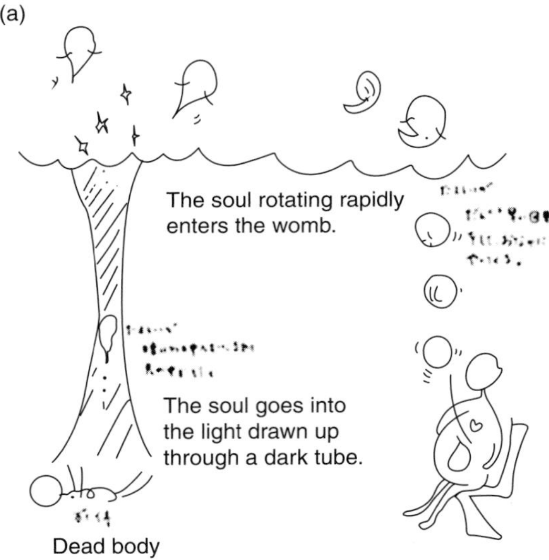


(b)

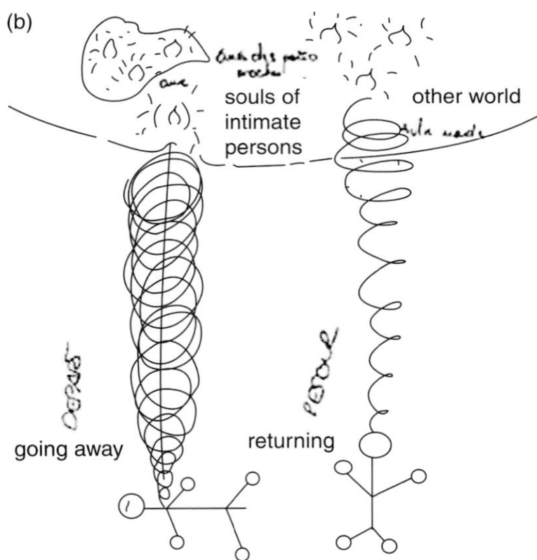


Figure 4.5 Japanese (a) and French (b) drawings of the return of the soul (Yamada and Kato, 2006, pp. 151 and 152): (a) Japanese case (j371) (b) French case (f118).

the life course – even if the name remains the same – the means of public address may change. Again, the Russian practice is interesting – a boy may be named after his father *Nikolai*, be adorably nicknamed in childhood as *Kolya* – with no direct trace of the father. Yet as he moves into middle age, at a certain point he and the people surrounding him feel it is no longer appropriate to address him as *Kolya*, or even as *Nikolai* – and insist upon the use of the patronymic – which is the same. So the son named after his father Nikolai becomes addressed as *Nikolai Nikolajevich* (Nikolai the son of Nikolai). The symbolic link with the previous generation becomes fortified as the person approaches the latter half of his life course!

## The generative lifecycle model

The 'staircase of life' as a folk model of the life course – as well as all stage accounts of the life course that occidental psychology has produced – are examples of the drop of the cyclical part of continuity (generation) in looking at the 'left-over' part. A general theoretical model that would integrate both occidental and oriental folk knowledge as well as providing a sufficiently generalized background for life-course developmental science is Yoko Yamada's and Yoshionobu Kato's generative lifecycle model (GLCM) – Figure 4.6.

The GLCM unites the cyclical and linear time notions into an open-ended spiral model. Spiral – or helical – models fit the ways of functioning of biological organisms. In GLCM:

> The linear time concept, implying progression from the past to the present to the future, is represented as horizontal arrows directed from left to right on the ground. The linearity reflects the life of each individual, which is characterized by a single stream of time from birth to death. In contrast to this unidirectional individual life, other kinds of lives, which are recycled in different spaces, are depicted as repeated multiple spirals in the figure. These are representations of multiple cycles from generation to generation, beyond an individual life. Note that these cycles are depicted as repeated spirals with variants.[37]

Every cycle in nature – seasons of harvesting of apple trees, and every new generation of human beings – brings into life new varieties of phenomena. Yet there remains a basic similarity (not sameness!) in these cycles – repeated in new ways. Every human being moves through a unique life course – yet its basic structure is organized by coordinated biological and cultural worlds. The particular belief systems can change in history – and a person of a new generation *may feel she or he needs to* get help from a

[37] Yamada and Kato (2006, pp. 153–4).

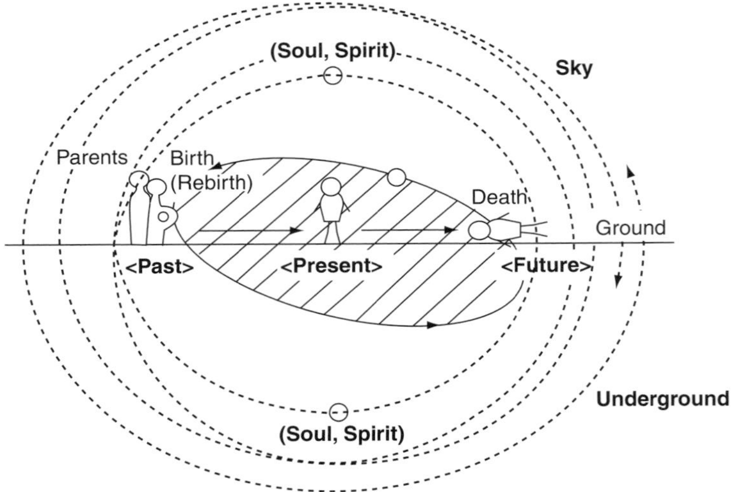


Figure 4.6 The generative life cycle model (GLCM) (Yamada and Kato, 2006, p. 153).

psychologist (rather than from a priest or from a shaman), yet the functions of turning to any of these specialists link her/his personal pilgrimage within the life course with the universes of mythology and science. Relating to these wider worlds is at times relevant for the person – and it is precisely here that the psychology of the life course can be situated.

Looking towards the future in the case of the life course entails the construction of meaningful transition myths surrounding life events – births, school exams, deflorations, weddings, divorces, childbirths, menopauses and deaths. The occidental 'life staircase' model (Figure 4.4 above) encodes in iconic form the move between the end of the life into the 'open gates' of 'the beyond' – be it a heaven, a hell or a purgatory. The object – the body of the deceased (or, more precisely, where it became located and what kind of social ritual was created for it) – is the centre for marking the life-course transitions for the living. In the history of European burial practices we can observe the transposition of the location of the dead bodies from the most sacred social places (burial under the church floor)[38] to that of immediate vicinity of the church (church graveyard) to special cemeteries at some distance from the churches.[39]

[38] The effect of such distancing for us in the twenty-first century can be felt personally whenever – as tourists or occasional visitors to medieval churches – we have to walk on many-hundred-year-old gravestones, and feel discomfort doing so.

[39] Koslofsky (2002).

### Living proleptically

The GLCM leads us to consider the coordination of the different open cycles in their everyday use in the human life course. The notion of *prolepsis* was meant to designate these meetings of temporalities. A prolepsis is a rhetorical device consisting in bringing elements from the future into the present.[40] Per extension, prolepsis designates:

> the representation or assumption of a future act or development as if presently existing or accomplished. [For example] ... adults totally ignorant of the real gender of a newborn will treat it quite differently depending on its symbolic/cultural gender ... For example, they bounce 'boy' infants (those wearing blue diapers) and attribute 'manly' virtues to them while they treat 'girl' infants (those wearing pink diapers) in a gentle manner.[41]

Expanding on that notion we might say that, at every moment of movement along the life course, people extend their imagination in three parallel directions:

→ How do I imagine the PRESENT SITUATIONAL DEMANDS as those converge on me?
→ How do I project into any particular FUTURE STATE of mine, and bring it to the present through semiotic markers (prolepsis)?
→ How do I imagine MY OWN PAST as I am involved in prolepsis?

All three processes are imaginings – yet they are viewed by the imaginer as if they were real. The whole process of living is thus *proleptic* – creating images of realities of the future and presenting these as if they were already present. Through our future-orientated communication processes and via the power of semiotic mediation people create meaningful worlds that in reality do not yet exist. They create their own *zones of proximal development* – from birth to the death.[42] This is possible because of ever-available imagination that in some sense *runs ahead* of the irreversible time.

Michael Cole's example of how the proleptic extensions organize the immediate moment within the life courses of a mother and her newborn baby (Figure 4.7) illustrates the different levels of developmental organization. The event – mother giving birth to the baby – has its clear physical time location address (e.g., 28 July, 2009 at 17.36 EST), which locates it in the background of BEFORE X or AFTER Y (where X and Y are other time points

[40] A prolepsis can be the anticipation of an objection ('you are going to say that', Dupriez, 1980), or of a specific event ('when this summer arrived we didn't know it was the first of a long series of happy ones').

[41] Cole (1992, p. 21).

[42] All persons who set up clear scripts for what should happen during their funeral services create their zones of personal development even beyond their own development.

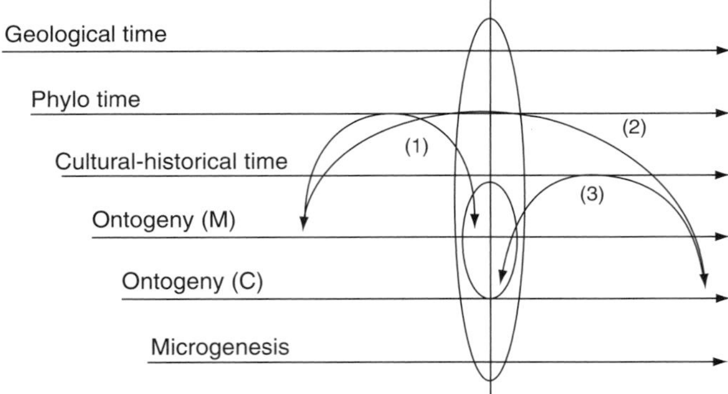


Figure 4.7 Coordination of multiple parallel time frames in the present of mother (M) and child (C) joint living (Cole, 1995, p. 38).

on the physical time scale). Yet functionally – for the mother and the newborn in a coordinated way – it is an *ontogenetic transition zone* (to parenthood for one, to life for the other). Extension from that zone to other time frames – both in the past and in the future – provides the meaning structure for the here-and-now movement forward by both mother and baby.

The mother extends her understanding of the baby into *her own* childhood through the prism of the cultural-historical time (1) (in Figure 4.7), from there – through the cultural-historical system – to the *child's imaginary future* (2) as invented by herself, and from there – back to the child's present moment (3) – again as viewed through the mother's present meaning system. The phylogenetic time frame – species-specific biological development – remains largely untouched by the event – yet it is always present as the outmost open spiral (in terms of GLCM – Figure 4.6)

*Feed-forward processes:* Figure 4.7 helps us to locate any particular moment on the human life course. The reason for projecting imagined scenarios from the present to the future leads to the construction of action plans in the present – based on consultation with cultural history. *Innovation* in a given society comes from such moments – 'I know that situation X must be done in way Y by our cultural standards, but I prefer to do it in ways non-Y'. In some cases there is a demand to start dissimulating that behaviour – so one has to add 'but have to *pretend to be* Y'. This is the case in the cultural history of bride's 'virginity testing' – display of blood-soaked bed linen after the 'first night' of the couple – together with the techniques of using chicken blood and the conspiracy of insiders to formally adhere to the custom.

In other cases, there is no need for such dissimulation – cultural history actually expects such an attempt to overcome limitations. Hence, since the Second World War, societies have undergone major change because young people live their present orientated towards a different future: 1968 enabled deep changes of gender relationship because some young people were living *as if* there were no more sexual restrictions – only to reconstruct different restrictions some time later in their lives. Likewise, young people in the 1980s developed new forms of music because they were living *as if* there was 'no future'.[43] Of course the future was constructed as they entered middle age – and nostalgic memories of 'living passionately' in their youth became stories to tell to others. The possibility of *psychological distancing* (Box 4.1) from the immediate ontogenetically framed microgenetic setting through referencing the imagery of the future in

**Box 4.1 Psychological distancing and de-distancing**

The notion of psychological distancing needs to be viewed through the opposite process of de-distancing. Its historical origins, to be found in German philosophy, are linked with the question of *Einfühlung* (empathy, or sembling). In conjunction with the process of 'feeling-in' with the world of the others, the person constructs the psychological distance relative to the object of 'feeling-in' – perhaps to be labelled as 'feeling-out'. The person in a particular situation 'feels outside' a specific situation, and through that feeling can survive and overcome the situation. Construction of special intramental experiences that substitute the actual here-and-now situation by some imaginary one, or creating a meaning for the given situation that neutralizes its relevance for the person, are different strategies of such 'feeling-out'. *Einfühlung* and psychological distancing can be considered interdependent psychological construction processes of opposite direction – *Einfühlung* feeds into the construction of distancing, and the latter allows for novel forms of *Einfühlung*.[44]

Bullough's description of 'psychical distance' illustrates the contrast between immediate relating to a context and a person's subjective separation of self from the context. Both immediacy and distancing are affect laden; it could be said that thanks to the affective personal-sense construction it becomes possible for the person to achieve *both* immediacy and distancing:

> Distance does not imply an impersonal, purely intellectually interested relation ... On the contrary, it describes a personal relation, often highly emotionally coloured, but of a peculiar character. Its peculiarity lies in that the personal character of the relation has been, so to speak, filtered. It has been cleared of the practical, concrete nature of its appeal, without, however, thereby losing its original constitution.[45]

[43] Actually, these changes were partly mediated by the industry that turned utopias into consumables – see Gonseth, Laville and Mayor (2008).

[44] Valsiner (1998, p. 116). [45] Bullough (1912, p. 91).

**Box 4.1 (cont.)**

In terms of the present sociogenetic perspective on personality, psychological distancing of such kind is made possible through human semiotic constructivity of the relations with the world. Distancing is possible thanks to the construction of hierarchically organized self- (and other-) regulation mechanisms – through meanings.

One of the results of such hierarchical construction of levels of abstracted meanings is the emergence of aesthetic experience, which unites the immediacy and distance of the object of such experience into a novel affective whole.

contrast to the cultural history of the past makes cultural innovation possible. As we adjust our imagination and memories, along with cultural rules, to a new situation, we necessarily create a new way of acting out known – yet selectively recollected – cultural histories.

### Anchoring life-course points

How do we remember what is before and what came after? What is it that gives our sense of time – in which year this or that event happen? And why is it that long periods of lives seem flat like the Sahara, while others seem to have compressed centuries in a month?[46] Our sense of time, our memories and our experience of our life course are actually punctuated by significant memories, or events that create punctuations in time. The significance of different life-course time points is socially suggested as well as personally constructed. If I am a twenty-five-year-old woman I may have forgotten the pleasures of my parents marking my birth by some celebration every month until I was a toddler – but expect that other persons in my network will acknowledge the day of my birth once a year. Symmetrically, we live with concrete deadlines and expected punctuations in the future. If I still am a twenty-five-year-old woman, I may expect to get married before I reach age thirty – but would have no clearly set timetable for my first divorce and later remarriage. The latter are socially undesired – yet very real – events. In the set-up of the future life course they are forgotten before they can be remembered! Time punctuations and anchors are all of semiotic nature and construct our subjective sense of our own historicity.

There are different ways of creating, maintaining and repairing our sense of time. Some time markers are biological; our heartbeats, our

[46] See Hviid (2008) on children's sense of growing older, and Draaisma (2004) on the subjective experience of the speed of time.

sleeping rhythm, the cycle of our digestive systems are all regular during our whole lives, even though their cycle may alter; other functions grow and decline, such as our thinking abilities or our physical strength – which remind us of the limits of our time. Changes in our bodies – wrinkles on the face of middle-aged persons, or change of hair colour (to be coped with by hair colouring!) are all about meaning markers on our bodies that are indispensable in the course of development. Thus, a young woman experiencing pregnancy:

> would wake up every morning to stand naked in front of the mirror, watching the developments that were overtaking her body. She would press her belly as if she wanted the intrusive swelling to disappear. She was disturbed by her bosom when it began to grow larger, but she only began to hate her pregnancy when the pink circles around her nipples began to change to a dark brown color. She had realized that she had lost a part of herself that she would never recover. When her belly began to swell further, she started to watch her navel with alarm. It was no longer just a small sunken area in the center of her belly, but began to protrude outward, changing in turn into another smaller swelling in the middle of the bigger swelling.[47]

Furthermore, social life offers strong markers – hours, days, or calendar events – celebrations of which we are aware. Between these, there are all kinds of markers which we constitute ourselves, on the basis of more or less specific events: we hear the neighbour coming back from work and we know it must be 6 am, or we celebrate the anniversary of a relationship. Time markers which are socially fixed, or socially acknowledged, usually carry normative expectations: Christmas constrains people to make gifts; people approaching their retirement are no longer expected to follow their unpredictable desires or they will be seen as behaving 'like teenagers'. In contrast, the study of diaries suggests that personal time markers give more freedom to reflect about one's past, or imagine one's future, regardless of these expectations.[48]

What creates personal time markers? A sense of significance of events probably comes from a conjunction of personal emotional impact, and the social value of the event. If we were to examine, side by side, a person's diary, and the fictional/autobiographical account given of his or her life, we could see which events had been retained as 'worth telling', that is, were significant enough to become anchoring points or turning points for a narrative.

That memories create past anchorages is quite clear. However, imagination enables us to create future anchors, or future endpoints. For example, a young man might decide that, if he hasn't had children by then, he will

[47] EzEldin (2007, pp. 32–3). [48] Zittoun (2008d).

not have children after the age of thirty five. When this young man gets to the age of thirty five, this imaginary endpoint might actually act as real termination; however, he might also reconsider. In that case, the age of thirty five might become (and remain) a memory anchorage – for instance, if he becomes a father aged forty, he may remember his thirty-fifth birthday as the year in which he expected no longer to have children.

## Multilinearity of life courses

We can consider Figure 4.7 as a generic starting point that describes the process of construction of the life course at any of its time moments; it also represents the depth of the coordination of levels (ontogenesis, cultural-historical, phylogenesis). Both the 'horizontal' (across PAST PRESENT FUTURE at each level) and 'vertical' coordinations provide a matrix for a high interindividual variability of life courses. First, and foremost, the phylogenetic level may appear in the microgenetic moments defined by ontogeny in situations where unique outcomes from biological features – inborn unique conditions (albino, twin birth, Down's syndrome, etc.) – enter into the construction of the given life course. A mother – in Botswana – who has given birth to an albino child gets a biological 'input' into the making of her own and her child's ontogeny. The impact of such a birth will be determined by the cultural-historical meaning of 'albino' in the given society (e.g. body parts of albinos are believed to have magical powers), which leads to the unique need to protect her child's daily well-being in the future.

## Summary: a non-naïve model of time for the life course

Our coverage of life-course development requires the use of concepts and methods that are applicable for any age of a person, and which are orientated to a person's pre-conceiving relevant ruptures in the life course in meaningful terms. The notion of *irreversible time* is central to such an understanding of the life course. This focus sets all developmental science – developmental biology, psychology, sociology, or anthropology – clearly apart from its non-developmental complementary counterpart. The latter creates the stable ground for the developmental sciences – but it does not substitute for the actual study of processes of change. Some of these changes are maintained – they become parts of developmental trajectories of the organism. Others will have no influence and vanish in the epigenetic landscape. As in music, thus, some patterns become part of an unique melody, while other variations simply disappear in the flow of the ongoing creation.

Development is in the unity of evolution (of new forms) and involution – disappearance and functional ignoring of old ones.

In this chapter, we have shown that time, as permanently flowing and irreversible, cannot be measured and cut into equivalent segments; such segments are social constructions that have pragmatic functions. From a subjective perspective, there is no such thing as a sense of present – we have only a sense of duration of what currently matters – a field of experience.

This has consequences for a more general model time: linear, arrow-like models of time fail to acknowledge the complexity of our sense of time – which is better captured by a broom-like model, suggesting that alternative futures coexist in the present (while left-out past alternatives have expired for good).

On the other hand, people's sense of time is always located in a certain social and cultural environment, in which dominant models of the life course exist, and are diffracted through mythologies, religious belief, naming practices, social expectations and language. Psychology has too often uncritically adopted these taken-for-granted models – for example the one according to which life moves through stages, and when people are treated as failures if they do not achieve these stages at the expected age.

We thus proposed models – the generative life cycle model, the prolepsis model along with the epigenetic landscape metaphor – accounting for both the irreversible nature of time, and the variability of experienced time – our sense of important events, our expectation of the future in the present, the time we share with others, the collectively elaborated imagination of time privileged by a given culture. This exploration of time and its model reveals how much time is real – and yet the product of our individual and collective imagination.

A thorough examination of a classical problem – that of time – usually explored either in the hard realm of science, or from a purely phenomelogical perspective, reveals another of the challenges of psychology. Indeed, the developmental science of the human life course needs to take into account the unity of real and non-real-yet-real: imaginary phenomena are as important as 'real' ones for development. As these dynamics between real and imaginary are produced by meaning-making processes, a developmental psychology consequently must study not only the changing person, but also the transformation of meaning-making abilities and processes in their social and cultural environments.

*Part II*

# Space for development

# 5 Social framing of lives: from phenomena to theories

A developmental science of the life course not only has to account for the irreversible time of people's trajectories, but also for the social and material environments in and through which people's lives unfold. To speak about 'context' is not enough. The environment, both perceived and imagined by people, very concretely creates the conditions for their lives.

In this chapter we define a set of notions that enable us to speak about the material and social spaces of development – how a person perceives her environment, relates to it, acts upon it and is eventually changed by it. That process can also be described from a third person perspective – of somebody who observes it, or who tries to intervene in that relating process. As in many other aspects of the scientific enquiry of human life, it appears difficult and artificial to fully separate these two perspectives – of the actor and the external observer/intervener – as they are actually always in dynamic interaction; we thus propose a model that integrates them.

Our lives are framed by fields of meanings through the whole life course. The clothes we are given to wear as infants – or as brides and grooms – or the ways in which we are expected to feel while watching regular world news on television, or entering the darkness of the night, are all markers of such framing. Yet we do not notice this ourselves – we immediately believe that it is *our preference* to wear a particular dress, and that it is the *inherent danger in the dark street* that faces us. We do not recognize that these experiences are linked to the meaning we attribute to them. We narrow down our attributional constructions to *either* ourselves *or* to the environment – while in reality both perspectives are mutually linked in a complex dynamic relationship. What happens with us is always the result of *both* ourselves and the environment – in some dynamic relation of the two. Social framing guides us to selectively narrow down what – if any – aspect of that relationship we are assumed to focus on.

*The ordinary nature of social 'influences':* the general principle of the social framing of human action covers the whole experiential field of the developing person – of any age. It is not a case of external 'influence' that forces a person into submission. Rather, the social world – through the environment available – offers action opportunities that are guided in socially desired ways. Complementing that, the active striving person looks for – and is offered – opportunities for involving herself within socially structured developmental pathways. While taking advantage of such opportunities, people are guided – by those who offer the opportunities – towards socially desired socio-moral or political identities. A young German boy – as he later narrated long after the he had become a famous person – at the age of ten years:

> the boy bearing my name voluntarily joined the *Jungvolk* ... At the top of my Christmas wish list for the year was the *Jungvolk*'s official uniform: cap, scarf, belt, and shoulder strap. True, I don't recall being particularly thrilled at the idea of carrying a flag at rallies or aspiring to the braiding that went with the rank of group leader, but I did my part unquestioningly, even when the endless singing and drumming bored me to tears.
>
> The uniform wasn't the only thing that made the group attractive. The wishful thought of its slogan, Youth Must Be Led by Youth! was backed up by promises of overnight hikes and other outdoor activities in the woods along the beach, of campfires among the erratic blocks dragged together to form a Germanic tribal meeting ground ... We sang as if our songs could make the *Reich* bigger and bigger.[1]

The contexts in which teenagers' activities take place are heterogeneous – and leave the young a range of possibilities for 'hooking up' their personal cultural meaning systems with the various features of the context. Thus, the uniform and the slogan of the importance of youth – together with outdoor adventures – did make a difference to the youngster, though he participated in the 'boring' drumming and singing as a part of the peer crowd, and did not find the 'pull' for upward mobility of any appeal. The different semiotic resources that are made available to people – uniforms, games, books, films, etc. – are guides for the construction of the self.

The framing of any personal act in a wider social meaning context is multilayered – usually involving mutually incompatible and contradictory social goal orientations. In such a heteregeoneous context, it is still the person who engages in one, rather than the another, action. Suggestions of guidance are present – the person follows one or the other, or resists. Very often, this multiplicity can also trigger an improvisation of action, albeit in the direction that some social institution may suggest – or even prescribe – as desirable. For example, when Agnes Wairimu – a young Gikuyu girl who had converted to Protestantism (and was attending a mission school) – left

[1] Grass (2007, pp. 19–20).

home for morning errands one day in 1926, the implications for her whole life of the events that were to unfold were not to be predicted. She came across a group of girls which included some of her peers and friends in a traditional Gikuyu circumcision procession. As a converted Protestant and an exemplary schoolgirl, Agnes should have ignored the 'pagan' procession. Yet:

> Suddenly, Agnes felt an urge to join the procession. The group would have been headed for the river, where they would not only wash away their childish ways, but where the chilly morning water would numb them in preparation for the operation. Agnes had already violated many tenets of the ritual, however, and once the group arrived at the ritual ground, her infiltration of the ceremony was discovered. Unlike the other candidates, Agnes did not have a *motiiri*, an official sponsor, a woman who would secure the initiate in a steady position of readiness for the surgery. But Agnes was determined to get circumcised. She took her position on the ground and awaited the *muruithia*, the surgeon, who enquired whose candidate she was. A woman stepped forward on the spur of the moment, adorned Agnes with the ceremonial bead necklace, and assumed the role of a sponsor. This woman had not anticipated the awkward situation, so it is assumed that she recognized Agnes and stepped in to save the situation.[2]

After having fulfilled her situationally triggered, yet deep wish,[3] Agnes's life at home changed dramatically. One of her brothers – a Protestant convert – condemned the circumcision. Her maternal uncle – who in principle approved of the tradition – was angry that Agnes had not asked for his permission. His wife – who would have played the crucial role of *motiiri* – was angry that Agnes had not let her assume that role. Her Protestant school expelled her once the fact of her having been circumcised was known. Yet that made it possible for Agnes's other brother – a Catholic convert – to get Agnes converted yet once more – to Catholicism – and enter a Catholic school. From an occasional temptation followed an altered life course, not only for the girl but her whole family.

Ideological divisions run deep in human lives. It is remarkable with what ease primary social units – families and kin groups – may become internally divided when higher-level ideological symbol systems become internalized by their members and begin to create divisions upon their externalization. It is therefore not surprising that all religious and political systems are interested in penetrating the social systems of families, by inserting their symbolic messages which, if escalated by the personal-cultural actions of the converts,

[2] Kanogo (2005, p. 75) – from the life story interview with the author conducted in 1993.

[3] Agnes's wish reflects the ambiguity of her social situation: when a Protestant convert she wanted to be with her peer group, as the age set of the Gikuyu is a strong cohort identity. Hence circumcision was a social status that needed to be obtained, at the expense of being excommunicated.

enhance the ideologies within families, from the inside. In an analogy with the biological world, different semiotic elements of outside agents are imported inside families, and inside people's minds, where they begin to act as 'internal semiotic viruses' to take over human hearts and minds.

## The reality – of the real, and of the constructed

The describing of people in relation to their environment has for a long time been polarized between two extreme positions. On the one hand, positivist approaches to humans and social sciences assume that science can describe humans and their environment as if they *really* existed. Yet what 'really' means becomes a contested notion – precisely because of the human capacity to construct meaning and create new versions of the environment. The architectural wonders of Europe first emerged in their architects' imaginations – and only when implemented in practice became *real* in the sense of being touchable and breakable buildings.[4]

The simple objectivist focus described here above prevails in the social sciences – some areas of sociology and environmental psychology attempt to describe the objective structure of the social world and the forces that organize it, while some fields of psychology try to describe humans as organisms that can be described and predicted from without. The role of human beings according to such approaches is to be passive recipients of 'environmental influences', rather than active co-constructors – or even resisters – of such 'environmental impacts'.

On the other side, there has always been an opposite tendency that insists on paying more attention to the person's perspective – looking at the active role of the people in organizing their environments. For authors adopting this standpoint, it is humans who render their world meaningful as they construct it. For these writers, the goal of social and human sciences is to understand how people understand what happens, or confer sense on it. In the extreme version of such a position, the reality of inevitable interdependence with the environment is dismissed, and we are faced with an exaggerated version of subjective constructivism. Reality becomes a human invention.

[4] Engineers – and architects – are *bricoleurs* as we all are in their creative process of planning – only their constructions have a socially shareable longevity. Furthermore, the significance of the implemented work for their users may be quite different from what was planned. Consider an unfinished architectural project – Antoni Gaudí's La Sagrada Familia in Barcelona. It is *real,* it exists, millions of visitors pass by and touch and photograph it. Yet at the same time it is not real, as it is an unfinished cathedral, the precise final version plan of which was lost with the death of its originator. The relationship between the plan and the implementation, in this case, was supposed to be a work of engineering. It emerged, however, as a case of 'collective' *bricolage* through the socially moulded attention it won in a social-historical process . . . On the notion of *bricolage*, see Chapter 1.

The problem is that these two types of description tend to see each other as mutually exclusive: if the world is made of subjective positions, then there is no objective description; or – in other terms – the world of causalities is incommensurable with the world of human intentions.[5] A solution to the problem is remarkably simple – a move to consider the constructive role of human beings in their lives working *through* the environmental set of constraints (Figure 5.1). Any construction of the external environment or of the internal mind entails the starting point of the real (personal experience of the past and the present objective condition). That basis feeds into personal construction – moving beyond the *so-far-given real* into the *imagined future real* and through that to the actual construction of that future *as the present real.*

Looking at Figure 5.1(a) and 5.1(b) it is clear that the question of person–environment relations has been inadequately stated in much of the social sciences. It has been captured by the notions of classical logic (if A then not non-A: either the environment determines the person or the person constructs the image of reality). The solution to the one-sided causal determinist views of the first two figures is in Figure 5.1(c) – and lies in the notion of *meanacting.*[6]

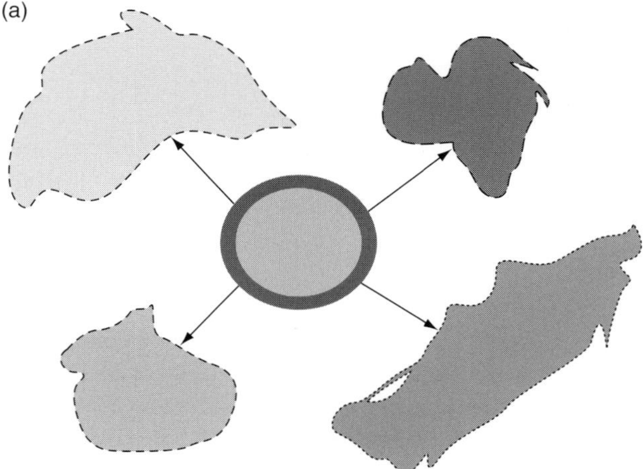


Figure 5.1 Three ways of looking at *the real*: (a) personal (subjective) determination; (b) environmental ('objective') determination; (c) the meanacting solution: acting *through* the other.

[5] See Brinkmann (2006). [6] Introduced by Thompson and Valsiner (2002).

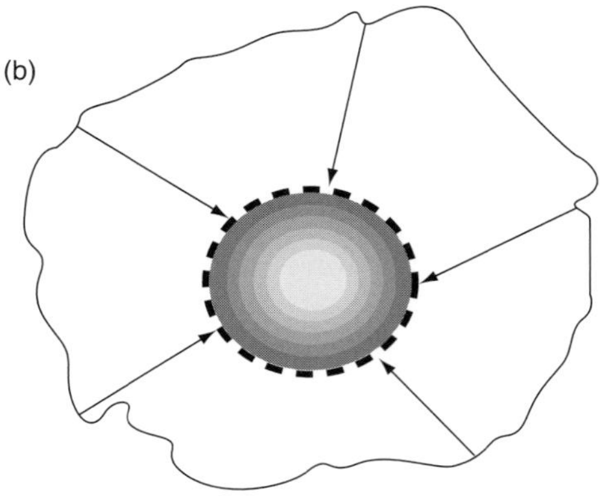


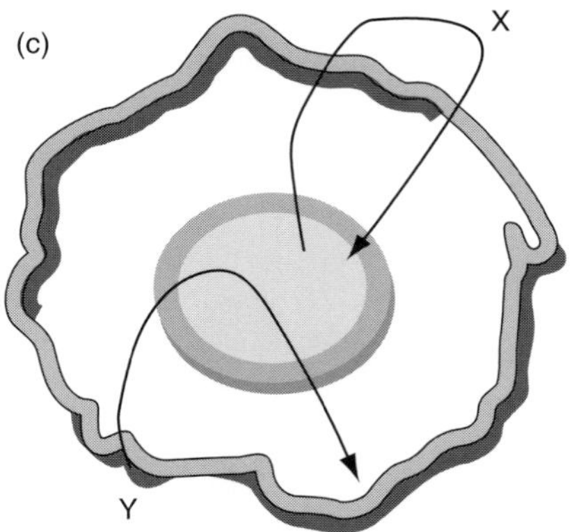


Figure 5.1 (cont.)

The notion of *meanacting* designates a fact that a person acts upon the environment in ways that feed forward to the development of the person him- or herself (arrow X); it is *through the resources of the environment* that a person develops. Similarly, the 'impact' from the environment (arrow Y) has an "effect" only as mediated by a person. The environment 'acts' – so to speak – *through the active relating* to that environment of the constructive person. Given our sociocultural approach, we are very much concerned with the person's perspective – yet we also know that her understanding of the situation results from a complex dialogical process with other persons and with her social and symbolic environment. This locates the sociocultural approach clearly within the meanacting (Figure 5.1(c)) version of defining person<>environment relationships. This implies that anything from the world that enters a person's perspective needs to be considered from at least another perspective too, that of another person, or a social, general other. Hence, it is admitted that, a person develops her *personal culture* (see Box 5.1), that is, all the personally meaningful features of her immediate external environment as well as her internal fields of feelings, thoughts and desires, within a given collective

### Box 5.1 Personal culture

The notion of *personal culture* developed by Valsiner in tandem with *collective culture*, continues the tradition of Georg Simmel[7] looking at subjective and objective cultures. For Valsiner, the human *psyche* is elaborated and regulated by semiotic tools, which are created (and recreated) under the guidance of social others. It is the others who created the conditions for a meaningful creation and use of signs. Individual human meaning/action is dependent on the effective use of these signs. The notion of personal culture is a corollary of this reasoning: if our human *psyche* operates through the developing semiotic system in a constant pursuit of adaptation to the uncertain immediate future, then the psychological realm can be coined as a *personal culture*.

> The notion of 'personal culture' refers not only to internalized subjective phenomena (intramental processes), but also to the immediate (person-centred) externalizations of those processes. The latter make personal culture publicly visible, as every aspect of personal reconstruction of one's immediate life-world reflect that externalization.[8]

Both internalization and externalization are constructive processes – hence the intra-psychological and externalized personal-cultural realms are not isomorphic relative to each other. Therefore, collective culture is constantly (re-)created through the externalizations of the person, but it is not a mirror image of the personal culture. Nor is the personal culture a mirror image of the collective culture. Rather, the collective culture of the person – meanings exemplified in interaction with peers and all others, experiences of places in the local community or (vicariously) as shown far away on TV screens – is the material that feeds into the further construction of personal culture.

[7] Simmel (1908/1971a).
[8] Valsiner (2000, p. 55). On the concepts of internalization and externalization, see also Chapter 3, Box 3.3.

culture. For example, a film – say *Casino Royale* – has a consensual meaning in a given cultural environment (the last James Bond, about a risky poker game) at the same time as each particular viewer in that culture confers a unique sense on the film (e.g. 'it reminds me of the dangers of betting, as my uncle did until bankruptcy').

Similarly, faced with any kind of general knowledge and social representations, a person may internalize some part of this consensual meaning – based on her previous personal knowledge base – transforming it as she integrates it into her understanding. On the basis of this personal knowledge base, she may then externalize it in the transformed version. Hence, in this approach, the necessary gap between the thing-as-understood-by-a-particular-person, and the thing-as-consensually-understood, is not a philosophical question; it is part of the continuous making and unmaking of meaning in the social world.[9] The process of *meanacting* mostly escapes linear predictions and planning; rather, as a developmental process, it is best described as *bricolage*.[10]

*The unity of construction and destruction in the personal culture:* A good example of the dynamic movement between self and the environment, mediated by imaginary experiences, comes from the autobiography of George Sand.[11] Aurore, as a young girl growing up in devoutly Catholic France, developed an aversion to external church rituals (to her meaningless), and instead created a new personal religion for herself in her adolescent mind. Her new deity – Corambé – came to her in a dream:

> Corambé was created by itself in my mind. It was as pure and as charitable as Jesus, as shining and handsome as Gabriel; but I needed a little of nymphic grace and Orpheus' poetry. Consequently it took on less austere forms than the Christian God and more spiritual aspects than the gods of Homer. And then, I also had to complement it at times with a woman's garb, because what I had loved best and understood best until then was a woman – my mother. Hence it often appeared to me with female features . . . I wanted to love it as a friend, as a sister, all the while giving it the reverence of a god. *I did not want to fear it, and for that reason I wished it to have a few of our failings and weaknesses.*[12]

[9] This is captured in communication theory by the *organon* model of Karl Bühler, discussed below in this chapter.

[10] It may take place as engineering, or as *bricolage* (cf. Chapter 1); yet we argue that the prevailing form of construction of the real is *bricolage*. In addition, this *bricolage* is rarely confined to a solitary workshop activity, but may be – or, more often than not – *is* embedded in a social-historical context, where people together co-construct a reality that is not necessarily preconceived in any individual's imagination.

[11] One of the first female novelists later considered as a feminist, Aurore Dupin (1804–1876) used the pen name of George Sand.

[12] Jurgrau (1991, p. 605), emphasis added.

The construction of the deity – 'out there' – is deeply personal ('in here'). The fantasy creation was not only projected on to the external environment – Aurore made a temple for her deity. A secluded forest spot became a construction site, where her

imagination transformed a three-foot high mound into a mountain, a few trees into a forest, a footpath which went from the house to the meadow into a road that leads to the end of the world, the pond bordered with ancient willows into a whirlpool or a lake, according to my whim. And I saw my fictional characters moving, running off together, dreamily walking alone, sleeping in the shade, or singing and dancing in this paradise of my idle dreams.

... At *first I was quite conscious of this labor of mine*, but after a very short time, perhaps a few days (for a child a day seems like three), *I felt possessed by my subject much more than it was possessed by me*. The daydream came to be a sort of sweet hallucination, but so frequent and sometimes so perfect, that it left me as if transplanted out of this world.[13]

The process of turning a mound, trees, a pathway and a pond into a temple corresponds to the sort of transitional phenomena described by Winnicott, characterized by a series of paradoxes: the temple is "both" found and created, ME and NOT ME.[14] Also, the crucial psychological move visible here is the dynamic *shift of the feeling of control* – from Aurore's own decisions about how to construct the temple, to that of aligning herself with and becoming subservient to the more powerful agent – the deity that she had created herself in her fantasy.[15] In the ongoing dynamics of living, the separation of loci of control (internal/external,[16] primary/secondary)[17] into mutually exclusive opposites would eliminate the very phenomena of control from a psychologist's further consideration. It is paradoxical that paying attention to a particular topic in a certain way may actually 'hide' that object from our understanding. By stating – it is *either* the person *or* the environment that 'has control' over the person's lives – we eliminate the *relationship* between the person *and* the environment from our investigative focus. Note that in the former statement it is the classical logical scheme – if something is X it cannot be non-X – that is being used in our commonsense and ordinary thinking. Yet for developmental phenomena classical logic is not adequate, and our investigative thought models need to proceed along

[13] Jurgrau (1991, p. 606), emphasis added. [14] Winnicott (1971).
[15] See also Valsiner (1999).
[16] This conceptual solution offered by Julian Rotter (1966) has proven widely popular in psychology – yet from the perspective taken here it is a construction of no use for science, since it overlooks the mutual dynamic relations between the opposites. What is 'internal' in control beliefs is supported by the 'external' and vice versa.
[17] Cf. Rothbaum, Weisz and Snyder (1982).

the lines of 'genetic logic'[18] or on open-systemic focus on person–environment relations. From the perspective of the latter, each of the control processes is internally external (or externally internal) as features from both feed forward into the other – generating the actual control.

The externalized deity – through the temple constructed for it – was an intimate place for Aurore. It was an external place created by her, for herself, and as such did not tolerate exposure to others. The sanctuary was discovered one day by a boy – a playmate, who tracked Aurore to her secret location. This violation of her private world ended the personal meaning of the temple:

> From the moment other feet than mine had trodden the sanctuary, Corambé no longer lived there. The dryads and cherubs abandoned it, and my rituals and sacrifices seemed to me no more than a puerility that even I myself had not taken seriously. *I destroyed the temple with as much care as I had taken to erect it.*[19]

The actual place is still the same; only Aurore takes back what belongs to her. Winnicott calls this the 'fate' of transitional phenomena: although they can be the most important thing for a person at some point, they can also lose their emotional and imaginary function and become *mere* objects again. Aurore's way of handling a symbolic construction has a counterpart in the practices of Buddhist monks who spend long time building *mandalas* – only to destroy them after they have finished constructing them. *Development over the whole life course entails the unity of construction and destruction* – and in the human case the dialectics between these two opposites fuels the emergence, the annihilation and the re-emergence of meanings. A person is never in possession of the meaning, except at that very moment when she is speaking[20] or otherwise making sense of something in her life.

18 See Baldwin (1915/2009) as well as Valsiner (2009b, 2009c) on the history of developmental ('genetic') logic.
19 Jurgrau (1991, p. 610), emphasis added.
20 As Mikhail Bakhtin has emphasized:

> The word language is a half alien [chuzoye – not belonging to me and unknown – in Russian] word. It becomes 'one's own' when the speaker inhabits it with his intention, his accent, masters the word, brings it to bear upon his meaningful and expressive strivings. Until that moment of appropriation [prisvoenie in Russian] the word does not exist in neutral and faceless language (the speaker does not take the word from a dictionary!), but [it exists] on the lips of others, in alien contexts, in service of others' intentions: from here it has to be taken and made into one's own. (Bakhtin, 1934/1975, p. 106)

### *Making meaning together: Karl Bühler's* organon *model*

The above example shows clearly our constant effort to make sense of our lives, both at a microgenetic and an ontogenetic level. Prima facie, making sense is 'constructing meaning'. However, the above example proves to be a somewhat simplistic statement. Through the semiotic function, humans are particularly apt at interacting with the environment in a *mediated* way, that is, their lives are not confined to the linearity of the here-and-now.

Historically, humans' ability to communicate has played a major role in their capacity to control their environment, because this communication has enabled them to have a common understanding of their environment, to share experiences and coordinate actions. Through internalization of such communication it became possible for the individual to keep in mind the past and the future, and to render present distant geographical places. Through externalization it also became possible for people to communicate these contents of their mind to others. It made possible the accumulation of experiences interindividually and historically, the most powerful source of collective and individual knowledge. This ability also laid the basis for imagination, which is, in turn, used to make sense of human life. It may be argued that it is also the basis for religion, as we have seen in the previous example.

Ontogenetically, the semiotic function first and foremost emerges in person-to-person interactions. Yet these cannot be separated from the person–environment relationship, as very clearly illustrated in the Corambé example – and reciprocally: person–environment relationships are always mediated by one person-to-person relationship or another (e.g. Aurore's relationship to her mother, in the Corambé example).[21] Of course, neither person–environment, not person-to-person relationships are static: all evolve through time.

Finally, the semiotic function constantly operates at the level of microgenesis – in the here and now of social interaction. This was elegantly captured by the *organon* model proposed by Karl Bühler to describe meaning-making in person-to-person communication.

According to Bühler all communication is *about* something – an external or internal object – from the sender's perspective. The intention to communicate finds its expression ('print-out' or *Ausdruck*) in a particular message form (the triangle in Figure 5.2) that represents the object or state of the communicative act. Yet this representation – which is simultaneously

[21] The 'other' may be real or imagined, a concrete or a 'generalized Other'. More generally, for the inherent 'triadic' nature of dialogical processes and the theoretical evolution of the idea, see Marková (2005).

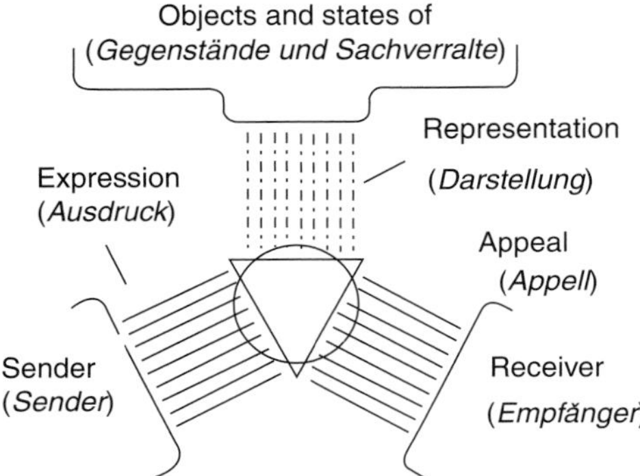


Figure 5.2 Karl Bühler's organon model.

a presentation (to the receiver) – is not an immediate 'copy' of the object, as it is presented in terms of signs. When I as a sender say the word 'chair' it may *refer to a class of objects* we can sit upon. The message has an appeal to the receiver, who, however, makes sense of it by way of his own history of creating meaning, and from the current point of view. The result is that the sender's intended message (triangle) is turned into a different meaning (the circle in Figure 5.2) by the active transformation of the receiver. Both the speaker and the listener inhabit the message with their – respectively different – *sense*. Communication is, as a result, negotiation of the meanings between co-constructing partners, rather than the conveying of existing information. Hence, meaning is always re-created in microgenesis.

Bühler's model allows us to view both co-regulation[22] and innovation within the same communicative act. This model surpasses the often mentioned communication model of Claude Shannon and Warren Weaver in the late 1940s, which treated communication as an as-accurate-as-possible transfer of a message from a sender to a recipient. In contrast, Bühler describes communication as the negotiation of meaning between co-constructing partners, similarly to current discursive, socioconstructivist or dialogical approaches.[23] Below, we will see that dynamic models such as Fogel's[24] suggest that in addition to their co-construction of the

[22] A concept introduced by Alan Fogel to account for the mutuality and simultaneity of social interaction and in communication, within which new meaning emerges from the joint action of the parties (see e.g. Fogel, 1993a, *passim*). We will return to the concept several times below. It is also explicated in Chapter 7.

[23] Linell (2009), Marková (2005), etc.

[24] Fogel (1993b).

### Box 5.2 Karl Bühler

Karl Bühler (1879–1963) can be seen as one of the thinkers in psychology whose work was of profound programmatic value for other disciplines – linguistics and the philosophy of language in his case.

Bühler's work has been important in different fields. It was relevant for 'speech act' theory, as well as for the role of language in human mental processes. Bühler also created a model of communication (the *Organonmodell*), and made notable contributions to semiotics – which he himself labelled sematology. He benefited from liaisons with phenomenology as well as the holistic thought of *Gestalt* and *Ganzheitspsychologie* of the beginning of the twentieth century. Furthermore, he became (together with Charlotte Malachowski, later Bühler) a substantial contributor to developmental psychology. He is certainly among the top German theoreticians of psychology of the twentieth century, alongside Ernst Cassirer, William Stern and Max Wertheimer. Yet Bühler is probably more consistent than the others in his linking of philosophical, theoretical and empirical domains in his version of psychology. The focus on *processes* of human reasoning that at times resurfaces in contemporary cognitive psychology can be traced back to the work of the Würzburg School of Oswald Külpe and Karl Bühler.

Bühler's role in the formation of psychological thought in the twentieth century is seminal. He attempted to overcome psychology's narrow focus on either mental phenomena, or behaviour, by a focus on the third component – the sign – that stands between both (in the inner-psychological sphere) and which mediates the interpersonal regulation of conduct. It is worth emphasizing that he was not a psychologist, in the narrow sense – his formative work was in medicine and philosophy. He took an active interest in very many topical areas – from the navigation of bees to processes of thinking, and – most importantly – the act of speaking. His contribution was of the kind that nowadays we are apt to label 'interdisciplinary'. Yet such labels mean nothing – usually they just cover up the inability of the label-user to create a synthesis between disciplines. Bühler did not use labels, he created bridges between ideas from different disciplines. His ideas were well rooted in the work of his predecessors – from Aristotle and Plato to the holistic traditions in European psychology (e.g. Edmund Husserl, Alexius Meinong, etc.). The richness of human speaking was the source for the richness in Bühler's thinking. Thinking was sheer intellectual pleasure, and its traces in Bühler's work are sources for the further advancement of our contemporary ideas.

message, participants actually co-regulate each other – thus leaving space to account for the emergence of new meaning.[25]

## The person–environment relationship: process of mutuality

How then can we speak of the world in which we live? One of the most common terms is the notion of *context* – which is extremely problematic. In psychological sciences, the term 'context' is used extensively to designate what is 'around' people. Usually it designates what is 'outside' a person, having an 'influence' on her: the media, public discourse, the weather are hence part of the context. From another point of view, however, the context is understood as something that is simultaneously partly 'given' to a person, and partly created through her interactions with the environment.[26]

We will start by exploring some of the available theoretical tools that a half-century of studies have provided us with in order to study these 'contexts'. There are two types of descriptions, the one examining a social situation – such as a classroom, an interaction at the baker's or the collective handling of foreign workers, etc. – the other focused on the processes whereby people make sense of the situation in which they are involved as it unfolds. Among these approaches, some are more focused on the 'situated' social frame – churches, rules, spatial arrangements or texts – while others are more interested in their psychological counterparts, thus capturing mental schemes or scripts, or discursive categories. Hence, first, these theories can be distinguished according to their focus on individual or social aspects. Second, some examine the social in its more material aspects, or in its more symbolic ones. Third, it is also useful to distinguish approaches more devoted to analysing human social framing in terms of structures from those more devoted to the study of their *dynamic* or developmental aspects.[27]

[25] See Bakhtin (1979/1996).

[26] Grossen and Perret-Clermont (1992, p. 117–18; 2001). See also the epigenetic landscape metaphor, where the rolling of the ball is constrained by the landscape ahead, but at the same time contributes to shaping that same landscape. Caution though – the landscape represents not only the present environmental context, but also the present internal epigenetic situation of the developing individual.

[27] Most of the structural approaches coming from social psychology or microsociology contributed to an understanding of the insertion of persons within their social life, calling our attention to the surrounding contexts and their variability and power. The dynamic approaches, generally more recent, tend to focus on how the system of evolving interpersonal relations is simultaneously involved in the creation of the human mind and in the (re-)creation of the social contexts themselves.

Of course, creating these divisions reinforces dichotomies. Science usually proceeds analytically, dividing and fragmenting reality, focusing on particular elements of a complex object of study, while such division should be just one step of the process, the next one, synthesis, usually being missing. Here, the notion of 'meanacting' enables us to bring together processes always related in reality; and we will consider persons and their social context as bound together and yet separated.[28]

## Space for living: creating the *Umwelt*

There is a long tradition that has attempted to define the phenomenological quality of local environments. Basically, this question is close to that formulated by William James, which seems to have guided this enquiry: 'Under what circumstances do we think things are real?' Contributions from this tradition are devoted to describing how our internal perceptions and feelings of the world have emerged, rather than characterizing the objective qualities of our living spaces. A very close attention to a person's (or an animal's) perspective leads to defining a specific understanding of what the environment is. This involves centring the perspective on the organism in immediate relation with the environment.

Johann Jakob von Uexküll[29] (1864–1944) proposed the term *Umwelt* to describe an organism's experienced environment. Etymologically, this term comes from the German combination of *Um* ('for' or 'around' – accusative preposition) and *Welt* (World). His notion of *Umwelt* suggests that we generate our own worlds within the limits of constraints[30] based on the physical properties of the environment, and set up according to the scope of our perceptual and meaning-making abilities. Thus, in the same living room, Jules and a fly are in two different *Umwelten*: because of their perceptual systems and cognitive abilities, for the fly the world is defined by the heat of candles and the sweetness of the drinks on the table; for

28 This wording is based on Marková's (2005) work.

29 Johann Jakob von Uexküll (1864–1944) was a non-evolutionary German Baltic biologist. He made contributions to the fields of muscular physiology and animal behaviour studies, and developed a theory of the general meaning in biological life. His notion of *Umwelt* had an influence on semiotics; through semiotics, on psychoanalysis; and through psychoanalysis, to some extent, on psychology. For a detailed coverage of von Uexküll's life and work, see Mildenberger (2007).

30 We act 'around' the environment 'for' our life's needs, creating the *Umwelt*. This is a very comparable idea to that promoted by William James (1890/2007) and developed by Alfred Schütz under the term 'life world' (Schütz and Luckman, 1973): their focus on a person's perspective on motivations brings them to see people as popping in and out of a plurality of life-worlds.

Jules, there is a whole romantic scene which may be taking place for humans having a dinner. For a dog, the same scene is of different functional significance. Hence *Umwelt* is a part of the environment that relates to the active organism – 'nobody is the product of one's *milieu* – everybody is the master of one's *Umwelt*'.[31]

Uexküll's relativization of the functional view on the environment – leading to the creation of the organism-centred look at its structure (*Umwelt*) – is a necessary starting point for a developmental look at the environment. The environment for us is what matters for our actions and reactions in the individual historical as well as the given here-and-now context. We act upon it from our current standpoint – and in accordance with our current goal-orientation – change it, and through that act of changing it move ourselves into a new position in relation to the environment.[32] The *Umwelt* develops together with the developing person – and through the actions of that person.

## Kurt Lewin's look at life space

Kurt Lewin was the pioneer in psychology who systematically defined what a person's 'life space' could be. Working with the principle of 'what is real is what has effects',[33] Lewin tried to define a set of notions enabling the capture of the range of possible actions in which a person could engage in a specific time and place.

The idea is that people's possible actions are limited by their perception of material, social and cognitive constraints. Hence, a person's life space could be described as three-dimensional (see Figure 5.3). The main focus is present, while the field structure grows and differentiates (giving multiple pasts and multiple futures) from birth to adulthood.

Lewin's theoretical perspective has a number of peculiarities. First, Lewin was interested not in the 'objective' material or social situations in themselves, but *insofar as a person feels them as limiting his action* (i.e. 'having effects'); Lewin thus spoke of *quasi-social*, *quasi-physical* and *quasi-conceptual* facts. Hence the following example:

Two six years old boys are sitting in a bathtub, the one very lively and over excited, the other quieter. The excited one (A) jumps around in the bathtub so much that the other one (B) feels cramped. Finally (B) draws a line in the water across the middle of the tub and tells A to stay within his own region. Whereas in the beginning there

[31] 'Niemand ist Produkt seines Milieus – ein jeder ist Herr seiner Umwelt' (Mildenberger, 2007, p. 117).

[32] For a contemporary extension of the look at *Umwelt*, see Sokol Chang (2009).

[33] Lewin (1936, p. 19).

was a single unarticulated region of possible movement for A with the result that for the other child (B) the actual freedom of movement was very much restricted, now there are adjacent but sharply separated zones of free movement for A and B.[34]

In this example, it is only what the child actually *perceives* that appears as relevant: first A has a great deal of space to move in, and after B's intervention, he has a much smaller space. Even though the bathtub may seem the same to an observer, its *quasi-physical* and *quasi-social* nature changes for the participants. Because of a social exchange, the space perceived as accessible is cut in two; and hence the life space of A has radically changed. Later, Lewin came to call *boundary zones* of the life space 'certain parts of the social and physical world [that] do affect the state of the life space at that time'.[35]

Second, the life space is organized in time. Only the present exists;[36] *past and future only exist if they are made actual in the present*, as plans, goals or expectations. Lewin was thus opposed to the idea of *historical causality*, that is, that the present is caused by past events. Past and future made present by imagination thus generate the division of the life space into different regions between which a person may move – metaphorically speaking (see Figure 5.3). These regions also have more or less impermeable boundaries, which makes them more or less available to a person. Lewin thus conceives of a systemic causality (in the present), as opposed to a historical causality across past–present–future time.

A third dimension is, however, required for a person to cross boundaries. Lewin distinguished between 'degrees of reality' in a person's life space.[37] In Figure 5.3, this dimension is represented by the height of the boxes. With this dimension Lewin makes his 'quasi'-qualification of different states and events in the life space *a question of degree*: an action is more real than a daydream; the perception of an object is more real than imagining it, etc.

Hence, for Lewin, the *total* present situation of the person includes her history, as well as aspirations and imaginatings; it is essentially a *psychological life space*. In this model, social, physical and conceptual facts do not exist. In contrast with the epigenetic landscape metaphor explored in the

[34] Lewin (1936, p. 42). [35] Lewin (1943, p. 210).
[36] For instance:

> we shall here strongly defend the thesis that neither past nor future psychological facts but only the present situation can influence present events. This thesis is a direct consequence of the principle that only what exists concretely can have effects. Since neither the past nor the future exists at the present moment it cannot have effects at the present. In representing the life space therefore we take into account only what is contemporary. [Lewin, 1936, p. 34ff.]

See also very explicit formulations in Lewin (1943).
[37] Lewin (1936, pp. 196ff.).

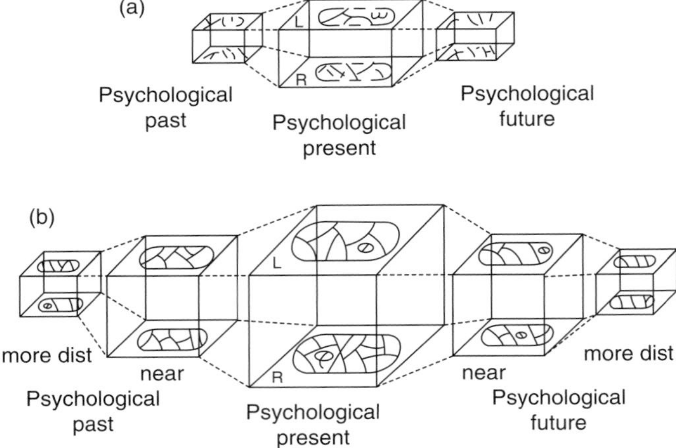


Figure 5.3 Kurt Lewin's scheme of life space in human development (from Lewin, 1951, p. 246).

first chapter, there is no representation of the history of a person (including genetic inheritance, physical history and history of experiences), or the history of the environment.

## From the theory of frames to dynamic positioning of the self

Erving Goffmann (1922–1982) pursued a parallel effort to that of Kurt Lewin within sociology. Rather than describing social structures, organizations or social forces, he proposed to account for individuals' organization of experience, and the ways by which they make sense of 'what is going on there' as they participate in social situations.

Goffman used the term *frame* proposed by Gregory Bateson[38] to describe the understanding that people have of what it is that is going on in a given social situation. Bateson suggested the notion of *frame* inspired by an observation of two monkeys play-fighting. This frame – 'we are just playing that we are fighting' – is very different from one in which the monkeys really were fighting. Also, this frame – 'we are just playing' – implies that the monkeys had some form of metacommunication that allowed them to distinguish play from 'a real' fight. Goffman departed from this notion of Bateson's to:

[38] Bateson (1972/1999).

assume that definitions of a situation are built up in accordance with principles of organization which govern events – at least social ones – and our subjective involvement in them; frame is the word I use to refer to such of these basic elements as I am able to identify. That is my definition of frame. My phrase 'frame analysis' is a slogan to refer to the examination in these terms of the organization of experience.[39]

If the notion of frame rejoins Lewin's quasi-social fact, Goffman's emphasis is not only on the immediate perception of a social boundary, but also on asking the crucial question of what enables this understanding – a question that could be raised in the monkey example above.

On the one hand, Goffman emphasizes kinds of 'schemata' – which seem almost cognitive – on which people uncritically draw to make sense of daily situations. These constitute *primary frames*: some are natural, and include physical objects and their causal relationships; others are social, including human agency and intentions, rules and principles. The latter require the former: playing chess requires playing within the *social frame* of rules and expectation, as the player moves the pieces on the chess board in the *natural frame* of objects defined by physical rules.

On the other side, Goffman was interested in how people, engaged in social interactions, actually keep on 'framing' their situation, that is, rectifying their understanding, and also negotiating the definition of the situation, that is, the frame. For example, even though people can tolerate being touched by an unknown person if the situation is framed as 'medical consultation', they may feel as inappropriate the gesture of the karate teacher who wants to check the strength of the muscle of his female students.[40] Hence, the description of the environment is here focused on the person's construction of it, but from the perspective of a social being, engaged in constant negotiations with others. Logically, then, Goffman considered that the sum of the primary frames of a social group constituted a central part of its culture. For a given group, there is also a 'frame of the frame', that is, a system of beliefs or a cosmology.

It is this dynamic, co-constructive dimension of framing that has been explored by researchers interested in interaction. In sociolinguistics and in domains of psychology analysing interactive discourse, authors have learned to identify, in language, cues revealing this work of framing within dialogues or group discussion.[41] But with a focus on discourse, there is no

[39] Goffman (1974, pp. 10–11). [40] Goffman (1974, pp. 10–11).

[41] In this line of ideas, Marková, Linell, Grossen and Salazar Orvig (2007, p. 73) have built on Goffman's work so as to distinguish *external framing*, including instructions given in a situation, or the physical environment of an interaction, and *internal framing*, that is, the

### Box 5.3 Erving Goffman

Erving Goffman (1922–1982) was a sociologist who studied and depicted everyday life in societies. He developed what was called a unique 'dramaturgical perspective'. Initially trained in Toronto, he then moved to the University of Chicago where his work was influenced by symbolic interactionism as developed by George Herbert Mead and Herbert Blumer, as well as by social anthropology. This led him to use participant observations to observe and describe everyday life interactions and rituals. His first major contribution was an analysis of the mechanics of everyday life through the metaphor of the theatre – hence, people can be described as if they take on a role, or manage impressions as they interact on stage (*The Presentation of Self in Everyday Life*, 1959). Goffman's further work led him to examine the social treatment of deviance and exclusion, as in *Stigma* (1964). In *Asylums* (1961) he followed the career of patients in a mental asylum, which led him to develop a reflection on the role of total institutions. His later work developed the stage metaphor in a more general theory of *frames* guiding, and emerging out of social interactions (*Frame Analysis*, 1974) and to focus on the micro-processes of discourse (*Forms of Talk*, 1981). Through the ideas of stigma, stage, frames and institutions, Goffman proposed tools enabling a very critical reading of our society. Although his work was criticized on methodological grounds, its heuristic power made it very influential, not only in sociology, but also in social psychology.[42]

real description of the materiality and presence of the social worlds that people feel and interpret, and that come to manifest themselves in their discourse.

*Are frames subjective?* In synthesis, these three authors contribute to our understanding of the context in which people live. First, they suggest that people's surrounding world is both sensed and constructed, and that it changes along with a person's perspective. Second, this experienced world is also socially regulated, implying that our 'subjective space' and our possible actions are set up by a complex perception of material, social

continuous adjustment occurring within an interaction and through which people keep on defining and correcting their definition of what is going on. In that sense, framing is part of the work of making sense of the situation using all the possible available cues. But in doing so, people may be blind to many of the social and cultural facts and elements that are actually also constraining their situation, but which are not visible to them. This is one of the reasons why we also need a vocabulary for describing the actual embeddedness of social interactions within their social contexts, etc.

42 For an exposition of his main ideas see for instance Branaman (1997).

and cognitive constraints. Third, the notion of frame itself expands our perspective on the social nature of our inner world, implying that we use some kinds of schemata in order to set the ground for what is going on. In other words, our understanding of situations has a social nature; yet even if it has been socially pre-prepared for us, it implies the active understanding of the person, who has to confer sense on the situation at stake. As we shall see later, this active understanding is not self-enclosed, since it also calls for social processes of regulation with the material and interpersonal world.

Hence, we might say that these authors present a very dynamic understanding of people's relationship to their environment: *Umwelts*, frames and life space are the result of constant dynamic and creative interactions between a person and her social environment, which defines her experiences. However, their emphasis on the environment is essentially symbolic, as it is given through people's interpretations. Of course, probably none of these authors would deny that there is something 'out there' which is given regardless of people's interpretation. Yet their theoretical effort is mainly concentrated on the subjective part of people's construction of the world. Consequently, they do not actually analyse the specificities of the socially shared realities in which these experienced worlds take place, and which may have a coercive power over a person. If we have a range of subtle notions to describe a person's experience of the world, what symmetrical vocabulary do we have to describe these same worlds from another – the researcher's – perspective?[43]

## The 'rock of reality': institutions and settings

How can we then speak about the 'rock of sociological reality',[44] that is there and constrains people's actions, independently of the nuances and variations of people's perception? While remaining aligned with the authors that have a nuanced understanding of the constructed nature of the social reality, we can identify a few notions that give us a firmer grip on what is beyond people's simple apprehension of their environment.

The authors we have already mentioned did spend some time defining the less mentalistic aspects of the social world, more consensually

[43] Bronfenbrenner (1979, p. 17) similarly noted the lack of available, precise notions for describing the 'objective world', especially compared to the theoretical abundance of terms for describing phenomenological experiences.

[44] After Alléon, Morvan and Lebovici (1990).

considered as 'objective', and important in situations in which the 'reality out there' becomes a problem very close to one's deep personal world.

*Settings – nested or not:* Urie Bronfenbrenner has proposed a well–known *ecological model* attempting to show the relations between multiple environments in which people live. He proposed the notion of *setting* to identify specific material and social places in which interactions take place: 'a setting is a place in which people can readily engage in face-to-face interactions – home, day-care center, playground, and so on'.[45] The author used the notion to show how people move from one setting to the other, for example, from home to the day-care centre, to playground and so on and so forth. For them to do so, these settings need to have some stability. Hence we might say that the notion of setting is useful in so far as it enables us to identify the actual surroundings in which an activity might take place; a setting is an actual (material) situation in which a given frame might take place and evolve.

But why do specific frames take place in such settings, and where do settings come from? This is where one has to look at a further context or environment.

In Bronfenbrenner's model, settings are mutually dependent and nested in wider systems of determinations. He thus proposes considering an actual setting as a microsystem, which is 'included' in a meso- and macrosystem.[46] The main limitation of this model for our present purpose of identifying terms to capture the 'rock' of the real is, first, that it eventually fuses objective aspects of settings and more symbolic

[45] Bronfenbrenner (1979, p. 22).

[46] For Bronfenbrenner, the settings, as defined above, are at the scale that can be analysed as *microsystem*: 'A microsystem is a pattern of activities, roles, and interpersonal relations experienced by the developing person in a given setting with particular physical and material characteristics' (Bronfenbrenner, 1979, p. 22). Because people circulate from one setting to another one, Bronfenbrenner proposes to examine the relationships between such microsystems, and calls them the *mesosystem*, or a system of microsystems: 'A mesosystem comprises the interrelations among two or more settings in which the developing person actively participates (such as, for a child, the relations among home, school and neighborhood peer group; for an adult, among family, work and social life)' (Bronfenbrenner, 1979, p. 26). Additionally, some systems have an influence on a person's microsystems although the person does not participate in them – hence the parent's workplace has some influence on the child's development, even at school: 'An exosystem refers to one or more settings that do not involve the developing person as an active participant, but in which events occur that affect, or are affected by, what happens in the setting containing the person' (Bronfenbrenner, 1979, p. 25). Finally, all these are included in a wider system, which defines the blueprint for a specific type of setting – e.g. French nurseries: 'The macrosystem refers to consistencies, in the form or content of lower-order systems (micro-, meso- and exo-) that exist, or could exist, at the level of the subculture or the culture as a whole, along with any belief system or ideology underlying such consistencies' (Bronfenbrenner, 1979, p. 25).

ones.[47] Second, the model represents relations of simple inclusion: broader systems have an effect on more local ones, based on a belief in simple causality (or so the model is operationalized). However, in the view proposed in this book, societal anxieties are no 'more' distant than a school's rule system; for a given learner, these semiotic streams equally shape his or her meanacting – or equally participate in the epigenetic landscape. Yet what we still need to capture is to what extent 'materially' social surroundings are present in the realm of the person's activity. For this, we turn back to other notions.

*Facing institutions*: people are living in a perpetual movement between frames. In a seminal paper, Schütz (1944/1964) described the experience of a person who enters in a new social situation. A stranger is thus any:

> adult individual of our times and civilization who tries to be permanently accepted or at least tolerated by the group which he approaches ... The applicant for membership in a closed club, the prospective bridegroom who wants to be admitted to the girl's family, the farmer's son who enters college, the city dweller who settles in a rural environment, the 'selectee' who joins the Army, the family of the war worker who moves into a boom town – all are strangers by the definition just given.[48]

The stranger is the someone who has not mastered rules or situations that are totally external to him. How to qualify these things that resist a person's understanding of the situation (in Goffman's terms, his framing attempts)? Schütz calls them the 'cultural patterns of group life', designating:

> all the peculiar valuations, institutions and systems of orientation and guidance (such as the folkways, mores, laws, habits, customs, etiquette, fashions) which, in the common opinion of sociologists of our time, characterize – if not constitute – any social group at a moment of history.[49]

*Institution* is one of the words we need to clarify if we want to describe those things that enable us to characterize specific environments or groups. In what would become classical sociology, the term *institution*

[47] Hence Bronfenbrenner insisted on the following key points: the unit of analysis of human development would actually be the *activity*; and the *role* of the person is usually defined by a specific setting, within specific relationships – all this as it is *experienced* by the person. The experience reflects the scientifically relevant features of any environment and thus includes not only its objective properties but also the way in which these properties are perceived.

[48] Schütz (1964, p. 91). [49] Schütz (1964, p. 92).

designates any system of beliefs, or collective modes of actions – and as such is the privileged object of study of the discipline.[50]

In contrast, Goffman uses the same term (institution) to designate a very specific type of social organization, likely to considerably constrain a person's actions:

> Social establishments – institutions in the everyday sense of that term – are places such as rooms, suites of rooms, buildings, or plants in which activity of a particular kind regularly goes on. In sociology we do not have a very apt way of classifying them. Some establishments ... are open to anyone who is decently behaved; others ... are felt to be somewhat snippy about who is let in.[51]

*Total institutions:* Goffman was actually interested in one particular type of institutions: *total institutions*, such as prisons and asylums, which are characterized by the fact that they have strong barriers, limiting social exchanges as well as movement in and out, often characterized by material obstacles: locked doors, high walls, forests or fields.[52] While people usually sleep, work and have leisure in different places, in a total institution these activities occur in the same space. All this takes place under one authority; there is a lack of privacy; time is strictly organized; and all these activities serve the general goal of the institution. In a total institution, all these features are the result of a bureaucratic system that collectively handles needs. Goffman also shows how a person is transformed so as to be turned into a good inmate, through a process of acculturation mediated by specific techniques. According to him, a total institution 'is a natural experiment on what can be done to the self'.[53]

Goffman noted that specific aspects of total institutions could be found in other situations. For us, this mainly means that many of the categories proposed by Goffman, such as time organization, rules, organization of space, networks of social and material exchanges, etc., can be used to analyse a wide range of institutions. These features exist independently of a person's explicit apprehension of them – and yet they strongly constrain a person's zone of free movement.[54] We can thus retain the idea that institutions are situated social environments, organized in some manner, with some boundaries to the external social world, and which people can enter, engage in some activities and leave, on

[50] '[I]l y a un mot qui, pourvu toutefois qu'on en étende un peu l'acception ordinaire, exprime assez bien cette manière d'être très spéciale: c'est celui d'institution. On peut en effet, sans dénaturer le sens de cette expression, appeler institution, toutes les croyances et tous les modes de conduite institués par la collectivité; la sociologie peut alors être définie : la science des institutions, de leur genèse et de leur fonctionnement' (Durkheim, 1894, p. 15).

[51] Goffman (1961a, p. 3). [52] Goffman (1961a, p. 4). [53] Goffman (1961a, p. 22).

[54] Or ZFM see below, Chapter 7.

some specific conditions. They offer one specific type of the actual 'things', containers, durable environments, in which people engage in framing activities.

*Quasi-total institutions:* most human lives are spent in institutional settings where people distribute their life activities – and therefore experiences – regularly between different socially constructed conditions. So, children live at home and go to school every weekday (unless they are at a boarding school, that is, a total institution). Children who have no regular home and do not go to school may turn the street into their major quasi-total institution.[55] They may at times wander away from that place and spend some time in the shelter for homeless children – a transitory quasi-total institution that has permeability of borders. In the case of such shelters the basic organizational rule is that the children can come and go at any time – in contrast to children attending schools. The boundary of school and home for schoolchildren is further socially organized.[56] In some school contexts that boundary is institutionalized even within the institution – by way of creating a system of 'transit visas' to places other than the classroom. The effort to set up 'border controls' within a quasi-total institution is similar to such controls between institutions. Fences or other forms of border zones around a place are borders that require specific rules and rituals for entrance. Their location may become symbolically marked long after the border is gone (Figure 5.4).

*Fluid institutions*: some institutional arrangements for human life are fluid – they are episodic, need not occur in regular places and may include a variety of people. Examples of such institutions are political rallies, football matches, rock concerts, pilgrimages, crowds of holidaymakers on beaches or buyers in a department store. The setting, or *locus* – a stadium, department store, or a concert hall – may be fixed in space and time, but who organizes what kind of event in these settings is highly variable. The institution takes the form of a temporary – yet persistently recurrent – performance where all relevant participants from time to time enact their roles.

Shopping may be an activity of our modern times that exemplifies the functioning of such fluid institutions. At first glance it may seem to be about individuals' needs – the buyer needs an object, the seller needs money for the transfer of the object. Yet it is the institutional nature of shopping that differentiates it from neighbouring frames within which

[55] See Hecht (1998) on the reflections upon their lives by street children in north-eastern Brazil.

[56] These borders can be symbolically marked – by special buses that transport children to/from the school, and by 'street crossing guards' who meet the school buses.

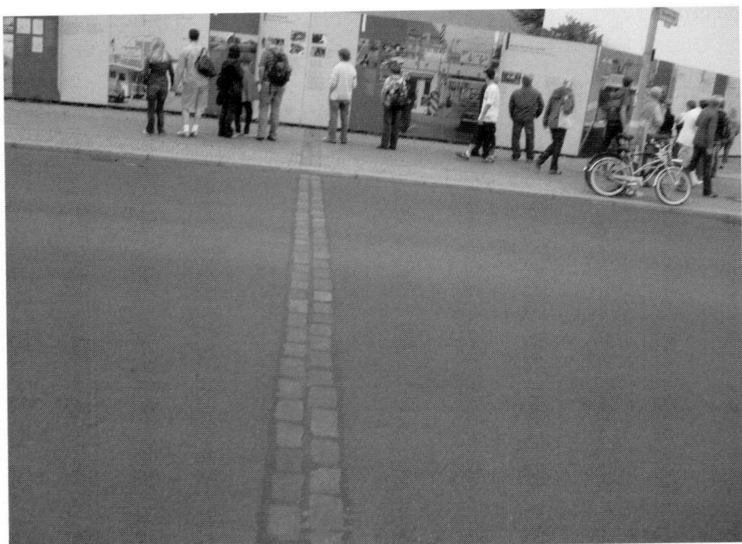

Figure 5.4 The Berlin Wall – where it used to be.

ownership of objects may be transferred (e.g. begging, robbing). This fluid institution entails a wide variety of functions:

> Shopping is not just about food, shoes, cars or furniture items. The avid, never-ending search for new and improved examples and recipes for life is also a variety of shopping, and a most important variety . . . There are so many areas in which we need to be more competent, and each calls for 'shopping around'. We 'shop' for skills needed to earn our living and for the means to convince would-be employers that we have them; for the kind of image it would be nice to wear and ways to make others believe that we are what we wear; for ways of making new friends we want and the ways of getting rid of past friends no longer wanted; for ways of drawing attention and ways to hide from scrutiny; for the means to squeeze most satisfaction out of love and the means to avoid becoming 'dependent' on the loved or loving partner; for ways to earn the love of the beloved and the least costly way of finishing off the union once love has faded and the relationship has ceased to please; for the best expedients of saving money for a rainy day and the most convenient way to spend money before we earn it.[57]

This multifunctionality of the institution of shopping guarantees its centrality in human lives of today. Shopping as a fluid institution – or as a *shopping act*, as we will see later – branches out from its parent institution

[57] Bauman (2000, p. 74).

Figure 5.5 Commercial guidance of identity through meaningful objects.

of *trading* – with the addition of direct consumer participation component. Stock markets – once the privilege of traders – are in our time open for shopping by almost anybody.

In Figure 5.5 we have captured an environmental setting that both commercializes a particular way of constituting an identity (of football fans) through the acquisition of specific objects and also promotes an identity of belonging. In addition, it is notable that a store designated for the fans of the given German football club – and located in Munich – is marked by English-language signs. Hence the promotion of club identity crosses traditional country boundaries – and may divide up the European Union into new mutually conflicting empires – that of the 'Manchester United Empire' fighting the 'Kingdom of Real Madrid'![58]

[58] This joking projection may be not too far from reality – if the football clubs' fans who already roam all over Europe looking for fights with their opponents were to exchange their colourful apparel for khaki uniforms and arm themselves, the joking scenario could become a cruel reality of new analogues of mediaeval wars, albeit based not on the need to conquer the *material* but *symbolic* resources. Extra-rigid identity of any kind – in relation to a company, football club, street gang, political party, religious organization or country – can lead to the construction of acts of violence.

## Putting personal positions back in the frame

Frames create the social landscape of action and consciousness of our lives. *Frames* can be seen as the general agreements that constrain the field of possibilities of one or several agents in a given setting, but they do not determine it. They institute a global field of experience and action, through which the person is in touch with the world, in its material (e.g. peeling an onion) and social dimensions (e.g. talking to others). They thus include both *personal experience* (usually coined under different labels, such as phenomenological or experiential fields, life space, cognitive representations) and *continuous interaction* with the world.

*Identity positions:* within this constituted frame, a person's history, needs and wants – together with present external circumstances – are in touch with each other, and the overall lived situation demands a response from the person. Yet that response is in no way an automatic one: at each lived moment, every human being is called on to form his or her unique response to the socially constituted world. The social world demands a person's answerability – and through this response, the agent assumes *a position* towards the current situation.

There are currently different theories of the notion of *position*[59] (or positioning). Here we draw on the dialogical tradition clearly rooted in Mikhail Bakhtin's work.[60] Among such approaches, Hubert Hermans has defended the idea of a *dialogical self*, composed of 'a multiplicity of I-positions',[61] each one addressing some other I-positions and/or some external positions. These positions result from the experience people have in various social frames, and from the internalization of various social others.

For instance, Mr Q. is thinking 'I would like an ice-cream', but immediately anticipates an inner critical voice saying 'you cannot eat more sugar today' which echoes his wife's usual remarks, that is, her getting angry with him for not watching his weight. Therefore, since people travel through different social frames, they are populated by different positions. These positions are sometimes metaphorically referred to as 'voices', which can be understood as 'expressions of a specific position'. From such a perspective, it is the dialogical intersection of these voices that creates meaning. Hence, intrapsychological, dialogical meaning-making can be seen as an *internalized co-regulation*. Therefore, a person will move

[59] See, for example, Harré, Moghaddam, Cairnie, Rothbart and Sabat (2009); Hermans (2001); Leiman (2002).

[60] See Salgado and Gonçalves (2007); Salgado and Hermans (2005).

[61] Hermans and Kempen (1993).

from one I-position to another I-position, according to fluctuations in time and context.[62]

*The notion of position* has been extended in several ways.[63] Here we will try to highlight some of the core elements of this notion. First, the notion of position involves a sociocultural background. *A personal position is always suggested by the social and cultural meanings – it is a cultural position.*[64] Within a sociocultural field, positions always emerge within specific frames.[65] Second, a personal position also involves an *intentional state*[66] – *it is about something*. A position involves the (self-)organization of, for example, perceptions, feelings and thoughts into an attractor, a general gestalt or field-like experience of 'what's going on'. Some particular object (or an organized set of objects) then becomes the focal point of attention within that field. The person is positioning herself or himself towards that object. Thus, the content of the positioning is always related to an object. Third, a position also has *agentive qualities*; it implies some form of *action* within the frame. The position implies purposes and goals, even if they are expressed in complex and paradoxical ways. For example, after being turned down at a job interview, a person who reacts by saying 'there is nothing I can do, I will never get a job' is actually *acting* as a powerless victim. Therefore, positions are motivated towards specific goals of adaptation. Fourth, positions operate with *semiotic means*. As we have seen, meaning implies a communicational relationship shaped by a frame. These frames institute signs – material actions, sounds or images – that by convention start to refer to something else. Mutuality implies sign-mediated action. Therefore, these signs enable communication with others – and from others to oneself. The high relevance of semiotics in this process leads Leiman to refer to such positions as 'semiotic positions'.[67] A sixth property of a position is the fact that it is always a *dialogical positioning* towards others. Assuming a position about something (the object) means to assume a position towards others through that object. This is a sort of corollary of the previous arguments. Some degree of mutual understanding is needed in order to create meaning. Therefore, all mean-acting takes place within a frame that warrants that minimal agreement and specifies what is going on and what sort of positioning the person is assuming. Through the position, a person engages in a relationship with others.

62 Hermans (2001).
63 Ferreira, Salgado and Cunha (2006); Salgado and Gonçalves (2007); Salgado and Valsiner (2010).
64 See Valsiner and Han (2008). 65 Salgado and Cunha (2012).
66 In the philosophical sense: *intentional* refers to something that stands for or refers to something else.
67 Leiman (2002).

Therefore, a position is actually a multi-position, since it involves multiple potential or real addressees. Finally, through this dialogical engagement, a person participates in the continuous reconstruction of the frame and the social broader context.

*Positioning movements within or between frames*: the notion of position, in the sense previously described, can be used at different levels of analysis, according to the time scale, or the frame chosen for the analysis. Are we studying quick movements between positions within minutes? Or are we following the promotion of an employee in a company, from a subordinate to a superordinate position in a period of months?

First, the choice of an appropriate timescale is essential when describing such positioning movements. Moment-to-moment movement from one position to the other might be described.[68] For example, if someone says 'I want to take a day off, but I have too much work to do', two successive positions can be identified: one position assuming a personal will, and another position assuming an obligation. Using another time frame to observe these movements, one can describe movements in a person's specific work day, drawing attention to the more frequent or dominant positions adopted during that day; or we can observe the same over an even larger time frame, giving us the picture of the positioning movements during a few months of work.

Second, people also evolve within social frames, and between social frames. People are constantly moving from one frame to the other[69] – and even when within one frame they may be operating outside the frame they are supposed to be engaging with.[70] There, as well, the observer has to choose a level of analysis, which will have implications for the phenomena described.

## *Developing through frames and the development of frames*

Describing such multiplicities of dialogical positions raises another question: how can a person remain stable and the same person?[71] How can we combine frames in time, or from a developmental perspective?

*Developing frames*: for many theoreticians, the focus has turned to the processes by which frames develop in specific interactive situations. Fogel proposed a temporal notion of frame[72] considering that a 'frame has a precise meaning and refers to a well-known aspect of the communication process: the need for communicators to establish a working definition of

[68] See Cunha (2007a, 2007b). [69] In that sense we are all 'migrants'; see Chapter 8.
[70] Goffman (1974). [71] Valsiner (2002). [72] Fogel (1993a, 1993b, 1995, 2006).

the communication situation'.[73] This leads to the study of *framing* which implies a process of dynamic social interaction, in which participants are involved in a dialogical activity of mutual co-regulation. Mutual co-regulation has simultaneous outcomes: on the one hand, co-regulation may contribute to the establishment of some consensual frame; on the other hand, and simultaneously, it is also a moment of affirmation or creation of one's unique position. Studies of framing emphasize the mutuality of this process; hence "a frame is a co-regulated consensual agreement about the scope of the discourse: its location, its setting, the acts that are taken to be significant vs. those that are irrelevant, and the main focus or topic'.[74]

To understand stability, we need to bear in mind that meaning has a social basis and implies some degree of agreement or mutuality. To achieve that agreement, some repetition and memory is needed. Even in a non-verbal phase, the infant and the adult need to repeat a sequence of actions in order to be able to play peek-a-boo. This will create a recurrent *pattern of position and reposition* from the participants, resulting in the possibility of a mutually coordinated action – a form of attractor. This recurrent pattern is what Fogel names a *frame*. It implies both stability – by the recurrent pattern – and change, by the slight modifications that take place from one occurrence to the next, with the same participants.[75] It is these changes that make the frame dynamic and alive.[76] In dynamic systems terms, this means that the attractor does not revisit exactly the same point in the given space. If that were to happen, the attractor would lose its dynamic impetus and the frame would eventually dissolve. An example would be when, in the discussion frame of a conjugal conflict, the same arguments are repeated over and over again, without wife and husband listening to what the other says. This will end in silence between the two, that is, the end of the frame. The arguments lose meaning and communication breaks down.

We are thus born into a social world and we are guided by social others to establish the possibility of the communication that renders meaning possible. We co-regulate our actions with these others, constraining our possibilities within a specific frame. At the beginning, these others need to be present; later in life, they do not need to be real people – they can be books, travel guides, signposts or clouds in the sky – in order to regulate our action and constrain our possibilities of meaning-making. This implies a reduction of our apparent infinite possibilities to those available in the frame we are playing in. Thus, even if there is no explicit constraint,

[73] Fogel (1993a, p. 36). [74] Fogel (1993a, p. 36). [75] Level 1 change, see here below.
[76] Fogel and Garvey (2007).

people tend to adopt the same position in order to maintain their self-understanding, as well as to render themselves intelligible to others.[77] This constant movement of repositioning thus more often than not takes the form of dynamically recurring stability that defines a frame, in Fogel's sense.

At the same time this stability is developing, by the slight changes that take place from one occurrence of the frame to the next. This also defines the historicity of frames. For example, when Mr Q. gets home, he always performs the same kind of actions: he arrives at the same time, puts his hat and coat at the same place, he greets his wife with a kiss, drinks a glass of water, while he starts asking about what happened with the kids that day. Thus, he enacts several positions (organized and punctual man, caring husband and caring father) that evolve into an organized chain, which is more or less the same every day. In this case, we are facing a stable frame – what can be called an attractor. However, the repetition of a frame within a relationship does not mean that it will be repeated in exactly the same way; frames develop, and their transformation may be more or less substantial. If the changes are important, this may challenge the limits of the attractor and the system will go through a phase shift, resulting in a new attractor, either to the detriment of the old one, or as a parallel frame, coexisting with the old one.

The dictinction between the three 'levels' of attractor changes defined in DST[78] can be used to describe the evolution of frames. For instance as an agent – and not an automaton – one evening Mr Q. may first ask how the kids were, and only afterwards kiss his wife; or he might choose to bypass the drinking of water. Here, the frame is not questioned, there are just adjustments of actions within the frame; this is a level 1 change in Fogel's terms. However, there will always be some variation, according to which the person readjusts to the situation. Mr Q. for instance, may arrive one day very concerned with a problem he had in his company, going directly to the kitchen and sitting down, near his wife, thus violating some of the daily routines and announcing that something important is going on. In that case there is a 'change in the pattern of change',[79] or innovation in the frame, which would be a level 2 change. His wife might be immediately alarmed by this strange sequence of events. At that moment, the frame 'arriving home' will be reformulated, and all the agents will try to adapt themselves to the new situation – for instance, that Mr Q. has lost

[77] See Cunha (2007a, 2007b). In Chapter 1, we have explored a little further this theme, using the notion of different levels of change, proposed by Fogel, Garvey Hsu and West-Stroming (2006).

[78] Fogel (2006). [79] Fogel (2006, p. 15).

his job or has met another woman. This might lead to a redefinition of the frame and with it, a whole new system of frames, which can be called a level 3 change. Of course the three levels of changes are mutually dependent: a transformation in one or the other is likely to move the others – unless inertia slows it down.

*The inertia of frames*: routines and habits occupy a great deal of our lives, and they free us from decision-making so as to enable us to focus our attention on various activities – such as when a person designs new plans as he washes the dishes. Hence routine can also enable creativity – in a given setting, routine conduct in a frame enables the deployment of another, imaginary frame. The processes by which we acquire routines and habits also have a creative dimension. When someone learns how to do something – how to cook rice or to read – new positions emerge for him.

However, sometimes, stable patterns of repositioning prevent change, as we will discuss in the next chapter. At a microgenetic level, Fogel and his collaborators have proposed differentiating between *creative* and *rigid* frames in the study of interactions. Within a creative frame, people can experience themselves as creatively building a consensus, working through disagreements or moving towards peak emotional moments with their partners. When individuals are constrained within rigid frames, they experience their I-positions as wilfully resisting or deliberately coercing their partners. They may also take the position of passively submitting or resigning themselves to a hopeless situation.[80]

At a sociogenetic level, institutions usually have regulating principles to prevent change. They may also impose themselves to maintain specific courses of action in individuals. Of course, people may actively resist the kind of social regulation imposed, a resistance that may contribute to social innovation. Hence, to acquire a new position implies, simultaneously, a process of novelty and a process of reaching some stability (in this case, an ability to achieve that position again and again, within one and the same, or several different, frames).

### *Development of social spaces: trajectories in the making*

Frames and settings operate in time and evolve as humans move through them. Yet the evolution of frames and development are mutually dependent.

[80] Fogel (1993a); Fogel, Koeyer, Bellagamba and Bell (2002, p. 193).

Consider a family setting – a child grows up into a teenager asking for new rights – such as working a few hours a week to earn some money. Their parents may resist, and then accept. In turn, parents will give less pocket money[81] to the adolescent who has entered the domain of adult economic relationships. With these savings, the family might organize a longer family trip – and it is there, abroad, that the child may meet a peer who becomes a long-term friend. The initial condition – a teenager's move to earn money – leads through systemic processes to unexpected outcomes, involving frame changes, and consequent transformations of each of the life paths involved and their mutual relationships.[82]

How, then, to consider people's development as they move through different settings and frames? How to consider the mutual dependency of frame changes, the individual developmental course and the progressive transformation of the social environment?

*Mutually dependent geneses:* if it can be said that frames can be seen as evolving, these processes can be observed as dependent on individual trajectories, as well as on social change. For analytic purposes these logics of change can first be distinguished. Duveen and Lloyd[83] proposed distinguishing between *microgenetic, sociogenetic* and *ontogenetic* processes of change. *Microgenetic* changes typically designate modifications taking place within the exchanges between a person and others, as well as with her non-social environment, that is, the activity of framing. *Sociogenetic changes* designate changes in the social world itself – including institutions, social representations and symbolic systems – which may be the result of ongoing regulations taking place at the microgenetic level, but which may also constrain these processes. *Ontogenetic* changes designate changes of a person herself through time. Both ontogenetic and sociogenetic processes are likely to be affected by, and to affect, microgenetic processes.

*Trajectory and biography:* as we saw in the first chapter, epigenesis implies that each moment in development is dependent on the preceding one. Thus, for instance, a person's experiences entering a specific setting – a new classroom – will first and foremost depend on the person's history of experiences in similar and different settings, while the person also has to deal with the material place, the other students and the teacher, and the informal and formal rules shaping the frame of the situation, which are

[81] On the cultural construction of the notion of 'pocket money' see Yamamoto and Takahashi (2007).

[82] This illustrates the principle of epigenesis (see Chapter 1). It could also be described in terms of our epigenetic landscape metaphor.

[83] Duveen and Lloyd (1990).

given partly by the institutional context, partly by the wider sociocultural environment.

We may describe each of the growing relations between the person and her classmates in terms of *microgenetic* processes, until they reach stability in recurrent and relatively stable patterns, here called frames. We may also describe the microgenetic processes through which the student becomes a class leader who reorganizes some aspects of these frames. These learning and position changes constitute her ontogenesis. From the person's perspective, the immediate options or possibilities for further action constitute the life space. Yet from an economist's perspective, the actual possibilities for the young student in the ninth grade, living in a country just entering an economic recession – a sociogenetic issue – have to be described differently. And the actual developmental pathway of a that person will be a result of actual interactions between her and her teachers, the school committees, potential employers, discussion with the young person's family, etc. We can call such a socially, interactively constructed pathway, a *trajectory*.

In doing so, we borrow the term from sociological approaches that use the term 'trajectory' quite specifically, for example when talking about the trajectory of a sickness: unlike the physiological evolution of the sickness, *the trajectory designates the whole organization of work required by the human handling of the particular sickness, in diverse social settings.*[84] Hence an 'illness career' results from the fact that a person has been labelled as 'sick' by others and somehow identifies with that label. Both terms – *trajectory* and *career* – highlight the fact that the movement of a person in the social space results from interactions with others; the second one emphasizes the work of collective meaning-making of the person's situation, with its feeding-forward properties (being labelled as ill leads a person to act as ill, and others to interpret her action as resulting from illness); the first one emphasizes the actual activities in which the social system is engaged and that construct the trajectory of a person. This sociological concept suggests that a trajectory is external to a person: the notion of *trajectory* does not designate a movement self-propelled by an agent; it is rather the emerging result of complex game of interactions. This concept of trajectory is different from the use of the concept in the epigenetic landscape metaphor, where the trajectory is not only external to a person, but is also constrained by factors internal to

[84] Wiener, Strauss, Fageraugh and Suczek (1979). It slightly differs from the term of 'career' used by Mehan, Hertweck and Meihls (1986, pp. 88–9), where it designates the path of a person under a specific aspect, as it is shaped according to the social handling and labelling of that aspect.

that person, for example, hormone levels and earlier experiences. However, it is true for both uses that the trajectory does not designate the self-propelled movement of an agent.

If we take a person's view, on the other hand, what a trajectory is becomes different. During her life, a person moves through a wide variety of settings – in parallel and alternately, as when moving from family to the workplace and a few leisure activities, or successively, as when leaving primary school for secondary school, or leaving a country at war for exile. These movements in time and space have received different names. With the term *biography*, we are located at the level of the construction of the person's narrative of life; with notions such as 'biographical trajectory', we designate this movement in and through social settings, within complex dynamic systems.

### *The trajectory equifinality model (TEM)*

A personal trajectory results from complex interactions between a person and her environment; and in many cases, the microgenetic processes by which a person's relationship to her environment take place actually lead to a transformation of the relationship itself. This happens through trying out new ways of being – in one's action (play) and in one's imagination:

> *The relationship of play to development should be compared with that of teaching-learning [obuchenie] to development. Changes of needs and consciousness of more general kind lie behind the play.* Play is the resource of development and it creates the zone of nearest development. Action in the imaginary field, in an imagined situation, construction of voluntary intention, the formation of the life-plan, will motives – this all emerges in play *and ... makes it the ninth wave of preschool age development.*[85]

Hence, if we examine people's movement across frames and settings – in their actuality – play and imagination are the main processes by which these can be transformed or avoided.

As we have seen above (Chapter 3), the present moment is the only thing that there IS for a person; what is immediately to come is always already a mystery and demands the elaboration of AS-IF possibilities. Play and imagination are the arenas where AS-IS<> AS-IF linkages are coordinated with AS-COULD-BE, AS-SHOULD-BE and AS-I-WANT-IT-TO-BE in the future, and with AS-IT-WAS (reconstructed actual history) and AS-IT-COULD-HAVE-BEEN (unrealized past possibilities).[86] The AS-IF mode is a

[85] Vygotsky (1933/1966, pp. 74–5, added emphasis). [86] See above Chapter 3, Figure 3.2.

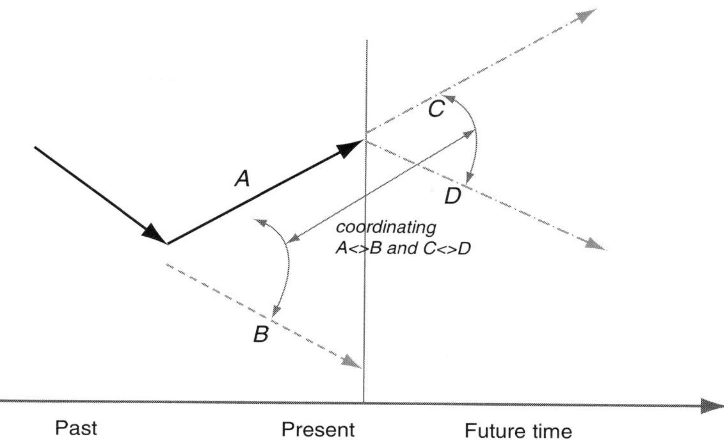


Figure 5.6 The minimal structural unit of TEM.

powerful tool for psychological change and social innovation; it brings us beyond what is HERE and NOW.

All these features are captured by the TEM. TEM[87] grows out of the theoretical need of contemporary science to maintain two central features in its analytic scheme – time and (linked to it) the transformation of potentialities into actualities (realization). It is the latter – the inclusion of the hypothetical (not real – or not yet real – or not to be real) – that separates TEM from all other time-inclusive models (time series analyses, etc.). The kernel of TEM is given in the scheme of the generic 'cell' of the processes that in their reality are hypercomplex (Figure 5.6). Structural units like the one in Figure 5.6 enter into a variety of configurations, yet – like the minimal unit of any complex whole – the one depicted in that figure is the core 'minimal gestalt' we need to consider.

The unit of analysis presented in Figure 5.6 includes three imaginary parts (B, C, D) and one real (A) part. This dominance of the imaginary over the real is crucial for understanding cognitive functions and their development – cognition is needed to create a meaningful thought basis for the construction of the future rather than merely serving as a factual commentary on the reality of the world. Second, it is not the presence (and nature) of these four components, but their *relations* (A<>B, C<D>) as well as their *meta-relation* ([A<>B] <> [C<>D]) that is the structural unit of analysis.

[87] Sato *et al.* (2006, 2007) and Sato, Hidaka and Fukuda (2009).

TEM breaks up the backbone of contemporary psychology – its reliance upon inductive generalization and its practical elaboration, conventionally called 'measurement'. It replaces that practice by careful investigation of the microgenetic level. Yet that level is embedded in higher levels.

## Summary: spaces for development

A life melody thus appears unique in the field of all other melodies. Yet as in a concerto or a jazz improvisation, its themes and tones can be the echoes of others, it can answer other instruments or refer to other motives. Similarly, people making sense of events are never alone. As we have seen, they interact with others, as well as with objects and pre-existing meanings and ideas. Thus, even when (objectively) alone, they carry within themselves the 'voices' of others – and their relationships with these others. However, what a relationship means, or what are the consequences of events, is very often highly defined by the social situation in which a person finds herself. Falling in love with a girl who has a different skin colour can be seen as a novel relationship that enriches one's life – but at many historical times and in most countries such enriching has been viewed with suspicion. And then, according to the political orientation of one's family, or the religious community to which one belongs, or the trade in which one is working, it could be seen as a malediction, as a drama or as a challenge. Many love stories have been destroyed because of the strong opposition of a young person's parents, his community or her social network. But how do these external institutions, or other people's opinions, interfere with what seem to be the most intimate feelings of love and passion? And how are these groups or institutions themselves reshaped by a *Zeitgeist*, the historical state of a society?

In this chapter, we theorized about people's belonging to different social environments, and the relationships between these environments in a given society. Starting with models that focus on the life-world-as-experienced by persons, we came to distinguish two kinds of concept that help us to understand development – *settings* and *frames*. *Settings* have a strong ontological status and apparently escape to the potential change of daily co-regulations. *Frames* are perceived, created and develop as people interact with their environment and each other over several occurrences. Furthermore, we saw that rigidified frames are threatened by dissolution, that their apparent stability (as strong attractors) may be only temporary, if they are not dynamic and developing. In that sense, even materially solid settings are also only one temporary state of things – in the very long term.

We were also reminded that individual development (ontogenesis), interactions and the frame they generate (microgenesis) and historical changes (sociogenesis) are mutually dependent. Dynamics at one level are likely to affect others – even if there are social or psychological forces that canalize or constrain these changes.

Finally, leaving the outside view on framing dynamics, we came back to an examination of a person's trajectory. In previous chapters, adopting an inner perspective, imagination appeared to bring humans to play with time and memories. Here, we finally suggested, imagination may enable a person to generate new alternatives, or explore the space between two possible courses of actions – thus bending her trajectory.

# 6 Stability and innovation in adults narrating their lives: insights from psychotherapy research

This book suggests that change is a reality of our world and of our lives. We are used to seeing things as having essential properties, as atoms or molecules, in physics; and traits, motives, processing information styles and the like, in psychology.

Newtonian physics has deeply influenced psychology and other human sciences and this has often led to processes being reified, turned into things, often leading scholars to create tautological explanations.[1] Both psychology and our common life discourse are filled with examples like 'John is aggressive because he has a tendency to be aggressive' – while evidence for such claims is taken from episodes of John's conduct in different life situations. Gregory Bateson called this type of explanation *dormitive*, based on a play by Molière:

> Molière, long ago, depicted an oral doctoral examination in which the learned doctors asked the candidate to state the 'cause and reason' why opium puts people to sleep. The candidate triumphantly answers in dog Latin, 'Because there is in it a dormitive principle' (*virtuas dormitiva*).[2]

Our common sense suggests to us cultural tools to emphasize the stability of our personal worlds. We are therefore not used to thinking that change processes are inherent in things.[3] In fact, a language to describe change faces a difficult challenge, given language's reifying tendency to turn what it names into a 'thing'. This property of human language haunted developmental biologists long before we met it in the science of human development.

The primary authors of this chapter (MG and JS) are grateful to Carla Machado for the comments done on the first version of this chapter. The writing of this chapter was supported by the Portuguese Foundation for Science and Technology (FCT), by grants PTDC/PSI/72846/2006 (Narrative Processes in Psychotherapy) and PTDC/PSJ-PCL/103432/2008 ('Decentering and Change in Psychotherapy').

1 See Bateson (1972/1999); Harré and Gillett (1994); Toulmin (1990); Salgado and Valsiner (2010).

2 Bateson (1972/1999), p. xxvii.

3 For a development of this argument, see Fogel, Garvey, Hsu and West-Stroming (2006). See also Chapter 1.

## Narrative meaning-making

Two of the authors of this book (MG and JS) have developed a research programme with the aim of studying how the narrative metaphor of the human mind can inform psychotherapy's efforts to understand change, helping us also to generalize these findings beyond the territory of psychotherapy – to the daily lives of any human being. After all, what is at stake is the constant adaptation of the psyche to the dramas and traumas of living, in peace and in war, in affluence and in poverty – and the role of the psychotherapist is itself a cultural invention to provide support for these life tasks.

Psychotherapy is in a sense an 'anthropological laboratory' (to use Harry Stack Sullivan's phrasing),[4] a setting where the promotion of changes in the personal life course is the main target. Treated as a field of knowledge acquisition in general – rather than just clinical psychology – psychotherapy process research is a valuable domain of study for the understanding of human change processes.

Change is inherent in people's lives, but how do people change? What are the main processes involved in changing one's life? What can we learn from psychotherapeutic change that can be generalized into other forms of change?

### *On the roots of a narrative approach to psychology*

The narrative approach emerged in psychology and in psychotherapy after the 1980s in several branches of psychotherapy, from psychoanalysis to family therapy[5]. However, this was part of a larger movement. Under the influence of literary studies in that period, narrative has started to be a persuasive concept for social sciences. Psychology was no exception – narrative has also become a very appealing concept to different research orientations.

Life is a succession of events in time, and the notion of narrative is, most of the time, associated with the idea of 'story' – a verbal organization of events in people's lives. In fact, those who initially introduced this concept into psychology were somehow highlighting two main features of narratives: their temporal dimension and their cultural embeddedness. These two qualities belong to the realm of everyday life, and the conclusion that human life has narrative characteristics sounded appealing: life can be

[4] Sullivan (1953) introduced this notion of psychotherapy as an anthropological laboratory long ago.

[5] See Omer and Alon (1997).

studied as if it were a novel. This interest also brought a great variation to the conceptual use and application of 'narrative'. We will analyse three dimensions along which we observe large fluctuations: the degree of centrality attributed to narrative in the human mind (ranging from positions assuming narrative thinking as a specific mode of cognition versus those who assume narrative to be the very basis of the human mind); the scope of what is meant by narrative (narrative as story versus narrative as verbal production, discourse or text); and the relation between narratives and experience (experiences as narratives versus description of experiences as narratives).

*Degrees of centrality of narratives:* nowadays, different lines of research place narrative as an essential feature of psychological processes. Taking it as a close synonym of 'story', it is clear that through narratives we are able to place events in spatial and temporal locations, and to organize these into a more or less (even if open-ended) coherent whole. For example, the cognitive orientation has started to consider narratives as a specific mode of cognitive organization. Under the notions of episodic and autobiographical memory, narrative modes of cognitive processes have been highlighted for their ability to identify episodes in a spatio-temporal frame, for their relevance to self-identity and their ability to promote emotions.[6]

In this sense, narrative psychological processes are a specific type of cognition. In a way, one of the most important figures introducing narratives to psychology, Jerome Bruner,[7] also considered the 'narrative mode' one type of meaning-making that contrasts with the 'paradigmatic mode'. The first is clearly grounded in the flow of experiences of human lives and their episodic articulation, while the second is detached, abstract, based on logical-deductive operations (more on this below). However, some psychologists[8] have been bold enough to propose that *all psychological processes* have a narrative basis, considering narrative as the main process of meaning-making, placing it at the core of the human mind. For instance, Sarbin suggested that 'human beings think, perceive, imagine, and make moral choices according to narrative structures'.[9] The idea is that we cannot pass through life without constantly finding events that always demand to be situated and narrated. These psychologists gave rise to a perspective coined 'narrative psychology'. Thus, it is clear that there are variations in the centrality assigned to the notion of narrative among researchers interested in human narrative abilities.

*The scope of narratives:* most of the time, 'narrative' is used in a sense close to its literary meaning – as a story, even if open-ended, that may be developed under different formats (written, spoken, but also dramatized,

[6] See Bluck and Habermas (2001). [7] Bruner (1990, 1991, 2003).
[8] For instance Sarbin (1986). [9] Sarbin (1986, p. 8).

sung and danced). In this sense, a narrative is a linguistic structure with several elements, for instance a context, actors, actions, plot, intentions and so on.[10] However, sometimes the notion is used in a broader way, and every verbal description or discourse is considered as 'narrative'. In that vein,

> I take narrative in its broad connotation as the act of telling, narrating or showing subjective experience. In such a way, narrative becomes the act of expression in which persons make known the meaning of experiences and the significance of their actions. Narrative psychology becomes the study of *expressive acts rather than just well structured and clearly bounded plotlines* or sequences of action.[11]

In this perspective the general argument could be more or less this: narrative is every linguistic production that refers to a specific event in space and time – that constitutes an *episode*. Consequently, since every verbal production is somehow related to concrete episodes, even more abstract verbal productions can be considered as narratives or as part of narratives. For example, a teacher of philosophy teaching her preferred theory will be producing a verbal account that is connected with past 'stories' belonging to others (e.g. battles of ideas between schools of thought) or belonging to herself (the narrative of her career). At the same time, each moment of teaching is also an event of life and, therefore, part of the autobiographical narrative of this teacher.

*Narratives and experience:* The third dimension on which treatments of the notion of narrative can vary is related to the connection between the verbal side and the lived side of narratives. As we have been discussing, life evolves through time. Humans divide the flow of time into episodes, creating verbal accounts referring to them, explaining them, articulating them into a narrative form. Thus, we may say that our human time is narratively structured. Then, while some recognize this tension between the flow of experiences (lived narrative) and the account of those experiences (verbal narrative), others restrict themselves to a verbal notion of narrative.

This tension between narrative as a phenomenological element of the mind and narrative as a told story is well documented in the following extract written by Daniel Stern:

> The *narrative format* is a structure for mentally organizing (without language) our experience with motivated human behaviour. *Lived stories* are experiences that are narratively formatted in the mind but not verbalized or told. A told story – *i.e.*, a narrative – is the telling to someone about the lived story.[12]

[10] Mandler (1984). [11] Schiff (2006), emphasis added. [12] Stern (2004, p. 46).

Table 6.1 *Various perspectives on narratives*

| | | |
|---|---|---|
| Narrative as *a* particular meaning-making device | Narrative as a specific verbal account (equivalent to episodic knowledge) | Narrative as a verbal interpretation of experience |
| versus | versus | versus |
| Narrative as *the* meaning-making device | Narrative as all verbal accounts | Narrative as a *lived account*, that shapes how life unfolds |

In this excerpt, Stern admits that we have a narrative mental template or structure that shapes our lived experience (lived stories), out of which we build verbal narratives (see Table 6.1). How is such a vision compatible with the developmental and semiotic perspective previously outlined? Our next task is to build a conceptual model that connects a semiotic perspective with a narrative one, while solving these conceptual riddles.

### *A semiotic perspective on narrative*

As elsewhere in this book, we assume a semiotic perspective, which endorses the idea that our meaning-making activities are performed under the mediation of signs.[13] Our mental activities are performed upon real-life settings using signs, under their symbolic and material forms, through which we aim to promote our adaptation to anticipated future conditions. In this social articulation we are thus contributing to the creation of a culturally structured environment. Hence, if signs are always already social, we are actually the creators of the meaningfulness of any life situation, thanks to our unique use of signs. These signs, on their own, are combined with each other, creating complex utterances in our speech. These externalizations allow us to make sense of our environment, and simultaneously, through these utterances, we assume a certain *position*[14] towards the world in which we participate.

For example, seeing a glass of golden liquid and experiencing a bitter taste, a person can say 'I don't like beer'; by doing this, she assumes a social position towards this object ('beer') within a certain social

[13] See especially Chapters 1 and 3, and the notes on Vygotsky (Box 3.1) and Peirce (Box 3.2).

[14] See Chapter 5. The notion of position and counterposition has been introduced in varied ways within the dialogical perspectives. Hermans (1996) and Valsiner (2002, 2007b) are two of the most important sources for this part of the work. See also Leiman (2002) for a different use of these notions, in a very interesting way.

background – for instance, stating that you don't like beer in an English pub has a different address from in a French restaurant. Since the production of these utterances has a social origin and they are socially addressed we may say that human beings are in a constant dialogical activity that gives meaning to their life situation (notice that this is true even when we have virtual audiences, for example, when we are producing utterances in our inner thoughts). This implies that our minds are *dialogical, meaning that a person is involved in a constant process of communication with a social and material world, assuming new positions from moment to moment.*[15]

*What is a narrative?* It is clear that at this micro-level of analysis, signs, and more specifically, utterances (combination of signs) occupy the centre stage of our argumentation. From this perspective a narrative is a specific semiotic structure, created from a combination of utterances, organized into an episodic description ('In the summer I went to the town where I was born and . . .'). However, in some other cases we face situations in which we identify events, while not creating a full-fledged narrative ('Maybe later I will have a cup of coffee' or even 'I like this'). *We propose to consider accounts that contain a reference to time and space as 'narratives'*. Other verbal products that do not involve such a description, such as 'I am worthless' or 'Verbs refer to actions' will not be considered as narratives. Thus, we will consider that not all verbal products are narratives.

However, from a developmental point of view, it makes sense to argue that even non-episodic accounts are always based on episodic ones, since the former imply higher levels of abstraction. As we have seen in the case of Emily (in Chapter 2), children start their verbal productions by making explicit references to people and situations – in other words, by describing episodic elements. Consequently, it is defensible to say that all kinds of utterances are developmentally based on previous *weak* narrative descriptions. In this sense, higher-order abstract verbalizations need to proceed from simpler forms. Then, if someone says 'I'm worthless', this conclusion must cohere with the description of life episodes – otherwise, it would not be sustained. Therefore, this utterance implies a positioning towards the social and material world in which the person assumes not having any value, and this positioning is the result of specific episodes in which this was somehow felt to be true.

In sum, a person has an embodied and *felt experience* in a given situation; yet she establishes contact with the surrounding world through the use of

[15] See Hermans (2001); Salgado and Hermans (2005); Salgado and Cunha (2012); Salgado and Valsiner (2010); Valsiner (2002; 2007c).

signs that mediate the ongoing interaction. Once she uses these signs, she assumes a certain positioning towards some 'objects' (of interest, curiosity, need, value). This positioning – which Leiman[16] names a 'semiotic position' – involves a sense of *felt meaning* in the situation and a specific kind of action. For example, a person who says 'I like your outfit!' is not only saying this: the person is also doing something to the other (complimenting, seducing or even making fun – all are viable possibilities). From all kinds of signs and of organizing signs, we are considering narratives (in a weak sense) as specific forms of sign-organization that involve a direct reference to episodic features of the situation. Therefore, a narrative is a sign-combination that refers to real life situations, upon which generalizations and abstractions may then be produced (see Figure 6.1). We may say that they are a vital element for setting the stage in which the person assumes a certain positioning.

Narratives are flexible. They are created in the present – as the person tells a story – but they can refer to many different space and time domains. They may refer to the present itself – to the real situation that is taking place at this moment – yet when they do so they are simultaneously re-presenting the present – that is passing just as the narrating happens – and presenting the future expectation on the basis of that present. Of course they also may refer to the past. In that situation, the person is 'retelling' a specific episode that has already taken place. So, following from Figure 6.1, the statement 'I like this ice cream' re-presents the disappearing – eaten or melting – object, as well as stating a future orientation

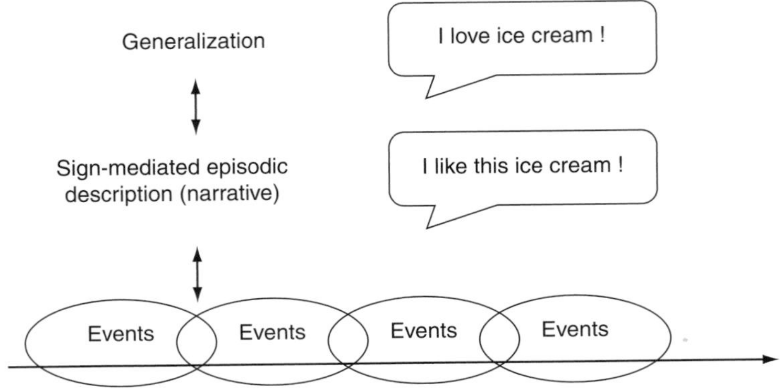


Figure 6.1 Narrative as episodic description.

[16] Leiman (2002).

towards ice cream in the indeterminate future. The generalized statement 'I love ice cream' positions the person *vis-à-vis* the given potentially recurring encounter.

The way in which a person positions herself towards the past may vary – for example, a person may have assumed a positioning of anger towards someone, and while revisiting the episode, may feel guilty; or she may maintain her positioning of anger. Narratives may also refer to the future: we project future circumstances and possibilities. Most importantly, *narratives of the present, past and future take place in the here and now* and in this process assume a position towards something at hand. From this variety of narratives, a person becomes prone to assume conclusions or generalizations based on episodic examples. There is no logical mathematics in this process: a generalization does not need to be produced by accumulation of facts; sometimes, one single event may become the basis for an overwhelming generalization (e.g. a single failure may lead to the conclusion that 'I have always failed'). Narrative positioning sets the stage for the use of abductive 'jumps' in meaning-making as a person lives into the future.

### *Narrating as semiosis: duality of storytelling and self-positioning*

Narratives are 'semiotic contents' that play a central role in the functioning of the human mind. They allow a person to make spatio-temporal reference to real situations and assume a position towards these events. Narratives connect people to specific life situations. They are a sort of intermediate level between sensuous experience and the higher levels of abstraction. At the same time, there is a constant bounded duality in this process. Using the weak sense of narrative, whenever someone produces an utterance referring to an episode, we may distinguish the *narrated event* from *the storytelling event*.[17] A person commenting on the outfit chosen by someone else is not only narrating this event (narrated event), but also acting upon it. In other words, through narrative construction, that person *enacts* a position (storytelling event). This enacted position is an event in itself and therefore feeds the possibility of new narratives. Therefore, these two levels are always intertwined. However, this does not mean that they coincide, and situations of deception illustrate this.

This semiotic perspective clarifies and integrates diverse ways of dealing with the notion of narrative previously outlined. First, narrative is in some sense only a type of discourse or verbal activity. Nevertheless, since it

[17] See Wortham (2001).

connects semiosis with concrete events of life, it remains a vital mode of meaning-making. Thus, it is consistent to distinguish narrative thinking from paradigmatic thinking, while still attributing a vital role to narrative, as Bruner did.[18] Second, it seems obvious that narrative must be treated as a specific form of discourse. However, using narrative in a weak or broader sense – as a verbal production that connects the person with specific concrete life-situations – a large part of our verbal activities will fall into this category and, moreover, there will always be a connecting element between the abstract and the concrete domains of life. Finally, narratives are events in themselves, in which a person assumes a certain position towards something else (an object) and especially towards others' positions regarding the same object. Thus, the production of a narrative – like any other kind of human activity – as a concrete event in a certain time and space, is potentially part of a new narrative to be told. If one tells to a co-worker the story of what happened last Sunday evening, when arriving at the workplace on Monday, the event of telling this story may itself become part of a new story, if one decides to put that experience into words.

## The pervasive role of narrative

Taking this perspective into account, narrative becomes a very important tool of meaning-making, since it connects our semiotic abilities with real-life situations. Narratives can be identified at various scales, though.

At a microgenetic scale, we keep developing narratives of our daily life (e.g. what happened to me this morning as I was going to work). However, the narrative mode of thinking is not always activated. If I am cooking a meal I am not necessarily creating a narrative to myself or to others, I may just be cooking. But let us imagine that while I'm cooking I set the kitchen on fire – that could in fact be the material for a good story! As Jerome Bruner has suggested, the narrative mode is more clearly activated *when one is facing something that is not ordinary, that falls out of the canonical.*[19] When we face an event that falls outside what is expected in our daily life, or that creates a sense of rupture, the need to assimilate it activates the narrative mode.

Imagine that you are in a class and your professor does something that falls outside what is expected in your cultural environment. For instance, let us imagine that he or she approaches students and starts lecturing with his or her head 5 centimetres away from a student's head. This would be very strange and inappropriate, as it would be in most sociocultural

[18] Bruner (1990). [19] Bruner (1990, 2003).

environments. How do you give meaning to this strange behaviour? The students may start asking questions to themselves like: 'What is the meaning of this?', 'What are his or her intentions?', 'Is he or she crazy?', 'How shall I react if he or she does that to me?', 'How will I cope with the embarrassment?', 'What are other people here thinking?', 'What should we do regarding this behaviour?', 'What are the purposes of this behaviour?' and so on. Notice that these questions are narrative orientated, in the sense that they allow the construction of different potential narratives that could, eventually, facilitate the integration of this strange episode in to students' lives and structure the near future (e.g. 'what shall we do to cope with this?'). Now imagine that the professor wants to demonstrate that rules of behaviour are largely implicit and shaped by culture.

This episode might indeed be something that one recollects easily some years after, even when the course is mostly forgotten! With this strange behaviour, the professor has clearly demonstrated that even apparently simple and straightforward behaviour (such as being in class) is shaped by culture in an implicit way, without conscious awareness – except when these rules are clearly broken.

Notice that telling this imaginary episode involves a narrative structure: *something happened* (the strange behaviour of your professor), *in a specific location in time and space* (a setting), *that affected other characters* (the students), *creating a tension* that finally was *resolved* when the explanation was provided (the professor was just demonstrating the implicit nature of cultural rules). This example also illustrates what Bruner refers to as making ordinary what is outside the canonical. That is, a strange occurrence is rendered 'normal' through the construction of a narrative.

Narratives that people tell about themselves get progressively generalized and can become macro-narratives – the way in which we give sense to our collection of memories. Hence, some scholars call *self-narratives*[20] the (macro-)narratives people tell about themselves, and which acquire some coherence during late adolescence and early adulthood. According to this perspective, self-narratives structure our lives, that is, our meanings, feelings and actions. Hence, a person who lives her life as a tragedy creates different meaning from someone who lives a life as a challenge, even if the lived events are similar. People 'do' something with signs and that 'doing something' implies a certain positioning towards the social and material world.

Finally, narratives can be said to shape our experience of time. Humans are future-orientated beings, creating stability and order out of an

[20] Hermans and Hermans-Jansen (1995).

irreversible and unpredictable flow of time. Hence, narratives can be seen as orienting the future and thus restraining[21] the present.[22] If a person is getting married the following week she will imagine the event. How she imagines the event will of course affect her present experience. It is quite clear that anticipating future events is very important in creating meaning and movement in the here and now.[23] When a person imagines a future event, she will impose a narrative structure on this projection of the future. She needs to imagine a setting, actors, actions and a plot that structures these actions, intentions, feelings and so on. In other words, a narrative of the future is thus created and as the person experiences this future-orientated narrative, events are rehearsed in the imagination. The same structure is imposed on 'real' memories of the past or, as Gabriel Garcia Marquez wrote, 'Life is not what one lived, but what one remembers and how one remembers it in order to recount it'.[24] Altogether, narratives appear pervasive in the process of meaning-making. The meanings of our daily events are largely structured by the stories people tell to others and themselves.

### *Restraints on narrative meaning-making*

Until now we have been discussing the ability of narrative thinking to create meanings and facilitate the assimilation of what falls outside the ordinary, allowing the organization of one's life. However, as one interpretation of events is created and consolidated, other interpretations are rendered less probable. Similarly, this is what allows us to recognize that what we see also makes us blind to other possibilities; as we have noted, our visual abilities are very different from those of a fly. As

[21] This concept is akin to the concept of *constraint*, as described and used in Chapter 1 (in particular as a concept for the epigenetic landscape metaphor, opposed to cause) and elsewhere in this book. *Restraint* is preferred in this chapter due to the tight connection the approach presented here has to G. Bateson's use of this word in explaining the role of cybernetic explanations (Bateson, 1972/1999).

[22] Valsiner (2001).

[23] From a cognitive perspective, this process has been related to motivation, since motives are thought to be related to a tendency to reduce the distance between the actual self and the possible selves. Markus and Nurius (1986) were pioneers within the cognitive tradition in the study of possible selves, incorporating the notion of time – and therefore, of expectations, daydreaming, fantasies – in the motivational dynamics of the human mind. Their work originated an extensive line of research on how these possible selves influence us in the present. Hence, for example, if a person is fat and wants to be thinner, the impact of 'I'll never lose weight' – a negative possible self – is very different in the actual self than if one believes 'I'm fat, but I can lose weight if I want' – a positive possible self.

[24] Marquez (2003, epigraph).

our life-narrative starts to take form, probably after the adolescent years,[25] it starts to impose criteria according to which episodes are worth relating (and of course, to live as we tell).

Life is more than its narrative account – the map is not the territory, to use the famous expression from Korzybski. Narrative constructions operate as restraints on other interpretative possibilities, excluding information outside that particular format.[26] A depressive patient, for instance, hardly integrates events in his life-story that are incompatible with the depressive account. If a person is centred on his inability to be a competent person (as usually depressive people are), he will not tell the therapist episodes in which personal competence was present, unless usually with the intention of contrasting them with the present state of affairs ('before I was able to do X, but now I'm a shadow of what I used to be'), making him even more depressive.[27] The harder the restraint on success, the less likely the person is to see himself as successful, the fewer episodes of success are narrated, creating in this way a vicious cycle that creates a form of self-stability. Hence, narrative construction allows meaning construction out of what, otherwise, would be a chaotic experience, but in this process, restraints on what is experienced are also created.

### *Narrative as restraints on development*

Narratives allow adjustment to the chaotic flow of events (internal and external), but are there narratives that facilitate development while others freeze self-meanings, making it harder to accommodate innovation? When do self-narratives restrain development? Or, to use the map–territory dichotomy, when does the map becomes a problematic tool in the adjustment to the territory? Several scholars and therapists have proposed diverse forms of narrative dysfunction.[28] Neimeyer, Herrero and Botella,

25 According to McAdams (2001), and building upon various traditions of thought, it is defensible that we only start to build a more coherent and stable life-story, and therefore, a self-identity, in the adolescent period. See also see Habermas and Bluck (2000) about different forms of narrative coherence and their development.

26 The example that follows corresponds to what can be called a *tragic narrative*. According to Gergen and Gergen (1988), three types of narrative structure and their combination account for the diversity of narratives that we have at our disposal (e.g. comedy, tragedy): progressive, regressive and stable. A tragic narrative is a combination of a progressive narrative (the aims of the characters are, as time goes by, closer and closer), followed by a regressive narrative (suddenly and unexpectedly the aims become more distant). Needless to say a stable narrative is one that goes nowhere; the aims of the characters are at the same distance as time passes.

27 See Bateson (1972/1999) for an interesting development of this argument.

28 See Dimaggio (2006) for a revision on narrative perspectives about psychopathological disorders or other kinds of psychological difficulties.

for instance, propose three types of dysfunction that can co-occur: narrative disorganization, narrative dissociation and narrative dominance.[29]

*Narrative disorganization* is very typical of intense stress experiences, experiences that 'are not only radically incoherent with the plot of a person's prior life narrative but that invalidate its core emotional themes and goals as well'.[30] The ability of the self-narrative to organize the flow of events is thus strongly disrupted and the experience that dominates the person is a chaotic one.[31] When we interview someone dominated by this sort of dysfunction, we soon notice that the conversation is very difficult to follow, the person often interrupts one topic to explore a different one, the topics are not consistently elaborated, parts of the narrative structure (e.g. setting, actors) are often missing, which makes it very difficult to elaborate a clear, consistent representation of the person's life.

*Narrative dissociation* occurs when parts of a significant experience are removed from conscious awareness or, at least, from narrative coherent elaborations, impeding the integration of important aspects into the life-story. Stiles and collaborators[32] have developed a model that predicts the path that an unwelcome self-position – that is, a voice – has to follow before being accepted by the other voices of the self. According to this model, most often a voice, which is an active representative of the person's experience, is easily accessed when it is needed (e.g. 'I as a supportive therapist even when my clients criticize me'). However, sometimes a voice is rejected because it is difficult to accommodate (e.g. 'I as a therapist that is very afraid of the possibility of suicide of my clients') with the self's 'community of voices'. When this occurs, the voice continues to be active, but it is not recognized by the person. This is a problematic experience, given that the voice will emerge in experience without any awareness and will be silenced by the self, the other voice. If the previous voice is not accessible to the therapist's 'community of voices', it may emerge as a form of discomfort in a session in which, for example, the therapist perceives a patient as being a suicide risk. Instead of making a correct evaluation of this risk, he may feel paralysed, without knowing exactly why, and start thinking about himself as a lousy therapist.

Stiles and collaborators have been developing in the last twenty years a very creative research programme in psychotherapy using this idea that

29 Neimeyer, Herrero and Botella (2006, p. 131).

30 Neimeyer, Herrereo and Botella (2006, p. 139).

31 Lysaker and Lysaker (2006) claim that, in severe cases, this kind of disintegration of the narrative structure of the self can lead to a collapse of the very possibility of meaning-making, at all, culminating in psychotic symptoms, such as delusions or hallucinations.

32 See Honos-Webb and Stiles (1998); Osatuke and Stiles (2006); Stiles (1999); Stiles, *et al.* (1990).

psychotherapy involves the integration of an alien, rejected voice. The assimilation of problematic experiences[33] (APES) thus describes the path that a *dissociated voice* would follow until being accepted and used in a mastered way by the self, when needed. The middle stage is *insight*, in which a meaning bridge is created between the formerly rejected voice and the community of voices (e.g. 'to accept fear is a courageous thing to do') where the person recognizes the presence of the unwelcome voice. Research indicates that *insight* is present in good outcome cases in psychotherapy, but never present in cases in which the changes were more modest[34] (poor outcome cases).[35]

The last form of narrative dysfunction is *narrative dominance*, a 'narrative reduced to a single theme',[36] which means that there is a redundant theme that systematically impedes alternative constructions. White and Epston[37] theorized this narrative dysfunction as a problem-saturated narrative that colonizes people's lives. Once, one of us (MG) worked with a woman who was a victim of rape when she was an adolescent; at the end of a successful therapy, when asked about what was most important for her during the therapeutic process, she replied 'learning not to reduce my life to a single day' (the day she was raped). This exemplifies very well what a problem-saturated narrative is: a day ruling an entire life, colonizing it. Dominant narratives are also well illustrated in the idea from Weakland that 'life is just one damn thing after another. Therapy can't change that. But people who seek therapy are no longer experiencing that – life for them has become the same damn thing over and over again'.[38]

Following a semiotic and development standpoint, Josephs and Valsiner[39] refer to these types of restraint as *macro-organizers of meanings*, characterized as highly abstract and generalized meanings that organize lower and more concrete meanings. The hypergeneralized idea 'I'm a failure as a person' is a macro-organizer, which imposes serious limitations on

33 See Osatuke and Stiles (2006). 34 See Detert *et al.* (2006).

35 Research in psychotherapy often compares cases in terms of the change achieved during therapy. Most often the criterion is based on symptomatic measures (e.g. depressive complaints) as evaluated by standard questionnaires (e.g. Beck Depression Inventory; Beck, Steer, Ball & Ranieri, 1996). From a developmental perspective this is a problematic standard, given that people can change (and most probably do change) even without changing some of their complaints. However, we lack other ways of differentiating successful and unsuccessful cases in psychotherapy, and for that reason we will use this criterion in this chapter.

36 Hermans and Hermans-Jansen (1995, p. 164). 37 White and Epston (1990).

38 Quoted in O'Hanlon (1998, pp. 143–44).

39 Josephs and Valsiner (1998). See also Josephs, Valsiner & Surgan (1999).

a person's life (actually the opposing meaning, as it occurs in narcissistic personalities could also be very hard to live with.)

These three forms of problematic narrative – dominance, dissociation and chaotic organization – represent different forms of imposing restraint on the creation of meaning. They impede the creation of alternative meanings outside their 'rules' (that is closure, dissociation and disorganization), through different processes, thus creating meanings compatible with the existing form of dysfunction. We can easily imagine exceptions to these classes of narrative – or a way to move out of them: closure would give way to flexibility and openness to different meanings; dissociation to assimilation; and chaos to organization.

## Therapeutic accounts as a special arena for adult development

In therapy, the therapist must adjust to what ever kind of dysfunction most severely affects the client and use several tools (therapeutic techniques) to create and sustain change. When he or she does this successfully, exceptions to the former narrative dysfunction are created. Thus, one can say that, from a narrative perspective, *the main aim of psychotherapy is to create the ability to break the narrative restraints that hinder the client from experiencing her life in a different way, allowing new meanings to be generated.*

Gonçalves and collaborators[40] have developed a system for tracking exceptions in psychotherapy especially for the narrative dominance type (closure of meanings), but which can be expanded to two other types of dysfunction. This system was inspired by the concept of *unique outcome*, from White and Epston.[41] These narrative therapists developed a model of therapy in which the first phase is characterized by the *deconstruction* of the dominant meanings. The therapist must try to loosen the narrative rigidity that dominates the client's life (e.g. depression), creating space for alternative meanings to emerge. This idea of deconstruction fits very well with the idea of breaking the restraints that impede alternative construction. The second step is *reconstruction*, in which the therapist tries to identify and expand exceptions (or 'unique outcomes') outside the main narrative restraints.

Our model was constructed inside the territory of psychotherapy and thus applies to narrative dysfunctions, but what about 'normal' life, when there is not necessarily any kind of psychopathological dysfunction or any need for professional help? How does our model fit changes in a person's

[40] Gonçalves *et al.* (2010). [41] White and Epston (1990).

life outside psychotherapy? First, life is also full of transitions to unexpected events or to expected but new events. This usually implies an effort of adaptation to new circumstances. This can be externally imposed, but it can also have a determinant contribution from the person. Sometimes people become dissatisfied with old ways of meanacting[42] – or start to desire new and better ways of acting and acting upon the world. In all of these cases, people usually face a need for 'change' – for a more clear effort to solve a rupture in development.[43]

Second, from a narrative perspective, when significant changes take place there is a modification in self-narrative dominance. In effect, even if there is no strictly 'narrative dominance' dysfunction, some dominance of the former narrative has to be broken in order to accommodate innovation and to allow a new self-narrative to emerge. That is, independently of why the narrative change is occurring, changes in the restraints that organize the former self-narrative also develop.

### *Culture and narrative restraints on meaning-making*

White and Epston[44] use the work of the French philosopher Michel Foucault[45] as an inspiration in order to analyse how cultural restraints are formed and sustained in problematic self-narratives.[46] According to Foucault, in modern Western societies we are under the surveillance of an internalized normative power, very different from what took place four centuries ago, when only major deviations (like crime) were subject to the exercise of power. Power nowadays is diffuse and exercised by each one of us. Foucault refers to an architectural structure that is a metaphor of this form of power: Bentham's panoptic (pan-optic = 'the eye that sees all').

This panopticon was a circular building (appropriate to prisons, but also to other social arrangements) in which there was a central tower of observation, that allowed the surveillance of each singular cell, aiming at permanent observation, without any possibility for the targets of the observation (in this case the prisoners) to know whether they were being observed at a particular moment in time. This omnipresence of the external power was quick to correct any deviance, which created the need for self-discipline, leading to the internalization of power. According to Foucault, this form of surveillance is aimed not only at the

[42] See Chapter 5. [43] See Zittoun (2006b). [44] See also White (2007).
[45] Foucault (1975).
[46] Of course these restraints are also present in non-problematic narratives, but they become stricter in problematic forms of narrative dominance.

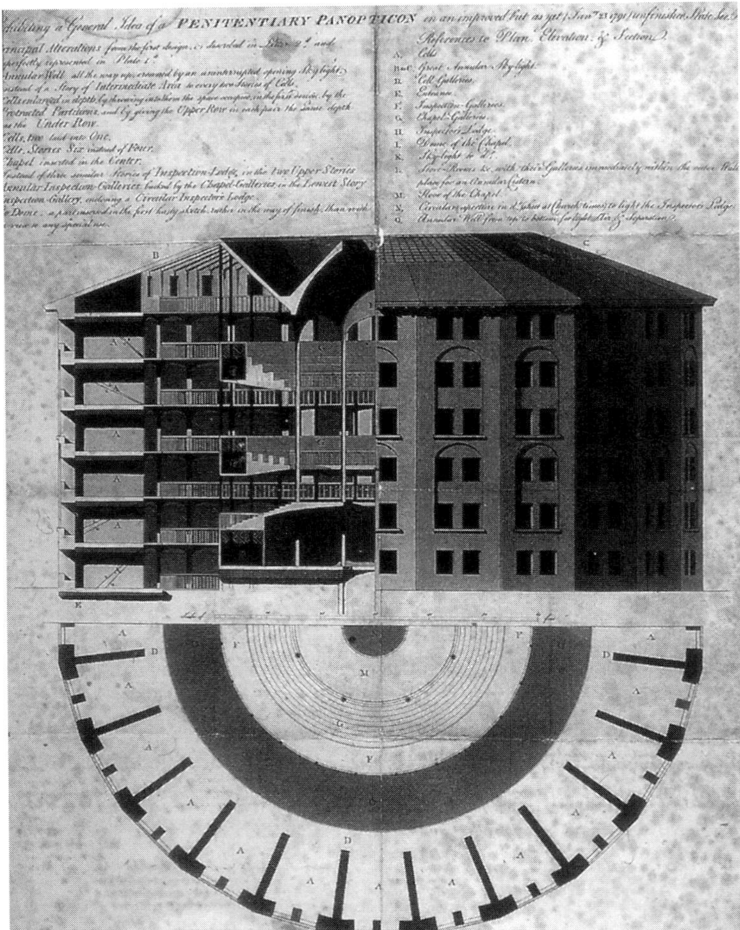


Figure 6.2 Panopticon blueprint by Jeremy Bentham, 1791.

correction of deviations, but also at making people productive, as occurred in the first workshops and after that in factories.[47]

The main point is that after this transformation in the structure of power the simplest actions in diverse social institutions (e.g. asylums, prisons,

[47] The movie *Modern Times*, from Charles Chaplin, offers a satirical view on such a Taylorist organization.

schools) are now the target of surveillance. Even more important, nowadays we have internalized this form of power and we are continuously adjusting ourselves to all kinds of norms, in our health, appearance, sexuality and relationships.

Based on these ideas, White[48] suggests that in the main forms of problem-saturated narratives (that is, narrative dominance), we can find several types of normalizing practice that implicitly produce judgements about what is acceptable, normal, valuable and so on. According to Foucault, the act of looking at one's self is inseparable from the norms internalized from culture, and is in a sense an exercise of self-surveillance. Inspired by this Foucauldian frame, White and Epston see the aim of therapy as precisely deconstructing this normalizing surveillance. This form of therapy tries to expose 'the taken–for-granted "truths" that dictate how to live and how to behave ... [and] liberate people from society's marginalizing practices that determine what is acceptable and unacceptable.'[49]

From a very different perspective, but with some striking similar features, Thomas Szasz,[50] more than forty years ago, proposed that the aim of psychotherapy was to allow people to develop their meta-learning skills. In a book published in 1965, Szasz states:

> I shall approach the subject of the analytic relationship [today we would say therapeutic relationship] from a broad psychosocial base, *viewing man as a person who uses signs, follow rules, and plays games* – not as an organism that has instincts and needs or as a patient who has a disease.[51]

One of Szasz's central arguments is based on a hierarchy of learning, composed of three levels: proto-education, education and meta-education.[52] As an example of *proto-education,* Szasz suggests a tourist in a foreign city, who asks for help to reach a certain location. If she has no map, she has to trust guidance from local people. If she does so and asks for help, she is in a situation is which she has no possibility of checking the validity of this knowledge and has learned only one item. Thus, the main prototype of proto-education is to give and receive advice and suggestions ('if I were you, I would do X').

The notion of *education* for Szasz refers to situations in which a person has the means to check the validity of knowledge. Moreover, learning is not limited to a single item. For instance, if a person takes a map with him

[48] White (2007). [49] Monk and Gehart (2003, p. 20). [50] See Szasz (1965/1988).
[51] See Szasz (1965/1988, p.3; italics added).
[52] See also Bateson (1972/1999) for a close, and yet different view on several levels of learning.

and knows how to use it, he will know how to go to different places and will not be dependent on others. Also, in a sense that person has the ability to check the validity of his learning outcomes, by verifying what occurs at any time by using that form of knowledge (that is, every time he uses the map of that city he will be able to verify its accuracy).

According to this model, all the things that we know about a specific subject (let us say, chemistry) were acquired through education and proto-education. But learning does not involve only the acquisition of contents; it also involves the use of tools. Thus, meta-education is learning about learning. In a sense *meta-education* is less than proto-education and education, given that no specific items are learned and that it is not about factual information. But, in another sense, it is much more than the other forms of knowledge, since it involves learning about the way we learn – as we will see in the next chapter.

Szasz considers the aim of psychotherapy to be located precisely at this last level. But how does the therapist facilitate this meta-level? According to Szasz, by discussing the therapeutic situation (in psychodynamic parlance, *transference*) and the extra-therapeutic situations 'in which the patient plays a significant part, (because) each of these "games" must be scrutinized to lay bare its structure, in other words, to ascertain *who makes what rules for whom and why*'.[53]

From this perpective, it can be said that what Foucault calls practices of self-surveillance ultimately result in 'items' learned through proto-education, given that they are internalized and the process by which the internalization occurred is not explicit, making the person unable to break free of them. The only route to liberation is meta-education – learning about the learning processes and the ways in which proto-education and education made us the way we are.[54]

Thus, from Szasz's perspective, the process of change in psychotherapy involves a meta-learning process, in which a person detaches from the meaning-making processes and takes an observer position (of course, this is also a process of meaning-making).

[53] Szasz (1965/1988, p. 53). From here, Szasz suggests that the traditional aim of psychoanalysis – making conscious the unconscious – should be reframed. What the therapist does is facilitate meta-education, which exposes forms of proto-education, from family and the wider culture, that are creating difficulties in people's lives and are not perceived as doing so (that is, the result of proto-education is outside conscious awareness). For example, repression 'is a particular form of obedience and hence a result of proto-education' (Szasz, 1965/1988, p. 60).

[54] This proposal has strong similarities with the suggestion from White and Epston that therapeutic change starts with deconstruction of former meanings, leading people to question the 'the taken–for-granted "truths" that "dictate"' (Monk and Gehart, 2003, p. 20) their behaviour.

Similar proposals can be found in several contemporary perspectives. For instance, Dimaggio and colleagues[55] studied extensively metacognitive abilities in psychotherapy, mainly with patients with severe personality disorders, and emphasized two main ideas: severe personality disorders are associated with failures in metacognitive functions and the development of these functions during the psychotherapy process is a curative factor. Also, several dialogical thinkers[56] have emphasized a creation of a metaposition during psychotherapy that transcends the multiple positions of the self, facilitating reflection about the diversity of I-positions, as well the organization of this multiple repertoire.

A word of caution is, however, necessary about the meta-learning processes. The analysis made up to now could lead the reader to imagine that such processes imply a kind of liberation from all the restraints, and that one then sees the reality of one's life 'as it is'. This would be a naive way of conceiving meaning-making transformations. There is no access to reality (of the world or of the self) without the lens imposed by our ways of knowing. We clearly assume a constructivist position on this point. To know is always to create meaning, which, in turn, will restrain our experience of the world. Our knowledge is always semiotically mediated, since we use signs to construct meaning. These signs, as far as the construction of self-identity is concerned, are narratively structured. Thus, change implies a transformation in the ways signs are organized and in the structure of our life narratives. As these transformations occur, new restraints are formed. Fortunately, culture allows us a very flexible use of signs and is complex enough to facilitate a multiplicity of constructions.

## Innovative moments and change

In order to track the emergence of innovation during the therapeutic process a system for coding sessions and interviews has been developed.[57] *Innovative moments* are all the moments during psychotherapy in which the main narrative restraints are challenged, even if the challenge is very small. Thus, we can say that *an innovative moment* (IM, also called an I-moment in some publications) *is an occurrence outside narrative restraints, whatever they may be*. Needless to say, in order to identify *violations* of the restraints we need first to identify the restraints. The way we do it is by

[55] See Dimaggio, Salvatore, Azzara and Catania (2003); or Semerari, *et al.* (2004). It should be emphasized that several other sources can be invaluable to the clarification of this metalevel of meaning-making. To name just a few: Cooper (2004); Georgaca (2001); Hermans (2003, 2004); Leiman and Stiles (2001).

[56] See Hermans (2003); Dimaggio, Salvatore, Azzara and Catania (2003).

[57] See Gonçalves, Ribeiro, Matos, Santos and Mendes (2010).

becoming familiar with the entire case and identifying the different facets of the problematic narrative. Every time in the conversation a theme (a thought, a feeling, an action) emerges that is situated outside the restraint of the problematic narrative we consider it as an IM. Thus, where the facets of the problematic narrative are the rule, IMs are the exceptions to the rule.

In Table 6.2 we present the example of a specific case, with the facets of the problematic narrative and the identification IMs.

### *Types of IM*

Five possible categories of IMs[58] were previously identified inductively, by analysing psychotherapy sessions (with a narrative approach) with women victims of partner abuse.[59] From this original study, we have been applying the *innovative moments coding system* (IMCS) to different samples (e.g. cognitive therapy, emotion-focused therapy) and the system has been changed in several ways, but the five types are still those that emerged in the original sample. Below there is a definition of each IM and a clinical vignette to illustrate them.

*Action IMs* are actions or specific behaviour against the problematic story. They should lead to the potential creation of new meanings and not be only the result or a direct consequence of the problem. Thus, for instance, in a situation where a woman is being abused by her partner, her instinctive protection of herself from aggression is not an IM. However, to protect oneself in a more intentional way is considered an IM (e.g. pressing charges with the police):

Vignette (agoraphobic client):

C (client): Yesterday I decided to go out: I went to the mall and I managed to stay there for more than one hour.

*Reflection IMs* consist of the emergence of new understandings or thoughts that do not support the problem or are not congruent with the dominant plot. A good story implies a landscape of action and a landscape of consciousness. A reflection IM relates to the landscape of consciousness, to the way a person feels, knows, and thinks.[60] On the other hand, the landscape of action includes the setting, the actors, and the actions (usually present in action and protest IMs):

[58] A version of this section was previously published in Gonçalves, Ribeiro, Matos, Santos & Mendes (2010). The use of this material was authorized by the publisher.
[59] Matos, Santos, Gonçalves and Martins (2009).
[60] This distinction between landscape of action and landscape of consciousness in narrative telling was introduced by Bruner (1986).

Table 6.2 *Lisa's problematic self-narrative and IMs*

| | Problematic self-narrative | Examples of IMs |
|---|---|---|
| Sadness | L[isa]: yeah, [I feel] neglected or rejected or um, just there for the purpose of being there as the provider for the kids and<br>T[herapist]: mm-hm, so kind of just left all alone holding the bag<br>L: yeah, I guess . . . I hold a lot on my shoulders. | L: I feel content because um I do have friends now.<br>L: yeah, I feel pretty satisfied at this point. |
| Guilt | L: yeah, when I, if I do go out to the store and you know, I may take, whatever, a couple of hours (laugh), an hour and hour and a half, um sometimes I feel guilty about doing that.<br>L: (talking to her husband in empty chair task) – – – um, there's a lot of making me feel like I'm a bad person and I've just got to keep on trying, just, no matter what happens; just accept you the way you are and just shut-up. | L: let me explore, mm-hm, let me grow and explore and just let me find myself.<br>L: um, I don't want to live like that, I want to be able to enjoy life, to let out my creativity and I want to blossom. . . I deserve that. |
| Resentment and difficulty in expressing her own feelings | L: maybe that's why I don't tell him (husband) how I really feel inside (sniff) . . . yeah, there's, or um, even though I express it, it's just kind of laughed at<br>L: for me to express this, yeah, it's a little, it's sad and it's scary.<br>T: uh-huh, what were the rules (in your family)?<br>L: uh, to respect, be nice to everybody, don't talk back. . .<br>L: yes scared (crying). Scared – I feel that I always had to be a good girl in front of him. . . and, if I'm not, then I'm no good | L: but then my feelings are my feelings and (sigh) and I'm entitled to them<br>L: I don't want to um, resent my mother . . . because then I find when I do that I stay stuck<br>L: yeah, just accept me the way I am... |
| Lack of assertiveness | L: he'll (husband) raise his voice and I simmer down and either walk away, or just forget about what was said and I don't fight it out<br>L: um, yeah, or just better shut up and that's it – I've never tried to go over my limit (laugh) | L: yeah that's what I say to myself, why don't I, you know, why, excuse me, why don't I stand up for myself<br>L: I'm not responsible for his actions (husband)<br>L: I am me and these feelings belong to me and if I want to tell you I will |

Source : From Gonçalves *et al.* (2010).

Vignette (depression):

C: I'm starting to wonder about what my life will be like if I keep feeding my depression.
T(therapist): It's becoming clear that depression had a hidden agenda for your life?
C: Yes, sure.
T: What is it that depression wants from you?
C: It wants to rule my whole life and in the end it wants to steal my life from me.

*Protest IMs* are moments of confrontation, defiance or assertion, which can involve actions, thoughts and feelings, either projected or accomplished. They assume the presence of two positions: one that supports the problem (entailed by a person, an internalized position of oneself, or by a given society or culture), and another that defies or confronts the first one. They involve proactivity and personal agency by the client.

Like reflection IMs, protest IMs can also involve thoughts or feelings, but they represent a way of repositioning the self through a proactive, affirmative, or assertive process (e.g. '*I think that nothing can justify this; I decided that I won't allow fear to interfere in my life any more*'). They involve a repositioning towards the problem and its effects, as well as towards others who are contributing, intentionally or inadvertently, the problem (e.g. *'I told my mother that I won't accept her ideas about my marriage!')*.

Vignette (parental critique):

C: I was trying to change myself all the time, to please them (parents). But now I'm getting tired, I am realizing that it doesn't make any sense to make this effort.
T: That effort keeps you in a position of changing yourself all the time, the way you feel and think . . .
C: Yes, sure. And I'm really tired of that, I can't stand it anymore. After all, parents are supposed to love their children and not judge them all the time.

*Reconceptualization IMs* involve a meta-reflection level, from where the person not only understands what is different in her- or himself, but is also able to describe the processes involved in this transformation.

This metaposition enables access to the self in the past (problematic narrative), the emerging self, as well as the description of the processes that allowed the transformation from the past to the present. While reflection IMs are related to innovation in terms of a thinking *episode* or *moment* (related to the past, present, or future) that is outside the influence of the dominant story, reconceptualization IMs are associated with the narration of a meta-reflection *process* involved in change. The perception of some transformation is narrated, making clear (1) the process involved in its emergence and (2) the distinction between the present moment and the former condition (the contrast between past self and emerging/changing self can appear implicitly (e.g. 'I am *more* mature now (than in the past')). These two elements must be distinct. Thus, for example, when the client says 'now I'm more responsible', this is not by itself a reconceptualization IM. To be a reconceptualization, another element has to be present, like 'now I'm more responsible and that allows me X or Z' (X or Z not being a mere re-description of responsibility). Therefore, the element associated with the process of change cannot be exactly the same as the transformation.

Vignette (victim of partner abuse):

C: I think I started enjoying myself again. I had a time . . . I think I've stopped in time. I've always been a person that liked myself. There was a time . . . maybe because of my attitude, because of all that was happening, I think there was a time that I was not respecting myself . . . despite the effort to show that I wasn't feeling . . . so well with myself . . . I couldn't feel that joy of living, that I recovered now . . . and now I keep thinking 'you have to move on and get your life back'.
T: This position of 'you have to move on' has been decisive?
C: That was important. I felt so weak at the beginning! I hated feeling like that . . . Today I think 'I'm not weak'. In fact, maybe I am very strong, because despite of all that has happened to me, I can still see the good side of people and I don't think I'm being naïve . . . Now, when I look at myself, I think 'no, you can really make a difference, and you have value as a person'. For a while I couldn't have this dialogue with myself, I couldn't say 'you can do it' nor even think 'I am good at this or that'. . .

*Performing change IMs* refer to the anticipation or planning of new experiences, projects, or activities at the personal, professional and relational level. They can reflect the performance of change or new skills that are akin to the emergent narrative (e.g. new projects that derive from a new self-version). These IMs imply the presence of an implicit or explicit marker of change, that is, the client has to narrate the perception of some transformation:

Vignette (victim of partner abuse):

T: You seem to have so many projects for the future now!
C: Yes, you're right. I want to do all the things that were impossible for me to do *while I was dominated by fear* [marker of change]. I want to work again and to have the time to enjoy my life with my children. I want to have friends again. The loss of all the friendships of the past is something that still hurts me really deep. I want to have friends again, to have people to talk to, to share experiences and to feel the complicity in my life again.

The IMCS is a qualitative method of data analysis that was developed to study psychotherapeutic *change*. Table 6.3 lists the various types of IM. However, it can also be applied to understanding life change processes,

Table 6.3 *Innovative moments grid (version 7.2)*

| Types of IM | Subtypes | Contents |
|---|---|---|
| *Action IMs (A)*<br>Actions or specific behaviours against the problem(s) | | New coping behaviours facing anticipated or existent obstacles<br>Effective resolution of unsolved problem(s)<br>Active exploration of solutions<br>Restoring autonomy and self-control<br>Searching for information about the problem(s) |
| *Reflection IMs (R)*<br>Thinking processes that indicate the understanding of something new that makes the problem(s) unacceptable (e.g. thoughts, intentions, interrogations, doubts) | (i) Creating distance from the problem (s) | Reconsidering problem(s)' causes and/or awareness of its effects<br>New problem(s) formulations<br>Adaptive self-instructions and thoughts<br>Intention to fight problem(s)' demands, references of self-worth and/or feelings of well-being |
| | (ii) Centred on the change | Therapeutic process – reflecting about the therapeutic process<br>Change process – considering the process and strategies implemented to overcome the problem(s); references of self-worth and/or feelings of well-being (as consequences of change)<br>New positions – references to new/ emergent identity versions in face of the problem(s) |
| *Protest IMs (P)*<br>Moments of critique, that involve some kind of confrontation (directed at others or versions of oneself); it could be planned or actual behaviors, thoughts, or/ and feelings. | (i) Criticizing the problem(s) | Position of critique in relation to the problem(s) or/and the others who support it. The other could be an internalized other or facet of oneself. |
| | (ii) Emergence of new positions | Positions of assertiveness and empowerment<br>Repositioning oneself towards the problem(s) |
| *Reconceptualization IMs (RC)*<br>Process description, at a meta-cognitive level (the client not only manifests thoughts and behaviors out of the problem(s) dominated story, but also understands the processes that are involved in it). If the RC includes PC we should code RC with PC (RCPC). | | RC must involve two dimensions: – description of the shift between two positions (past and present) and – the process underlying this transformation. |

Table 6.3 (*cont.*)

| Types of IM | Subtypes | Contents |
|---|---|---|
| *Performing change IMs (PC)*<br>References to new aims, experiences, activities or projects, anticipated or in action, as consequence of change. | | Generalization of good outcomes into the future and/or other life dimensions<br>Problematic experience as a resource to deal with new situations<br>Investment in new projects as a result of the process of change<br>Investment in new relationships as a result of the process of change<br>Performance of change: new skills<br>Re-emergence of neglected or forgotten self-versions |

such as specific life transitions or regular daily changes. It can be applied to qualitative data, namely discourse or conversation, as therapeutic sessions, in depth interviews, or biographies, preferably in video/audio systems or transcripts support.

### *A model of change and stability*

In our research programme we have been studying several types of psychotherapy (e.g. emotion-focused therapy, narrative therapy) with different kinds of client. Our research involves the intensive study of small samples and case studies. We have also conducted two studies on daily life change.

From these several studies we have constructed a model of change and a model to explain stability (as a form of failure to produce significant changes, again in psychotherapy and daily life). This model is supported by several findings that have systematically emerged in these studies:

1 IMs appear in poor and good outcome cases, although in good outcome cases the duration[61] of the IMs is longer and it tends to increase as the process develops.
2 Reconceptualization almost fails to emerge in poor outcome cases, or has a residual presence; on the other hand, it represents an important proportion of the IMs that emerge in good outcome cases.

[61] Our measure of IMs is not the frequency, but rather the duration in time that each type of IM occupies in each session, and in the entire process. The reason for this is our claim that duration reflects better the narrative elaboration of IMs than their mere frequency.

3 In good outcome cases reconceptualization IMs tend to emerge in the middle of the therapeutic process and increase until the end of it. Performing change tends to appear after the development of reconceptualization.
4 Poor and good outcome cases tend to be similar in the beginning of the process, both presenting IMs of action, reflection and protest, but become different in the middle of the process (as reconceptualization emerges and the duration of IMs increases in good outcome cases).

It is our proposal that narrative change starts with *action*, *reflection* and *protest* IMs as elementary forms of innovation (level 2 change in DST terms). They mark the beginning of the change process, being signs to the self and to significant others that something new is under way. They defy the expectation of the redundant behaviour imposed by the narrative dysfunction, as they are occurrences outside the restraints imposed by the former self-narrative.

Sometimes innovations start to develop from new actions, at other times from new reflections, and at other times from forms of protest against a life dominated by the problem. These three types of IM at the beginning of the process reinforce each other. For instance, as a person starts acting in a new way, she also starts thinking in a form that is congruent with this new action or vice versa. As cycles of action and reflection develop, the protest against the problem increases, also increasing the probability that more IMs will emerge. At a certain point in this process, which in short-term therapy (between twelve to twenty sessions) coincides with the middle phase of the process, reconceptualization IMs emerge. We found that reconceptualization IMs are very important to sustaining change. Poor outcome cases in psychotherapy present a low duration of IMs and almost fail to include reconceptualization IMs.

In order to understand why reconceptualization is so important the reader should remember that reconceptualization has two necessary features: the description of a past self and of a present self (we can have only one part explicit and the other implicit) and the narration of the process which allowed that transformation.

Reconceptualization necessarily has a higher narrative coherence than other more elementary IMs. This could mean that reconceptualization may act as a gravitational field for other IMs. Figure 6.3 tries precisely to capture this idea. As the person narrates him- or herself differently, new actions and thoughts (that is action, reflection and protest IMs) that are congruent with the narration of change are still emerging. This creates a virtuous cycle in which reconceptualization supports, and is supported, by the emergence of the three other forms of IM. The narrative structure of reconceptualization, which can give coherence to what, otherwise, would

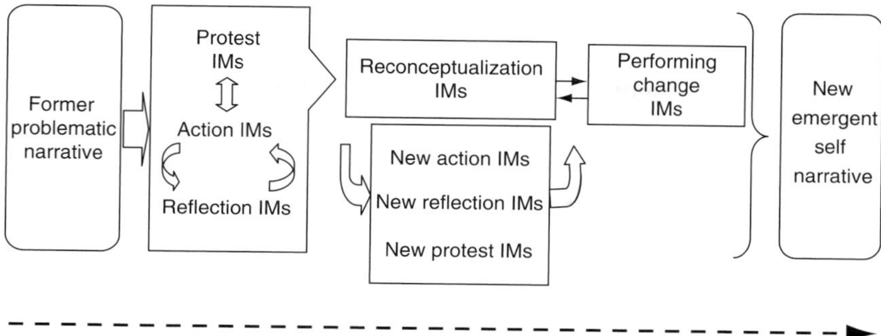


Figure 6.3 A heuristic model of sustainable change in human psychological development (adapted from Gonçalves, Matos and Santos (2009)).

be dispersed occurrences of innovation, attracts and gives purpose and meaning to other IMs. Another feature of reconceptualization that clearly increases its narrative structure is its power to integrate the old and the new (one of the requirements for its coding).[62] Hence, not only do innovations emerge, but innovations that integrate and transform the old patterns. This means that, when reconceptualization emerges, a semiotic bridge is created between the former and the emergent narrative[63].

Reconceptualization IMs also posit the person as the author of the change process. The client is not only an actor, but given her access to the way the plot is changing, she is also authoring it.[64] With the other IMs a violation of the restraint emerges, but the person has no access to the processes that allowed the innovations, they simply occur. With reconceptualization the person narrates the transformation process, which put her in the position of an author of change (in the next section we will return to the reasons why reconceptualization is so central in the development of change). Finally, IMs performing change emerge and expand the change process into the future since good new stories have to have a future.[65]

[62] As does re-equilibration in Piaget's sense, see Chapter 3, Box 3.5.

[63] See Osatuke *et al.* (2004) on the concept of semiotic bridge that occurs in insight, between the alien voice and the community of voices.

[64] We are using here a distinction from Sarbin (1986): he operates a narrative translation of the Jamesian distinction between I and Me, introducing a differentiation between the author (the one who is telling the story, the I) and the characters of the story. Since one of these characters happens to be oneself, therefore, it will be Me.

[65] For a similar argument, see Crites (1986); Omer and Alon (1997); Sluzki (1992).

The change depicted here involves a modification of restraints, in which the previous restraints are cleared and rejected and the experience is transformed.[66] All IMs represent a rejection of the former restraints and a rehearsal of new ones, even if the larger part of this process occurs implicitly.

As seen above, various levels of change can be distinguished – from level 1 changes, within an attractor, to level 2 changes, which demand a change of attractor, to level 3 changes, which demand a radical reorganization. Here, all the modifications that occur inside the problematic self-narrative (see Figure 6.3) are level 1 changes. Mostly people perceive this variability as no change at all, or at least as change that is not significant. A depressed patient can feel more or less depressed, can devalue himself more or less. For him, this is stability, not change. But clearly, this 'frame' varies and from a DST perspective this is considered level 1 change.[67] The changes that take place inside the middle of the figure – which correspond to the emergence of IMs – are level 2 changes. Some of them are attenuated and change is aborted. But others are expanded.[68] In particular, the emergence of reconceptualization and its amplification in time can start a cascade of processes that lead to level 3 changes. Clearly, the emergence of the new self-narrative represents level 3 changes, as it occurs in successful psychotherapy and in successful life-changes.

We believe that the model depicted here also applies to major transformations in life. In fact, Gonçalves and collaborators conducted two projects where the results supported the idea that changes in adult lives develop in a similar way to what occurs in therapy.[69] It would be really interesting to study whether something similar occurs in other life transitions (e.g. during adolescence). For instance, do young children reconceptualize their experiences, transforming their life narratives? Children use many comparisons with former states, to highlight new competencies (e.g. 'before I did X, but now I'm able to do Y', 'when I was *young* I didn't

[66] We are not talking here of an intellectual process, as we think this rejection is a form of experience that can occur through different paths. Psychotherapies explore these different avenues for change. For instance, behavioural therapy produces change through new actions, experiential therapy by emphasizing changes at the experience and emotional level, and cognitive therapy by challenging the assumptions behind the problematic behaviours. Independently of these paths, we believe that the model depicted here applies. Of course, this claim still needs to be supported in several models of therapy, but until now the results found with narrative therapy, emotion-focused therapy and client-centred therapy are encouraging.

[67] For DST (dynamic systems theory) see Chapter 1. For the concept of frame and for the 'levels of change' concept, see Chapter 5.

[68] See Ribeiro and Gonçalves (2011), on this issue.

[69] See Cruz and Gonçalves (2009); Meira, Gonçalves, Salgado and Cunha (2009).

know how to write, but now I realize that it's so easy'). All these contrasts are similar to what we refer to as reconceptualization. They are probably preceded by other types of IMs as well.

### *Stability and abortion of level 3 change*

Let us explore now what happens when level 3 change does not occur. From a psychotherapeutic perspective, this corresponds to unsuccessful cases. Poor outcome cases are, at the beginning of therapy, amazingly similar to good outcome ones, as far as action, protest and reflection IMs are concerned. Thus, an important question is why, in these cases, these IMs do not evolve to more complex forms of innovation (that is, reconceptualization and performing change) in the middle phase of the therapy.

We suggest that level 2 changes start to occur as action, reflection and protest IMs emerge. However, in the absence of reconceptualization, the change potential of these IMs is aborted and the person again organizes her behaviour with the same rules, that is, with the same self-narrative. Thus, despite the emergence of level 2 changes, level 3 does not occur (see Figure 6.4). Some of the reasons referred to above about the change potential of reconceptualization can explain this failure to produce level 3 changes, namely the absence of a narrative structure that attracts other innovations and allows the integration of the old and the new, and the

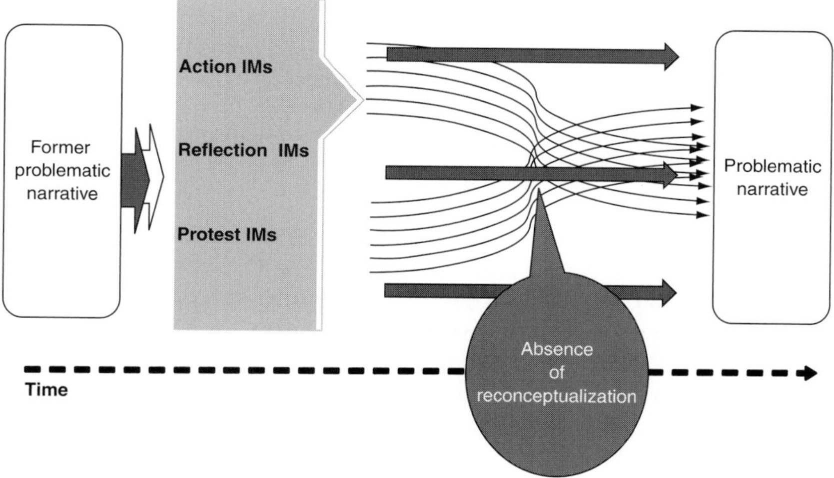


Figure 6.4 How change fails in human development.

absence of an authoring stance allowed by the meta-position inherent in reconceptualization. However, if reconceptualization is the main process through which level 3 change emerges (more on this topic below), the interesting question, of course, is what are the reasons that explain why reconceptualization sometimes does not occur?

We suggest that if IMs that emerge in the first phase are not developed enough, this will prevent the emergence of reconceptualization, blocking the way to level 3 changes. Thus, we think that the accumulation and consolidation of new emergences, in the form of action, reflection and protest IMs, are necessary before a metaposition such as reconceptualization can emerge. This explains why – despite the large amounts of narrating that human beings do, about themselves, or others or anything – the desired change in orientation of their psychological development happens relatively infrequently.

The accumulation of earlier more elementary IMs may prompt the emergence of the more complex ones – given some enabling conditions. In other words, there must be a repetition of several violations (IMs) to the implicit narrative restraints, as well as an expansion of these challenges to the problematic self-narrative (translated to increased duration IMs), before the person admits to herself and to the others that she is *really* changing, thus eliciting the meta-level position that emerges in reconceptualization. One particular strategy to avoid this development is by attenuating[70] the innovative power of the IMs that emerge, by returning to the problematic narrative, as the follow example illustrates.

Clinical vignette:

Client: I can't stand this situation anymore. I want to feel able to do whatever other persons do in their lives, I want to get up in the morning and feel good with myself. I'm just tired to feel sad all the time. [Protest IM] *But I just can't do it! It's too difficult for me.* [Return to the problem].

From a dialogical point of view, the client has performed a cyclical movement between a position and a counter-position (emphasized in the previous clinical vignette), a voice and counter-voice, that does not allow the development of the system of meanings out of the dichotomy (see Figure 6.5). This has led to an insoluble dilemma and makes change difficult to achieve. Valsiner coined this dialogical process, in which two opposite positions keep feeding each other, dominating the self alternatively, as *mutual in-feeding.*[71]

[70] See Valsiner (2008a) on attenuation and amplification of change. [71] Valsiner (2002).

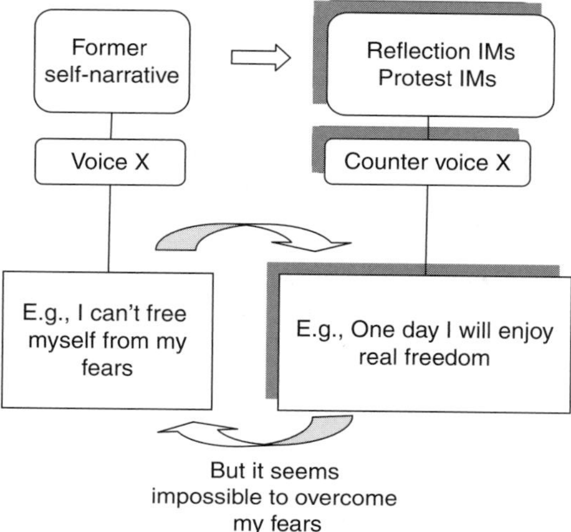


Figure 6.5 Reflection and protest IMs and mutual in-feeding.

Mutual in-feeding is, at an elementary level, a process of ambivalence. Similarly, Arkovitz and Engle propose to call some forms of therapeutic resistance *ambivalent resistance*, which:

> refers to patterns of behavior in which people express some desire to change, believe that change will improve their lives, believe that effective strategies are available, have adequate information about executing those strategies, but nonetheless do not employ them sufficiently for change; these pattern are usually accompanied by negative affect.[72]

Among other therapeutic models that discuss similar processes,[73] Stiles and collaborators describe the cross-fire phenomenon, a process of oscillation between two contradictory voices that seem 'to fight for possession of the floor'.[74] Neither voice speaks for long without being contradicted by the other. In this self-contradictory speech, the emergence of one voice seems to trigger the emergence of the contradictory one, and vice versa.[75]

Mutual *in-feeding* has been tracked in our studies by identifying all the times an IM is followed by the re-emergence of the problematic narrative.

[72] Arkovitz and Engle (2007, p. 172).
[73] See Gonçalves *et al.* (2009) for a review on this topic.
[74] See Brinegar, Salvi, Stiles and Greenberg (2006, p. 170).
[75] This rapid cross-fire precedes *insight* in the model of APES, in which the dissociated voice is recognized by the self, allowing insight (see above).

Most of the time a semiotic marker (e.g. 'but', 'however') is present, representing a contradiction of the emergent innovative content.

The empirical studies that we have done with this model are still very exploratory but clearly show that mutual in-feeding (1) occurs more in poor than in good outcome cases; (2) typically follows reflection and protest IMs, being more rare in the other types and almost absent in reconceptualization and change-performing IMs.

Curiously enough, we also found,[76] when we studied reflection and protest IMs, that the levels of return to the problem are higher in the IMs more detached from the problematic self-narrative which represent a higher potential for change. This means that, as a way of preventing development to level 3 changes, the person attenuates precisely those IMs with the most developmental power. One can question if this is so, why it is that these IMs emerge at all. We hypothesize that they emerge to facilitate the management of the problematic self-narrative, creating a sense of liberation from its oppression. However, significant change creates a sense of discrepancy with the familiarity of the previous state, promoting a sense of insecurity with the future development. That is, while innovation occurs, it is too far away from what the person is able to change in her life at that moment.[77] The person therefore oscillates between elaborating those IMs, temporarily freeing himself or herself from the oppression of the problematic self-narrative and, as soon as the discrepancy created is too large, returning to the problematic narrative (IMs attenuation) – thus reducing the sense of discrepancy and the threat it represents. Therefore, the problematic self-narrative and the IMs act as two opposite self-positions, with a feedback loop relationship, and end up feeding each other in a cyclical movement, maintaining stability.

## The dialogical magic of change

Through this work on therapeutic change, *reconceptualization* appears as essential to developmental change in adults (and perhaps even in children and adolescents). As new thoughts, feelings and actions emerge (action, reflection and protest IMs), the former self-narrative becomes challenged to the point at which the person starts narrating as a different person (reconceptualization IM), which prompts more experiences of innovation (more action, reflection and protest IMs), facilitating more reconceptualization, and so on – until a new self-narrative is clearly present and consolidated.

[76] Borges and Gonçalves (2009).

[77] The notion of zone of proximal development from Vygotsky seems quite appropriate here, as Leiman and Stiles (2001) argue.

We also suggested that by attenuating the early IMs in the change process, reconceptualization IMs may be aborted, impeding the emergence of level 3 changes. *Mutual in-feeding* is one process by which the attenuation can occur. Other processes, such as social invalidation of change by significant others, may similarly facilitate the attenuation of early IMs. Mutual in-feeding could also emerge at a macroscopic level through different forms, such as trivializing change (e.g. 'feeling a little less depressed is not important, because I'm still depressed'), taking change as temporary (e.g. 'I felt less depressed but I'm sure tomorrow I will be worse again'), or by re-attribution of change to something outside the person's agency and control (e.g. 'I felt less depressed, but that was only my meds starting to having an effect'). All these examples would be rated as involving a mutual in-feeding process, given the presence of a dance between the innovation and the return to the problematic narrative.

Why is reconceptualization so central in the change process and what are the different facets of an *authoring position*? This position is dependent on the access the person has to the change process. Which are the other processes involved in the production of such an active and developmentally productive position? We need to discuss three dimensions of reconceptualization in order to analyse its transformational power: direction of change, integration of different opposing self-narratives (past and present) and performance of change.[78]

### *Reconceptualization as directing the innovation potential*

Reconceptualization, given its narrative structure (involving the past, the present and the process of change), allows the aggregation of different IMs, operating like a gravitational field that gives purpose to a diversity of new statements (action, reflection and protest IMs) that are much more molecular in terms of their narrative structure. The power to aggregate the diversity of IMs is very important in the change process, given the coherence conferred on what could otherwise be the emergence of innovations in very different directions and not perceived as related to each other. This aggregating power creates a redundancy in the emergence of other IMs, giving a clear direction to the challenges of the former self-narrative. As some therapists and scholars[79] suggest, the *amount* of change is not the most important factor in the change process, but rather the direction of

[78] Most of these proposals are still very speculative and more research is needed to check their viability.

[79] De Shazer (1991) and Valsiner (2008a) are exemplary in this respect.

change. Strategic therapists even claim that smaller changes are more meaningful, given their 'domino effect',[80] that is their ability to generate other changes in the *same direction*, without creating too much discrepancy and resistance. Valsiner advocates that 'it is the direction of meaning construction – rather than the actual meanings constructed – that can tell us something about development',[81] in so far as it mediates the construction of the range of possible future life course trajectories.

It is clear that reconceptualization IMs have an amplifying effect in a given direction, aggregating other IMs in that new developmental path.

### *Reconceptualization as an integration of opposing self-narratives*

What is at stake in reconceptualization is a contrast between the old position and the emergent one. The restraints involved in the old position are rendered visible, as Szasz suggested, by a process of 'meta-education', through which the person has disengaged from the rules of behaviour learned by proto-education. The new position is clearly involved in a rejection of these restraints, by depicting how things could be different from what they were before. In fact, the content of a reconceptualization is usually something like 'before I did/thought/believed/felt X', X being the restraints of the former self-narrative; 'but now I do/think/believe/feel Y'. Moreover, the person knows how to pass from X to Y, which represents the meta-level position or, using Szas's terminology, the meta-education process. This level allows the integration of the old and the new, by creating a bridge that connects the past with the present (suggesting also some future paths), through the description of the process of change. The access to the change process operates as a historical bridge between past and present, avoiding the fragmentation of the self.

However, if the person had constructed something like 'I was X (depressed, for instance) and now I'm Y (cheerful)', this would create an enormous risk of fragmentation, as this self-narrative account is similar to a disorganized or chaotic narrative. It is precisely the meta-position involved in the comprehension of the process that, in turn, allowed the move from X (depressed) to Y (cheerful) that allows fragmentation to be escaped and allows for the construction of an integrated account of the new self-narrative. In a sense reconceptualization is the opposite of the mutual in-feeding process. In the latter there is a movement between two opposing dualities, without any transformation in either of them; in

[80] Watzlawick, Weakland and Fisch (1974). [81] Valsiner (2008a, p. 3).

the former the dualities are integrated by a third position (the metaposition).[82]

*Reconceptualization as performance of change*

As we have been discussing, one of the main features of reconceptualization is the metaposition involved in it, which allows the self-observation of one's change process. Such transformational power of self-observation has been present in the psychotherapy literature for a long time. Hence, Ouspensky referred to it more than sixty years ago:

> In observing himself a man notices that self-observation itself brings about certain changes in his inner processes. He begins to understand that self-observation is an instrument of self-change, a means of awakening. By observing himself he throws, as it were, a ray of light on to his inner processes, which have hitherto worked in complete darkness. And under the influence of this light the processes themselves begin to change.[83]

In the psychotherapy literature there are several constructs very close to the concept of self-observation.[84] Clearly, *insight* is one of those concepts, and there has been a long tradition of seeing insight as curative, at least since the work of Freud,[85] and can be defined as 'a conscious meaning shift involving new connections'.[86] Although *reconceptualization* and *insight* overlap, their definitions are different: reconceptualization, like insight, involves a 'meaning shift involving new connections', but reconceptualization necessarily involves past, present and a connection between them by a metaposition that describes a process. Moreover, there are reflection IMs (mainly level 2, see Figure 6.4) that clearly fit the notion of insight provided above better than reconceptualization.

The kind of processes suggested by White and Szasz may actually involve, not only an insight, but also an *outsight*,[87] in the sense that what is discovered is inside as well as outside the self, that is, in the societal and cultural rules that organized proto-education. From this perspective,

[82] See Ribeiro and Gonçalves (2011).

[83] Ouspensky (1949/2001), quoted in Hayes and Cruz (2006, p. 282). Note the representationalist stance of this quotation: self-observation brings light into darkness . . . Of course, one may wonder what kind of light is this and how it is created. What would be the features of a non-representationalist position on self-observation?

[84] Mentalization (Fonagy, Gergely, Jurist and Target, 2005) and meta-cognition (see Dimaggio, Salvatore, Azzara & Catania, 2003) are other constructs that can easily be related to self-observation.

[85] See Messer and McWilliams (2007) for a development of this argument.

[86] Hill *et al.* (2007, p. 442).

[87] See Gonçalves and Salgado (2006).

when the narrative restraints are rendered visible through reconceptualization, a process of 'illuminating' the way these societal rules were internalized takes place. In psychotherapy there are two extreme positions: one that states that insight is necessary and leads to therapeutic change (e.g. early psychoanalysts) and the other that claims that action leads to insight and not the reverse (e.g. strategic therapists). Gelso and Harbin[88] suggest that probably both paths are possible: as a person has new insights the ability to act differently is enhanced, but as that person experiences new actions, new understandings will occur. We might say that the interaction between some forms of reflection and action (or protest) IMs represents such a bidirectional process. However, we believe that at a certain point in time reconceptualization needs to emerge and to be developed in order for level 3 changes to take place. In other words, insight needs to be involved in a reconceptualization process, as we described above, in order for development to occur.

From our perspective, reconceptualization involves more than self-observation, although meta-cognitive abilities are certainly necessary for reconceptualization to emerge: it necessarily entails a performance of agency and compromise.[89] The emergence of IMs is always a matter of deviation from the familiar. When they emerge, the restraints of the former self-narrative are challenged. We propose that this challenge operates on two levels, the one represented by action, protest and reflection IMs; the other being a meta-level represented by reconceptualization IMs. In the first, the person challenges the rules of the former narrative, without developing a clear compromise with a new way of being. The meta-level involved in reconceptualization IMs allows an emergence of a clear compromise between one position (the narrating one) and the self (that is, the other I-positions). Thus, we are suggesting that the self involves two interrelated processes: the content being narrated and the act of narration. Similarly, Wortham suggests that an alignment between these two components (the content and the narration act) can be a very powerful way to create a particular view of the self:

> While telling their stories, auto-biographical narrations often enact a characteristic type of self, and to such performance they become that type of self.[90]

The meta-process involved in reconceptualization allows the development of this performance, the repetition of this performance being a

[88] Gelso and Harbin (2007).

[89] This view would allow escaping the representationalist view of self-observation's power, see note 83.

[90] Wortham (2001, p. xii).

very powerful way of asserting a new self-narrative. One could ask why reconceptualization continues to appear until a new stable self-narrative emerges. Precisely because one needs to experience the change before it becomes familiar. The repetition of reconceptualization IMs marks a transition in which a person explores a new state of affairs, a potential new self-narrative, or if you prefer, a new form of living. That is why other cycles of action, reflection, and protest IMs emerge again, prompting new reconceptualizations and so on. The change process is not linear but circular. Note that if the only thing that mattered was the content of the narrative, only *one* reconceptualization would be necessary to change. But clearly this is not the case*; repetition is a central process in changing our lives.*[91]

### *Social recognition in change*

The performance of reconceptualization in psychotherapy is not only an internalized process between the position that narrates and the other positions that operate as audience, but also between the narrating position and an external other: the therapist. The therapist is an involved partner who is supposed to facilitate the exploration of new positions. Thus, the repetition of reconceptualization IMs having the therapist as interlocutor is certainly another form of consolidating the change process. We could certainly assume that besides the therapist there are other people – significant others – who are positioned as an audience for this performance. In that sense, social recognition is likely to play an important role in change and development. Of course this role is itself mediated by the local frame.

In a four-month longitudinal study on how people – who were not in psychotherapy – change in their daily lives, we found that reconceptualization emerged mainly in the last session, when the interviewer asked questions about the experienced change process.[92] Thus, it is interesting that the majority of reconceptualization IMs emerge by the explicit invitation of the interviewer, unlike what happens in psychotherapy. However, people who rated the change experienced during that period

[91] Cunha *et al.* (in press) explored through a case-study how this repetition is a form of consolidating a progressive identification with a new self-narrative and a process of disengagement with the old one. In this case-study, even after the emergence of reconceptualization IMs, a back and forth movement between the old and the new narrative kept on going, suggesting the need that a person has to slowly accommodate the changing process.

[92] Meira, Gonçalves, Salgado and Cunha (2009).

as a *minor* were not able to elicit reconceptualization IMs, even when prompted by the interviewer.

One way to interpret these differences between therapeutic and daily life change is that the therapist is a much more involved partner than an interviewer, regularly inviting clients to *play* with life-change and, thus, a performance of reconceptualization emerges at the middle phase of good outcome cases. In a more neutral context, like in this research, in which the interviewer assumes a more peripheral role, we can speculate that when reconceptualization emerged, it did so in the presence of significant others, more involved in the change process (e.g. family, friends). Only when clearly invited by the interviewer, in the last session of the project (that is, when the relational context for the performance of change was created), did people who had changed meaningfully elicit reconceptualization IMs. It is very likely that if those IMs were prompted before by the interviewer they would have emerged, as happens in psychotherapy.

### *Reconceptualization IMs and change*

Summarizing the argument developed in this section, we propose that reconceptualization IMs:

1 create a developmental direction to the more molecular IMs;
2 promote the integration of the old and the new emergent self, preventing a sense of self fragmentation; and
3 involve the performance of change between one part of the self and the rest of it, and between oneself and others, thus consolidating the identification with the new emergent self.

We also proposed that an *authoring position* is more than the mere access to the process of change, that is, the meta-level position. Furthermore, it necessarily involves the three elements: directionality, integration of the old and the new and the performance of change.

## Summary: therapeutic change and life development

In this chapter we have explored how a narrative metaphor of the self can inform our understanding of change and stability in people's lives. The majority of our proposals were constructed from research done in the territory of psychotherapy, and some are more speculative than others. However, if psychotherapy can be seen as a special setting for producing change and development, it is also quite likely that some of the processes observed here also occur, to some extent, in other settings. Hence it is worth exploring how these processes apply in developmental trajectories.

A first important question is how much these findings can be applied to daily life transitions: transitions are periods that demand adjustment to new situations in people's lives, and these in turn demand change. It may be worth exploring how much reconceptualization assumes the same importance in other frames and settings that it does in psychotherapy. Our intuition is that reconceptualization is a universal process involved in self-narrative changes. If these processes occur in daily life, it would then be interesting to know whether they occur similarly in changes triggered by expected ruptures (e.g. having children when it was planned) and by unexpected ruptures (e.g. suddenly losing a job).

A second question, linked to the previous one, can be raised: does something similar to reconceptualization occur in life changes that are not narratively structured – for instance motor development in childhood, or the decline of motor functions in old age? If most changes which come to people's consciousness are likely to trigger semiotic process, only some types of change may demand the sort of meaning changes structured by narratives. In these cases, our guess is that whenever people give meaning to a significant life-change – especially in adult life – that prompts a narrative construction, reconceptualization is likely to occur. However, in other periods of life and other skills (e.g. development of cognitive abilities), narrative construction may not be required or happen only as a post-fact occurrence, if at all.

One of the most fascinating issues that the development of human lives poses to our scientific explanations is precisely how people transform themselves, being actors and authors of these transformations.

# 7 Paradoxes of learning

We change through life – and do so thanks to the role of cultural means, which mediate our ability to remember, imagine, anticipate, act and interact. All this happens in the course of confronting the ever-new tasks that our continuous exploration of the environment creates for us. Moreover, our actions result in change – of the environment and of ourselves.

Change in our lives may imply development, but not all change translates into development,[1] as demonstrated widely in this book (see the difference between levels of change, mutual in-feeding as examples of non-development changes,[2] etc.). However, if everything changes and is potentially developing, can we also say that everything constitutes *learning*? The topic of learning has occupied the minds of psychologists ever since Edward Lee Thorndike made it important at the end of nineteenth century. Yet despite the fact that the term 'learning' has been prominent in psychology over the twentieth century, its meaning is still unclear.

Knowledge is not something that is *transmitted* from a teacher to a learner: it is always constructed, or *reconstructed*, in the process of teaching and learning – with innovations emerging from the previously established knowledge (see Figure 7.1). If person A is in the role of the teacher (the more knowledgeable Other) who attempts to communicate the established knowledge (X′) to the learner ('novice' – person B), the knowledge becomes transformed into a new state (X″) in this process of *joint reconstruction* due to the active role of the learner (B). In effect, as shown by the bottom arrow from B to X′, the actions of B will not only contribute to the construction of his own learning, but may also transform the knowledge being taught (or the modalities of teaching, as when students' 'resistance' to learning maths brings teachers to define a new programme), and perhaps even person A in his experience of being a teacher or a

[1] Cf. definition of development of Carolina Consortium on Human Development (1996), Chapter 1.

[2] For 'levels of change', see chapter 5; for 'mutual in-feeding', see Chapter 6.

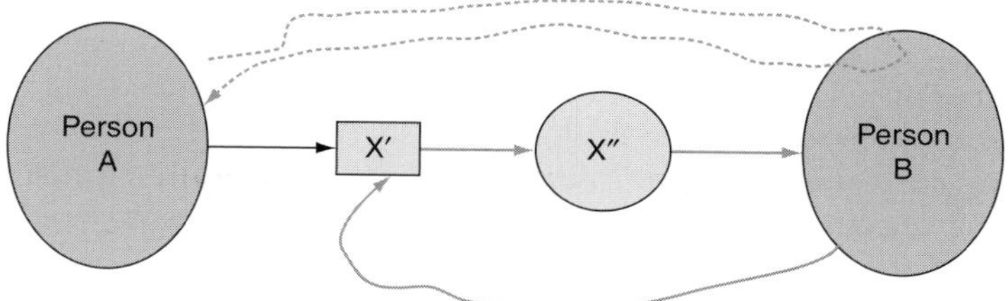


Figure 7.1 Communication as mutuality of construction: emergence of novelty.

person.[3] So in what sense does person B 'learn from' person A – and what is it that is 'being learned' – X′ or X″? And if such a model might account for the way in which children learn at school or adults learn in the workplace, learning is much more than this. We can learn from a book, from the contemplation of insects or from life. This is what we have to account for.

*Teaching as power?* Built upon animal models – of Pavlov's dogs, Watson's ideological claims and Skinner's pigeons – the traditional notion of learning implies a unidirectional model of knowledge transfer. A similar view is present in the commonsense understanding of knowledge. Within that view it is assumed that there is somebody who knows (the teacher, the parent, the government) who 'brings knowledge' to the learner. This unidirectional knowledge transfer model is based on the implicit *social power differential* that is in force here. The powerful – who have full control over the fate of the powerless – assume that they have the possibility of 'pouring knowledge' into the minds of novices who are assumed to take the form of a tabula rasa.

The unidirectional 'transmission' model is privileged by the power of social institutions that attempt to subordinate human minds to their rules. These institutions – at least in their public self-reflections – overlook the active role of the subordinate 'novices' who – within their limited freedom of movement – can neutralize, resist or reorganize the 'knowledge bombs' thrown at them. The recurrent discourses about the 'downfall of our educational systems' or the 'moral decay of the next generation' that can be heard from power holders (parents, teachers, politicians, activist moralists, etc.) are a reflection of the inefficiency of the unidirectional transfer model. The socially powerful blame the

3 See discussions of the notion of co-regulation in Chapter 5, and below.

actively resisting powerless 'novices' for not performing as well as they expect. This unidirectional conception is clearly monological, as if people could be instructed from the 'outside' and were devoid of any agency. We encountered earlier in this book several theoretical positions that deny the possibility of transferring knowledge without a transformation of the 'transferred' content: dialogical perspectives on the one hand, but also on the other hand systemic theories that conceptualize people (and groups) as self-organized systems (that is, determined by their own parameters, constrained by external conditions but not determined by them).

Yet it is precisely these resisting and counteracting learners who transcend the knowledge base of powerful teachers – as the history of technological advancement has amply demonstrated. A high-school 'drop-out' or poor performer may become the inventor of a new technological device that changes the world – benefiting from his or her innovative recombination of the available knowledge ($X'$ in Figure 7.1) and creating new, previously unknown, versions ($X''$).

*Beyond the narrow look at learning:* the traditional unidirectional view of knowledge transfer has been present in the version of developmental psychology that centres on children – as schoolteachers, parents and all kinds of social institutions carry further the symbolic glory of the teacher's role. The traditional focus has been on schools and on children who relate to whatever happens in schools. However, with rapid technological advances it is becoming increasingly clear to adults that they also have to learn constantly – the traditional power differential is being changed. The social and technological, as well as the ecological environment changes; and children themselves develop skills far beyond those of adults in relation to technological objects. A teenager who teaches the classroom teacher or parent how to use a new technological gadget reverses the teacher/learner social power role. The traditional view that adults know more than children can be questioned.

We need new definitions and understandings of learning. For instance, as part of a recent attempt to summarize efforts in that respect, the concept of learning has been defined as: 'any process that in living organisms leads to *permanent capacity change* and which *is not solely due* to biological maturation or ageing'[4]. This effort to make sense of learning is paradoxical as it includes the vague negative marker ('not solely due') aside from the usual focus on change that becomes permanent. Any attempt to define learning raises the question of the relationship between

[4] Illeris (2009, p. 3, added emphasis).

learning and development, an old question in psychology and the educational sciences.[5]

To address development in the lifecourse, we first have to open that discussion again: if science still does not know much about how people develop and learn as adults and older persons, this means that it has generated 'intellectual blinkers' that it uses to avoid the general nature of the phenomenon. Many scientists and practitioners admit today that adults in the mid-years or older need to learn continuously – but what does that mean in the real life-worlds of teachers and learners alike? And, when the learner – an adult – is also one's own teacher, the social power differential is eroded. Looking at learning during the whole life course will thus help us to understand some of the variations of life-course development.

## Defining learning, in contradistinction to development

There is a long-standing debate in psychology and the educational sciences about the relationship between learning and development. The debate has different social-institutional histories – the question of learning has been historically created in the framework of schooling, while the issues of development came to psychology through discourses in embryology, evolution and natural philosophy. The interests of the first notable developmental thinkers – William Preyer, Charles Darwin, Alfred Russell Wallace, James Mark Baldwin and Henri Bergson – were all far from the concerns of educators in the context of school learning. Their primary focus was on development in biology.

Development is often considered as *change including the biological and psychological maturation of the individual, usually seen in its interaction with the environment.* This fits with the natural-philosophical history of the concept. In contrast, learning is often seen as *the acquisition of specific skills and knowledge by a person, mostly through specific interactions with the environment.* The implied environment is first of all any kind of school-type environment where somebody is involved in efforts of teaching – a teacher, a parent or a peer. In some cases, learning is seen as relatively

[5] The problem has also been prominent in biology – Alexei Severtsov's (or in German version Sewertzoff) distinction between *idioadaptations* (changes in the biological species under pressures of environmental changes that will not be permanent when the pressures are gone) and *aromorphoses* (changes that become permanent – Sewertzoff, 1929) is an example. The question of development becomes that *of conditions under which idioadaptations are maintained when the environmental pressures are no longer in place.* Likewise, learning in psychology leads to development if it is maintained outside the institutional contexts of education.

superficial and short lived, while development is considered to be deeper and more long-standing.[6] Learning can be 'lost' – authors usually admit that people seem at times to 'unlearn', that they seem to forget what they have learned. In contrast, it is impossible to say that people 'undevelop'.[7] The developmental process may involve seeming reversals that look like 'losses', but such regressions are themselves a crucial part of development. Human development – as well as biological or social development – is irreversible.[8]

*Learning, unlearning, and forgetting:* Development can, however, also be viewed in terms of ruptures in the life course. Is it not the case that people sometimes 'regress' – when they seem to 'forget' to behave as educated adults and cry and feel helpless like children, or when they quit their wives and jobs to look for their lost teenage freedom? Temper tantrums, whining, getting drunk, dramatization of moral performances in social contexts, etc. are examples of carnivalesque temporary transformations of the ordinary functioning at a person's expected developmental level.[9] As such they are an integral part of epigenesis, that is, of each person's history. The social functions of such displays are established in social power games. The developing person can act AS IF he or she were in some previous state of development. Under some circumstances such 'acting out' of 'childish ways' is positively socially sanctioned – a father involved in play with his child on the floor, displaying complementary actions as if he were a child could be seen as a 'good father'. If the same father took such playful ways of acting to his workplace he might lose his job or end up in a psychiatric facility. In any case, such behaviour will, one way or the other, have an impact on the further development of the individual.

On the other hand, we may ask, do people really 'unlearn', that is, completely lose once established skills or integrated knowledge, or do they simply *not use* knowledge? The readiness to exercise one's will – intentionality – as the organizer of actions makes it possible to refrain from using some already established psychological functions. Furthermore, we all seem to forget our once learned knowledge. Yet that does not undermine development. Probably any adult who has been through school would miserably fail any examination on school knowledge if tested many years later. Much of the exact knowhow that was

[6] Granott (1998, p. 17). [7] Mercer and Littleton (2007, p. 4).

[8] As seen in Chapter 1, development follows the principle of epigenesis – at any moment the developmental 'state' of an individual is dependent on the chain of previous states ('state' is here to be considered as a figure of speech, as a living organism will never be in an immutable condition at a standstill).

[9] Carnivalesque inversions have been identified by the literary critic Bakhtin (1984) as well as by anthropologists.

mastered at school has been forgotten, yet that is also part of epigenesis. The present job situation of any individual is most certainly dependent on that individual's educational history. The impact of school learning becomes transferred into ever new forms through adulthood – an educated person develops new ways of approaching the world, while most of the actual knowledge acquired from the process of 'becoming educated' becomes a background for the acquisition of new knowledge and skills. The history of the individual consists of reorientations and specializations, depending on the circumstances, including life transitions. Furthermore, the individual can deliberately decide what kind of knowledge, is to be used in any given situation and refrain from acting in knowledgeable ways. Here is the problem: if someone does not use knowledge, how do we as outsiders know that he or she has actually learned it in the first place? The absence of never-acquired knowledge, the loss of once-present knowledge and the intentional non-use of knowledge may all look similar from the outside.

*How does* learning *relate to* development? Fundamentally, the relationship between learning and development depends on the definitions of learning and development that one adopts.[10] 'Cognitive' theories of learning, which mainly examine cognitive schemata or brain functions in learning or solving tasks, generally consider that the brain needs to have some maturational basis for specific forms of knowledge acquisition to happen. On this basis, learning can be studied quite independently from development: one can learn specific behaviour or acquire certain schemes without this being regarded as development. The 'socio-constructivist' tradition of learning studies admits the mutual dependency between biological development and social interactions in learning. In this tradition interactions participate in the construction of competencies, where as previously these were seen as simply 'accelerating' processes that were otherwise meant to be biological – which suggests that learning and development are the 'two faces of the same coin'.[11] More recent approaches in the so-called 'learning sciences' try to combine discoveries in the fields of neuroscience, sociocultural theory and research on learning–teaching design; they tend to examine how teaching–learning situations and their biological substrate interact, although their programme is more about increasing learning than development.[12]

[10] See for instance Schunk (2003) for an overview.

[11] As phrased by Charis Psaltis (Psaltis, Duveen and Perret-Clermont, 2009). This tradition has for instance consistently shown that peer work can substantially increase the complexity of tasks that a child can later solve alone (Perret-Clermont, Carugati and Oates, 2004), and has explored the social and relational conditions facilitating these dynamics.

[12] Bransford *et al.* (2009).

Learning *as a dynamic system:* from the perspective of DST, learning may be conceived as the self-organization of earlier and present experiences into an attractor basin in the *microgenetic*[13] context of a particular function or task, as opposed to the *ontogenetic*[14] or sociogenetic or macrogenetic contexts of development.[15]

A dynamic understanding can help to account for observations of children's learning. The fact that a five-months-old child looks for a toy under the pillow where it used to be hidden, although the child observed how it was hidden under a second pillow, has been called an A-not-B error (the child looks under the 'wrong' pillow). In a reading *à la* Piaget,[16] the child is *lacking* the understanding that the toy has a permanent existence (she seems not to know that the object is still the same in its new location); yet the critics of such interpretation considered that the child has manifested *having* such knowledge (the childs seems to think that 'the same' object should be under 'the same' pillow).[17] This discrepancy of views is a good example of the developmental (Piaget) and non-developmental (his critics) orientations – whether an infant at age A 'has' (or 'does not have') function X is a basically non-developmental question. Most of our contemporary child and infant psychology has been asking non-developmental questions (e.g. 'do infants <younger that we believed before> *have* X?'). Behind such questions is the axiomatic belief in predeterminism in the unfolding of the inherent 'developmental course,' rather than an epigenetic view. In contrast, the epigenetic perspective starts with Baldwin's and Piaget's focus on how development happens, through emergence, between the states of X not being present and its becoming present.

Esther Thelen and her collaborators, adopting an approach inspired by DST, propose an alternative interpretation of the same observation. For them, both conclusions are wrong, as they presuppose that object permanence resides in a mental representation of the object. Instead of attributing the A-not-B error to a lack of knowledge in terms of some inner symbolic structure, Thelen and her collaborators propose to consider the system constituted by the child and her contexts of experience.

13 Learning episodes are specific events in the person's life – *microgenetic* events where novel construction unfolds in real time.

14 *Ontogenetic* in the sense of taking place at the scale of the person's situated life development.

15 Implying a transformation of the context itself, up to cultural learning – 'in humans, emergence of collective cultural frameworks for regulating person-environment encounters' (Valsiner, 1997, p. 169).

16 Piaget (1952).

17 Baillargeon and De Vos (1991); Baillargeon, Spelke and Wasserman (1985).

In a first part of the task, the child is exposed to the repeated hiding of the toy under the first pillow. The child can be said to be learning that the toy is hidden under the first pillow – it creates in the child a strong attractor guiding behaviour. The younger child relies on this attractor, and although the context changes in the second part of the task – toy changes pillow – the child fails to take the change into account. In order for that to happen, the child needs to reorganize her perception that the habituation attractor is coordinated with a visual attractor of the actual placement of the toy; the attractor has to be reorganized with the context change.

From this dynamic system perspective, the difference between the younger and the older child is not a change in cognitive function; rather, both draw upon resources from earlier experiences and the present situation. However, they organize these resources differently, one organization being more adaptive than the other. One might thus think that the more experiences the child accumulates, and the more he practises a certain organization of these resources, the more skilled he will be in finding flexible solutions to similar, yet at the same time different, tasks.

In such understanding, then, *learning is seen as the adequate transformation of patterns of interactions between a person and her environment, enabled by the person's identification and use of relevant resources*. This example also suggests that, very often, identifying which 'learning' occurs depends on the unit of analysis chosen by the observer.[18]

## Learning together with its counterpart: the whole of *obuchenie*

Lev Vygotsky (1896–1934) also linked the issues of the *microgenetic* contexts of learning with the *macrogenetic* contexts of development. He proposed the notion of *obuchenie* to link these two levels of development. *Obuchenie* denotes a 'complex', and can be translated as the *teaching–learning–complex* (TLC). It entails both *active learning* (by the pupil) and *active teaching* (by another person). The latter, however, need not be manifest – the avid reader will learn the wisdom from a book written by some author even hundreds of years earlier. Or the active learner can be subject to *obuchenie* in a context for individual learning that is set up to guide him/her to some new knowledge. The whole process of *obuchenie* is depicted in Figure 7.2.

[18] Hence the observer focusing on the system constituted by the cognitive schemes of the child sees reorganization of cognitive schemes as learning, while the observer that sees the child–environment interaction considers learning as a reorganization of these relationships.

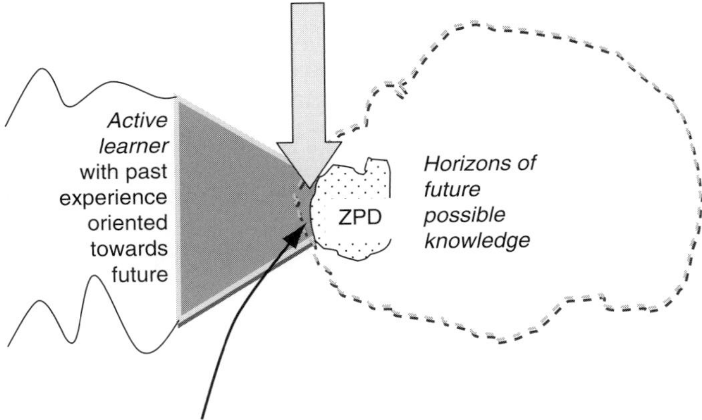


Figure 7.2 The teaching–learning complex (TLC) – *obuchenie*.

As depicted in Figure 7.2, the learning process is that of individual learners who – while actively oriented towards the future – carry into any here-and-now teaching/learning setting their past experiences. The local setting – microgenetic locus for *obuchenie* – is guided by one or two social organizational forms. The macro-social context is always present in the learner's efforts – human learning is inevitably embedded in a socially structured environment. Yet despite the social organization, the horizons of future possible knowledge are never fixed. No matter how much a social system of a political, religious or educational kind tries to fix what 'required knowledge' is, the learner moves beyond these limits through active imagination and experimentation.

The other form of social guidance – a specific agent (human or other) in the teacher's role – may be present as well. Yet the presence of that immediate 'teacher' is not mandatory – a learner will be involved in *obuchenie* even in solitude, yet always in a state of social embeddedness. A person rises above his or her current knowledge with the help of another agent – or without (i.e. by solitary, personal learning).

At the intersection of the activities of the learner in relation to the field of future knowledge is the *zone of proximal development* (ZPD).[19] This is a

[19] This concept dates back to Lev Vygotsky's work in 1933–4. For a full history see Van der Veer and Valsiner (1991) and Van der Veer and Valsiner (1993).

field (dynamically changing zone) of *these psychological functions that are currently in the process of formation* but are not yet established. The person creates the ZPD in play (in the case of children) or in imagination (in the case of adolescents or adults), or – possibly – in the interaction with others. The latter – social embedding – is an enabling but not determinative feature of ZPD. As a notion, ZPD is thus situated 'in' the person, or more exactly, at the boundaries of what the person is and what he or she may become: it is in effect always relative to the past history of the learner's knowledge, and linked with the immediate future possibilities. In that temporal sense, ZPD occurs at points of bifurcation and creation of future pathways, as captured by the TEM model (see above, Chapter 5 and Figure 5.6). Finally, from a spatial perspective, it is essentially a term centred on the active, developing person, who creates that zone in the context of relating to always uncertain environments.

On the basis of the Vygotskian heritage, one tradition in learning psychology and educational sciences of the latter half of the twentieth century has largely focused on the role of assistance from the other in the TLC. ZPD has thus been used to study and explore the learning and development of children and young adults in informal and formal settings – family, school and the workplace – where the role of more able others or experts can be clearly defined; a parent, the peer group, co-workers, teachers or trainers participate in the creation of a ZPD and enable – or disenable – the less able to learn and develop, through participation, collaboration and co-construction.[20] Without doubt developing human beings closely relate to social groups, develop affective ties with other persons, are guided by the features of specific frames and are perceptive of cultural codes embedded within the environment. In the view of Vygotsky, however, the entity that develops – from birth to death – is the person him- or herself. The social Other is an independent counterpart that acts through the culturally structured environment.

*Learning–teaching as mutual co-regulation:* one way to overcome the misleading idea that ZPD necessarily requires a more skilled partner to guide a less skilled is to see TLC as co-regulation. First of all, the presence of a physically existing 'social other' for TLC is not a necessary condition for learning. Yet this presence surely has a guiding role. Secondly, when learning and teaching involve a dyad (or a group), not only do the persons change, the dyad itself has a history of change. In such a case, each person has a story as a learner; and the two persons involved have a history of *shared experiences*, especially if their dyad takes place in a continuous

[20] For instance Perret-Clermont, Carugati and Oates (2004); Mercer and Littleton (2007); Wells (1999).

relationship, and not as a unique interaction.[21] This history sets the frame of the interactions, and hence may constrain the unfolding of the interaction (microgenesis) and the evolution of the frame itself (macrogenesis). Fogel describes such dyadic interactions as implying *co-regulation*:[22] 'Co-regulation occurs whenever individuals' joint actions blend together to achieve a unique and mutually created set of social actions'.[23]

In a teacher-learner dyad this means that the two partners might together achieve a result that neither of them would have been able to achieve alone. An asymmetric understanding of the teacher–learner relationship is thus replaced by a mutuality scheme. Yet this mutuality does not mean that learning is 'the same' on either side. Rather, it suggests that both teacher and learner can profit from the interaction, but in different ways, as they have different developmental histories. Such analysis invites us to consider not only the development of individual learners, but also the development of a dyad, or group, in the setting of a particular frame – most often itself developing. Thus, whether the description focuses on the interacting dyad and its frame, or on the varying zones of movement they generate, TLC can be seen as implying dynamic co-regulations.[24]

*Overcoming the symmetry* versus *asymmetry problem: co-regulation and resource use:* descriptions of TLC dynamics face a recurrent problem: on the one hand, there is necessarily an asymmetry between the learner and the teacher; yet on the other hand, co-regulation implies mutuality of the teacher–learner relationship. In theories based on the idea of a unilinear *transmission* of knowledge or skill from teacher to learner, the problem is simply bypassed. Yet in more dynamic approaches, this double relationship has to be accounted for.

One solution to this problem is to consider that the system is constituted not only by a learner and a teacher, but by a learner, a teacher and a certain object of knowledge. Once the TLC is described as a *triadic* relationship,[25] there is much more room for each person to develop his or her own relationship to the object of knowledge, and/or to the other person. The 'teacher' may be more knowledgeable in respect of the object, yet the 'learner' and the 'teacher' may still have a relationship of

[21] Hinde, Perret-Clermont and Stevenson-Hinde (1985).
[22] Fogel (1993a, 1997).
[23] Fogel (1993a, p. 6).
[24] A clear example of this is the experience of every teacher teaching a new subject. The organization of the teaching is obviously a new opportunity for the teacher to understand in a deeper way what he or she already knew before. In this case, as the teacher prepares his or her classes the subject of the teaching is transformed.
[25] Houssaye (2000).

mutuality.[26] The teacher may mediate the learner's relationship to the object, or the learner may need to 'use' the teacher as a resource.

### *The structure of social guidance in the TLC*

The idea of TLC admits the 'Other' of the learning dynamic to be an absent other, an imagined other or even a generalized other. Any situation in which a person acts in her social and cultural environment may be an occasion for learning. In such cases, the 'other' is a generalized, abstract yet pervasive, *social guide*. Under this social guidance, the 'objects of knowledge' can become resources for the learning and development of the learner; the teacher himself may be used by the learner, for his skills and expertise toward the object, as a person resource in the learning endeavour. These perspectives thus invite us to examine how a learner identifies and uses what is available, in his zone of free movement, as a resource to support his own learning. They also invite us to consider the conditions in which such autonomous use of resources is possible – what can be the teacher's role in enabling such a process, what sorts of co-regulation foster learning and what frames support it.[27]

In the life-course perspective, who is an expert – and for what – becomes relative; a particular person, in some capacity, may be acknowledged as a possible resource, to solve certain tasks, under some conditions, by another person.[28] Hence, co-regulation invites us to separate expertise from social status, and to see them as dialogical, situated properties that can always be negotiated and redefined.

## How social guidance works

That social guidance is important in human development over the whole life course – and across individual life courses in history – is no surprise to anybody. Yet, while accepting its central role, the social sciences have a very limited understanding of how such guidance works. The

[26] The differentiated relationship can also be seen as an asymmetrical relationship to the object of knowledge, accompanied by a symmetrical *mutual recognition* of each person by the other, and of each other's specific object use (Zittoun, in press).

[27] Among many see the whole educational movement inspired by Dewey (1916). See also, for instance, Bjørgen (1993), Little (1995), and Yang (1998).

[28] As shown by the studies exploring the role of peer interactions in development, and the complex conditions in which children perceive the other as 'equal' and to what extent (Nicolet, 1995; Muller Mirza and Perret-Clermont, 1999; Perret-Clermont, 1980; Psaltis and Duveen, 2006; Psaltis, Duveen and Perret-Clermont, 2009, etc.).

developmental theoretical model developed by one of us (JV) over the past three decades[29] – based on the notion of selective limiting of uncertainty (constraining) – may be applicable here for understanding the phenomenon over the whole life course.

The basis of the model is the observation that developing systems – as open systems – can only be approximately guided in some directions (rather than others). The actual developmental course will be constructed by active individuals – creating their personal cultural world as a *bricolage* at the intersection of all social suggestions. The model consists of three zones, the zone of free movement (ZFM), the zone of promoted action (ZPA) and the ZPD.[30]

*The ZFM:* this model is rooted in other theoretical systems. The ZFM has affinities to Kurt Lewin's region concept – it denotes an approximately given region of what could happen – in contrast to what is 'ruled out' and cannot happen. It is a *socially constructed cognitive structure of person–environment relationships.*[31] It is *social*, as it is based on the social suggestions from others – the teacher or parent or a policeman may stipulate for the learner what is allowed and what is not allowed. It is *cognitive*, as it is co-created by the active person (who builds personal relations with the environment through *bricolage*, that is, assembling varying relationships into an integrated whole to be reflected upon). It focuses on *relating to the world*, as the person constantly acts upon the environment, attempting to extend or modify the boundaries of the ZFM.

The difference of the ZFM from Lewin's earlier life space model[32] is that the ZFM (and the whole ZFM–ZPA–ZPD system) implies an ongoing interaction between persons acting within their social roles – the teacher and the learner, who constantly renegotiate these boundaries. Furthermore, various signs that organize the meaning of the environment participate in the interaction. Mutuality is thus a basic part of the ZFM. On this crucial point, this model distinguishes itself from Lewin's life space and concept of region by allowing *real* (as opposed to 'quasi') social facts into the person's life space.[33]

Finally, Lewin's notion of life space appears as a *closed system.*[34] However, this is only true for systemic causality, sharply distinguished by Lewin from historical causality. The present system transcends

[29] Valsiner (1987, 1997, 2007b).
[30] A modified version of Vygotsky's well-known concept, as seen above.
[31] Valsiner (1997, pp. 188–92). [32] See Chapter 5.
[33] As well as, by the way, vice versa, that is, the teacher–learner relationship is a *real* social fact also in the teacher's life space.
[34] Lewin (1936, p. 69): 'The psychological events are determined by the life space according to the formula B = f(S).'

Lewin's: *systemic causality here is both conditional and historical.*[35] That a person's life space at the next moment is built by the same person on the life space at the preceding moment makes the system *open.*[36] This is the historical focus of the development of the life space. Yet that development does not proceed solely from 'causes' in the past. Instead, it is constructed by considering the local conditions of the present, and anticipating conditions in the future – in co-regulation with the reconstructed past.

*The ZPA:* this a region within the life space of the teacher, implying what he or she wants the learner to do. This zone may be characterized by its directivity – the unilateral (as opposed to mutual) social suggestions involved:

> ZPA is a set of activities, objects, or areas in the environment, in respect of which the person's actions are promoted. Parents may get involved in special efforts to promote the child's actions with an object that they consider important for the child's development. The child may, but need not, be interested in interacting with that object.[37]

The ZPA is unilaterally defined by the teacher, parent or any other social power holder. Yet in its functioning it is also mutual – the recipient of the directed, suggested or promoted messages can construct a variety of life courses based on them. The recipient can *comply*, *neutralize* or *counter-act* the suggestions set in the ZPA. Since the ZPA (in contrast to the ZFM) boundaries are not obligatory limits,[38] such active relating to social suggestions is the usual state of affairs. We all utilize these counter-strategies to the ZPA on a daily basis – ignoring or countering those social suggestions that do not fit our current path of action.

The act of climbing by a child is a good example of how ZFM and ZPA can be encoded into the cultural properties of human-made objects. The specific object – meant for children in the playground (another cultural object) to climb up and slide down without getting hurt (its usual location in a sandbox) – sets up *climbing* and *sliding* as actions within the ZFM, ruling out jumping from the elevation (there are often protective barriers). Within the ZFM, the ZPA suggests the sequence of action in the direction climb the ladder→ slide down by the slide. However, the opposite action – a *counter-act* to ZPA – climb the slide→ climb down by the ladder is also possible. All over the world we can see such sliding devices in children's playgrounds – and all over the world we can observe children deeply

[35] Valsiner (2011).
[36] On the distinction between open and closed systems, see Chapter 1.
[37] Valsiner (1997, p. 192).
[38] The only condition where it becomes obligatory is if the ZFM = ZPA ('you must do X and X is the only thing you can do').

engaged in climbing up the slide side of these devices. Yet such counter-action to the ZPA – *as it is all within the ZFM* – *fortifies* the very ZFM–ZPA system.[39]

What looks different on the surface may work for similar objectives if considered in a wider framework. It is through the counter-action that the meanings of *both* socially suggested normative ways of being *and* their opposites are established. *Acting against a social norm works for the maintenance of that norm in ways coordinated with the promotion of the application of the norm itself.* It is only by neutralization of the given norm and its transformation into a new one that the old norm is successfully eliminated. Counter-acting a particular norm actually supports the very norm against which the counter-actors perform. The children's slide thus affords support for the existing social order in the case of children climbing in both directions. The attention of actors – children and parents – towards the possibility of constructing an alternative activity context in the same location, and on their own, is circumvented by the promotion of the action/counter-action system.

*The ZPD:* while the ZFM–ZPA system characterizes the social embeddedness of the person in the world, the ZPD concept – borrowed from Lev Vygotsky (see above Figure 7.2) but modified – links the social and biological functions of human development. ZPD 'entails the set of possible next states of the developing system's relationship with the environment, given the current state of the ZFM/ZPA complex and the system'.[40]

Within the ZPD, the ZPA will be constantly challenged by the current psychological functions-in-the-making of the developing person. This is one of the components that constrain the ZFM: the learner can only do what he or she is in the *process of becoming capable* of doing. If the teacher defines the ZPA outside the ZFM, the learning objective will fail. On the other hand, the ZPD defines a border condition, where the learner does not master a particular knowledge or skill by him- or herself, but will be able to do so with the support of the teacher.

*How the ZFM–ZPA–ZPD model transcends other models:* the contrast of this model with Lewin's and Vygotsky's models shows how the integration of two classic models into a new context can be theoretically productive. The third component – the ZPA – is an addition to both the ZFM and ZPD, giving them a joint structure and innovative role.

[39] The difference between totalitarian and democratic political systems can be phrased in simple terms – in totalitarian systems ZFM = ZPA, in democratic ones, ZFM > ZPA. This provides an explanation of the function of oppositional voices in democracies – their presence is necessary for the dominance of the social power.

[40] Valsiner (1997, p. 200).

First, unlike Lewin, we abandon the principle of the contemporaneous nature of all developmental factors, and the distinction between historical and systemic causality, and renounce the idea that the life space goes through a succession of states. Instead we allow for the flow of time and the continuous and uninterrupted development of the life space – the transformation of the life space with time. Henri Bergson's concept of *duration*,[41] defined in terms of what Lewin would have called psychological events, offers units of analysis in the life space. Also, we work with the methodological principle of DST according to which it is in the hand of the researcher to define what the system is and what is its environment. This has important implications for the analysis of social frames along the lines outlined above for the case of the teacher–learner relationship. We also need to assume social life spaces, not only psychological.

Second, we need to give a more explicit meaning to *dynamics* than Lewin did. For Lewin it was the influence of *forces* that made the system (life space) dynamic: 'The study of dynamics concerns the way forces apply and how they change and exert an influence on the world'.[42] This proposition holds as long as the system consists of only two entities, which is, from a formal point of view, a simple matter (e.g. a system consisting of one billiard ball in movement and another stationary one, the two colliding and the first ball setting the second in movement). However, if there are three entities influencing each other, the matter becomes much more complicated; this complexity actually led the French mathematician Poincaré to solutions that laid the foundation of dynamic systems approaches.[43]

Thus a dynamic system is *an ensemble of more than two entities where these entities continuously exert influence on each other over time*. The system would not be dynamic if the forces cancelled each other out, leading to an entropic, thermodynamic equilibrium. A dynamic system may achieve stability, but only if it is not a thermodynamic equilibrium. That would be the case if these forces balanced each other so that the system self-organized into the dynamic stability that we call an attractor state. If there is an imbalance between the forces in the system, the attractor will be destabilized, possibly changing into another attractor state, where the distribution of forces is different, and thus also where the self-organization will be different from that of the first attractor. To conclude, *dynamic means the same as for Lewin, only, more exactly formulated as a system of forces that exert mutual influences on each other over time, whether in stability or instability*. Dynamic systems may continue to strive towards the same attractor state

[41] As seen in Chapter 4. [42] Van Geert (2003, p. 643). [43] Van Geert (2003, p. 644).

over time, or they may be cyclical, oscillating between different attractor states,[44] or they may be truly developmental, that is, attractors may change in an epigenetic fashion, thus implying history. Our focus is the latter form of dynamic system, notably human systems. We have used a version of the epigenetic landscape metaphor to illustrate such a system.

Thirdly, we need to take into account the mutuality of *real* social interactions. We may accept the idea that social facts appear as quasi-social in the personal life space, where these are experienced by the person and have an effect on his behaviour. However, social interaction takes place between real people, and it is more than effects on the behaviour of the person. The zone model – presented here above – is based on *real* social interaction, where borders of the ZFM are negotiated between teacher and learner, and the ZPA is (or at least ought to be) continuously revised as the result of a continuous re-evaluation of the ZPD as learning progresses. Thus this model is based on an assumption of *mutuality* between teacher and learner. Likewise, and even more strongly emphasized, in Fogel's concept of co-regulation, also presented in this chapter, it is the *joint* actions of the parties that make possible the emergence of new information, of new meaning or new solutions to challenging tasks. Thus also new attractor states may be reached.[45]

As said above, a dynamic approach leaves the researcher free to decide on the scale of a system – and here, the scale of the dynamics between ZFM, ZPA and ZPD: we can focus on the whole learning situation, or alternatively focus on a personal trajectory.

If we want to understand how, from an outside perspective, the social world evolves, we can examine a situation and trace a history of earlier experiences, both within individuals and *between* – or *among* – individuals, that is, *histories of shared experiences*. Such histories of shared experiences are the basis for the development of social frames.

Yet as our goal is to understand the development of a person in the life course from an inside perspective, we need to see how a person becomes who she is, in present experience, through such shared history. Again, we can use Lewin's principle[46] according to which for a person here and now, experience is everything that has an effect on the present – whether it is conscious or not. For a child solving a task, this may include the hidden agenda of the school systems, the very clear expectations of parents based

44 There are many types of attractor, see Chapter 1 and, e.g., Milnor (1985).

45 'Meaning, similar to any other pattern formation process in a dynamic system, can be thought of as emerging and stabilizing dynamically through a process of self-organization' (Fogel, 2006, p. 8).

46 Lewin (1936, p. 19); see also Chapter 5 above.

on their own school failures, the child's own past experiences of math-solving, the friends with whom a school task is discussed, the colourful classroom, the background noise, the birds singing outside and the knowledge that she will play football in one hour. But what is a person's *accumulated life experience*? For Lewin, development is a progressive differentiation of one's experience.[47] Indeed, through all learning and development, something is developed, and that may imply accumulated and differentiated knowledge about life experiences.

*TLC and the human life course:* if we take TLC to be the central feature of learning, and if we admit that TLC and, in particular, ZPD can be generated in all kinds of situations, which are always social, then learning appears as a central feature of development, not only in childhood, but also in youth, adulthood and old age. Then, the particular forms of these ZPDs, and especially the resources that the person will use to generate and progress through these zones, will change as life progresses and experience is accumulated. This experience progressively crystallizes in an always evolving *personal life philosophy* (PLP) – a generalized reflection on life experience (see Box 7.1).

**Box 7.1 Personal life philosophy (PLP)**

The notion of PLP – personal life philosophy – emerges at the intersection of personalistic psychology (exemplified by William Stern) and contemporary sociocultural psychology which emphasizes the internalization of social suggestions through transforming them into new forms of subjectivity, and processes of generalization within the psychological lives of persons. The PLP is organized by *hyper-generalized semiotic mediators* – signs that capture vast areas of person–environment relations giving them meaning as wholes. For example, *values* (as we refer to our basic ethical stands in our everyday talk) guide a person through the whole life course, providing the basis both for individual accomplishments and merging with social units. We live by these values, but – given their hypergeneralized nature as signs-as-fields – we cannot describe them precisely. The PLP belongs to the realm of higher psychological functions (emphasized by Lev Vygotsky) and guarantees personal resilience across the life course – coping with all possible adverse circumstances. PLP is also a generic resource to deal with ruptures, as it organizes a person's repair of the destruction brought about by rupturing. PLP is the basis for personal resilience across diverse life circumstances.

[47] Lewin (1936), p. 155.

In adulthood, PLP enters as a part of the macro-social setting as the person moves through adulthood.[48] This is the *wisdom* – or the personal understanding of the living process itself – that starts to guide human learning over the life course. In the development of such personally co-constructed social guidance it may be the *less* knowledgeable 'social others' – one's own children or grandchildren – who provide an impetus for the advancing adult to enter into new knowledge domains.

### *Learning as a component of development*

Co-regulation means creativity, and may lead to the emergence of new meaning. However, co-regulation may also be hampered, along with creativity. In the approach outlined in this book, development is seen as emerging through the activity of a person as she tries to adjust to situations, remembering and anticipating, in interactions with others and the world. All this takes place through constant meaning-making, semiotic attractors emerging from the self-organization of past and present experiences. We literally go through the world creating meaning out of anything – or sometimes – out of (seemingly) nothing. Consider the view out of your window into the darkness of the night – nothing can be seen, but your imagination can create the meanings of *danger*, *pleasure*, etc. from the perceptual field of impending darkness. There is no 'thing-like' feature of such properties *in* that darkness – these feelings are created *in ourselves* as we relate to the environment. We observe such semiotic dynamics as the phenomena that enable us to understand how the social becomes psychological and the psychological social.

Like any human psychological function, meaning-making has biological substrates. Although in this book we do not directly examine the basis for these dynamics, we know from biological research that the anatomical and physiological features of our bodies enable and constrain our psychological functioning,[49] and that they can be modified by psychological and social dynamics. We basically recognize the extreme flexibility of human thought and action, where new possibilities of action are precisely generated by a person's activity in the social and symbolic environment. What is then reorganized is captured, at the semiotic level we have adopted here, as the reorganization of a person's capacities or semiotic system, where a

[48] See also Chapter 6 on life narratives.

[49] As seen in Chapter 1, enabling factors are also to be considered *constraints*, since the term designates everything that contributes to the trajectory of the ball in the epigenetic landscape – as a metaphor for the life course. See also Panksepp (1998), Rizzolatti and Sinigaglia (2008).

person develops more general, or more differentiated, or newly synthesized, ways of selecting, interpreting, organizing and transforming the traces of her action in the world. As a person faces new tasks, or situations that resist her actions or understanding, she engages in a form of *bricolage*, the soft assembly of resources from past and present experiences, both physical as well as social and symbolical resources in the environment.[50] This general capacity itself develops at a biological level, in terms of the transformation of a person's semiotic system, or at the more manifest level of a person's ability to engage in new *bricolage* in life.

Attempts at solving daily life tasks, as well as their outcomes, constitute new experiences that are commonly conceived as learning. Such experiences will be integrated into a person's history – and will be integrated into her earlier experiences, her identity, her PLP and her resources.

Consequently, learning can be considered as an integrated part of development; it usually designates the part of the process of development including the person's use of socially recognized chunks of knowledge (including activities such as sewing or drawing, reasoning, or retrieving learned-by-heart foreign words, names of organs or rules). In theoretical terms, studies traditionally devoted to learning can be seen as particular cases of development; and the study of acquiring life experience, rather than being limited to issues of developmental psychology, can also be seen as a particular case of learning from experience.

## Forms of learning

If learning is part of development, then, like development, learning is likely to occur in all kinds of situations, throughout life, and to be constrained by the dynamics of local interaction, and also by complex and diffuse forms of social guidance. Let us examine the diversity of learning – as recognized in research and beyond.

### *Formal learning*

Generally speaking, researchers and policy-makers consider institutional education and the school system as *formal learning*, in which activities are clearly organized with the purpose of teaching specific knowledge to learners. Formal learning is supposed to take place in specially established locations which are separated from their environment by visible (see Figure 7.3(a) and (b)) or invisible borders. Such separation reflects the

[50] See Chapter 1.

Figure 7.3 Boundaries of the institutions of formal learning: (a) entrance to a gymnasium in Berlin, Germany; (b) entrance to a school in Novos Alagados, Salvador, Bahia, Brazil.

history of formal education – to bring to the learners knowledge 'from afar', not available in – and at times not matching – informal education within the community.

Studies on formal learning mainly address learning and instruction in childhood and youth and consider these processes as they occur in the classroom. Historically viewed, it is clear that formal education is a missionary enterprise: it turns minds towards better futures – defined by the mission's goals. Educational efforts take place from the perspective of a social power that introduces new sets of activities – as well as often new symbolic locations such as churches, schools, mosques and madrasas – together with an elaborate system of canalization of these activities.[51] The combination of action-regulation and feeling-suggestive tactics is expected to lead to the transformation of the persons who are made into targets of formal education.

Yet the success of these institutions depends upon learners and their experiential self-organization as well as on the learning resources offered by the institution. How well these resources are used may to a considerable extent depend on the didactics used in the particular institution.

The missionary spirit of formal educational efforts exists in any society – it is a universal cultural invention at the summit of a society's self-directed intervention. It entails the dialogical separation of 'what we are now' and 'what we should be', and a series of strategies for moving from the former to the latter. In the case of colonial education this contrast becomes expanded by the 'we'<>'they' distinction that entails the tension of viewing 'the other'.[52]

The mission of introducing formal schooling has been explicit in its effort to produce a rupture in current ways of living – a break that will keep

[51] Such as the interplay between ZPA and ZFM, see above.

[52] Education in Africa during colonial rule brought this distinction out very clearly – to alter their minds the children were to be taken away from their communities:

> The relative value of boarding and day schools ... is to be determined largely by the community environment, the objective to be attained, and the available school facilities. Experience and observation in every part of the world prove the necessity for both types of schools. *Boarding schools are necessary to cultivate sound habits of life in communities that lack the home conditions and influences essential to the formation of such habits.* The brief contacts of the day school are in many instances insufficient for forming character when the influences of the home and the community are potent in the wrong direction. It is almost equally futile to send young men or young women with sound habits formed in the more or less artificial environment of the boarding school to cope single-handed with the traditions and customs of their home community. Experience in Africa and elsewhere has revealed tragic examples of such thoughtless use of those who have profited by long years of training away from their homes. The cruel and futile results of such action are far more certain in case of young women than that of young men. [Jones, 1925, p. 350, added emphases]

the learners within the field of educational efforts, without allowing these to be jeopardized by the background conditions of home and community. Not surprisingly, such purposeful breaking of local ties through formal learning entailed a focus on deductive logic in contrast to its inductive counterpart. Formal schooling brought with it thinking in 'scientific concepts'[53] with the promotion of undoubted loyalty to the premises of such thinking as introduced by the authoritative power holder – the teacher or the priest. Thus, in the formal learning context the learner is commonly persuaded to accept without question general – and empirically unverifiable – statements ('all metals are heavy') from the source of the information giver ('but, teacher – how do *you* know that?') and then carry out a reasoning task based on that formally promoted and unquestioningly accepted premise ('all metals are heavy → copper is a metal → copper is heavy'). Transfer of such a use of deductive inference from technical to social themes can lead to socially controlled actions of stigmatization or violence (e.g. 'all Martians are evil→ this man in the street *looks like a* Martian → he is evil → [I avoid him/I attack him]). Cognitive mechanisms of deductive logic – applied to social realities – can lead to conflicts, violence and genocide. A task of lifelong learning is the development of distanced and differentiated relationships to such social control efforts.

*Varieties of life-course learning:* talking about formal learning over the course of adulthood, the social institutions of education come to include studies on vocational training, higher education, professional development and adult education.[54] Other situations of formal learning, according to this definition, could include taking music classes, sports classes or undergoing a religious education. They also include knowledge-exchange networks[55] or a language 'tandem' (where two people teach a skill to each other). Finally, such studies also start to include studies on old age learning when these occur at university, or in formal settings – as when retired persons develop computer skills, for instance.[56] All these frameworks add to the childhood learning context an important correction – adult learning settings are not completely governed by the social institutions that provide such learning.[57] The formal nature of socially

[53] This notion was used by Lev Vygotsky (see Van der Veer and Valsiner, 1993) in contrast to 'everyday concepts'. Alexander Luria (1976) and Peeter Tulviste (1991) have elaborated the relations of the use of both kinds of concepts in situated activity contexts.

[54] For instance Sutherland and Crowther (2006).

[55] For instance, Muller Mirza (2001).

[56] Although there is currently a general interest in developing intergenerational exchange and enabling seniors to be still active and competent, there is still little research on actual, socially situated learning in older persons.

[57] With some exceptions – all military training of adults utilizes the social organizational forms that we can observe in childhood formal schooling.

established learning contexts takes into account the needs of the learners within their current life-course trajectories. The formal learning becomes intertwined with its non-formal counterpart.

However, from the perspective of the developing adult, lifelong learning generally takes place in non-formal settings. Even formal learning – taking courses – will lead to a person-centred (and hence far from formal) assembly of new knowledge. Human living is primarily informal – *we all live in our private life-worlds in which our relations with ourselves are deeply non-formal.*[58] Yet that informal self-development at times becomes embedded in formal or quasi-formal learning settings. However, the mid-range learning settings which are constituted by learning at the workplace, learning in out of school activities, have been called non-formal – and there is no consensus on this definition.[59] Because of this lack of clarity, the International Organization for Economic Cooperation and Development (OECD), which promotes lifelong development and aims at the validation of adults' knowledge, has proposed a distinction between forms of learning based on whether the learning is intentional (or not), or whether it happens as a side effect; and whether the activity, whatever it may be, has [a] learning objective(s) or not. Table 7.1 illustrates these contrasts.

This proposition has the double advantage of considering the *intentions* of actors, as well as the purpose and the structure of the context of activity in which they are located. Of course, these intentions may be shared between the persons involved or not, or the intentions of the actors may be more or less compatible with the setting – accordingly, teaching–learning is more or less likely to occur. *Such a definition is important for identifying learning sites in the life course.* Indeed, these divisions suggest that people learn far beyond their compulsory schooling years. Let us simply mention some of the areas in which learning as a modality of development has been, and can be, investigated.

### *Non-formal learning*

Studies on non-formal learning include studies on activities in which people are aware of developing skills or understanding in settings not initially defined as having learning objectives. Yet the social promotion of different values is present in non-formal learning. They would include attention to what people learn as they work,[60] are engaged in scouting activities, in out of school activities (sports, theatre, music practice, etc.),

[58] We solve our daily life tasks through *bricolage*. [59] See review by Werquin (2007).
[60] Boud and Garrick (1999).

Table 7.1 *Modes of learning – proposed new definitions*[a]

| There is intention to learn / The activity is planned as a learning activity | Yes: learning is intentional | No: learning is not intentional |
|---|---|---|
| **Yes**: the activity has [a] learning objective(s) | *Formal learning (type I learning)* [People] may learn during courses or during training sessions in the workplace; this is formal learning. The activity is designed as having learning objectives and individuals attend with the explicit goal of acquiring skills, knowledge or competences. This definition is rather consensual | *Semi-formal learning (type III learning)* [People] may learn during activities with learning objectives but they learn beyond the learning objectives; this is semi-formal learning. This is a new term that is proposed here. Individuals have the intention of learning about something and, without knowing it, learn also about something else |
| **No**: the activity does not have [a] learning objective (s) | *Non-formal learning (type II learning )* [People] may learn during work or leisure activities that do not have learning objectives but individuals are aware they are learning; this is non-formal learning. Individuals observe or do things with the intention of becoming more skilled, more knowledgeable and/or more competent | *Informal learning (type IV learning)* [People] may learn in activities without learning objectives and without knowing they are learning; this is informal learning. This definition is rather consensual |

[a] After Werquin (2007, p. 5). Note however that the distinctions presented in this table have not been accepted by the OECD, which continues to identify only formal, informal and non-formal learning (Werquin, 2010).

during their leisure and hobbies,[61] etc. Important life changes may bring people to engage in non-formal learning, such as learning to become a parent[62] or a grandparent;[63] learning to live in a country at war, after a job loss or after an accident.

[61] See Perret-Clermont, Pontecorvo, Resnick, Zittoun and Burge (2004) for a discussion on youth learning.
[62] For instance LaRossa and LaRossa (1981).
[63] For instance, Cesari Lusso (2004), Hagestad (1986).

### *Semi-formal learning*

This term is not consensual, yet, interestingly, designates phenomena in which people learn beyond the learning–teaching objectives of a given setting. Studies on formal learning incidentally notice that key learning and acquisition occur in the 'margin' of the expected: hence, formal school learning has a 'hidden agenda' of socialization and modalities of interaction with adults; it requires 'implicit learning' of social roles and social routines; settings providing vocational learning actually often emphasize the 'social knowledge' that people should master as they enter the work place (e.g. self-presentation, ways of being).[64] Also, practices more based on the evaluation of skills or portfolios then reveal that, while engaged in one sort of activity – say, sales management – a person also acquires other skills – for instance, organization and communication skills.

*Occasional nature of learning:* an example of non-formal learning in childhood – which has been of importance through the whole life course – comes from the past. The decade is that of 1860s, the place a small country home of a former officer of the Russian army, not far from St Petersburg. Repairs are being made to refurbish the house. It turned out that not enough wallpaper had been brought from the capital and the decision was made to use left-over paper to cover the children's bedroom walls. By coincidence, lithographic lecture notes of the father on mathematics – found in the attic – were used. A retrospective adult account of what happened in the life of the eleven-year-old girl captures the flavour of the new life this makeshift wallpaper created:

> As I looked at the nursery walls one day, I noticed that certain things were shown on them which I had already heard mentioned by Uncle. Since I was in any case quite electrified by the things he told me, I began scrutinizing the walls very attentively. It amused me to examine these sheets, yellowed by time, all speckled over with some kind of hieroglyphs *whose meaning escaped me completely but which, I felt, must signify something very wise and interesting.* And *I would stand by the wall for hours on end, reading and rereading what was written there.*[65]

The experience of encounter with the patterns on such makeshift wallpaper entails social guidance of the creative play of the inquisitive girl – the wall paper becomes a semiotic resource that feeds into the playful processes of mathematical reasoning. Instead of the usual gender-role expected orientation to dolls, the girl's attention was drawn to the wallpaper which triggered her curiosity (which could end after

[64] For instance, Audigier, Crahay and Dolz (2006).
[65] Kovalevskaya (1978, p. 215), added emphasis.

finding out that these were 'math scribbles') about the mentioned uncle, who had regularly chatted with the girl:

> Uncle used to tell me fairytales and teach me how to play chess. Then, unexpectedly carried away by his own thoughts, he would initiate me into the secrets of the various economic and social projects through which he dreamed of benefiting humanity. But more than anything else, he loved to communicate the things he had succeeded in reading and learning in the course of his long life.
>
> It was during these conversations that I first had occasion to hear about certain mathematical concepts which made a very powerful impression upon me. Uncle spoke of 'squaring the circle,' about the asymptote – that straight line which the curve constantly approaches without ever reaching it – *and about many other things which were quite unintelligible to me and yet seemed mysterious and at the same time deeply attractive.*[66]

The girl's attention to the wall developed within her relationship to her uncle. She found in the wall a fascinating playground. Here, not only could she engage in transitional phenomena, but in addition, she had to master a specific language and technique, mathematics (a semiotic system), to play that particular game.

For Winnicott,[67] science or the arts play the same transitional function as children's play, only, these are located within cultural traditions and the 'player' needs to accept and master these in order to be creative. Which is what the girl, Sofia Kovalevskaya, did and became one of the most celebrated and original mathematicians of the nineteenth century and beyond.[68] Unlike in our times, there was no educational discussion of there being too few women in the sciences, or the 'math phobia' of girls in schools. Women were simply not in academia – being forbidden to attend university courses[69] – yet those who were highly dedicated and motivated prevailed and excelled. No social institution was offering to 'help' them to 'overcome' their supposed 'inferiority'. But as is usually the case, the unconditionally repressive social system triggered various trajectories of resistance. Some of these proved to result in excellence in the sciences – aside from Kovalevskaya there were numerous highly talented women who made their way in the basic sciences, against all odds and social limitations.[70] Sofia Kovalevskaya's

[66] Kovalevskaya (1978, p. 214), added emphasis. [67] Winnicott (1991).

[68] There exists a Sofia Kovalevskaya Prize for talented young scholars – female or male – given annually by Alexander-von-Humboldt Stiftung in Germany.

[69] For example, Kovalevskaya's studies in Berlin had to take place outside the university – through private guidance of the (male) university professors recognizing her talent, and subverting the official rule of women's exclusion from sciences. The exams were also organized outside the university territory.

[70] See for example the case of Anna Maria Sibylla Merian, who published the first description of the lifecycle of butterflies in 1679, Caroline Herschel who became the first woman astronomer acknowledged by the British Royal Astronomical Society in 1835, etc.

circumstances – unity of the interpersonal (listening to the talkative uncle who liked to talk about the mysteries of science rather than telling fairytales or moralistic stories) and personal encounters with the environment (reading the wallpaper) combined with many other circumstances of her life – led her to the life course of an academic. The 'traditional' role for a woman – to marry and bear children[71] – became secondary to her personal desire to '*live in*' mathematics.

What emerges as an important point from this example is the role of *episodic synthesis* – a new personal overwhelming desire, or commitment, that can emerge in an instant in the developmental course of a person – young or old. This episodic nature of core moments[72] – rupture points, or innovative moments[73] – in human development makes them very hard for any researcher to access. As these moments are not planned by anybody – least of all by the person who develops – they can occur anywhere, anytime – and waiting for them on the side of the researcher would be akin to *Waiting for Godot*.[74]

### *Informal learning*

Informal learning, in which people unintentionally learn in a setting not designed for that purpose, covers any forms of learning by experience. Studies on informal learning are still rare, but they would include studies on youth socialization, for example examining how young people learn to become members or to display specific signs of belonging;[75] they might include studies on learning through cultural experiences such as novel reading or film watching, etc. Note that, as there is here no intention to teach and no intention to learn, we fall back on the general issue of change and development. Most development over the life course relies on the processes of informal learning – a person explores the world and learns through self-generated experience. Rarely are there 'social others' in the

[71] Sofia did marry, but a husband who supported her search for knowledge and never curbed her independent quest for it. Marriage was a necessary social façade for many personal accomplishments by the persons who married, men and women alike. In contrast, the efforts of social institutions – in many countries and historical periods – to instil 'family values' for married people constitutes an effort of social control of the conduct of individuals through local social (family) norms that conform to those of the social institutions.

[72] See *Transitions* (Zittoun, 2006b) and Lev Vygotsky's (1971) analysis of the ways in which reading a short story can lead to episodic synthesis – a hypergeneralized new feeling (Valsiner, 2005, 2007b) about the world.

[73] As in Chapter 6. [74] Beckett (1952/2010).

[75] For instance Hundeide (2005), Zittoun (2008c).

form of teachers, tax collectors or prison wardens on their way to teach us how to live our lives.

If there is neither intention of learning nor of teaching, and the setting is not intended for that purpose, then why is it worth talking about learning? In such situations, a person is simply facing a situation that *resists* her action or her interpretation.

There are two possible answers. One consists in considering that there is learning if a person engages, intentionally or not, in a negotiation with her environment, and a quest for appropriate resources, so as to be able to overcome the situation (or avoid it or find an alternative route). In any case, there is a form of reorganization of the person's actions in her environment. The other answer would reserve the idea of 'learning' to occurrences in which a person is actually intentionally aware of how the experience has changed her.[76]

Social suggestions surround arenas for informal learning. Wherever we may turn in our life space we encounter some – elaborate or tentative – social suggestions attempting to guide us in some direction. True we can ignore them, yet their presence remains a fact. Thus, although a person may be non-religious the sound of church bells, the passing of a funeral car or a wedding procession and the presence of crosses and crucifixes in different locations in everyday life remind us abut a meaning system that may be foreign to us (now) but that can be available to us when we feel we need it.

The realm of intimate relationships contains a cluster of arenas for a central learning focus in adulthood that leads to the grand dramas and operas of everyday life. Such relationships capture both internal and external infinities (in William Stern's terms), while being strictly socially organized by legal and moral constraints. Love for one's children is not to be sexual (as it leads to sexual abuse), it is not sanctioned by society that people become involved in extra-marital love affairs (yet they do – and have done so over centuries and across culture boundaries), the emergence of intimacy with partners of the same gender results in public and private outcry, and the loss of a relationship can lead to deep psychological problems. The deeply personal-cultural phenomena of love are highly socially contested – it is an affective personal phenomenon that is carefully observed by the moral watchdogs of society. A person may herself emerge as one of them.

[76] Some authors reserve 'learning from experience' for a person's active reflective grasping of her experience, with its emotional and relational implications. See for example Bion (1984).

Examples abound. A young woman of twenty-five, married for seven years, reflects upon her family life in quite traditional terms – having a 'good husband', reporting a happy childhood. Then the husband's cousin comes to live with them. The woman's retrospect of the events shows the birth of the play of love during his four-month stay:

During the first three months he was not in my thoughts at all . . . but during the last month my heart began to beat for him. It was a novel sensation for me and I did not know the meaning of this attraction; I said to myself: I love my husband and my children, why then this strange fascination for my husband's cousin? *He surely must have done something to me to arouse this feeling in me*, I thought. Fortunately, the young man soon lost his position and left for some distant place. *I felt very happy at his departure, though I longed for him very much.*[77]

The newly experienced feeling – leading to the crossing of the social boundary set by marriage ties – emerges without planning, but once it has emerged it creates a deep ambivalence. The environment becomes disquieting, and the taken-for-granted organization of the woman in her environment is questioned. This is typically a situation that 'calls' for change. Two years later the cousin returned – and the woman tried to protect herself from the affective escalation on her horizon:

I had a presentiment of dark clouds that would soon gather over my head, so I requested my husband to find other quarters than our own for his relative, on the pretext that I was not well enough to care for another person in the family. But as my husband reproached me and charged me with lack of interest in his relatives, I had to yield and give my permission for the man to stay with us.[78]

Hence, the woman first tried to modify the environment – the cousin should be located elsewhere. This solution is not acknowledged by the husband – who is not aware of the threat – so when the cousin moves in with the family, the woman engages in another strategy, that of changing self – she thus tried to control her feelings:

I had *decided to be indifferent and act as stranger* toward the boarder that was thrust upon me, so as to avoid trouble. I did not wish to ignite the feeling in my heart toward him by too close contact. I almost never spoke to him, and never came near him. God only knows how much these efforts cost me, but with all my energy I fought against the *diabolic feeling* in my heart. Unfortunately, my husband misinterpreted my behavior as a lack of hospitality. His resentment compelled me to assume a more friendly attitude towards his relative, as I wished to avoid quarrelling.[79]

Reducing the interpersonal distance in home interaction brought with it a breakdown in the woman's self-defence efforts. The young man started

[77] Thomas (1923, p. 15, emphases added). [78] Thomas (1923, p. 15).
[79] Thomas (1923, p. 15, added emphasis).

to occupy her whole mind so that everybody else felt non-existent for her – yet she did not show that sentiment interpersonally. Until the feeling had to come out into the open:

One day I *decided to put an end to my sufferings by confessing all to my boarder* and *requesting him to go away or at least leave our house to avoid a scandal.* Unfortunately, my hope for a peaceful life was not fulfilled, following my confession to the cousin. He remained in our home and became more friendly than ever towards me. I began to love him so intensely that *I hardly noticed his growing intimacy with me* and as a result I gave birth to a baby whose father is my husband's cousin.[80]

Thus the solution found by the woman can be seen as another example of unity of the internal and external 'control' effort – she (having before assumed that the young cousin 'had done something to her' – love magic?) turns to *him* in request to control *her internal* turmoil (by leaving the scene). Not surprisingly he does not comply – and she 'hardly notices' how she became pregnant from him. Yet the aftermath of the birth led to further intra-psychological turmoil:

I am unable to describe to you one hundredth part of the misery this has caused me. *I always considered an unfaithful wife the worst creature on earth* and now . . . I am *myself a degraded woman* . . . The mere thought of it drives me insane. My husband, of course, knows nothing of this incident. When the child was born he wanted to name it after one of his recently deceased relatives but . . . *I felt as if that would desecrate the grave of this late relative.* After oceans of tears, I finally induced him to name the child after one of my own relatives.[81]

At this point, the woman is engaged in intra-psychological attempts to render the situation meaningful. The internalized semiotic organizer – '*unfaithful* wife' – guarantees continuous intra-psychological turmoil. Her uses of semiotic resources such as the image of the *desecrated* grave of the relative create the 'oceans of tears', and result in a negotiated settlement about naming. The compromise found – a name coming from her own relatives – can be seen as an implicit *externalization* of that conflict.[82] Yet the implications for everyday life are reported as persistent:

I cannot stand my husband's tenderness toward the child that *is mine* but not his. When he gives the baby a kiss it burns me like a hot coal dropped in my bosom. *Every time he calls it his baby I hear someone shouting into my ear the familiar epithet thrown at low creatures like me* . . . and every time he takes the child in his arms I am tempted to tell him the horrible truth . . . When my husband is not at home I spend my time studying the face of my child, and when I think it appears to resemble its

[80] Thomas (1923, p. 16, added emphasis). [81] Thomas (1923, p. 16, added emphasis).

[82] First names are thus often the crystallization of conflictual issues, in the life of parents, in relationship to their partner or their own family – beyond the parents' conscious recognition (Zittoun, 2005).

father at such a moment I become terrified at the possibility of the baby's growing up into a real likeness to its father [added emphasis].[83]

The feeling of ownership ('my child' – in contrast to 'child as a human being') here becomes ambivalent, and is linked with the acceptance of an internalized derogatory perception of self ('low creature like me'). Yet the woman's fear is of being dismissed by her husband, thereby leaving a 'stain' on the child that would be there for the rest of its life.

In this example, the woman facing an obstacle in her environment tried to modify it – yet, after non-acknowledgement by her husband, she eventually engaged in new conduct, contradicting with internalized values; the intra-psychological conflicts are grasped through the use of semiotic resources leading to a derogatory sense of self and complex relationship to her child. The woman uses various resources at her disposal in her attempts to reorganize her place in her environment, and through an iterative, try-and-fail and exploratory process, she changes – and is changed by – the situation. Can we say that she has been *learning from experience*?

If we consider that a person's experience takes place in the flow of time, yet at the same time, that everything that contributes to the situation can be felt as relevant, the person has always the possibility of acting as her body or her affects demand, or as the social environment requires; but she can also use her capacity to suspend her action, to imagine other situations, to consider alternative pathways for herself and for others, to question norms, and so on. Such processes demand *distancing* from the flow of being-feeling in the world.

The dialogical nature of human relationships – with others, and within oneself – is the basis for human construction of new experiences. The intra-psychological regulation of the self entails constant *modulation of psychological distancing* – as recommended also by the wisdom of Telugu courtesans:

Better keep one's distance
Than love and part –
Especially if one can't manage
Seizures of passion
Make love, get close, ask for more –
But it's hard to separate and burn.
Gaze and open your eyes to desire,
Then you can't bear to shut it out
Better keep one's distance.[84]

[83] Thomas (1923, p. 16, added emphasis).
[84] Ramanujan, Rao and Shulman (1994, p. 440).

In more theoretical terms, distancing, or the possibility of inner dialogue, is what humans can do given the fact that thinking and acting are mediated by signs. Interactions with others, words, social knowledge, mantras or any other thing or person, present or internalized, that mediates a real or an inner dialogue, can contribute to the distancing. Distancing is hence what enables ZPD reflection, or the opening of a field of WHAT IF thinking.

In this case, the enamoured cousin found semiotic mediators to distance herself from her actions and elaborate a dramatic meaning of the situation. We might say that, in a broad sense, she has engaged in the hard work of living, and perhaps learning – with neither an intention to teach nor to learn – in the sense that new solutions are tried out and found. Yet did the protagonist take enough distance to question her husband's action, her cousin's deeds, the nature of her own feelings, the very fact that she remained in a given household, or the implicit rules of fidelity or extended incest? To some extent, she seems to have remained blind to all these social, symbolic and emotional aspects that constituted the frame and field of her action. Also, she seems to have ignored the fact that she herself, in her capacity as a person, may have been in a process of change. In that respect, the woman has adjusted *to* life; but it seems very difficult to say that she has learned *from* life.

Hence, in a more restrictive sense, we might propose considering that informal learning – learning from life – occurs only as *the person engages in such distancing from experience as allows some grasp of what has changed in the self or the other.* In other words, it is afterwards that the person recognizes a past experience as a learning one (this would be a form of reconceptualization).

*When no learning occurs – therapy as additional learning setting:* new events and challenges do not necessarily imply higher complexity and higher adaptation. Sometimes, challenges far beyond ZPD need to be met for the individual to function in society. There may be no development and adaptation might be at risk. In such a case, we may say that no learning takes place. How can the above proposed version of ZPD help us understand how learning problems in such a situation can be overcome?

Clients that seek psychotherapy have these kinds of learning problems. Psychotherapy is not 'formal' instructional learning – at least, most therapies do not rely solely on explicit and didactic models of 'transferring information', as the perspective on 'education' from Szasz suggests,[85] privileging meta-education (that is meta-learning) as a central aim of the

[85] Szasz (1988).

therapeutic process. Nevertheless, it is a formal setting, ruled by specific legal and social constraints, involving a 'professional' helper, sometimes seen as a 'healer'. It is also, in some sense, a context of learning, but in a more loose sense than discussed here. All psychotherapies seek to transform people's lives in a way that leads them to usually feel that they are learning something new. In therapy a therapist needs to accommodate her client's needs to real-life needs! In other words, psychotherapy deals with real episodes of life, which people have strong difficulties dealing with.[86] In that sense, people are 'stuck' in their development, probably rehearsing old habits to deal with new challenges. It is as if they were not able, on their own, to use their ZFM in order to change the current situation, because the situation places demands outside the border of their ZPD.

In like with this perspective, Leiman and Stiles[87] describe the process of change in therapy as a joint activity, in which the therapist introduces new semiotic tools (redescriptions, clarifications, interpretations, etc.) in which new viewpoints about the problematic issue are rehearsed in a dyadic intersubjective interaction. Usually, the issue at stake is not 'cognitive' – it is not a difficulty in rationally understanding something, but a difficulty in assimilating emotionally painful experiences.

In the context of the approach to learning outlined in this chapter, we may say that, in order to help the client, the therapist must be particularly attuned to the emotionally marked ZPD of the client – and therefore the ZPA must be dialogically articulated in relation to the ZFM. This has implications for the client–therapist dyad, considered as a TLC, as described above. Who is teacher and who is learner in therapy? The learning situation is about the life of the client. Yet the client is herself the expert on her own life. So actually the therapist cannot be the teacher. The therapist needs to learn about the life of the client in order to help her. We assume the theoretical knowledge and professional experiences to define the ZPD of the therapist. However, the client does not assume a role as teacher. The therapist is usually looked upon as the teacher. Again, the concept of meta-education (Szasz) suggests that the therapist should help the client to become her own teacher. The double roles taken by both therapist and client make the co-regulative processes in the therapy even more salient. Through co-regulation, therapist and client may dialogically change both parties' ZPD towards a goal where the client will be able to face her challenges. If that happens, the tools introduced by the therapist sustain a perspective that enables the client to anticipate new possibilities when previously she envisaged a dead end. Therefore, therapy can – and

[86] On problematic self-narratives, see Chapter 6. [87] Leiman and Stiles (2001).

should – be seen not only as a matter of removing symptoms and promoting well-being, but also as a way of promoting lessons of life to both participants – therapist and client. Curiously, when therapy is developing successfully a very interesting communicative phenomenon often occurs – the client produces an assertion, and while the therapist is just listening, the client abruptly says 'I know what you are going to ask me next!' and often the question framed by the client, *through the therapist's position*, is a very relevant one. This also means that a particular frame, with rules of co-regulation, is now established at this point in time.

*Learning as development, development as learning:* learning occurs in multiple forms. Some of these include explicit teaching efforts (school learning, teaching by parents), but in other forms the intentions are hidden from the learner, yet present teaching in the background of their actions. Hence all teaching/learning processes are socially framed – explicitly and implicitly. If formal, semi-formal and non-formal learning settings can be considered as forms of situated development where there is an intention of learning or teaching, we may then say *that informal learning can be considered as the central mechanism that leads to general development*, which, a posteriori, might be considered as a learning experience. Since most of the human life course is filled with contexts of informal learning, it is through the focus on such learning that life-course learning becomes the focal core for all human developmental science.[88]

The idea of *adult learning* or *lifelong learning* has became of major importance in discussions about world education at the turn of the millennium. The study of adult learning and lifelong learning has complex implications in terms of policy-making, economic development and didactics. This has led authors to question social settings in which learning may occur and forms of knowledge that may be acquired, questions that go along with issues of recognition and validation of skills.

We will examine development in specific niches that have been traditionally identified as 'learning' sites. These sites are complex social activity settings, which are set up to guide learning processes. It may be useful to talk about 'learning' to designate developmental events in which someone

[88] Formal schooling settings in a given society are unevenly distributed over the life course, and never cover personal experience twenty-four hours a day, seven days a week (unless, of course, prisons – as total institutions – are considered establishments of formal education). As the discourse of psychologists on human development has been linked to existing formal schooling systems and the role of teachers (power holders) the coverage of human developmental psychology traditionally ends when the institutional order of education stops – at secondary education or university – and restarts at the new institutional coverage at old age – now no longer in the educational but in the social and health services domain. The absence of focus on mid-life development is an indicator of the role of social guidance in the science.

(or a social entity) has the intention of teaching, or in which someone has the intention of learning, or, when there is no such intention, there is an awareness of learning or of having learned something. This questions the processes of learning involved – *what is learned*, and *how it is learned* – and how these are connected to development in general.

## Lifelong learning and adult education

Attention to learning across the lifespan is a relatively new cultural invention. Although mentioned in the 1930s, lifelong education started to be written about in the 1960s'.[89] From the 1960s onward, researchers and policy-makers began to become interested in learning beyond the years of schooling and initial training, in the lives of adults and older persons. *Adult education* designates 'all forms of learning undertaken by adults after having left initial education and training'.[90] On the one hand, continuous adult education includes the processes by which professionals can, as part of their continuous adjustment to their working life, develop new skills and competences, either to follow technical progress, or to progress within a company. On the other hand, the notion of adult learning includes all forms of education in which adults engage to develop new interests, hobbies and in general contribute to their well-being. Decades of adult training in or out of the workplace have led educators and researchers to realize that learning in adults requires specific adjustment and cannot be carried out via the same modalities as with children.

However, at the turn of the millennium, the question of adult education has fallen under the general umbrella of *lifelong learning*. Indeed, lifelong learning has become a priority for policy-makers and those in the educational field under two main pressures. On the one hand, the extension of life duration and the increase of life quality in the elderly in Western countries enables more and more older persons in good health to engage in new activities – although their initial training is often no longer up to date. On the other hand, one of the most important means to address South–North inequalities (and to a lesser extent East–West) is by providing basic education to populations that have been deprived of it, be they children or adults. Rapidly – from 2000 on – lifelong learning has become a major social, economic and political issue. For instance, in Europe, the Bologna agreements, which have brought institutional standardization and the accreditation of education at the university level at the beginning

[89] 'Lifelong Learning'. *Encyclopedia of Career Development*, 2006, SAGE Publications, 21 September 2009, http://sage-ereference.com/careerdevelopment/Article_n166.html.

[90] European Commission (2006), p. 2.

of the second millennium, enable lifelong education to be acknowledged (and not only initial training).[91] In 2006, the European Commission published guidelines by which the European Union should become a 'learning area'[92] in order to deal with demographic changes, inequalities within Europe, social exclusion and the challenges faced by its economy. In the United States, in 2007, a governmental thinktank produced a comparable document, urging the development of lifelong learning as the only mean to compensate for the ageing of the population.[93]

## Contexts of learning: realities of life-course tasks

An important implication of the increased interest in lifelong learning is that it has encouraged educators, researchers and policy-makers to examine what people actually know, whether they acquired this skill and knowledge at school, in their vocational environment or in their daily lives. In other words, interested people who have taken on administrative roles are starting to pay attention to the obvious everyday fact that learning never stops over the life course, and that much of it happens outside the school walls. Yet the particular forms of learning – formal, informal, occasional, and quasi-formal – differ at different times over the life course. Aside from 'school-type' knowledge that may indeed be of importance for maintaining the professional competence of adults, there are a number of other forms and domains of learning through the whole life course.

Everyday life creates endless numerous situations that invite learning. The invitation to learn comes both from people's need to adjust to situations, and from cultural guidance. In effect, societies generate life-course 'tasks', usually formulated in vague and approximate terms – indicating general desired or required direction in development – and supported by various social representations that give these directions a moral flavour. What psychologists – following common sense – have called developmental 'tasks' thus often correspond to *normative* expectations about what the life course should be. People more or less readily engage in these tasks; although they may be occasions for learning, learning may also occur in spite of these tasks, or at their margin – learning is an open-ended process.

[91] See for instance the report on the Bologna Seminar on 'Recognition and Credit Systems in the Context of Lifelong Learning', Prague, Czech Republic, 5–7.06.03, http://www.crus.ch/dms.php?id=3843.

[92] European Commission (2006). [93] Bosworth (2007).

*Life course task: 'to become adult'*

The major life-course task of 'becoming an adult' is socially defined in conjunction with social role assumptions ('be a man', 'be a policeman') – as well as with a social encoding of moral imperatives ('be a *real* woman', 'be a patriot'). This happens through hypergeneralized meanings ('be honest', '*become* responsible'). Very often these 'tasks' implicitly invite people to act differently from what the social representation of being a *child* implies.[94]

Much of the learning over the life course entails *entering into a social frame* that is defined by social roles and fortified by social representations.[95] The specific learning tasks follow such directions of frame entrance. Thus, all societies over the world have socially normative forms of body movements – dancing, lamenting, singing – that are evoked in different social situations. Such activity frames unite the cultural guidance of human bodies and, through them, minds in social relationships, while providing arenas for affective self-actualization and the publicly acceptable expression of sensuality.[96]

*Guidance by social representation:* European cultural history provides us with many examples of how adult informal learning has been socially guided in directions that not only establish norms for social conduct (in public) but also guide people towards internalized versions of such conduct that take the form of personal or subjective culture. After the Protestant Reformation in the sixteenth century we can observe the emergence of borrowings from ancient Greco-Roman mythologies that guide persons to learn how to be in society while accepting – and even idealizing – personal pleasure. The myth of Cupid (Amor) and Psyche, which re-emerged as a socially highlighted story retold in the sixteenth century, reached its peak in the eighteenth and nineteenth centuries. The myth was a story of love, retold in various versions, and encoded in visual forms in large and small (miniatures) versions. The Cupid and Psyche story constitutes an example of an artefact promoting a social representation (here, of love), and meant to invite people to use it as a

94 For instance through injunctions such as 'be an adult – not a child!' rather than 'be an adult – not an old man!' See also Chombart de Lauwe (1979).

95 *Social representations* is a term proposed by Moscovici in the 1970s (Moscovici, 2008) to designate socially shared systems of beliefs, images and feelings, which canalize people's communication and action, and are generated and transformed by these. See also above Chapter 3 and Duveen (2007), Marková (2005).

96 Sensuality – bodily feeling into the world – rather than sexuality – is the basis for human psychological meaning-making (Valsiner, 2003). It takes a multitude of forms – from massaging the infants' bodies by mothers, co-sleeping, sunbathing, eating, etc. We experience the world through our bodily exposure – and its hiding (the PRIVATE <> PUBLIC dialectics in our social lives). Some forms of bodily experiencing – dance (Hanna, 1988) – are a collective arena for regulating such personal dialectics socially.

**Box 7.2 *The Tale of Cupid and Psyche*, by Apuleius**

A king and a queen have three daughters; the youngest, Psyche, is so beautiful that no one dares ask for her hand; the others have made good marriages. The goddess Venus is so jealous to hear everyone praising the beauty of Psyche that she asks her undisciplined son, Cupid, to make Psyche fall in love with a horrible creature. The parents of Psyche go to an oracle that announces a terrible fate for Psyche: she has to be abandoned on a high rock where she will be given to some monster. Psyche is brought there as she would be to her death – however, a soft wind brings her to a beautiful palace, where invisible servants take care of her. At night, in the dark, a manly creature visits her and makes her his wife. She soon learns to like the visits of that creature, and respects his demand that she should not try to unveil his identity; she becomes pregnant. Psyche's sisters, full of sorrow, want to know what has happened to her, and Psyche invites them to visit her. Immediately, the sisters become jealous of the palace in which Psyche lives, and envious of her fate; they push her to try to uncover the identity of her husband and to cut his head off. Under the pressure of her sisters, and against the warnings of her husband, Psyche eventually discovers his godly beauty as he sleeps, and cannot kill him – it is Cupid himself, who actually had fallen in love with her and could not accomplish the instruction given by his mother. Psyche touches one of Cupid's arrows and falls deeply in love with him. Cupid and Psyche are parted, and Cupid, who had been burned by Psyche's lamp, has to be cured by his mother, Venus. Psyche wants to see him again, and Venus sets a series of impossible tasks for her. Psyche's good heart encourages people and gods to help her, and she fulfils the tasks. On his side, full of despair, Cupid asks for the support of Mercury, his father, who decides to bless their union. Finally, Psyche's sisters, blinded by greed, die; and in a final banquet of gods and goddesses, Cupid and Psyche are made husband and wife and Psyche becomes a goddess; their daughter is Pleasure.[97]

symbolic resource, so as to encourage the internalization and reconstruction of the values it promotes.

In effect, the Cupid and Psyche story gave rise to new social activity settings – role plays of the story by European aristocratic society members[98] – with a result of promoting the social representation of *passionate love* – yet in service of social obligations.[99] The proliferation of iconic

[97] Our summary from Apuleius (1993).

[98] See Holm (2006, Ch. 1) on the history of *Gemeinschaft der Heiligen* (Society of the Sacred) in Darmstadt, 1771–3 – which crossed the intellectual paths of Herder and Goethe as participants in the social roles of games of love.

[99] Psychology is largely built on another myth of similar origin – the Oedipus myth. The difference of Cupid and Psyche is in its focus on the appreciation of pleasure in the larger context of deep feelings of love, in contrast to the guilt linked with crossing the limits of

images of Cupid and Psyche in European everyday life environments guided affective socialization towards new norms of expressing affect to others – and feelings in one's own internal self. Just as Cupid's arrows captured Psyche, so images of the myth as well as novels revitalizing the Apuleian original story of the second century AD captured the minds of Renaissance Europeans.

The hypergeneralized notion of 'love' is a favourite topic of various cultural artefacts – poetry, songs, novels, films, newspaper articles about a marriage or divorce of a celebrity, etc. All these may become resources that operate as a texture for guidance of meaning-making in social interaction, giving flavour to the otherwise mundane organization of everyday living of family groups. The mythologies of love fortify the social role expectations of people who are – or might be – or desperately want to be – in love, loved or in a *different* social relation. Such semiotic resources also set the stage for identity promotion (what being a '*true* woman' or a '*loving* husband' means in a given society at a given time) and guide people's narratives. In turn, they also create norms on the basis of which some people's love lives can be a cause of rejection or stigmatization.

Similarly, but with a contrasting content, images of Kali are visible in many public places in Orissa (India). Kali symbolizes the transformation of a 'loving mother' into a 'killing mother'; the presence of the statue thus reminds the passers by of the need to be ready for drastic transformation of attitudes (Figure 7.4.). Such artefacts promote certain social representations in a given historical and cultural environment; these are made available as public cultural elements, which then still need to be appropriated by people before they can used them as symbolic resources.

*Sub-task: learning to 'be married' (and its corollaries – 'staying married' or 'getting divorced'):* Marriage in the history of human societies has been a framework for survival and procreation – through cooperation between the wider kinship groups whose representatives are married.[100]

marriage within one's kinship network. The issue of personal affect – bodily pleasure – has always been in the centre of social organization of human lives. In mediaeval Europe it was blocked from being socially acceptable other than in the life-course transition into marriage, while in the Indian *bhakti* devotional tradition sensuality (and sexuality) were elevated to the level of highest value to serve the deities. Cultural continuity in European societies with the Greco-Roman mythologies was in full swing by the eighteenth century – with the promotion of male ideals in reinventing the Heracles myth, etc.

[100] For example: 'marriage is much too important to be left in the hands of two kids who have lost their heart to a pair of beautiful eyes or nice hair, who think life is like love films they see on television. What do they know of the difficulties of life? A marriage should be based

Figure 7.4 The image of goddess Kali/Durga in Orissa, India.

The *neolocal* and *monogamic* arrangement by way of interpersonal attraction as a marriage framework is a relatively recent European invention.[101]

on compatibility of the couple and their families ... A marriage based on respect and harmony brings love, but a love marriage that lacks harmony ends in fights and disaster' – an elderly Egyptian woman, a mother of eight (Hoodfar, 1997, pp. 62–3).

[101] See Valsiner (2000) on the contexts and mutual transformations of marriage forms.

Guiding young adults into taking on marital roles is a central social organizer in any society in the world – independent of which marriage forms are practised at a given historical time. Conversely, all kinds of relationships having a potential impact on reproduction (which includes all sexual relationships) outside the marital situation are socially stigmatized and often legally ruled out – with major punishment for such acts if the participants are caught. Sexual activity does not differ from any other activity of everyday life that is of an episodic kind – eating, sleeping, chatting, etc. Yet in its social normativeness it carries a special symbolic load – it becomes appropriated into marital roles, and regulated by norms of age appropriateness. Ordinary human life activities – eating, making love, sleeping, celebrating various occasions – are guided from the social position of *being married*. Everything that happens within that social position – the birth of children, reconstructing housing, etc. – gains value from that position. Children born within 'wedlock' are valued – children born outside are not. Good sexual relations within marriage are valued positively – similar ones in extra-marital relations are denounced (even when intra-marital sexuality is problematic).

However, such alignment of the self with the social role position is a perspective from the 'outside in', from the socially normative institutional view towards that of persons who live their lives. The latter – to consider their learning in life – have to face various contradictions in their relations with the socially normative positions of 'now you are a *married adult* and should act accordingly'. Being in that role leads to new demands upon personal exploration of one's life space – some of which may be in contradiction with actual social circumstances. Thus, a person may suffer from physical or emotional abuse within marriage – from the spouse, parents-in-law or her own children – and yet be under pressure to construct solutions that are compatible with the position of 'married adult'.

However, a person may move into new – formal or semi-formal – learning contexts, or create meaningful activities outside the confines of given social role positions. Such activities are also part of adult development over the life course. From that perspective, adults' invention of hobbies, joining various social groups, going to the cinema or a library or entering into an extra-marital secret love affair are all examples of constructing meaningful life events. A person constantly *strives for meaning* – and many efforts of such striving entail embarking on adventurous paths.[102]

From that person-centred perspective, what is usually called a 'mid-life crisis' is a situation of exploration of intense learning efforts that constitute

[102] Many inexplicable acts – usually viewed (normatively) as 'delinquent' or 'irrational' by others – are of crucial function in the development of the self. Adolescents' 'thrill-

a rupture in relation to the ordinary confines of social role positions. This may lead to new learning tasks. Thus, learning how to end marriage, by separation and divorce, becomes a modern learning task for adults in societies where divorce is legally allowed and socially accepted. If in contemporary occidental societies about 50 per cent of marriages end in divorce it would be appropriate to ask how marital relations end, how these endings are socially structured, what kind of re-constitutional options for further living are available from the ruins of the previous marriage.

### *Life-course task: learning to 'be a parent' (and a 'grandparent')*

Issues of having children and bringing them up to adulthood have become prominent in child psychology over the past half-century. However, the focus in issues of *parenthood* has been on its 'effects' on *child* development – not on the *development of adults* through their roles as parents. Here we reverse this perspective – the 'middle ages' of the life course are years of extensive social learning under the impending process of development of the first, then the second, and – last but least – of the Nth child. As is well known, the number of offspring per birth-giver is reduced with advancing of education and economic status. A mother of ten children over her twenty-year parenting career would necessarily learn how to 'be a parent' very differently from a mother of one – especially if the latter was in a position to expect to share the task with her husband, while the first one was not. In contrast, the mother of ten would most probably be embedded in a supportive wider kinship group in a rural (i.e. food-producing) environment, where there were many knowledge sources (grandparents) and activity support resources (relatives of equally large families) to help in child care when needed.

An example of a socially promoted fantasy is the focus provided for young adults of becoming parents. The desire for offspring – assumed to be deeply engrained in the evolutionary nature of any species – acquires its social organization in *Homo sapiens*. The adult state of motherhood (and, more recently, fatherhood) becomes highlighted as a personal desire guided by social institutions. The indirect guidance ranges from supporting 'family values' – including the necessary ingredient of the family being one (e.g. China's 'one child policy'), some or many children. This is obviously linked to the social suggestions to

seeking' in adventure construction has been well described (Lightfoot, 1997), and the role of adventure in human living has been of interest in classic sociology (Simmel, 1911/1971b).

women as to their roles in a given society at the time – either emphasizing participation in public life ('to hell with the kitchen') or – some decades later, when low birth rates set future the labour market in jeopardy – focus on women's social duty to have more than two children (Figure 7.5).

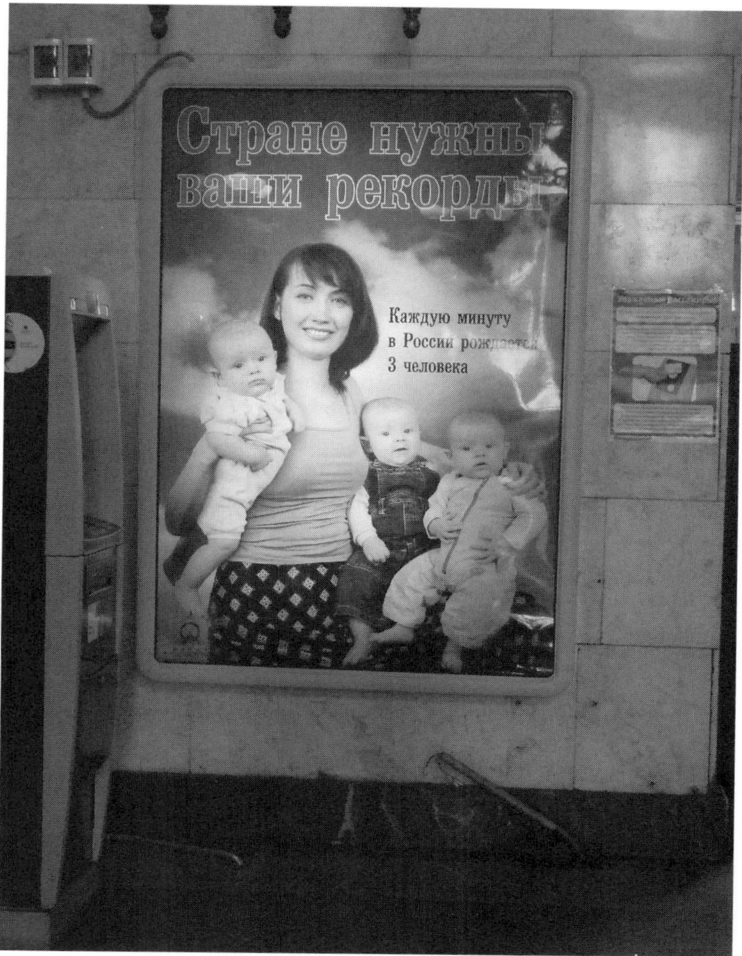


Figure 7.5 Russian poster advocating a three-child preference in 2008 (photo courtesy of Jessica Golliday) ('The country needs your records', 'Every minute three persons are born in Russia').

Under conditions of declining birth-rates – by choice or by war – social institutions can take over their own role in the otherwise family-centred practice of childbearing and furnish it with different fantasy-supportive social suggestions. No longer is the beauty of having a child the individual prerogative – it is moved into the domain of loyalty to the nation. In the middle of World War II, the German National Socialist leadership introduced a project of granting the state new (racially pure) children – by taking selected women to child-bearing colonies where they would meet selected fathers-to-be (racially 'pure' Germans) and give birth to children who would belong to the state. The *Lebensborn* project that started in 1936 was supposed to give the National Socialist regime that result.[103]

*Naming a child – setting the social stage:* although the general project of parenting can be shown as fed and guided by social representations and specific myths and narratives, it also meets the personal doubts, projects and desires of the couple. The name that parents choose for a child very often reveals the tension between the individual project and its related feeling of uniqueness, and social myths. In contemporary societies, in which choosing a name is both 'compulsory and free',[104] most people take into account family, religious and national traditions and myths at the same time as they cherish their own imaginary worlds of values and expectations.

First names chosen for children thus usually have at least four symbolic functions: they are signs of the child's belonging to a given group (an Italian name, a name that goes for both the country of residence and of origin); they have a strong aesthetic aspect and hence reveal what parents consider as 'sounding good' – which is extremely variable and sensitive to the general semiosphere (e.g. names commonly heard on TV programmes, the 'fashion' for short, long, etc., names). Names designate parents' preferred or meaningful cultural experiences – a story they liked, a movie they adored, a song they heard together; and finally, names often contain a programme for the child (as when a name might suit the butcher's son or someone who might become a CEO). In that sense, although a name for a child is personal and intimate, it is also shaped by all the myths, cultural experience, shared values, etc., to which the parents have been exposed, and then results from unique *bricolage* – an unique rearrangement of these references so as to correspond to the parents' feelings and projects at that time and moment.[105] In that sense, names become semiotic resources used by parents to fix and communicate complex webs of meaning.

[103] See in detail Koop (2007). [104] Besnard (1995). [105] Zittoun (2004d, 2005).

*Life-course task: entering into public social roles*

Human adulthood is about work – and work roles are socially differentiated in any given society. Persons assume varied roles in relation to work which are mutually complementary (workers and work-givers). Even the social roles in the economically unproductive sector of any society – those of petty bureaucrats and political leaders – are closely embedded in the economic realities of work and its productivity.

Learning to be in a work-related role entails learning how to move between work roles – the 'be employed' and 'be unemployed'. The tension around worker<>non-worker roles appears episodically in the life course – ranging from 'being made redundant' (losing a job) to 'deciding to stay at home' (to take care of a child, become a 'home-maker'). An extreme case comes towards the latter part of the life course in relation to retirement – which can be seen as a state of age-related unemployment.

*Learning to be loyal:* Social suggestions for organizing one's life course necessarily include the promotion of loyalty – to one's family, religious institution, political leaders and country. Human life activities are organized in ways that confine a person to act by way of a script, to feel the social role assigned to her/him and internalize the social expectations of that role. Society entails numerous 'dry testing' cases where loyalty to an idea or a leader figure is critically tested. Moral discourses triggered by such testing situations are ways to guide the person towards further internalization of the loyalty. Places like monuments to political leaders or – won or lost – wars of the past,[106] as well as places for public or institutionalized confession (see Figure 7.6) are signs that are supposed to guide a person to reinstatement of loyalty. The introduction of ritualistic prayer routines[107] is the social mechanism of guidance of the self.

The confessional is a solution to the publicly private nature of the person's confession. As an example, consider the internal flow of feelings when facing the act of confession, described by James Joyce in the introspective account of his subject Steven Daedalus:

> The penitent came out. He was next. He stood up in terror and walked blindly into the box.
>
> At last it had come. He knelt in the silent gloom and raised his eyes to the white crucifix suspended above him. God could see that he was sorry. He could tell all

[106] For instance Zittoun (2004c).

[107] See Del Río and Alvarez (2007) on the analysis of Lord's Prayer. Creating scripts for recurrent actions that enforce the actor to create meaning of a particular direction – quasi-privately as in confession or publicly as in our contemporary new genre of public apologies (Brinkmann, 2010) – is a way of guiding human non-formal learning over a lifetime and across any setting of a public/private kind.

Figure 7.6 Activity context for loyalty promotion and maintenance (a confessional in Arlon, Belgium).

> his sins. His confession would be long, long. Everybody in the chapel would know then what a sinner he had been. Let them know. It was true. But God had promised to forgive him if he was sorry. He was sorry. He clasped his hands and raised them towards the white form, praying with all his trembling body, swaying his head to and fro like a lost creature, praying with whimpering lips.[108]

In that example, the whole setting acts as staging guiding the person's action and feelings – feeling guilty – leading to a certain outcome, the surrender to the priest, with the promise of a relief. Social institutions lead individuals – and groups – to action scripts that propel the internalized meaning-making in the socially desired directions. The begging forgiveness in the confessional happens *before* the actual interaction with the confessor takes place.

### *Learning to survive: in peace, in war and under occupation*

Human societies pass through phases of construction and destruction – wars have raged over the whole world, and there is no indication that they

[108] Joyce (1964, p. 143).

would end even if one dearly wished for such an outcome. Social power groups have conquered the territories of others and tried to govern them.

Some wars go on in the middle of peacetime. A country that irregularly bombs targets in another country – but does not 'declare a war', or capture the other's territorial resources, operates in such a zone of limbo. In that zone, the war can be felt even though there are no destructive actions in the local neighbourhood. And then an upsurge of unexpected violence, or a suicide bombing might happen, only to be followed by a return to calm everyday life. Such a situation is very similar to intermittent criminality in urban environments – robbing or stealing sometimes happens, but otherwise life goes on in its ordinary way.[109] Any exaggeration of a local war situation leads to the adjustment of such normality. People maintain their quasi-ordinary ways of living under occasional sniper fire that may make crossing the street to fetch bread from the bakery potentially fatal. Or they may be subject to public education séances in the community by opposing forces in a guerrilla struggle, who suggest the 'security' offered under their administrative control of the everyday environment. Living under occupation – even without a war actually happening in the locality at a given time – nevertheless sensitizes ordinary people, as such an experience is:

> a permanent condition of 'being in pain': fortified structures, military posts, and roadblocks everywhere; buildings that bring back painful memories of humiliation, interrogations, and beatings; curfews that imprison hundreds of thousands in their cramped homes every night from dusk to daybreak; soldiers patrolling the unlit streets, frightened by their own shadows; children blinded by rubber bullets; parents shamed and beaten in front of their families; soldiers urinating on fences, shooting the rooftop water tanks just for fun, chanting loud offensive slogans, pounding on fragile tin doors to frighten the children, confiscating papers, or dumping garbage in the middle of residential neighborhood; border guards kicking over a vegetable stand or closing borders at whim; bones broken; shootings and fatalities – a certain kind of madness.[110]

Learning to handle unexpected violence – and to avoid it – is a crucial adulthood learning task. The creation of near-war atmosphere through a complex of discrepant actions that fail to fit into a peacetime context is

[109] Military actions by the twenty-first century have been 'privatized' – rather than continuing as the monopoly of states, governments, or companies (e.g.The Dutch East India Company and its army in the seventeenth century). Currently 'privatized violence escapes the distinction between war and peace. Where it holds sway there is no peace. But there is no war either. Because of this, military superiority does not have the final sway' (Eppler, 2002, p. 47, quoted in Beck, 2007, p. 148).

Privatized destructive actions are meant for mass media transfer amplification; these set new learning tasks for adults facing them in the comforts of living rooms or public TV viewing places all over the world.

[110] Mbembe (2003, p. 39).

part of this third, intermediate state. Our contemporary societies undergo temporary episodes of panic in the middle of seemingly peaceful life contexts – due to politically oriented acts of destruction or the idea that these may occur. The move from learning to development is a buffer against traumatic impacts.

## Knowledge and development

Adult life in societies creates numerous occasions for learning, from quasi-explicit tasks to endless variations of events. In turn, institutions have developed techniques to acknowledge the skills and knowledge that people acquire through their life course, in informal and non-formal settings.[111] As this chapter pursues the theoretical reflection developed throughout this book, we will not engage with the particular issue of the practical recognition of skills and competences, but rather ask how these worldwide general changes in the apprehension of learning bring to question the nature of knowledge itself.

The notion of *knowledge* is defined by the *Oxford English Dictionary*[112] as designating:

1 'facts, information, and skills acquired through experience or education; the theoretical or practical understanding of a subject'; in a philosophical sense, knowledge is a 'true, justified belief; certain understanding, as opposed to opinion';
2 'awareness or familiarity gained by experience of a fact or situation'; and
3 'sexual intercourse' (in an archaic sense).

Although the third definition interestingly points out the intimate nature of a person's relationship to knowledge,[113] we will just consider the two first designations here. One question classically asked when considering these definitions refers to a philosophical debate that can be traced back to Plato: is knowledge necessarily true and justified, in contrast to belief?[114] The second issue of these definitions is more relevant to our discussion: can knowledge designate both information acquired through formal education, and simple awareness gained through experience? This question is often answered from a normative standpoint; one might think that chemistry was 'more' about knowledge than, say, weaving carpets because, unlike the most beautiful carpet craft, chemical formulae can be depicted and their

[111] Werquin (2010). [112] Soanes and Stevenson (2005, entry 'knowledge *noun*').

[113] Note that in Latin languages, knowledge comes from the Latin '*cognoscere*', in which '*co*' means 'with', and '*gnoscere*', 'knowing, to know': the idea of a relation with the thing-to-be-learned is etymologically embedded in the term. The very basic kind of co-knowing is the act of procreation.

[114] See for instance Audi (2002) for an overview.

effects systematically explored. Yet, as with all norms, such valuations are relative and reversible. We come to the crucial intersection to answer the question – where is knowledge situated? It is centralized, or distributed?

### *Knowledge in learning as cognition*

At one extreme, psychologists focus on the cognitive aspect of learning and tend to see really important differences between different forms of knowledge: for instance, doing mathematics is a very different cognitive operation from weaving carpets. Following and expanding Piaget's work, these approaches try to understand the specificity of the cognitive processes involved in different types of tasks (e.g. learning grammar or solving mathematical tasks), and the relationships between these (e.g. is the task of solving an equation in physics 'the same' as solving an equation in mathematics?). In that sense, one body of knowledge is defined by the cognitive operations it implies; and learning demands the mastery of the specific operations it requires.

These approaches allow the stating of the cognitive logics of learning. However, they fail to account for two issues. First, an exclusive focus on cognition fails to account for any circumstance related to the social situation of knowledge learned. Thus, one cannot explain irregularity in the activation of knowledge – why in an examination situation a person cannot solve the task she could solve at home. Similarly, this approach cannot account for social or cultural inequalities in learning (for example, the fact that adolescents who have been socialized at home in a manner differing from the implicit norms of an educational setting have unequal chances of succeeding).[115] Second, these approaches cannot account for the fact that it is very difficult to ensure that a person who has mastered a specific skill can activate it in another, comparable, situation (this is discussed below under the idea of *generalization*, or *transfer*). Indeed, people do not simply 'activate' a skill in their mind (or fire a network in the brain); they first have to understand the situation in which they are and what it requires. However, these contextual dimensions are not treated as part of knowledge itself by these approaches.

### *Cultural-historical activity theory*

At another extreme, a strong current in psychology considers all kinds of knowledge as always situated, and therefore different from one another.

[115] Rochex (1998).

The possibility of generalized knowledge is often denied because of the situatedness of knowledge. The empirical research programmes here emphasize the ethnography of knowledge as it is being constructed in a particular context. These approaches work partly on the basis of an anthropological approach to the workplace, and partly, within the theoretical frame, usually called *activity theory* (*teoria deyatel'nosti*), as developed by the Russian Soviet psychologist Alexey N. Leontiev in the 1970s.[116] According to Leontiev activity should be the basic unit of analysis for psychology. A parallel to an activity theoretical approach grew out of the German psychology of Klaus Holzkamp in the 1960s which was also built on Marxist philosophical grounds.

By the beginning of the twenty-first century, the 'cultural-historical activity theories' in education and psychology have engaged in the effort to understand how knowledge is constructed through activities pursued by people, in a specific community, with the help of specific instruments, people sharing certain goals, a body of rules or the organization of work.[117] Consequently, learning is seen as a transformation of the activity and its components – small actions, roles in a system, goals or tools; in that respect, knowledge can be seen as a specific configuration of these elements. A person does not have 'mathematical knowledge' in her head; rather, as an active agent she knows how to use the calculator to solve a specific sort of questions asked by a teacher considering her as a student.[118]

*'Communities of practice'*: a specific orientation within situated learning approaches examines *communities of practice*, that is, small communities sharing an activity, with a micro-culture and system of mutual recognition. Such participation by community members changes according to different group tasks. The idea of 'peripheral participation' has been used to designate how a newcomer or novice 'learns' the practice characteristic of one of these communities – a workplace, a specific interest group. The newcomer first stays 'at the periphery' of the activity, observing, and then progressively imitating and entering within the network of interactions. As the practices she can perform become more and more complex, the newcomer is also progressively more and more acknowledged as an able part of the community. The trajectory of becoming an expert and a member of the community is metaphorically designated as a movement from the

[116] Leontiev (1975) – see also Van der Veer and Valsiner (1991).

[117] Engeström (2005); Cole and Engeström (2007); Hedegaard and Chaiklin (2005).

[118] At a group level, from that perspective, it can be said that it is not a group of teachers that acquires a new body of knowledge about teaching methods; rather, it is a community whose activity, goals, instruments and internal relationships have been transformed (Engeström, 2005).

periphery to the centre of the community of practice. In such a description, then, knowledge has both practical and identity components: one learns nursing by practising as a nurse and being socially acknowledged as a nurse.[119]

*Learning systems of activity*: one particular version of cultural-historical activity theory, integrating the idea that communities rather than individuals should be studied, is that of Yrjö Engeström. He has considered change as a complex system of activity. In his model, Engeström[120] never considers the learner and her relationship to an object to achieve a goal as isolated; rather, he considers this person as part of a wider system. In Figure 7.7, we may imagine that the person, an apprentice, is using a hammer (instrument) to fix a chair (object). The action is motivated by a tension towards a goal – for example, to please one's vocational teacher. However, for Engeström, this action has to be understood as taking place in a wider social system: the meaning of the action is given by the fact that it takes place in a specific *community* – a particular workshop, with its particular history, regulated by *rules* (people are here to learn the trade, they should do what they are asked) and a certain organization of labour (according to which the apprentice is subordinate to the teacher, and should please him).

This, however, is just the first half of the story. For Engeström, the interesting bit is when the system itself starts to change, as *collective learning* takes place. In this system, change is motivated, or triggered, by

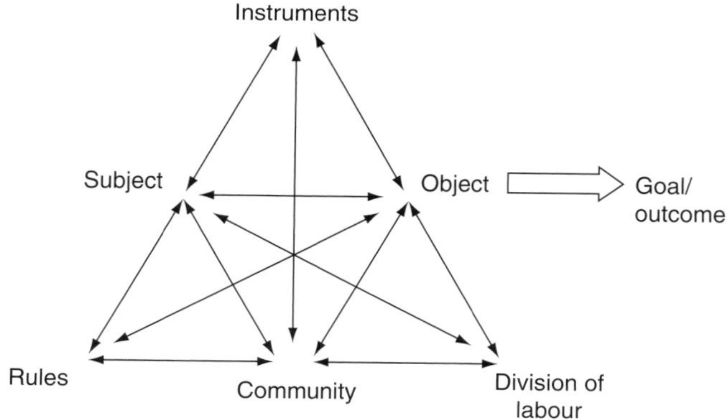


Figure 7.7 Yrjö Engeström's activity system (for example, in Engeström, 1999).

[119] Lave and Wenger (1991). [120] Engeström (1999, 2005), Cole and Engeström (2007).

internal contradictions: for instance, the division of labour is perceived as unproductive and does not allow people to achieve their goal; or the instruments – the methods to be used, or the hammer – are not adequate for their intended use. Once identified by the members of an activity system, such contradictions can be resolved – and their resolution is thus a collective change, that is, a learning experience. This model has been widely used as a tool for intervention – Engeström's 'change laboratory' enables working teams, school staff, etc. to analyse the dysfunctions in their activity system and to reorganize it accordingly. The goal of these interventions – and of the use of that model – is to enable the system to change or learn. Consequently, each person's activity – that is, what each person does in the revised system – has to be redefined and thus there should also be learning for each person.

From a DST[121] point of view, such interventions can be seen as attempts to 'engineer' learning in the dynamic system constituted by an organization. Ultimately, however, the outcome of such interventions depends on the organization of the activity between the members of the organization, where the personal understanding of the intervention will be crucial. Even if all members of the organization change their activity according to what is intended (which often is not the case), the productivity of the organization is totally dependent on the collective *bricolage* of the members coordinating their activity to achieve a new attractor in the production of the organization that corresponds to what was intended before the intervention. Therefore, individual learning is not enough. The achievements of a new attractor in the functioning of the organization, which may be understood as a collective learning, cannot be engineered (not without extreme control, cf. the relationship between ZPA and ZFM discussed above). It may emerge through the soft assembly of the activities of the individual members, that is, *bricolage*, into a new (self-)organization of the production. From that perspective, the 'material available' are the members of the organization – as a resource for the organization – who, in turn, have achieved their personal *bricolage* by integrating their understanding of the intervention – reduced to a resource for individual members – with their earlier experiences, skills, preferences into a personal attractor, that, in turn, is the most important resource for the system of the organization trying to reach a new attractor. Thus, individual learning and collective learning are achieved at two levels with a hierarchical relationship between them.

*Methodological implications: where to look with CHAT?* The implications of these approaches are both methodological and theoretical. In such

[121] DST, see Chapter 1.

approaches, learning or knowledge acquisition or construction occurs at the level of activities and interactions. Most studies adopting a CHAT or a community of practice approach (or their variations) focus on the parts of knowledge and activity which are material and visible, not on the mental operations implied. They also tend to be focused on specific settings. Hence, when a 'learning community' is described, what is examined is how a currently functioning community (with its goal, organization of work, rules, tools) faces a conflict which prevents its activities running smoothly. What is then required is the change of some of the components of the system (reshape the rules, change the means, etc.).

The main contribution of such approaches has been to show that any form of knowledge requires a specific community of people who share that knowledge and consider it as relevant – that is, considering learning as part of a dynamic system including a community – and organize specific activities depending on it.[122] It also highlights the identity dimension of knowledge: knowing a specific body of knowledge is part of a person's identity, and defines the social inscription of a person; in turn, learning requires also that a person or a community be changed or transform their activities – their goals, instruments to be used and so on.

However, the problem raised by these approaches is that knowledge risks being understood in very relativistic and incommensurable terms: different communities (chemists in their laboratory, physicists in the classroom, potters in their workshop) develop different forms of knowledge; and there is no point in considering some sorts of knowledge as 'more formal' than others.[123] Also, this approach ignores the psychological counterpart of such activities, both in terms of the emotional or symbolic value of knowledge – what it means for a person to know about cooking or music composition – and the nature of the psychic processes – in terms of the mental operations these demand.[124]

### *Where is knowledge? The quest for a synthesis*

Situated learning and cognitive approaches to knowledge may be seen as the extremes of a continuum – focusing, respectively, on the social situation, or on the mind or the brain. Yet they may also be seen as

[122] It thus joins the work of sociologists of science showing how even a scientific fact was actually the result of very situated practices and exchanges (Latour and Woolgar, 1986).

[123] 'What is called general knowledge is not privileged with respect to other "kinds" of knowledge. It too can be gained only in specific circumstances. And it too must be brought into play in specific circumstances' (Lave and Wenger, 1991, p. 34), quoted in Tanggaard (2008, p. 223).

[124] See Salomon (1997), for a critique.

depending on two radically different paradigms – one according to which knowledge is 'in the mind' and can be tested or measured, and the other for which knowledge is produced and activated within interactions. From that perspective, only the latter approach is compatible with the perspective developed in this book. However, as said, the main limitation of the body of work inspired by situated learning is that it overlooks the psychological component of learning and knowledge construction.

Different studies have tried to overcome these limitations. Over the past twenty years, a very productive tradition which claims to be inspired by Vygotsky's work has led to different theoretical and methodological propositions enabling both the situated nature of knowledge and its cognitive aspects to be accounted for. Some of these studies have tried to account for the 'conceptual fields' that people develop in relationship to a series of situations, and to describe the nature of the cognitive operations actually required by specific tasks in such situations.[125] Others have rather a specific focus on the interactive dynamics at stake.[126] These studies have made consistent propositions, enabling us to deepen our understanding of the relationship between interpersonal and intrapersonal dynamics. However, these approaches, usually empirically focused on one specific task at a time – logical, historical and so forth – have generally not questioned the similarities or specificities of different types of knowledge.

*Knowledge demands generalization*: A different look – through the symbolic and cultural-psychological prism – at situated learning emerged within the *symbolic action theory* of Ernest Eduard Boesch.[127] In the latter case the development of action systems in ontogeny leads to the establishment of symbolic systems that make human living cultural.[128] Generalizability is not only possible but expected – from the sound of the violin[129] we extrapolate the notion of beauty in all of our encounters with the world. In such understanding, knowledge is both in the mind and in the culture – and it is because of the specific organization of our semiotic and social environment that our mind develops certain modalities of knowing and understanding, and develops meaning, skills and values that have a generalizable value.

Among the researchers in teaching and learning who have tried to take into account both the operation required by a specific sort of knowledge,

[125] Vergnaud (2009).
[126] See for instance social psychology of development, current development of sociocultural approaches to learning and instruction (Carpendale and Muller, 2004; Perret-Clermont, Carugati and Oates, 2004; Psaltis, Duveen and Perret-Clermont, 2009) or studies on argumentation and learning (Muller Mirza and Perret-Clermont, 2009); the dialogical approach to learning construction (Mercer and Littleton, 2007), etc.
[127] Boesch (1991, 2000). [128] Eckensberger (2011). [129] Boesch (1993).

and the contexts in which they are usually used, the French sociologist of education Jean-Yves Rochex[130] attempts to understand the specific 'relationship' to knowledge that people develop in different frames. For him, one has to take into account not only the specific norms and expectations of a social environment, but also the sorts of cognitive postures and operation required for a person to develop a relationship to a given object of knowledge. From that perspective, and drawing on Piaget and Vygotsky, Rochex considers *secondarization* to be the main characteristic of the sort of knowledge developed in formal settings. Hence, one can read novels at home and calculate the price of bananas at the grocer without thinking much about it; in contrast, the school (as institution) has the very specificity to invite learners to reflect upon the processes by which they read or understand a story, or calculate, and provide them with a formal language for representing these psychological activities.[131]

A formal education system thus invites students to learn grammar, which demands stepping outside speech to describe the structure of discourse in a formal language; formal education in mathematics demands mastering the formal language of arithmetic or equations, etc. The process of secondarization is thus one form of distancing or reflection upon one's experience (such as in meta-position and meta-education) with the help of specific language. Secondarization thus emphasizes the semiotic difference between informal knowledge and formal knowledge: formal knowledge is based on the assumption of a semiotic system that makes it possible to represent and describe the processes involved in thinking and activity. Thus, secondarization is a strong argument in favour of a distinction between informal and formal knowledge.

Indeed, a semiotic approach to knowledge considers both the nature of the setting in which knowledge is taught and learned, and the operations involved. On the one hand, only institutions with a specific tradition of teaching and learning have developed a secondary discourse upon the practices developed by their members or upon the sort of knowledge they wish to teach.[132] In that sense, schools, scouts, music education, dual vocational systems, some initiation systems, can be said to transmit formal knowledge. In contrast, learning by imitation, participation, problem solving, experience can be said to promote informal knowledge as no

130 Rochex (1998).

131 This observation thus confirms the proposition made by Scribner and Cole in the 1980s according to which it was much more the format of education, rather than the fact of being literate or not, that was organizing a person's mode of reasoning: for them, formal education promotes knowledge to 'talk about' other knowledge (Scribner and Cole, 1986).

132 See also Scribner and Cole (1981/1986).

discourse on the practices involved is occurring. On the other hand, if any sort of knowledge requires cognitive, social and physical activity, and if many forms of learning or using knowledge require distancing from actual practice – reflecting on what is happening, examining further steps, connecting them to past events – *only formal knowledge* actually provides people with *formalized semiotic systems* to guide these practices. This also means that not all the settings considered as sites for formal learning (see above) promote formal knowledge. Hence, *formal knowledge* appears as a semiotic instrument for the re-examination of the acquired knowledge, subsumable under a formal system; it is one very specific form of distancing.

Of course, using formal knowledge does not occur in the void, and usually requires creative explorations and innovations; it is a form of sophisticated play.[133]

### Summary: the many ways (of learning) to contribute to life-course development

Development is a continuous affair of the organism relating to the environment, and includes all aspects of life – and all kinds of learning. Traditionally, learning has been considered as one particular sort of development that can be short lived and undone – in contrast to development. It has been seen mostly in the history of education and psychology as the result of the process by which some person or group, socially constituted as more knowledgeable, imparts some expertise to another, less knowledgeable, organism, person or group.

In this chapter we have questioned this view and have proposed to see learning – in its varied forms – as a set of self-organizing processes that feed into the life course, modifying developmental trajectories in one direction or the other. From that perspective, learning occurs not only in formal settings (like school or the workplace) but also in informal, daily settings, in which a person has to adjust to the new demands of a situation (e.g. becoming a parent, being exposed to the injustice of life, becoming loyal, living a war, moving places, etc.). In all these cases, learning can be said to occur through the process of *obuchenie*, proposed by Vygotsky, by which, in a given situation, past experience (personal and collective) and the role of specific others (even an imaginary other) enable a person to

[133] Formal scientific research, demanding the use of formal knowledge, is thus based on *Conjectures and Refutations* (Popper, 1972). Only refutations require formal thinking. Creativity lies in the conjectures, that is, in the informal processes where new approaches are fancied. Conjectures imply imagination, fantasies, counterfactual thinking, etc. More generally, both conjectures and refutations are dependent on the semiotic function and are part of the processes of learning and development in the life course.

generate her 'zone of proximal development' – the zone out of which new forms of acting and understanding can emerge.

Learning hence draws on earlier experiences – one's own, and notably those of others, personal or collective, the latter existing as received knowledge and represented in one semiotic form or other in books, discourses or any other material form that carries its representation. These external sources of knowledge are drawn upon as resources for the solutions to the tasks that the individual faces. Through direct social interactions and taking advantage of the natural or, more commonly, the culturally set environment, the individual learns through constantly reorganizing her own life space (in Lewin's sense) to face ever new daily tasks (such as changing diapers on a new-born infant).

In this view, learning is one of the motors of the creation of the continuities and variations of one's life melody. Like imagination, learning demands a distance from immediate action, distancing which is enabled by the semiotic and social nature of human experience. In contrast to imagination, learning is always orientated toward present situations of what IS and past situations, and it aims at facilitating the definitions of new actions in what will be, in reference to past and new conditions. However, learning requires imagination precisely to reflect upon experience, and to imagine alternative solutions; and even the most socially guided knowledge always demands personal reinvention. Thus, learning – from facts, books and life – is one of the ways through which melodies of life are expressed, created and transformed.

*Part III*

# Beyond time and space: imagination

# 8 We are migrants!

That life is a journey is a very old metaphor. In this book, we have tried to show that the life course can be seen as a trajectory unfolding in a multidimensional landscape, itself in development. We have focused on three dimensions along which people experience the journey that is their life: first, a life course unfolds in time – we have to advance toward our future, and we welcome it thanks to our past; second, it moves through space – within social frames, between social settings; third, it moves through experiences that can be considered as more or less real, or socially shared, versus fictional or imaginary spaces.

If we consider *time*, *space*, and the realm of *reality-through-imagination* as three axes of a three-dimensional space, then the life course can be represented as a person's trajectory in, out and through various spheres of experiences – various settings, frames, in different material and social locations. From this perspective, every person lives like a migrant[1] – leaving places and people, learning to be part of social spaces, trying to combine multiple belongings and keeping a sense of consistency through a plurality of situated experiences.

As we are all migrants in that three-dimensional life-course framework, then – as psychologists – we have to understand the processes whereby a person enters and leaves a social frame, how her experiences in various settings combine with each other, what difficulties are raised by these moves, how the power of institutions shape these trajectories and what facilitates them. In order to do so, we have to consider separately two types of moves: those that involve substantial experiences of ruptures, that can trigger processes of transition, and those that require the linking of the various daily activities and encounters.

[1] 'We are all migrants' is a metaphor used in developmental psychology, as well as social theory (Pieterse, 2009; Valsiner, 2007a, p. 249).

## Ruptures and transitions

From a person's perspective, some events in her life course imply substantial changes. Some authors have called these 'turning points'; here we call them *ruptures*. Ruptures are events, which can be experienced positively or negatively, that substantially question a person's daily life or current routines. They can be seen as major disturbances of an attractor and they call into being new stabilities. Ruptures can be expected (as when one moves to another country to start a new school programme) or unexpected (as when a close relative requires permanent care after a sudden accident). Experiences of rupture demand unprecedented changes, because the newness of the situation requires new ways of handling one's daily reality which usually have far-reaching consequences and do not allow a return to the initial state. We can then call *transitions* the processes of change in which a person is likely to engage while facing an experience of rupture. Transitions are the processes by which new forms of actions are explored, new ways of understanding are developed, new ways of presenting oneself to others arise.

Transitions can be seen as catalysed processes of change. Such processes, triggered by the rupture, have to be engaged in for a person to establish ways of handling a new situation. If ruptures are experienced when routine actions no longer suffice, transitions eventually end when new forms of routine are established (or when the unprecedented changes have led to a state of affairs in which familiar changes suffice to handle daily life). Typically, experiences of rupture and subsequent transitions can include entering primary school,[2] moving from one country to another, entering the army,[3] travelling in Asia,[4] being called to the war effort,[5] leaving a religious community,[6] retiring, losing a spouse, etc.

Note that such understanding of ruptures and transitions, based on a person's apprehension of change, differs from an observer's perspective which would a priori consider specific events as ruptures (e.g. moving house, or a war) and which defines transitions according to social expectations (e.g. the school-to-work transition). *Here, what becomes relevant is what aspect of the reality is experienced as rupture* (e.g., not war as such, but the fact that one can no longer sell petrol in one's garage),[7] *and the subsequent transition processes* (e.g. find another way to survive, to spend the day, learn a new trade, etc.).

[2] Winther-Lindqvist (2009). [3] Hale (2008). [4] Gillespie (2006).
[5] Gillespie, Cornish, Aveling and Zittoun (2008); Zittoun, Cornish, Gillespie and Aveling (2008).
[6] Zittoun (2006c). [7] Zittoun, Cornish, Gillespie and Aveling (2008).

*Three aspects of transition processes*

Transitions demand extremely diverse processes of change to adjust to a new situation. They are connected with the means a person has of conferring meaning on the situation, her modes of action in that environment and her ways of interacting with others. As an attempt to synthesize what we have seen, and to articulate such life-course psychology with existing studies, we can say that transitions triggered by ruptures entail three main types of deeply mutually dependent processes.[8]

First, transitions involve *learning processes*: for the person concerned, moving to another country typically requires mastering the local language, understanding the neighbourhood, knowing in what shop to buy aspirin or milk, learning what personal questions may be asked of a new colleague without appearing rude. From a theoretical perspective, every rupture – moving out of an attractor – implies exploration, and the generation of a TLC, by which a person, in her social and cultural environment, has to define new forms of action and understanding.

Second, transitions involve *identity changes*. In new situations, a person is identified by others (as a foreigner, as a newcomer), starts to fulfil new professional or social roles (as soldier, as father), has to act as competent or not, experiences being able to handle the situation or not. Hence, transitions imply the transformation and creation of identity positions, as well as the dialogical processes by which these positions can be linked to each other, together with the person one thought one was or expected to be.

Third, transitions involve *sense-making*. Ruptures trigger positive or negative experiences. Whether these are expected or not, people need to 'understand' why these occur. They need to link present changes to past experiences, they need to revise their past plans according to new opportunities, to revise their scale of values to accommodate new facts. Hence, sense-making implies working through affective and immediate experience, by distancing from these experiences, linking them with others, transforming them or reconceptualizing them. Sense-making is a core process of human existence and so any considerable reorganization of a life trajectory demands such processes. We have seen that narratives offer a very powerful means by which people organize and confer sense on their experience.[9] There are other semiotic ways of conferring sense on one's experience, only partly captured by the diverse modalities by which people

[8] Perret-Clermont and Zittoun (2002); Zittoun, Duveen, Gillespie, Psaltis & Ivinson (2003); Zittoun (2005, 2006b, 2008a).

[9] Bruner (1990); McAdams (2006).

externalize these processes (e.g. via painting, film making, writing, singing, dancing, displaying specific bodily postures, etc.).

### *Mutual dependencies in transitions*

Describing ruptures and transitions along these three lines of processes enables us to identify some of the dynamic properties of change in the life course.

First, identity positioning processes, learning and sense-making are three aspects of the same processes of transformation of one's ability to think and act with signs. They represent different aspects of change, which are phenomenologically distinct, as well as socially and scientifically often treated as independent. Yet these three lines of processes are deeply mutually dependent (see Figure 8.1). Changing one of these processes usually requires changing the others: as an adult, learning to read changes one's perception of oneself and also recognition by others (identity positions) and may lead to a deep change of understanding of one's life and future options (sense-making);[10] becoming a parent (new identity positions) requires new skills (learning) and a new reading of one's position in a family or in life in general (sense-making);[11] becoming more committed to Islam requires new learning, but might bring back social recognition (identity) and in turn, might bring more self-value and sense to one's actions.[12]

When one of these processes is required by the social demands or the local situation, yet seems impeded, it is often because another aspect resists: hence, one child may resist learning mathematics (NO learning) if

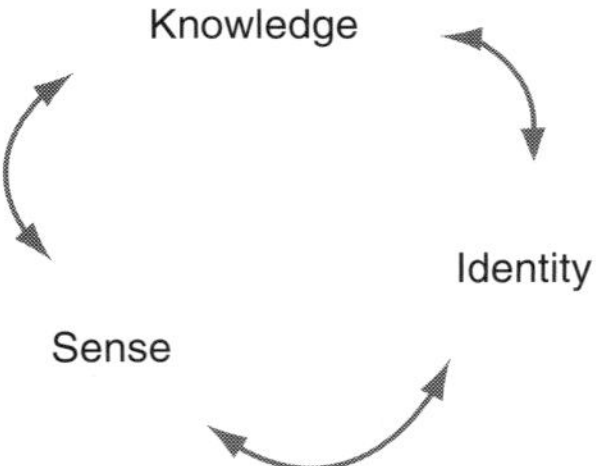


Figure 8.1 Mutual dependency of dynamics of transition.

[10] Hundeide (1991). Hundeide (1991, 2005) also proposed the notion of 'identity packages' to designate certain expected behaviour associated with specific identity changes, themselves constraining further developmental routes.

[11] Zittoun (2005). [12] Schiffauer (1999).

his family have repeated that school is not important as they are going back to their original country (NO sense because no shared meaning), or changing a professional position and one's social identity (NO identity repositioning) may seem frightening because of the new responsibilities and subsequent learning it requires (NO learning).

As we have seen, a person also participates in a plurality of social frames in her daily life. A rupture can be experienced as affecting one sphere of experience only, or as affecting many at once. A priori, moving from primary to secondary school affects only one's participation in formal learning settings, but not one's family life. In contrast, for an ageing person, entering a nursing home affects all aspects of life at once, as most aspects of one's experience – living at home, meeting friends in tearooms, going to the church – become concentrated in one and only one social setting – the nursing home. In the case of an isolated rupture, a person may rely on her own sense of continuity with other spheres of experience: the student who moves to secondary school can still share her experiences with her family, or see the same friends after school, or pursue her swimming classes. On the other hand, a person moving to a nursing home experiences so many aspects of life change at once that she may feel that her own sense of consistency is being threatened.

However, beyond this too simple opposition, because of the constant inner-dialogicality of human life, it appears that a person's changes in one setting often influence other settings. Hence, a woman who starts working again after having taken care of her children may engage in transition processes that lead her, through the development of new skills (learning), to experience her competencies and her identity in such a way (identity positioning) that she no longer accepts having her opinions ignored at home by her husband. So she engages in identity repositioning in the family setting as well, which may generate further changes. Similarly, a young man who experiences his growing competence as a musician (learning) in the frame of his leisure musical activities as authorizing him to teach music to younger students (identity position) discovers the pleasure of such teaching (sense). He might then, in the setting of his vocational school, conceive the project of being able to teach and consequently commit himself into learning how to become a vocational teacher. Of course, such transfers of skills or understanding from one social setting to another one are not always possible, as we shall see.

### *Uses of resources in transitions*

A system tends to use available resources to maintain and sustain itself. Similarly, when people experience ruptures, they are likely to mobilize, in themselves or in their environment, resources that facilitate transition processes. These resources may be used to maintain stability in changing times, or to mediate transformation processes.

Hence, on the one hand, a transition may occur in one aspect of a person's life only, and thus the person can rely on her sense of continuity in other aspects – changing school while keeping close contact with her best friends, for instance, or engaging in new learning while being able to maintain her sense of identity for a while. More generally, inner dialogues (dialogical processes between identity positions) are part of self-maintenance processes. Reflecting on one's experience, inferring principles of generalizing on the basis of various experiences, are typically part of such processes, as well as what we have called sense-making.

On the other hand, as people's lives change, they can very often find means of maintaining stability in their environment: they may have stable relationships with friends and family who have accompanied them through various life events and with whom they discuss these changes. They may also find that new social situations appear as 'already known'. In effect, institutions create social settings that share many commonalities; hence, although one school differs from another school, its 'schoolness' renders it recognizable; the act of buying coffee in a coffee-shop belonging to an international company is 'the same' in any country. People can easily establish links between these settings, and thus such social institutional aspects facilitate the construction of a stable environment.[13] Also, the social environment is filled with objects and artefacts that have some stability through time and space. Pictures, novels read in one's youth, the Bible offered by one's grandmother, enable a person to reconnect, in the present, to other places and times. These cultural elements are stable both because of their materiality, and because they belong to a socially shared semiosphere – the social environment has a memory of their existence and evolution. As a consequence, they can be 'the same' in various settings, in different times and places. These cultural elements may then become symbolic resources that not only support one's sense of self-continuity beyond change – as when a young student, after moving out of his parental home for the first time, puts objects from his home town on the walls of his campus room[14] – but that also may facilitate transformative processes themselves – as when a novel enables the reader to imagine an alternative life path, or a way to overcome a difficult life situation.[15]

[13] Grossen and Salazar Orvig (2011). [14] Habermas (1996), Zittoun (2006b).
[15] Vygotsky (1971).

In addition, there are social institutions and settings whose function is precisely to facilitate transitions, such as certain vocational training, Alcoholics Anonymous groups or birth preparation classes. Finally, some people may specifically facilitate such processes, either because they are professionally trained to do so – such as counsellors or psychologists, priests and personal coaches – or because they create interactions that facilitate these changes through dialogue and consequent position change.[16]

### *From kindergarten to primary school*

One example of early rupture and transition is that experienced by children as they move from the kindergarten to primary school. Clearly here, a move has to be made between two social settings, and the changes demanded are irreversible: not only will children not be able to go back to kindergarten, but as they will enter the world of literacy, they will also durably change their whole understanding of the world. But can we say that children experience a rupture and its subsequent transition?

In a recent research on transition at school, Ditte Winther Lindqvist[17] has examined children's externalization, and on this basis has shown how children anticipate, fear and work through changes that they perceive as ruptures. She followed two groups of children for eight months, before the end of nursery school and after their admission to primary school, and before and after their move from primary school to secondary school. Here we report some of the observations of children aged five and we read them with the help of the notions we have proposed.[18]

James is a popular child in the nursery school. In that social frame, children are free to organize their time as they please, and the activity most valued by the boys is soccer. As James is very good at it, he is recognized as very competent by his peers and he himself feels quite happy. In contrast, Benjamin is friends with girls and is bad at soccer; the other children consider him as incompetent, and he says he doesn't like them; he often withdraws and seems bored when adults do not organize his time for him; his main commitment is to adult conducted activities. The researcher describes how the two children construct anticipations of what might happen when they change schools:

James is sitting on the couch reading when Ollie asks him if he is coming outside to play soccer. 'Yes, when I have finished reading this book', he says. I sit down next

[16] Gillespie (2006). [17] Winther-Lindqvist (2009).
[18] This analysis has been presented by one of us in a chapter on the life course (Zittoun, 2012a).

to him. It is a spelling-pointing book. He pronounces every word carefully as he points at it. Sometimes he asks me to read a word aloud if he is not certain. He sits a long time concentrating with the book. 'I know my dad's telephone number', he says and recites it for me. 'I am attending school next Friday', James says. 'Only after the holidays', I correct him. 'No, we are to visit them next Friday and they will show us around and everything', he says with excitement. 'That is why I rehearse reading', he says, as he puts the book away and joins his friends in the playground.[19]

Benjamin and Mark are drawing at the table with the adult Mia. All children are supposed to make a drawing for Liva as it is her birthday. Benjamin concentrates and works with commitment on the task. He works steadily as required by the teacher; he is also exposed to the school norms explained by the teacher to Mark:

Mark: I am done (stands up).
Mia: But Mark you only just arrived! When you start school you can't just quit when you feel like it . . . Draw some more . . .
Mark: (grabs the pen and draws for 10 more seconds without sitting down) Now it is done!
Mia: Mark, you know in school there is no such thing as not being bothered! (Sighs) Alright, this will have to do then.[20]

James seems to be positively anticipating school, and playing AS IF he were already at school. He is actively creating a ZPD, with the help of a book, and his experience developed in another sphere of experience – knowing his father's phone number. Benjamin does not appear engaged in such active exploration, even though he is part of the interactions that signal to him what is expected in the primary school.

After the children have changed school, things appear quite different. James is put in a different class from his good friends. Soccer is no longer the main activity, and is even difficult to practise: it can be played only during breaks, yet the sports ground is far away, and always very busy. Eight weeks after the beginning of the school year, the researcher writes the following:

(protocol notes from the school interview) James draws an unhappy face to the general question: How do you like school? And the class teacher asks him what it is about school he does not like. He shrugs and cannot tell her. 'Is there something you miss from day care?' she asks him. 'I miss my friends' he says. 'But you have nice friends, also in school, don't you?' He shrugs. Regarding the questions about scholastic activities James also says that lessons are boring, and learning rhymes and singing is dull.[21]

[19] Winther-Lindqvist (2009, pp. 134–5). [20] Winther-Lindqvist (2009, p. 134).
[21] Winther-Lindqvist (2009, p. 138).

In contrast, Benjamin seems to do fine:

> in school he is not supposed to decide for himself what to do with his time, and he is engaged in the project of learning and being a good student, recognized by all teachers and peers for his hard work with drawing, counting, writing letters, remembering rhymes and lyrics, putting his hand up when wanting to speak, etc.[22]

He still does not have many friends, but this fact seems to worry his teacher and his parents more than it worries him, and he seems to enjoy school work.

These examples enable Winther-Lindvist to highlight how, in different social frames, children's 'orientation' and social identity are welcome or not, and lead to identity integration vs. disintegration (in Erikson's terms).[23] In our terms, it seems that, in the frame constituted by the old school, James was relying on his positive identity position as a good soccer player, reinforced by his friends' acknowledgement, and supported by the related skills. In the new social setting, there is no occasion to practise these skills, and to reactivate his friends' admiration so as to support his own identity. On the other hand, the expectations he had for school, through which things could have acquired a personal sense – reading and knowing telephone numbers – have not been met by reality: so far children do 'boring' things like rhymes and singing, which are much less grown up activities than writing phone numbers! Hence, the whole frame seems void of sense – which is suggested by the general emotional tone of James's externalizations (his unhappy face, his comments about missing friends and finding things boring). James has thus experienced the move from one school setting to an other as a rupture, and it seems that he can rely on none of the dimensions identified above as a means to establish some sense of continuity: his identity positions are questioned, his main skills have become redundant, and the sense he confers on the school frame degrades. In contrast, Benjamin was described as having had, so far, difficulties with establishing a strong positive identity, and his skills enabled him to execute 'only' what was asked of him in the first school setting. The entrance to the primary school enables him to actualize such skills in a social frame where they are valued, and where he becomes acknowledged as a good pupil; in turn, one may think that through this emerging position, and perhaps, through the genuine epistemic pleasure hence generated, Benjamin seems to confer some sense on the new school frame as a place to learn – as manifested by his enthusiasm. Here, some pre-existing skills are reinforced, supporting an identity in the making.

[22] Winther-Lindqvist (2009, p. 138). [23] For instance Erikson (1968).

In this example, we see the intricacy of learning, identity processes and sense-making – ranging from affective connotation to anticipation of the future and evaluation of the adequacy of the situation – as these may take place at any moment of the life course. We also see that such mutually dependent dynamics take place in specific social frames, in which relevant social others play an important role. Others do indeed acknowledge or not, validate or ignore, a child's externalization; this may facilitate or hinder the exploration or the change in which the child is engaged – his attempt to understand something he previously did not, his work of conferring sense on a situation, or of redefining himself. In addition, the role of these others may be guided by institutional rules – a kindergarten teacher can let children play, while a primary teacher has to teach them to read according to a certain agenda. Hence, this example shows that transitions are not linear processes: they demand complex reorganization of life configurations, and their outcomes are not predictable. However, the dynamics involved in transitions appear quite comparable through the life course. Migrating out of the natal home to a school or a university or to another village or getting married are all ruptures embedded in any life-course trajectory. Towards the end of the life course persons are faced with a set of reverse ruptures – relinquishing their autonomy and moving into the domain of being cared for by somebody else.

### *From an independent life to the nursing home*

The transition from a formerly autonomous independent life to a nursing home may be considered as one of the most challenging transitions in the human lifespan since it covers nearly prototypically the three characteristics associated here with life transitions: it involves learning processes, it involves identity changes and it involves sense-making of a sometimes dramatically changed life situation. First, a person has to learn to adapt to a new frame with new explicit and implicit rules and regulations; second, he or she has to compensate for the loss of significant parts of the self, namely the physical and social environment associated with life before relocation. Third and associated with this, a person has to integrate new experiences into the model of the self and of the world in such a way that these changes are experienced as meaningful, that is, serving a goal or a purpose.

The effects of moving to a nursing home on the psychophysical wellbeing of an elderly person have frequently been studied; in particular the increased mortality associated with such a transition has motivated reflections about its protective and risk factors.[24] Perceived predictability as well as perceived control could play a significant role here and different results for the person concerned may be expected depending on how voluntary the decision was. It is evident that the consequences of the relocation will differ if the decision to move to a nursing home has been a personal choice rather than being decided by significant others – the latter mostly comprising family members together with care personnel and medical doctors. In close association with this, the functional, physical and mental status of the person has to be taken into account as a second factor that influences the effects of this transition. Here, divergent or convergent views of the other – and the self-defined autonomy status – can be observed. One person may feel quite independent and able to lead an autonomous life while 'others' may not share this view. The second divergence covers a disagreement between an individual with comparatively good functional status who sees him- or herself as dependent despite the divergent evaluation of his social network. Depending on the convergence or divergence of these views differing effects on adaptation criteria may be expected.

The changes in identity inherent in any transition can be evaluated as particularly demanding within the context of relocation. This event almost always implies the partial or total loss of the physical and the social environment of a person, which is even more serious since both can be considered as extensions of the self. Relocation thus implies the loss of significant parts of the self, and it is no wonder that its impact on adaptation criteria is sometimes so tremendous. When moving into a new home, one always experiences a significant change of the *life space* (or '*Lebensraum*', to use the concept brought in by Lewin to describe the perceived and affectively valued life space of a person, comprising both the physical and the social environment). Having lived in a specific context for a given time always signifies adaptation to and active construction of both the social and the physical environment. In particular, the reduction in social networks associated with age has been in the focus of several psycho-gerontological theories. Carstensen and colleagues assume that network reduction in elderly people may be explained by changes in the underlying functions of social relationships. Particularly, if lifetime is perceived as getting shorter, the function of emotion regulation will become prominent and this will induce a specific socio-emotional selectivity of network partners.[25] The social network of elderly adults will thus comprise few

[24] Thorson and Davis (2000). [25] Carstensen (1991).

confidential relations and comparatively fewer relations with less emotional significance than in earlier parts of the lifespan.[26] This approach would predict that elderly adults only choose those persons as network partners who support their emotion regulation. This will also put limits on the creation of new confidential relations within a new living context such as a nursing home. On the other hand, this may also explain why elderly people in nursing home contexts develop close relationships with staff, given that former relations are no longer available.

When it comes to the physical environment of the elderly adult, the creation of senior friendly and supportive environments has become a particularly prominent research topic in psycho-gerontology during recent decades. The personal significance of a physical environment that has been established across the lifespan has not received such attention, although it constitutes a significant part of personal life space. The 'objective' physical environment – the setting – comprises physical objects at the observable level with a specific 'subjective' meaning. Similar to the development of network structures, a person actively creates his or her physical environment throughout life. The composition or arrangement of one's room is important for children's well-being; the leaving of the parental home implies the task of constructing a new physical environment with furniture and other accessories that may suit one's own taste. As we grow older we accumulate and collect many objects that have accompanied us through life and it seems obvious that we will keep only those objects that are of specific importance to us. These may comprise furniture, clothes, pictures and other artwork, jewellery, photos, objects with a spiritual meaning, etc. But also 'larger' objects like a house or a residence, a garden or land that one owns constitute the physical environment. A person always has the choice of keeping some objects or giving some away across the life span. A child will no longer play with the toys he or she played with as an infant, the adolescent will gather new objects to constitute the physical environment, as will the adult. The way one creates the physical environment and the objects one chooses to have around one always convey a specific individual importance, constituting a personal *Lebensraum*.

Conceptualizing the physical and social environment as part of the self signifies that the transition to a new physical environment is always

[26] However, precisely the reverse would be the case in societies where the elder*ly* are treated as *elders* – community leaders who carry accumulated wisdom that is a resource for community self-organization. Their social networks can be widened and acquire emotional-political roles.

associated with the choice of keeping or leaving things behind.[27] This marks again why the move to a nursing home almost always represents a loss event. It is no wonder then that when moving to a nursing home, most people try to re-establish their physical environment, for instance, by taking along selected furniture and other objects, but also pictures and photos. The following sketch of a transition story illustrates this. It is a story of a lady living in a nursing home in Luxembourg:

When Catherine finally decided at the age of seventy-five to move from her small rural village into a nursing home located in a nearby town she left a big house and two gardens behind. The youngest of ten children, she had lived in this village since her birth. She trained to become a tailor and she married her husband in 1939, before the Second World War. The war left her as a widow with two sons aged four and six. She never remarried and when she left the village, she was living in a house that had been built with the help of her brothers after the war. The building was constructed to house two families since she always expected her sons to live with her. Because this could not happen for several reasons, she had lived there for more than twenty years on her own supported by the regular visits of her sons and their families. Furthermore, she was well integrated in the village community and during the day she often chatted with her neighbours or had visits from two of her siblings and relatives who also lived in the village.

When her physical strength was weakened by arthritis and asthma and her siblings had died her sons tried to convince her that it would be best to move to a nursing home and she then decided to move to a Catholic nursing home in a nearby city. When leaving her house she took along her bed, an armoire and a chair. All these were handcrafted and she had already bought them when she moved into her house. She gave special importance to the bed by saying that she wanted 'to die in her own bed'. Furthermore, she took along a wooden crucifix and several framed photos that mostly showed persons of her family during different times of their lives. She also selected some of her 'best clothes' and left everything else behind, asking her sons to take care of them.

Having lived in a spacious house, she now had to arrange herself in a room of 15 $m^2$. She left this room only for meals that were served in a refectory or for some short walks in the monastery garden. In the winter she did not leave the house at all. When she received visits she looked to be well dressed and always offered drinks or sweets that she had stored in her armoire. She also tipped the staff for every little extra service and all in all she was very popular. When she talked about what she had left behind, she always said that her house had been associated with so many sacrifices and that she wondered about 'how it was doing' – just as if it were a person. Once she said that she had abandoned her house. She never talked much about her larger family but always pointed out that life had taught her 'to accept things as they are' and not to worry about things that could not be changed.

[27] The importance of the physical environment to the self is well illustrated by the work of Goffman on total institutions (see Chapter 5). In these settings often inmates are not allowed to have personal objects with them, which further contributes to their feelings of depersonalization.

One year after her relocation she told her family that she wanted to die and stayed in bed during the day although she had no clear medical diagnosis. She came out of this apparent depression after two weeks and lived on until the age of eighty-three when she died of physical infirmity, due to a life full of manual labour and physical work.

Catherine took a decision to take only some objects from the physical world with her, although the representation of her house and her gardens were still the objects of a constant inner dialogue. She decided what to keep and what to leave behind, and her behaviour in the nursing home illustrated this as well: as she had always done, she tried to be a good host and paid for little services. She also received visits as she used to do. She did not change her habits and did not change her identity, but she tried to make sense of the move by 'accepting it as it is'. In this sense, she *lived forward* by preserving what she could preserve and changing what needed to be changed. That it was her own decision to change and leave things behind did certainly help as well, since she had been in control of things. Her depression may have shown that the process of accommodation had costs as well. However, depression may also be seen as a period needed for internal adjustment before the last part of her life.

Indeed, some of the transitions that people experience as migrants in their lives are not triggered by changes of setting, but may be born of internal processes.

### *Ruptures growing from the inner flow of consciousness*

Particular cases of rupture and transition processes are those motivated by the flow of consciousness and inner dialogue. In such cases there is not necessarily an 'external event' experienced as rupture and triggering the subsequent transition; rather, processes of inner dialogue enable the experiencing of rupture and transition processes.

In this sort of situation the flow of thought may suddenly put a person in a symbolic scenario, positive or negative, that places her in a challenging position towards some particular 'object' of concern. This 'thought event' is felt in such a way that past routine procedures do not seem sufficient to handle the situation – it is felt as a 'rupture'. Hence, the rupture is caused by a thought that has unpredicted consequences. A rupture-causing thought may be a new understanding of something (an innovative moment); yet it is not the 'novelty' of the thought that is at stake here, but rather, the inner reaction of feeling a deep challenge. In this sense, we can define these sorts of ruptures as personal reactions to inner thoughts that demand new ways of meaning and acting, implying a personal repositioning.

A typical situation is the experience of an important 'insight', in which a new understanding of something arises. This can be, for example, for a person to find a new way of handling an old intriguing problem with great consequences for his professional life; or to realize that he plays an active role in avoiding intimate relationships, based on prior experiences of abandonment, something that is perpetuating a problem of loneliness. In order to generate a rupture, the new ideas or understanding have not only to be thought about, it is also necessary that the person adheres to some extent to that new perspective: she has to consider it viable or possible. As a consequence, the person faces a new challenging scenario, regardless of its positive or negative connotations.

Hence, the example of the person solving a professional issue seems positive, since it implies a solution to a problem. However, the novelty of the situation will also be challenging, since this change will also imply new and unknown issues. In the example of the person facing the origin of her loneliness, she is immediately confronted with the challenge of overcoming the avoidance, and even though this can be positive, it is also demanding. However, in other cases, personal insights can reveal terrible situations: lies, betrayals, personal pitfalls can suddenly fall under a revealing spotlight. The process of adaptation to these new negative scenarios can be tremendously challenging to the usual self-organization.

Extreme cases of inner rupture, such as those reported in clinical work, can also contribute to our enquiry. Hence people who are going through a period marked by obsessive cognitive processes frequently report another type of situation that implies a rupture motivated by inner processes. In such cases, obsessions are originated by negative, contradictory thoughts (egodystonic), which people feel to be so threatening that they try to suppress them (e.g. the idea of being a pedophile or a serial killer). The originating thought is always something that the person evaluates very negatively. It is here that we see the processes of semiotic auto-regulation in place: a threatening thought emerges, which leads to an affective negative feeling escalation and is subsequently suppressed.

However, such self-suppression of a threatening thought can also be felt as a rupture – as something that demands new answers. If that were not the case, the person concerned would simply ignore the thought and would not give it any credence. Since such thoughts are felt as ruptures, they may lead a person to engage in a process of rational verification of her validity, or an explicit attempt not to think about them. In the active process of meaning-making through building semiotic hierarchies this tends to actually accentuate the presence of the thought and therefore to feed the need to verify and think about it. The person becomes trapped in her inner cognitive processes, and the rupture leads to a transition towards a rigid form of self-organization. The clinical picture of this semiotic self-trapping can be recognized as obsessive-compulsive neurosis. However, such extreme clinical cases also highlight the strengths of the psychological need for meaning-making generated by ruptures, *ad absurdum*.

## Moving through social settings

Ruptures and transitions occur in cases of intransitive changes – people experience moves in time and space in such a way that they need substantial adjustments, which may durably reshape possible futures.

On a daily basis, however, people move in and out of various settings in which they participate regularly – and in that sense we are all migrants as well: we move from home to work, from the workplace to our preferred dancehall or beach, from the beach to the church or the temple and so on and so forth. Although our daily activities in and through these frames may progressively change us, they may not require or involve an experience of rupture. For clarity's sake, then, we will not call such transitive changes transitions.

Nevertheless, these important moves raise important questions for a life-course psychology. Obviously each of us remains as one and the same person who lives through these diverse settings – yet, as these settings require very different activities, modes of relating with others and self-presentation, how are such diverse experiences related? How can we describe how we use what we do in one setting in another, and under what conditions?

### *Dynamics of migration*

We are migrants whether we change social settings and never come back, in our daily moves from one place to another, or when we engage in the sort of inner reflection that deeply changes ourselves. One recurrent problem for psychologists is the question of how we can be the same and yet be transformed, or how we can use past knowledge in a new situation.

The general process of change can be described in dynamic terms, as we have seen in other chapters: patterns of action, interaction or sense-making are progressively transformed, until they demand deeper re-organization. Yet such a description is so general that it does not account for the fact that change is at times very different, and that the experience of having to change one's identity – as a young father, for instance – is not the same as that of learning a new theory. Thus, science has proposed various ways of describing how we can be migrants. Notions that have been used for this include dialogical processes, generalization and distantiation, transfer of knowledge and boundary crossing. These notions emphasize the learning and identity aspects of transitions, and sometimes a combination of two – yet we will also need to consider sense-making.

### *Identity – dialogicality*

When the emphasis is on identity, dialogical models have proposed ways to address the interplay of continuity and change that we experience. Indeed, they assume that the past and future of a person are always part of the present field of experience or that there is a constant dialogue between identity positions. Processes of inner dialogicality take place within a person, but also with imagined or interiorized others (the inner *alter*)[28] or as the result of the internalization of specific setting and community experiences.[29] Hence, the very fact that these processes take place enables change to occur – even if at times there are emotional or social resistances.

### *Knowledge and transfer*

Studies emphasizing knowledge have abundantly thematized the question of using a skill developed in one frame in another. The traditional approach proposed the notion of *transfer* of knowledge from the realm of learning theory. It happens by the overlap of sets of elements between the situations:

> Transfer of learning occurs when learning in one context or with one set of materials impacts on performance in another context or with other related materials. For example, learning to drive a car helps a person later to learn more quickly to drive a truck, learning mathematics prepares students to study physics, learning to get along with one's siblings may prepare one for getting along better with others, and experience playing chess might even make one a better strategic thinker in politics or business. Transfer is a key concept in education and learning theory because most formal education aspires to transfer.[30]

The notion was meant to question the processes whereby not only children, but also adults, can efficiently learn throughout life notably, and ideally, by transferring knowledge acquired in one setting to another.

However, as simple as it seems, transfer is far from occurring systematically and may not even occur in a predictable way. The 'overlap in elements' model does not account for the fact that people may, or may

[28] Marková (2006). [29] Gillespie, Cornish *et al.* (2008).
[30] Perkins and Salomon (1994, p. 6452).

not, use a skill acquired in one situation in another – such as a mathematical rule in a science class – or in one setting in another, such as from a school class to the workshop in the case of vocational training.

Typically, physics teachers despair when their students, having learned to calculate the speed of a ball falling from a tower, fail to calculate the speed of a ball falling into a deep hole.[31] Perkins and Salomon[32] have synthesized studies carried out in the field and they seem to suggest that transfer can occur through two main ways, a 'low road' and a 'high road'. The low road demands quasi-automatic patterns of answers which are activated in situations resembling the contexts in which they have been learned or used before (which we have called level 1 change). Typically, an experienced driver does not need much thought to drive a rental car. The high road requires abstraction and the identification of general patterns or structures between situations or domains, for example, identifying analogies between a political situation and a chess game (which probably demands level 3 changes). The high road can be triggered because the low road does not function, and needs mindfulness. For the authors, these two routes require different thinking processes; they can complement each other, but are usually exclusive.[33] This raises two issues: one is that the 'higher routes' needs further specification; the other is that, precisely, the high route often does not happen.

*Abstraction, generalization, and distancing:* the description of the low route and high route is strongly consonant with the discussion of semiotic processes so far. In semiotic terms, we may say that the low route is based on close similarities between a concrete apprehension of situations, signs which are extremely close to the here and now of experience and bodily embedded, while the high route requires more semiotic distancing and thus enables the identification of similarities between situations. Typically, the 'high route' implies *distancing* (the capacity to use signs to take some distance from the immediate experience), *abstraction* (identifying some common features in different settings) and *generalization* (rendering some meanings general enough for these to become available in

[31] Perkins and Salomon (1990). [32] Perkins and Salomon (1990).

[33] Perkins and Salomon also recommend two educational strategies for facilitating transfer: they invite teachers to facilitate 'hugging', that is, presenting learners with situations that have very strong similarities with what they know so as to trigger automatic responses, and 'bridging', which consists in actively constructing paths towards the high road of distancing. If it has been shown how rare mechanisms of transfer are in formal education with children, and if specific mediating techniques have to be developed, then it is reasonable to ask whether one might expect to see transfer processes at all in non-formal or informal settings, that is, without the deliberate intention of an educator or an expert, and beyond childhood.

further situations). However, these processes are precisely those that do not always occur as wished, and not in all domains of experience.

*Distancing is socially bounded:* in effect, the signs and means by which these processes of distancing occur are located within specific social settings in which people participate in activities, and interact with objects and others. Once considered within their context, people seem less to reactivate a mental skill for a new task than actually to engage in a situation making new demands. Such reasoning and empirical observations have led various researchers to question the relevance of the notion of transfer,[34] showing that it actually does not add much to that of learning: the issue is basically about how a person engages in certain forms of thinking or acting in a situation, seeing some connections with previous situations.[35] Yet this, as we have seen, demands reconnecting learning with identity and sense-making: often, people do not 'abstract' because they do not understand the situation as requiring it, or they feel insufficiently engaged enough to do so, or because the social frame forbids them to ask certain questions, etc.

### *Linking identity and knowledge: boundary crossing*

Instead of considering a learner activating a former skill in a new setting, research along the lines of cultural-historical activity has emphasized the situatedness of learning. For this strand, being competent in a setting actually has the requisite of being a member of the specific group involved. A consequence of this is that being able to use some skill in a new setting has been conceptualized as a process of *boundary crossing.*[36] The idea of boundary crossing emphasizes the *boundaries* that define a particular setting, and the notion of crossing, the processes by which one enters in that new setting.[37] In this sense, the difficulties for

[34] See Lobato (2006) for a review of critics. [35] Säljö (2003, p. 315).

[36] See Tuomi-Gröhn, Engeström and Young (2003) for an overview.

[37] In psychology the focus on boundaries (and their crossings) dates back to the work of Kurt Lewin in his years in Berlin (1917–33) where the focus on actions on the boundary was central for his field theory. The boundary can be viewed as a membrane – a centrally relevant notion in cell biology that is taken into psychology (Marsico, Komatsu and Iannacone, 2011; Valsiner, 2007b). However, current studies in learning and boundary crossing rather draw upon the use of the notion in social sciences, where it has a double origin. One the one hand it comes from social anthropology, where it has been used to define inter-ethnic relationships: members of a given group feel that they are 'playing the same game', while those outside the boundary 'lack shared understanding' (Barth, 1969, p. 15). The notion of *boundary*, as well as the processes whereby groups or individuals attempt to obtain social recognition from other groups, often in a situation of social dominance, are currently analysed by a growing tradition of migration and minority studies; hence, the dynamics by which a migrant is 'assimilated' into a new society can

a new professional trainee of using knowledge learned in the classroom in the work situation is reframed as a difficulty in crossing the *boundary*[38] – that is, of becoming a member, recognized or legitimized as such. It may also be described in terms of being able to use boundary-crossing objects,[39] that is, objects that can be used in different frames or that can bind together different frames.

The approaches developed by sociologists working with the metaphorical notion of boundary emphasize the deep connection between learning, identity and use of knowledge. Yet they raise further questions: is it really enough to describe the processes by which one becomes a member to describe learning – if learning demands specific thinking processes? And if what is transferred is actually a boundary-crossing object, how can we be sure that it can actually be used in different frames?

### *Obstacles to transitions and moving through settings*

These two traditions – work on *transfer*, work on *boundaries* – highlight interesting processes to understand the way in which people engage in transitions or create links between various frames of activities (or not). On the one hand, they suggest the importance of generalization and creating linking between social frames; on the other hand, they remind us of the issues of power engaged: if a person's identity could change, there could be others who do not do what is needed to enable these changes to occur.

Adult development has often been considered from the perspective of learning. In turn, many studies that emphasize what facilitates, or renders more difficult, the processes of transitions or moving between

be described in terms of boundary *crossing*, while the dynamics by which a group obtains more social recognition is a process of boundary *shifting* (Dümmler, Dahinden and Moret (2010); Korteweg and Yudakul (2009)). On the other hand, the notion of boundary crossing has been developed in the field of sociology and anthropology of sciences. Scientific creations (such as a museum of science, Star and Griesemer, 1989) very often require the collaboration of various social actors, with various agendas and knowledge; it could be said that they live in different social frames; the notion of *boundary objects* designates the sorts of objects that are stable yet flexible enough to circulate through these frames and enable the various actors to communicate and work together.

38 Tanggaard (2008).

39 ' "Boundary objects" . . . is an analytic concept for those scientific objects which both inhabit several intersecting social worlds . . . and satisfy the informational requirements of each of them. Boundary objects are objects which are both plastic enough to adapt to local needs and the constraints of the several parties employing them, yet robust enough to maintain a common identity across sites. They are weakly structured in common use, and become strongly structured in individual site use. These objects may be abstract or concrete. They have different meanings in different social worlds but their structure is common enough to more than one world to make them recognizable, a means of translation. The creation and management of boundary objects is a key process in developing and maintaining coherence across intersecting social worlds' (Star and Griesemer, 1989, p. 393).

social settings come from these traditions. One of the problems recurrently observed by researchers in lifelong learning is the strength of 'preconception' – that is, the experience that a person has acquired through her life and on which she draws as she meets new, formal knowledge in a situation of adult learning-teaching.[40] Preconceptions seem resistant, and are substantial obstacles to the acquisition of formal knowledge. Indeed, adults engaging in education have a strong basis of existing knowledge developed through their life course, as well as their professional experience. What a person knows (or knows how to do) is deeply embedded in the sense of who she is and how she confers sense on events in general (see above). Learning – especially in adult life – requires renouncing one's expertise and its related identity and sense-making. Thus, even if an adult engages deliberately in a learning programme, she is likely to hold on to her knowledge and resist other bodies of knowledge, which are, more or less consciously, seen as a threat to identity (in similar ways, as seen above, people resist change in therapy).[41]

Some researchers have tried to use these conceptions as grounds for more systematic knowledge, for instance through interventions inviting people to develop a reflective stance on their practice.[42] These procedures mainly rely on people's abilities to develop a semiotic translation of their actions, which would then enable some distance from them, and then, a

[40] These have been observed also in children, who have naïve or intuitive ideas about whether a kilo of feathers is lighter or not than a kilo of iron (Brousseau, 1983) – yet one may question whether these are really obstacles, or necessary steps in children's exploration for good enough explanations of their environment (Kohler, in preparation).

[41] In addition, adults in a formal educational setting may draw on the only experiences of formal education they have had, which were often their initial education; in doing so, they also tend to activate similar identity positions and their related senses – for example negative emotions, defiance, etc. (Aumont and Mesnier, 2005; Cesari Lusso and Muller, 2001).

[42] See also Tiberghien (2003). A field of studies is exploring the possibilities for adult to learn from their actual experience of working. In France, under the idea of 'learning through work', researchers have designed research and teaching interventions to enable such learning, partly drawing on cultural-historical theory (Vygotsky, Leontiev, Engeström and others). These techniques include 'crossed-confrontation', when workers have been video-recorded and are asked to comment on their action as they see themselves, 'double-crossed-confrontation' – when they comment on the activities of another professional – or 'instruction to the double', in which professionals have to give sufficient instructions to another person so as to enable her to carry out her own routinized activity (Clot, 2002). A second French tradition, inspired by phenomenology, has developed parallel techniques to bring people, through very specific interviews, to explicate the detail of non-reflective actions (Vermersch, 2006). Both these techniques create a distance between a person and her actions, and generate semiotic elaboration – people have to translate into an advanced semiotic system, language and conduct which is partly automatized and extremely embodied. In that sense, we can say that professional expertise becomes 'secondarized' (see above): it becomes a discourse about action, as grammar is a discourse about speech. In addition, these authors generally emphasize the

reflective understanding – which enables deliberate guidance and generalization of one's experience. In other words, they may be said to aim at turning experience into a form of semiotic resource.[43]

However, many practitioners have thus developed specific techniques to enable adults to learn *in spite* of their previous knowledge and experience, such as deconstructing their a priori representations through group discussion, writing their biographies as learners,[44] or engaging in new postures – such as that of researcher.[45] Interestingly, then, these techniques are meant to support learning through *distancing* from knowledge and its re-semiotization, either thanks to a *change of position*, or via sense-making and the creation of a new *narrative*. Hence, learning seems possible after the two other dynamics of meaning-making and change of identity position have been triggered.

On the other hand, as knowledge or skills are connected to identity, they are also connected to power – some people may prevent others from using certain sorts of knowledge, thus preventing them from changing their identities. A teacher may consider that it is not legitimate for students to mention personal experiences as they discuss a literary text, although creating such links between a daily frame and the school setting may help them to confer sense on the text.[46] Students are thus socially prevented from 'using' their personal experiences as resources to make sense of a text – teachers in turn remain the owners of expertise about the text. More generally, denying access to learning to women or foreigners, or excluding children from certain social classes from access to higher education, are means by which society controls people's access to knowledge and skills which could otherwise become tools for leaving certain social settings and entering others.

### *Imagination and sense-making*

Describing the difficulties of learning or identity change calls for a close observation of the dynamics of sense-making. Sense-making enables people to connect new situations to their experiences; it makes it possible to evaluate and reject them; and it is at the core of the association between identity and learning issues.

The proposition made throughout this book is that play and imagination – AS-IF processes – are actually at the core of sense-making. They

'emancipatory' function of such knowledge. In any case, once turned into a semiotic mode through a specific interactive setting, such knowledge should ideally become 'ready' for use in further situations.

43 Gillespie and Zittoun (2010b).
44 Dominicé (2007); West, Alheit, Andersen and Merrill (2007).
45 Aumont and Mesnier (2005). 46 Grossen, Zittoun and Ros (2012).

may thus be seen as the processes by which it is possible to move out of difficulties in learning and identity change, as well as to overcome the social and material constraints of a given social setting.

Of course, imagination is not always possible: in some conditions people feel in too much danger, or under too much pressure, or are too exhausted, to adventure beyond what IS. But as we have seen in various examples, even in the most extreme situations, imagination opens new possibilities – and some of them will turn into actualities. Also, this can be facilitated by various means – and the social world and various resources are there to support this, as we will see in the following chapters.

Imagination, a key process in learning and change (TLC), occurs in terms of the semiotic begetting of new sign complexes, new fields of experience, etc. Imagination is the first step in the process of sense-making – demanding distancing from experience, binding together past and future, as well as the possible and the actual. In that sense, imagination is often the first step to moving out of a stable situation.

Yet for learning to occur, distancing may need to be changed from a generalized experience to a more precise and communicable notion, such as in reconceptualization innovative moments, and often, in languages or gestures which are socially acknowledged. Also, changes leading to new identity positions and innovative moments often demand social recognition – in social terms as well as in terms of inner dialogicality. Finally, sense-making, which demands creative synthesis, may then need to find temporary new forms in narratives or others forms of symbolization – such as personal life philosophies.

## Summary: the play of transition

Life melodies have rhythm, breaks and acceleration. One of the ways to capture the rythms of people's life melodies is to highlight the alteration of melodies – ruptures in continuities and the creation of new patterns.

In life-course studies, the notions of ruptures and transitions have been proposed to identify major shifts in people's trajectories – from an observer's perspective. For the person herself, it is often from the perspective of the present that past ruptures are experienced as transition. It is often by rereading the past, constructing memories and narrating them, that people realize that change has occurred, and confer sense on it in a conscious way. In addition, it is by rereading the past, or constructing new expectations, that people may generate ruptures. Either way, ruptures appear as the most important occasions of change and development in the life course. Yet beyond these major ruptures, daily lives are paced by changes of settings and frames, imaginations and interactions. In both ways, we are migrants and we play an open-ended game – but how we make sense of it turns it into a repetitive experience, or an always renewed adventure.

Theoretical and empirical explorations of transitions usually put great emphasis on the surrounding social or material circumstances leading a person to face new conditions and imposing new social frames on varied aspects of life – if not the totality of daily life, as happens in the case of a move to a nursing home. However, this process is not only governed by externalizations – there is also an internalized process going on. The origin of the rupture may be an inner dialogue, leading to the creation of a new perspective about something. In these cases, it is not the social setting that is changed, but the personal way of framing some specific situation. However, in the process of adapting to this new framing, different externalizations will take place. In any case, externalizations and internalizations are both involved in the process of migrating from one framing to the next.

This chapter has offered a perspective of the life course centred around ruptures and transitions, and based on three core interrelated processes: sense-making, knowledge acquisition and identity positioning. In order to face the immediate future, unknown but nevertheless constructed from previous experiences, a person is involved in a purposeful act of meaning-making that calls for new identity positions. The dynamics of migration thus involve processes of inner dialogicality and outer dialogicality, by which self-identity re-emerges continuously. It is by assuming a position and in the movement from this position to the next that microgenetically the life course is drawn. Migration also involves knowledge transfer. If we are constantly facing new situations, this novelty must be faced with previous personal resources. Thus, knowledge is situated, but transferable by processes either of more or less automatic resemblance (or mindless efforts of adaptation to a new situation) or of higher abstraction (or mindful, purposeful and effortful thinking). This last process, probably more common in situations of rupture, implies a semiotic process of distancing by which not only is knowledge adapted to new circumstances, but also a person is challenged to cross some social boundaries.

Finally, if we had to account for what enables a person to develop new forms of acting, thinking or self-defining after ruptures and once she finds herself in a new frame, then imagination seems a core process. If imagination is thinking about what is not and how things could be, imagination is the first move beyond the here and now – thinking back in the past or forwards in the future, about what could be instead of what is, and about the most impossible options before thinking back to a realistic one – it may be the core process, and the first step toward all forms of psychological distancing. Yet imagination can do even more – it opens all the arenas of adult play.

# 9 Playing while being serious: the lifelong game of development – and its tools

Play is central to human lives. Of course that standpoint is a truism when we – as adults – look at children. Yet in seeing children as endlessly involved in play we overlook that very same way of being in ourselves. We all play – in different forms – throughout the life course. That play is socially guided – for different age levels there are different cultural expectations of how to play – including the charade of playing at 'being serious' – acting as a 'grown-up', 'career politician' or 'an elder'. The social norms of playing at different times of the human life course guide people to reflect upon themselves as if they were not doing so. Moving to playing one's life dramas as if these were not play (the idea of *emerged adulthood* of 'no longer playing') creates a convenient conceptual blinder to separate oneself as an ordinary adult in one's social roles (parent, policeman, pirate) from 'the others' – the 'children', the 'elderly', the 'immigrants', the 'silly next door neighbour who plants flowers rather than invests in the stock market' and so on. The self-reflection of 'being serious' is a semiotic device to set up the in-group of 'us, the serious people' in contrast to 'them, the non-serious'.

## Human play as semiotically organized activity

Our central premise all through this book is that playing is a phenomenon that exists – and is needed – throughout the human life course. The cultural psychology of the study of the human life course is based on one central premise – *human beings are constant active meaning-makers in their relating with their environments*. It is through that relating to their environment – constructing it in meaningful ways – that further meaning-making is triggered. This leads to yet further reconstruction of the environment – which leads to further meaning construction, and so on – without end. Such forward-oriented construction of the new is the core of all living beings. At the level of the *psyche* such construction entails both inventions of new forms of acting and – in the human case – construction of ever new meanings. When a person dies – from old age, illness, war, execution as a criminal or by accident – the others who remain continue in this never-ending process of meaning-making.[1] Only the end of the species of *Homo sapiens* could stop this production of meanings. The human world creates its *semiosphere* (see Box 9.1).

In the making and maintaining of the semiosphere, play occupies a central role. In this chapter we chart out the many ways in which *play* – and

### Box 9.1 Juri Lotman and the notion of *semiosphere*

The concept of *semiosphere* was introduced by Juri Lotman (1922–1993) – the originator of the Tartu School of Semiotics. He moved from Leningrad (now Saint-Petersburg) to Tartu after the Second World War, and was for the rest of his life a faculty member at Tartu University.

In 1984 he suggested the notion of 'semiosphere' as an extension of Vladimir Vernadsky's notion of biosphere.[2] The term 'biosphere' was originally coined by Swiss geologist Eduard Suess in 1875, and he defined it as *the place on Earth's surface where life dwells.* Vladimir Vernadsky elaborated this in 1926, proposing the notions of the *geosphere* (inanimate matter), the *biosphere* (biological life) and finally *noosphere* – to designate the third stage in a succession of phases of development of the earth due to the cognitive processes of humankind: just as the emergence of life fundamentally transformed the geosphere, so the emergence of human cognition fundamentally transformed the biosphere. Lotman's notion of semiosphere sets the focus on the signs-mediated nature of the mind that constructs the environment. The semiosphere is viewed as consisting of large numbers of meaning-constructing monads – hierarchically organized – that guarantee the meaningful nature of all human activity.[3] The notion of semiosphere is holistic – the semiosphere is a semiotic space outside of which sign construction cannot happen.

All semiotic space may be regarded as a unified mechanism (if not organism). In this case, primacy does not lie in another sign, but in the 'greater system', namely the semiosphere . . . Just as, by sticking together individual steaks, we do not obtain a calf, but by cutting up a calf, we may obtain steaks – so in summarizing separate semiotic acts, we do not obtain a semiotic universe. On the contrary, only the existence of such a universe – the semiosphere – makes the specific signatory act real.[4]

The semiosphere exists in the form of a bounded semiotic universe – through partitions of the 'inside'/'outside' – it is the transformational relation between the separated parts that becomes the arena for

[1] Josephs (1998). [2] Lotman (1984, 2005). [3] Lotman (1993, p. 368).
[4] Lotman (2005, p. 208).

**Box 9.1 (cont.)**

semiosis. The borders – and rules for their crossing – are constantly renegotiated. By ritualization of actions in everyday life semiotic borders are created, which then become objects for transcending. The semiotic monads[5] relate to one another within the semiosphere creating the heterogeneity of the human meaning system. The notion of semiosphere is linkable with other core constructs within cultural psychology – social representations[6] and psychological distancing.[7] In this heterogeneous system of semiotic field the act of play is of importance at all age levels – from the child's construction of a meaningful toy to the adult's construction of the lovable child,[8] and to the need for many older people to pre-set the stage for their final social encounter.[9]

its counterpart *fantasy* – relate to one another throughout the ontogenetic life course. In our contemporary world, playing and fantasy are becoming a purpose in themselves – to engage in playing in order not only to create a reality, but also to create further imagination.

### *A discriminating fantasy: adults are serious as they work, while children play*

Play is central for human living. We all play – even if pretending not to! All human beings are involved in play – including here the pretence 'I do not play' – from birth to death. From childhood to adulthood, play may change its forms and supports; what is socially acceptable for a child – running through the house saying 'I am a tornado' – is not for an adult; yet adults find other, more socially acceptable ways of playing that are more

5 Lotman (1993, p. 372). 6 Raudsepp (2005). 7 Del Río (2002).

8 Despite the obvious inconvenience of taking care of babies, children in any society become admired and loved – the social construction of such irrational feelings is crucial for the continuity of the human species. As human reproduction becomes framed within the semiosphere – rather than biosphere – it is the power of signs that starts to guide a person over the life course.

9 That final encounter is a person's funeral – where the participant is no longer capable of immediately setting the stage for this occasion. The need to make one's own funeral arrangements – which has become fashionable in the occidental societies – is a form of play act that transcends the biological end of the life.

relevant to their preoccupations and abilities.[10] Taking on a role – a mask – of full seriousness is a form of play. Play – when framed by social norms – leads to a whole variety of human social acts.

Thus – the usual contrast made in everyday life – 'children play, adults are serious' is a convenient lie, used by adults to mask all kinds of playful actions that they cannot accept, given their 'serious' play.[11] Consider a parent joining his or her child in some play. The parent may see his or her involvement as 'educating' or 'parenting', or 'child-minding' – while for an external observer it becomes clear that the parent accomplishes many of his or her playful fantasies through joint action with the 'playing child'. Thus, if play for the child has been seen as the arena for creating her ZPD,[12] then for the adult partner it surely creates the opportunity for the freedom to play as well, even in the guise of 'serious' child-orientated activities.[13] Yet the capacity to play indicates the flexibility for further development of both participants.

The special role of play in moving beyond the present state of human development was already recognized in the 1890s, as Karl Groos wrote extensively on play in animals and in man. His ideas were the basis for Vygotsky's later link of ZPD with play. Groos stated that:

> The child, playing with a doll raises the lifeless thing temporarily to the place of a symbol of life. He lends the doll his own soul whenever he answers a question for it; he lends to it his feelings, conceptions, and aspirations; he gives to it the pretence of mobility by posing it in a manner that implies movement, or by simple fiat when

[10] Freud (1908/1959) thus noticed that as children grow older, the realm in which they live their fantasies or imaginary experiences moves: if children can openly play, adolescents have to 'hide' their play in a more private sphere – writing diaries or poetry, while adults keep alive their personal fantasies, love for arts, etc. Winnicott (1991) similarly sees all forms of adult creativity as well as cultural experiences (music, physics or church) as growing out of children's play.

[11] As Freud put it: 'Might we not say that every child at play behaves like a creative writer, in that he creates a world of his own, or, rather, re-arranges the things of this world in a new way which pleases him? It would be wrong to think he does not take that world seriously; on the contrary, he takes his play very seriously and he expends large amount of emotions on it. *The opposite of play is not what is serious, but what is real*' (Freud, 1908/1959, pp. 143–4, our emphasis).

[12] Vygotsky (1933/1966) – ZPD is the area of psychological functions that have not yet emerged at the present time, but are in the process of coming into being. Hence play is the appropriate framework for that development. It can occur individually – the child rises above the actual level of current development in play – or in a social context – under the guidance of some more knowledgeable peer or adult. See also Chapter 7.

[13] Perhaps, in parallel with ZPD, we can call the adult version *ZARA: zone of available regressive actions?* Through the flexibility of modulating one's actions – between 'play' and non-play ('work', 'serious action', 'important tasks' etc.), the adult maintains the necessary range of reaction to various everyday life challenges. Consider an adult that can never 'play', and another that can 'only play' – *both* of these examples are mal-adaptive for the whole range of real-life situations.

he asserts that it has nodded, or beckoned, or opened his mouth. Here the resemblance to aesthetic sympathy is already strong, and still further augmented by the use of the child's own body as the instrument of this mimic play. His attitudes and positions are then symbolic.[14]

The basis for play is the propensity to feel into the other – a doll, or its equivalent, or another person. Play is an act of externalization of the internalized subjective worlds. Through the constructive internalization/externalization processes it is possible for the playing person – child or adult – to transcend the confines of the current reality – and construct a new one.

### *The basic contrast of reality and pretence: the importance of unreality*

Play is action in-between what is known (AS-IS) and what is imagined (AS-IF). Hans Vaihinger's philosophy of 'the as-if' – as we described in Chapter 3 – sets up the framework for conceptualizing play. His *Philosophie des Als-Ob* was the first move in twentieth century science[15] to capture the realities of the human *psyche* that constantly transcend the here-and-now given realities. When viewed in our flow of living – in irreversible time – every statement we make is at least partly orientated towards the future. So even mundane claims – 'Today is a nice day' or 'I am a happy person' – are not merely statements about a day or a person, but semiotic tools for the future events that are about to happen during the day ahead and to the person who has declared herself to be happy.[16]

14 Groos (1908), p. 327. The German original of *Die Spiele der Menschen* was published in 1899. Before that – in 1897 – Groos published *Die Spiele der Tiere*. Note that the starting point for Groos is the aesthetic aspect of human living that play makes possible. The notion of *rising beyond oneself* in play antedates Lev Vygotsky's later look at the ZPD as a result of child's play (Vygotsky, 1933/1966).

15 Vaihinger (1911/1935) – in reality his work was finished in the 1870s. He was followed, decades later, by Ernst Mally's values-based logic in the 1920s. In the first decade of the twentieth century James Mark Baldwin (1906, 1908, 1911, 1915/2009) created his system of developmental (genetic) logic that remains the basis for developmental science. In that logic, play had a central place since it creates the arena for *sembling* (feeling-in, *Einfühlung*) in relations with the world: 'The player... says to himself, *this is real, or would be, but for the fact that I know that it is not*; it stands for reality in so far as I choose to let it so stand – but not altering or abolishing it' (Baldwin, 1906, p. 111). Through this train of thought non-existent objects, created in play, become quasi-existing objects (Valsiner, 2009a, 2009b).

16 This notion is also at the root of the dialogical self theory of Hubert Hermans (Hermans and Hermans-Konopka, 2010) – any statement of an ontological kind (A) is actually a visible part of an inherent dialogue between A and something else, e.g. a claim 'I am happy' is a part of a dialogue with 'I am not happy' (or with at least 'I am neutral'). See also Chapter 6 in this book for elaboration.

## Differentiation of the AS-IF domain: the moral imperatives at work

What can be acted out in the AS-IF domain is relative to how the AS-IS is being considered. Thus, you can ask sisters to 'play brother' to each other, but you cannot get them to 'play sister' to each other.[17] Thus, the reality of AS-IS creates one boundary for the AS-IF construction zone – the AS-IF needs to transcend the AS-IS, yet the latter is the anchor point for such move beyond 'the real'. AS-IF domains can take different forms – they can offer people a way to escape from the here and now, as when bored students look out the window and imagine going to the swimming pool – but also to actively explore future possibilities. Hence, what is often called 'vocational choice' actually requires a complex exploration of alternative AS-IFS ('what if I start college?', 'what if I go on a one-year trip?').

This exploration of AS-IF is bounded by social norms and actual recognition of achievement – they fix what SHOULD BE or not. Hence, boundaries for AS-IF actions are created by the limits to the zone of possibilities (AS-COULD-BE) which are further specified by social norms that insist upon their imperatives (AS-SHOULD-BE) and their opposite (AS-MUST-NOT-BE) (see Figure 3.2). Much of our everyday reasoning and decision-making proceeds between these 'attractors' of the immediate future; 'I should do X but *I do not feel like* doing it . . . I could do Y but *it is immoral*' – are discourses often present in the mind and in social interactions.

It needs to be recognized that the borders of AS-COULD-BE and AS-SHOULD-BE (and AS-MUST-NOT-BE) are *episodically re-organized*. This means that the specific AS-IF form of action is constantly being renegotiated by a person at the AS-IS||AS-IF boundaries. The move from the AS-IS domain towards the AS-IF leads to the ambiguity of the field structured by AS-COULD-BE, and its sub-fields AS-SHOULD-BE and AS-MUST-NOT-BE. It is predicated upon the basic ambiguities of living in the move from past towards the future, and ambivalences built upon these ambiguities.[18] A young woman who has put on a miniskirt at home, liking the image her body presents in the mirror, moves through the public space, and constantly pulls down her miniskirt – attracting the further attention of others – now playing the role of not being mini-skirted. More generally, the simple play acting of adolescents to dress in a way that they find appealing, but which happens to overlap with the religious ideologies

[17] This example comes from John Sully (1896) and was later used by Lev Vygotsky.
[18] Abbey (2007).

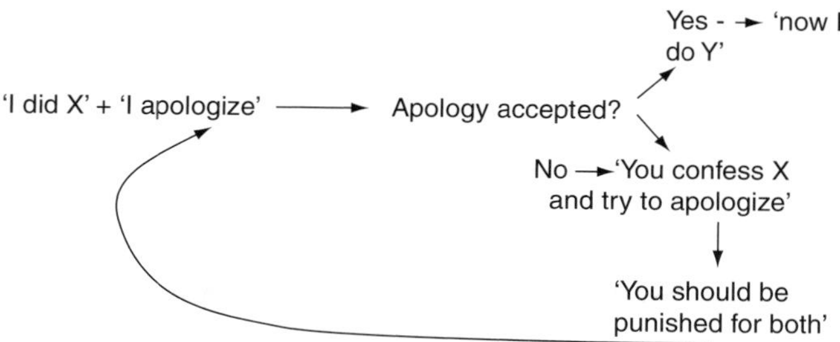


Figure 9.1 Bifurcation of symbolically repaired transgression.

of a given country, can become escalated into other plays ending up in ideological oppositions.[19] Indeed, imagery about social norms of self-presentation in the public place may feed into the AS-COULD-BE domain of body presentation, calling for such *symbolic repairs*.

### *The general form of symbolic repair*

The idea of symbolic repair is taken from genetics (it is an analogue for *mutation repair*) and is applied to the dynamics of human meaning-making actions. It is an 'exit route' or play – which becomes an act of further play. Thus, in terms of the AS-IS | |AS-IF fields in Figure 9.1, play includes the person's movement at the borderlines of

[AS-COULD-BE |border zone| AS-MUST-NOT-BE]

Play is the framework for testing – and renegotiating – the boundary. The playing person – starting from a state of AS-IS – moves towards a future social encounter exploring the 'border zone' – navigating between the possible and the disallowed. Hence transgressions are important for development, as these can bring with them renegotiation of boundaries. Once the boundary is violated – and the violation is recognized – symbolic repair tactics will follow to 'withdraw' behind the boundary. However, such a 'retreat' is symbolic – the act of transgression becomes a marker of boundary change as the mark of having been transgressed before sets the precedent for future renegotiations. The previous AS-MUST-NOT-BE becomes a part of the future AS-COULD-BE by the mere act of repair of a transgressing act. This is the function of apologies in social life – to mark the part of the boundary that is open for transformation.

[19] The 'scandal' about wearing 'Islamic headdress' in French schools is an appropriate example (Bowen, 2007). The issue of such negotiations has a long history (Auslander, 2000).

*An example of the play of public apologies:* one example of a public apology is that of former US president Bill Clinton to the general public after he had been accused of having an affair with his secretary, Monica Lewinsky:

Good evening. This afternoon in this room, from this chair, I testified before the Office of Independent Counsel and the grand jury. I answered their questions *truthfully*, including questions about my private life, questions no American citizen would ever want to answer . . . Indeed, I did have a relationship with Miss Lewinsky *that was not appropriate.* In fact, *it was wrong.* It constituted *a critical lapse in judgment and a personal failure on my part for which I am solely and completely responsible.* But I told the grand jury today and I say to you now that at no time did I ask anyone to lie, to hide or destroy evidence or to take any other unlawful action. *I know that my public comments and my silence about this matter gave a false impression.* I misled people, including even my wife. *I deeply regret that . . . Even presidents have private lives. It is time to* stop the pursuit of personal destruction and the prying into private lives and *get on with our national life.* Our country has been distracted by this matter for too long, and I take my responsibility for my part in all of this. That is all I can do.[20]

In his public apology, Bill Clinton asks for forgiveness for two things: having an affair with Ms Lewinsky – which was inappropriate, wrong, that is, AS SHOULD NOT BE; and for not acknowledging this earlier – which gave a false impression, AS SHOULD NOT BE either. Note that even in this highly uncomfortable public apology, Clinton manages to bring back the fault to his detractors, because even though it is true that he did things that a president should not do, presidents also have private lives, and the public should care about public affairs, not private ones – in other words, the public SHOULD NOT be interested in their president's private life and SHOULD NOT turn their attention away from national affairs.

How does a symbolic repair turn further into play? The repair – when play-acted – becomes a further step *in the very same play* that led to the need for such repair. In the irreversible sequence I DID X → BUT X MUST NOT BE DONE → I APOLOGIZE FOR DOING X → BUT *X WAS DONE* ANYWAY → X *COULD* BE DONE the particular act (X) is moved from the 'taboo zone' (AS-MUST-NOT-BE) to the AS-COULD-BE. In other terms, transgressions become neutralized through symbolic repair.

The inclusion of symbolic repairs in the further course of play makes it possible to plan transgressions with the intention of symbolic repairing if need be, to continue the play on the boundaries of AS-COULD-BE||AS-MUST-NOT-BE. Yet such continuity requires social response from the others – the symbolic repair needs a symbolic acceptance. If it is rejected

20 'Bill Clinton's August 17 speech to the American public re: Monica Lewinsky', available online at, http://www.zpub.com/un/un-bc-sp1.html, accessed 3 May 2009, emphasis added.

it this may feed into repercussions against the repairer. Symbolic repairs can become semiotic means used to punish people who have attempted a symbolic repair (Figure 9.1).

The act of rejecting a symbolic repair effort constitutes the defence of the AS-COULD-BE||AS-MUST-NOT-BE boundary (Figure 9.1). Specific semiotic markers can be attached to the decision making at the bifurcation point ('is THIS apology SINCERE, or not?' – versus – 'can X be accepted NO MATTER WHAT APOLOGY is given?'). The 'doubling' of guilt allocation ('you did it' *and* 'you DARE TO apologize' or 'you dared to give us a NON-SINCERE apology') may lead to further negotiation through yet another apology effort.

*Innovation*: Innovation, at the social as well as at the individual level, depends on a particular form of symbolic repair. It is often generated by the fact that a person or a group proposes an idea or an action which is unrealistic within a certain society ('let us act AS-IF sexuality could be separated from procreation', 'let me behave AS-IF I could write a great novel'), hence pushing the boundaries between AS COULD BE/AS MUST NOT BE, so as to bring self or others to symbolic repairs that can ultimately reconfigure these borders around a specific semiotic set. At a collective level, the first women who wore trousers were obviously transgressing the admitted boundaries (and actually looking 'AS-IF they were men'). Some of them were probably refusing to engage in a symbolic repair cycle; and being persistent enough, possibly other people – on the side of the norm – engaged in symbolic repairs: SHE DID X => X MUST NOT BE DONE => BUT X WAS DONE ANYWAY => MAYBE SHE HAS A GOOD REASON FOR DOING X (APOLOGY) => (YES SHE HAS: THERE IS AN UNFAIR NORM/TROUSERS ARE COMFORTABLE) => X COULD BE DONE. We can make the hypothesis that such a mechanism takes place in most social innovations, as it did in situations in which minorities were engaging in some behaviour or discourse that seemed 'unrealistic' to the majority (ecology, socialism, a Sunday without using a car, etc.).[21] On a personal level, a person coming up to retirement may also suddenly daydream about becoming an adventurer, exclude this as unsuitable for a respectable person having saved money all his life, yet on the basis of this fantasy, find the idea good enough to engage in a new life of travelling around the world. In many cases, engaging in AS-IF thinking or action creates bifurcation points and new pathways for action. Yet of course, not all AS-IF thinking involves real actions; otherwise we could not *think about* strangling our boss *without* doing it.

[21] See the work of Moscovici on active minorities (1985).

The social act of apologizing can become a social means for relationship regulation. Aside from immediate public apologies at times of revelation of private acts – as the celebrated cases of Bill Clinton or Tiger Woods[22] indicate – the genre of apologizing may become an issue of collective relations between institutions, and can become a personal act undertaken long after the clandestine 'wrongdoing' has been hidden in the mists of the past. Thus, the Danish celebrated cyclist Bjarne Rijs – suspected by journalists repeatedly of taking performance enhancing drugs (and denying this during his active years in top-level sports) decided to confess eight years after his retirement that he had indeed been taking such drugs. He asked to be pardoned by his still numerous fans.[23] Yet his demeanour in making the confession indicated no 'sincerity of guilt' – which led to anger in the audience.[24] A person whose body – in the process of achieving high-level athletic performances – could be supported by nutrients (some of which were categorized as 'performance enhancing drugs') – has become a symbolic object for others as a celebrity. The person enters into a liminal social role similar to that of fictional characters in novels[25] – yet with a difference: *as a live person* the celebrity can be expected to act as an ordinary person (e.g. to apologize for misdeeds), yet *as a celebrity* s/he is expected to adhere to the socio-moral expectations projected onto them.[26]

## Human propensity for creating fantasies

It becomes clear from these examples of very adult play that our lives are spent in creating fantasies.[27] We are also constantly negotiating – both within our subjective worlds and in relation to others – the relations of

22 The 2010 scandal of the top golf player in the USA concerning his private marriage issues indicated the extent of public appropriation of the private domains of a 'celebrity' for collective meaning negotiations.

23 Brinkmann (2010, pp. 260–4).

24 A similar anger at the 'trade in indulgences' led to the Protestant Reformation in Europe in the sixteenth century.

25 The fictional characters in novels are known to be fictions – on whom the readers' fantasies are projected (Eco, 2009). Yet no reader expects fictional characters to make public apologies to the public – no matter how much a Raskolnikov is desired to live a non-murderous life.

26 Which can be coped with by creating a liminally buffered status – see the case of Maradona (Salazar-Sutil, 2008).

27 The notions of fantasy (with an 'f') may designate more or less deliberate forms of day-dreaming, but also unconscious forms of imagination. In contrast, psychoanalysts usually call *phantasy* (with a 'ph') the unconscious processes of fantasizing, to which belong dreams, and all unconscious thinking that may lead people to slips of the tongue or neurotic symptoms. More generally, however, we need to consider the anthropological

these fantasies with the real everyday world. Children, adolescents, adults and the elderly are all involved – in their age-course specific ways – in the same psychological building enterprise. Through play-like activities, people travel in their minds, explore parallel social realities and sometimes open new routes for the futures or their societies. It is therefore not surprising that psychological systems that emphasize the whole of human action and its constructive nature have intuitively utilized the readiness to play for research and intervention purposes. Yet in these systems, the relationship between reality and play, or facts and drama, may vary.

### *Victor Turner – human living between ritual and theatre*

Victor Turner's anthropological heritage[28] is crucial for developmental science because of his consistent focus on the borders – the liminality of living (see Box 9.2). Developmental science deals with *time-bound liminal states* – development happens on the borders (rather than in the centre) of

> **Box 9.2 Victor Turner**
>
> *Victor Turner* (1920–1983) was a cultural anthropologist of Scottish origin who moved to the United States. He was best known for his work on symbols, rituals and rites of passage.
>
> His main empirical focus was on the Ndembu (a society in what is now Zambia). Turner became intrigued by ritual and rites of passage, and his work concentrated on rituals and dynamic dramas. As a professor at the University of Chicago, Turner began to apply his study of rituals and rites of passage as these are reflected in religious systems. His work centred on the liminality – in-betweenness – of human actions in ritualized contexts. This focus is very productive for cultural psychology in our present times, and should play a crucial role in developmental science – since all processes of development can be characterized as being in between WHAT ALREADY EXISTS AND WHAT DOES NOT EXIST YET.Turner's main books are *The Forest of Symbols: Aspects of Ndembu Ritual* (1967), *Schism and Continuity in an African Society* (1968), *The Ritual Process: Structure and Anti-Structure* (1969), *Dramas, Fields, and Metaphors: Symbolic Action in Human Society* (1974), *Image and Pilgrimage in Christian Culture* (1978) and *From Ritual to Theatre: The Human Seriousness of Play* (1982).

evidence of the cultural role given to fantasy – such as the role of 'daydreaming' (Pereira and Diriwächter, 2008) and dreams – a place for serious decision-making about non-dream time community (Stephen, 1982).

28 See Turner (1973, 1995).

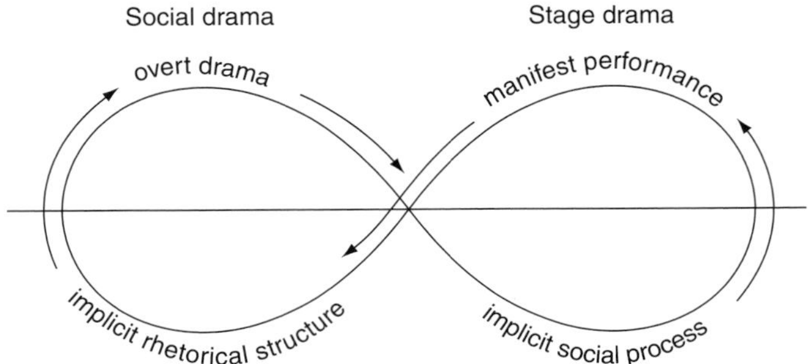


Figure 9.2 Dynamic relationships between life and theatre (Turner's use of Richard Schechner's figure).

the currently existing state of the organism. Turner makes the dynamic nature of his focus on meanings clear:

> *from the very outset* I formulate symbols as social and cultural dynamic systems, shedding and gathering meaning over time and altering in form, I cannot regard them merely as 'terms' in atemporal logical or protological cognitive systems.[29]

Through such dynamic means human beings not only understand order, but also make creative use of disorder. This is done by reliance on the opposite of structure – anti-structure – which relates to the former. Anti-structure

> can generate and store a plurality of alternative models for living, from utopias to programs, which are capable of influencing the behaviour of those in mainstream social and political roles (whether authoritative or dependent, in control or rebelling against it) in the direction of radical change.

Human play and fantasy create the formation of anti-structure. The dynamic tension between structure and anti-structure is embedded in each act of playing or fantasizing. In society, the dynamic process can be viewed as constant movement between the mundane and the theatrical (Figure 9.2), where:

> The left loop represents the social drama; above the line is the overt drama, below it, the implicit rhetorical structure; the right loop represents stage drama; above the line is the manifest performance, below it, the implicit social process, with its structural contradictions.[30]

Such dynamic relations between the stage in theatre and arenas of living create a liminal state for the persons involved – they are simultaneously

[29] Turner (1982, p. 22). [30] Turner (1982, p. 73).

actors in the dramas or tragedies that they direct as 'theatre directors'.[31] Under some circumstances – in theatre proper – these two roles become distinct (the spectator is not the actor, nor director, watching *Hamlet*), yet all the reasons why one or other theatre performance is (or fails to be) appreciated by the spectator *is in the unity of the actor and director roles in real life.*[32] The theatre- or cinemagoer who exits from the location of the performance into the arena of everyday life reunites the actor and director roles as needed for daily living. The idea that people play on different stages, in the theatrical sense, has then been developed further in the social sciences by Erving Goffman,[33] among others. Here, we may say that people move through different frames, and/or in different settings, which they can perceive as distinct spheres of experience, in which different identity positions come to the fore.

## Transitional space: contributions from Winnicott

A complementary way to describe the dynamic relationship between inner experience and the socially shared experience, or between individual fantasy and the semiosphere, has been proposed by Donald Winnicott, a British psychoanalyst known for his work on play (see Box 9.3). Winnicott[34] proposes to distinguish three zones within human experience (see Figure 9.3):

1 a zone of '*inner psychic reality*', which is possible when a person is sufficiently integrated to have a sense of distinction between inner and outer world, and where a person has wishes and desires that do not need to be shared with others;

2 a zone of 'external reality', or *socially shared reality*, in which actions and uses of things are limited by social rules (e.g. not stealing from neighbours) and natural rules (e.g. a body located at altitude is attracted by gravity towards the ground);

3 a 'third zone of experience', or 'intermediary' zone, in which transitional phenomena are possible. In that zone, one may play, or engage in cultural experiences: that is, these experiences are enabled by cultural objects (dolls, strings, books, symphonies) yet they become experiences because we populate them with our inner fantasies and emotions. This zone thus includes children's play as much as adult imagination.

31 See the distinction of actor and author of life narrative, as proposed by Sarbin (1986), also here Chapter 7.

32 Relevant material about that feature would come from the length of time between a playwright finishing a play and a theatre agreeing to stage it (e.g. Samuel Beckett's *Waiting for Godot* was finished in 1949, staged in 1953, his *Eleutheria* was written in French in 1947, published in English in 1995, and staged for the first time in 2005).

33 For instance Goffman (1961b). 34 Winnicott (1967, 1989, 1991).

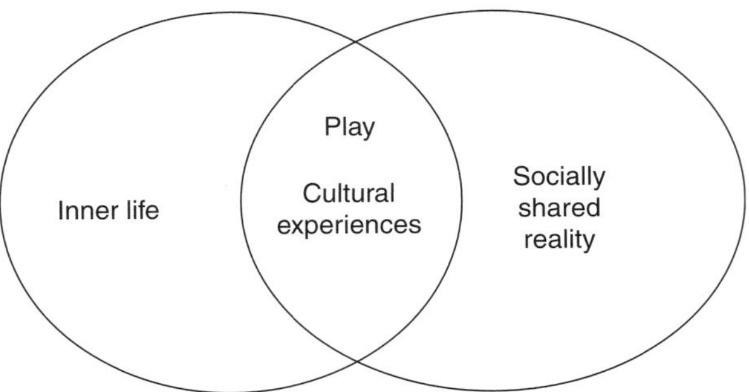


Figure 9.3 Three zones of experience after Winnicott (1971).

### Box 9.3 Donald W. Winnicott

Donald Woods Winnicott (1896–1971) was a British paediatrician and psychoanalyst. He worked with displaced children and children disturbed by the war, as well as mothers and children that came to his consultation. Active in the British Psychoanalytical Society at the time of the tension between the 'Freudians' and the 'Kleinians' he developed his original line of thinking and was thus considered as 'independent'.

His work led him to expand the theoretical models mainly available at the time, examining early interactions, the child's constitution of a sense of self and of her capacity to explore the world. He developed a special interest in human creativity and playfulness, as well as in cultural experiences, as presented in his best-known book *Playing and Reality* (London, 1971). The unusual transcripts of some of his whole therapeutic treatments were published, thus offering rare longitudinal case studies, such as *The Piggle: An Account of the Psychoanalytic Treatment of a Little Girl* (London, 1977) and in *Holding and Interpretation: Fragments of an Analysis* (London, 1986). His many public lectures to specialists and laypersons as well as papers for various audiences were published in a series of collected papers among which are *Collected Papers: Through Paediatrics to Psychoanalysis* (London, 1958), *Maturational Processes and the Facilitating Environment* (London, 1965) and *Psychoanalytical Explorations* (London, 1989). His main theoretical ideas are summarized in the unfinished posthumous *Human Nature* (London, 1988).

*The object as a tool for bridging the past and the future:* Winnicott described the ontogenesis of our ability to engage in such playful experiences; for him, the very young infant, still somehow 'fused' with the mother, comes at some point to experience the absence of the mother – for example, when he is not fed immediately when he feels hungry. In order to be able to feel separated, he turns an object – a blanket, his thumb or a teddy bear – into a sign that will symbolize for him his relationship to the mother, and the fact that she will come back and thus that he is not alone. It is this 'transitional object' that enables him to tolerate his separation from the other. For Winnicott, this thumb or blanket is thus both 'found' (i.e. given by the environment) and 'created' (i.e. generated by the child's psychic life and intentionality). This first 'transitional experience' opens the way for more and more complex experiences located 'between' the inner world and the socially shared reality, or partly 'found' and partly 'created', such as play, pretend play and cultural experiences (ranging, for Winnicott, from theatre to science and religion). Also, for Winnicott, humans develop, from that type of experience, a generalized creativity – an ability to 'reinvent' any given object: this is the ability to see the tree in front of one's window each time as a new tree.

More generally, and especially when talking about young adults and adult development, rather than mentioning a 'zone', Winnicott speaks about *transitional phenomena* – a dynamic, constantly evolving range of playful phenomena in which people engage as part of their constant transactions between self and their environment. These transitional phenomena are thus composites of inner tendencies and subjective apprehension of the world, and semiotic forms given by the social environment. Fantasies and imagination are guided by culture, yet can also always expand its limits. Hence the notion of transitional phenomena is very close to Vygotsky's notion of ZPD. The transitional objects are the cultural tools, or resources, that a person uses to guide his or her development towards the proximate future – yet in ways that relate with the affective history of one's past.

*The capacity to be alone:* Winnicott understood the growth of relative autonomy over the life course. He recognized the sociality of our private experience in his reflection on 'the capacity to be alone', which corresponds to the actual capacity to be alone yet in dialogue with others. Again, the origin of this capacity is identified, ontogenetically, in the infant's interactions with the mother. If the child has the experience of a 'good enough mother' (or her substitute), then he can trust that she will take care of him even when he is not maintaining an active interaction with her, and thus he can relate to himself (engage in a sort of inner, or intramental dialogue):

> Gradually the ego-supportive environment is introjected and built into the individual's personality, so that there comes about a capacity actually to be alone. Even so, theoretically, there is always someone present, someone who is equated

ultimately and unconsciously with the mother, the person who, in the early days and weeks, was temporarily identified with her infant, and for the time being was interested in nothing else but the care of her own infant.[35]

Hence, what renders the person able to be alone is the fact of having introjected the caring other; and hence the psychic presence of the other is what enables the child *to feel alone – self-sufficient – in the presence of* a close person (e.g. the mother, that is, pursuing the relationship with her without actual interaction). This capacity to be alone *in the presence of the other* leads to the adult's capacity to be autonomous while being *actually* alone, without feeling lonely. This is an example of the distancing from the social embeddedness that makes a person self-sufficient. Later, this capacity is what enables adults to have 'mature' relationships with others, without being dependent on their attention.

We thus see how this capacity to be alone is related to the previous issue. For one, it suggests that the capacity to be alone is dependent on an earlier interaction with significant others, and on an internalization of the relationship. Thus, even the zone of experience that corresponds to *inner life* is of a social nature. Additionally, we see that the capacity to be alone is linked to the capacity to be creative, or to engage in play and cultural experiences. Playing and engaging in cultural experiences, as well as engaging in an exploration of the socially shared reality, require the capacity to be alone – which is social in nature.

### *Fantasies constructed – within the mind*

The most hidden, and important, location of the human move beyond AS-IS reality – mediated by the internalization/externalization processes[36] – is in the realm of our own more intimate thoughts and desires. This is a fact that has been long acknowledged by psychoanalysis (contrary to the fact that it is often wrongly considered as the study of the 'private'). For instance, Sigmund Freud considered *culture as shaping the ideas we have about our lives*:

No feature, however, seems better to characterize [culture][37] than its esteem and encouragement of man's higher activities – his intellectual, scientific and artistic achievements – and the leading role that it assigns to ideas in human life. Foremost among those ideas are the religious systems, on whose complicated structure I have endeavoured to throw light elsewhere. Next come the speculations of

[35] Winnicott (1958, p. 36). [36] Valsiner (2007b).

[37] The German word *Kultur* used by Freud has been translated as 'civilization' in the standard edition of his work; in other editions it has been translated as 'culture', which we privilege here.

philosophy; and finally what might be called man's 'ideals' – his ideas of a possible perfection of individuals, or of peoples or of the whole of humanity, and the demands it sets up on the basis of such ideas.[38]

Hence, all the dreams analysed by Freud are full of instances of social norms, rules, others people's opinions about the self, etc. Here an example taken from the *Interpretation of Dreams*:

She was descending from a height over some strangely constructed palisades or fences, which were put together into large panels, and consisted of small squares of wattling. It was not intended for climbing over; she had trouble in finding a place to put her feet on and felt glad that her dress had not caught anywhere, so that she stayed respectable as she went along. She was holding a BIG BRANCH in her hand; actually, it was like a tree, covered with RED BLOSSOMS, branching and spreading out. There was an idea of their being cherry-BLOSSOMS; but they also looked like double CAMELLIAS, though of course those do not grow on trees. As she went down, first she had ONE, then suddenly TWO, and later again ONE. When she got down, the lower BLOSSOMS were already a good deal FADED.[39]

Freud's commentary is identifying the reported objects: fences, flowers, branches, white and red. He sees them as 'hieroglyphs' that have two levels of meaning. At one level, there is an explicit meaning (a woman climbing a fence, etc.). At the other level, each of the objects, their perceptual qualities and their geographical organization, designates other thoughts and emotions. To find them, Freud will ask the dreamer to freely associate around each of the objects mentioned in the dream. Through these associations, other webs of meaning will emerge; these constitute what he proposed to see as the 'latent' discourse.

This latent discourse can be more or less dissimulated. In this example, the association of the dreamer goes from the flower, which the dreamer identified as a camellia, to the religious paintings representing the *Annunciation* – in which a white flower usually represents Mary's virginity; yet the flowers are red, as in Alexandre Dumas's *La Dame aux camélias*. Freud sees here a juxtaposition of ideas of virginity, and of menstruation – and of the end of purity, as here the number of flowers referring to the number of his patient's fiancés. In Freud's theory of symbolization, signs find their meaning because they point, on the one hand, to socially shared meanings, and on the other, to personal experiences. Hence, the white flower belongs on the one hand to a complex cultural tradition, in which flowers are used by religious painters to represent virginity and, on the other hand, to the dreamer's experiences of such flowers. A person who thinks about such flowers can at once mobilize these two networks of

[38] Freud (1929/1961, p. 94). [39] Freud (1900/1953, pp. 347–8, emphasis in original text).

ideas, feelings, representation, etc. The flower is an object provided by our culture, where it acquires a semiotic value – and as such, it becomes a semiotic resource supporting and guiding thought. From that perspective, dreams – the supposedly most private of places – offer social semiotic guidance from within, in which signs become oversaturated by their locations in the semiosphere. Semiotic elements can symbolize private experiences precisely because they are social – they can guide one's experience because they carry the ramifications and echoes of their location in a cultural system.

### *Myths and counter-myths*

All human life takes place in the middle of various forms of stories told, rituals constructed and values exchanged – by trade, conquest, appropriation or other forms of social transfer. Parents may read books to the children, priests may read sermons to the parents and politicians may manage to utter one-liners on TV, interspersed with advertising for computers, beer and travel opportunities. TV channels fight for the attention of the viewers to tell them stories about how to live right and buy all the things they do not need. Priests only tell stories about the former. Dieticians tell mothers how to feed their babies, or how to eat 'properly' themselves. Teachers tell stories about the world outside the immediate reach of children. Policemen tell stories about immediate conduct – by their actions, words or even mere presence as complex signs in the public environment.

Similarly to the notion of landscape, one can think of the different narratives surrounding the developing person as a multifaceted surface – a 'mythscape'. The 'mythscape' of a given social unit – community, country or geographical region (e.g. 'European' or 'Asian') – and person – is always inherently ambiguous. Different myths can suggest mutually opposite values within the same society. This is not surprising, given the unity of opposites within the myth story (as described above). Simply in some myth stories, the meaning-value A is highlighted as socially suggested, while in another set of myth stories its opposite meaning-value (non-A) becomes socially suggested. In a society where these two kinds coexist, the dialogical nature of social discourse is likely to be observable.

The second kind of story – 'counter-myths'[40] – serves an important function in maintaining society's pool of possible meanings. The public discourse including such myths and counter-myths is filled with dialogical

[40] Ramanujan (1991).

tensions. If in standard myths a particular set of meanings (e.g. honesty, etc.) is emphasized and wins after a battle with opponents, then there may exist different counter-myths in the given mythscape which promote the opposite meaning (e.g. cheating) as victorious in mythical battles. When the mythscape contains such dialogical tensions, it also carries the seeds of its own change.[41]

*'Official' and 'non-official' history narratives:* Myth and counter-myth are roughly equivalent to the opposition of different kinds of histories of countries – official and unofficial – that operate along the lines of dialogism. The 'official history' of a given country is the equivalent of a myth, while its opposite – 'unofficial history' – functions as counter-myth. History narratives are created – and censored – in accordance with the goal orientations of social institutions. The colonizers usually create myth stories of the glory of 'discovery' of the lands of the colonized, while the latter are ready to tell the story of being conquered, rather than 'discovered'. The fate of smaller ethnic and linguistic communities within the historic artefact of political borders (e.g. Basques and Catalans between Spain and France, or the partition of India and Pakistan in 1947) are critical. The tensions generated by borders lead to the creation of a large variety of histories that operate as myths in the regulation of current intercommunity relations, which in turn modify these borders. The establishment of the European Union sets up a different social demand for myth stories to enter into a dialogue with those of Catalan, French or Spanish identities.

## How we navigate the semiosphere: structuring experience

Within the highly saturated semiosphere, myths and counter-myths can also offer an arena especially suitable for a strong engagement in imaginary worlds. If semiotic guidance is pervasive in daily action, to enter into these spaces people willingly accept disengaging from their daily lives and surrendering to a 'story' or an imaginary cultural experience. Watching a film, contemplating art, reading a novel or playing a videogame are in that sense specific cultural experiences characterized by a major jump into an unconstrained AS-IF world. Entering into the world of fantasy is engaging in a 'transitional' sphere of experience, in this case enabled by cultural artefacts such as books, films and, songs, and yet nourished by one's inner life.

41 See for example Zittoun, Cornish, Gillespie and Aveling (2008).

Cultural experiences are socially framed and authorized fantasies; as such, they are the elaborated forms of 'playing' offered to adolescents and adults in our society.[42] Phenomenologically, such cultural experiences are distinct from socially shared experiences. We can play at killing policemen in a computer game or at identifying with a 'bad-guy' character in an action movie yet this does not kill anyone for real. Such fantasies can also be distinct from our inner lives – in a difficult period of our life, we can abandon ourselves in a comedy, forgetting all about our usual grief and pain.

### *Boundaries*

There are different kinds of social and psychological markers that enable us to establish the difference between our personal reality, socially shared reality and imaginary cultural experience. Hence, a cultural experience implies embodied practices and discourses that create a boundary, a frame or threshold between what is 'real', AS-IS, and what demands a jump into the imaginary, WHAT-IF.[43] For instance, a traditional storyteller 'frames' his tale, both by creating a special setting (he meets his public at night, around a bonfire), and using specific semiotic devices, such as an introductory 'call' ('Good people, come and listen to the tale of . . .'). Similarly, going to an art exhibition demands certain threshold activities: buying a ticket, leaving one's coat and bag in the locker room, walking down a noisy corridor, before being suddenly pushed into an open, luminous and whispery space. Hence, for the museum-aware person, these practices may have already created the state of reception necessary to engage with a given painting or sculpture. The cultural practice of framing pictures – in museums and in people's home environments – provides social guidance for such reception expectation. Symmetrically, most cultural experiences also need a threshold, a semiotic practice that enables us to leave the imaginary and return to 'socially shared reality'. A crowd going out of a movie usually seems surprised and disoriented, as if waking up from a very intense dream. Here the social sharing – in the crowd – of the deeply personal lived-through experience of a 'movie-dream' creates a catalytic condition for such social guidance within deeply personal worlds. Different social settings can be deliberately set up to enhance such dream states – religious services involving large crowds, football matches with collective chanting by fan clubs, political

[42] Freud (1908/1958). [43] See Köpping (1997).

manifestations, dance parties and even occasional encounters of street performances or accidents observed in public places.

Interestingly, such framing activities are often meant to be 'invisible', or not relevant when thinking about the cultural experience (we think about the novel, not the fact that we read it on a red sofa after we had a cup of tea). Most of our social guidance is embedded in the background – it is a form or ornament that creates its guiding impact through peripheral input into our sensory systems and meaning-making activities. However, current research on TV watching shows the progressively greater control that people acquire over these framing activities, as means to modulate their full or partial participation in the imaginary cultural experience. Playing with the remote control is a way to immediately bring closure to an unpleasant scene on the screen.[44] It is also a vehicle for fragmenting one's flow of ongoing experience creating 'positive ruptures' when the flow is going in a direction we don't like. Similarly, contemporary videogames enable players to be more active in the manipulation of framing devices (enabling them to jump in and out of certain scenes or characters).

A second range of devices exist that enable people to frame some activities as belonging to 'make-believe', or fiction: these are semiotic indications that help the watcher or reader to attribute the cultural experience to a specific range of experiences. Hence, an image of a falling tower in a film describing the adventures of an MI6 spy using gadgets is identified as fictional, and can be appreciated for its aesthetic or narrative values; the same images shown and marked by the logo 'CNN news' are identified as belonging to a socially shared reality and are evaluated very differently by the watcher.[45] Children, who are not yet familiar with these cues, may need the help of their parents to identify whether the image invites a play-like openness or not. Trouble seems to arise – in clinical reports as well as in daily dramas – when adolescents or adults fail to make the distinction between social shared reality and fiction, for example, when they treat real information about the uses of weapons as an invitation to play a new game. On the other hand, it may be said that current cultural experiences tend to play more and more with the cues that are classically used to indicate whether an experience is fictional or real, hence creating many more blurred and ambiguous zones – think about 'fictional documentaries', fictional biographies,[46] simulation games, etc. The experience of semiotic ambivalence may open new ranges of exploration of real and new forms of poetic creativity in our daily lives.[47] Yet they may also be

[44] Lembo (2000), Tisseron (2005). [45] Tisseron (2005). [46] Tisseron (2005).
[47] Abbey and Valsiner (2004); Abbey (2007).

sources of individual confusion and anxiety, if not exploitation. For the comfortably situated television viewer in the living room news images from a current war zone may appear similar to a videogame or movie. When the same person is taken to the very real battlefield the 'gameness' of real conflict may lead to psychological trouble (as various films suggest). This also generates social debate or hostility (as there has been about the immorality of confusing archive images of a genocide and a Hollywood re-creation of these, or a biography and a fictional biography).[48]

Third, people have the ability to distance themselves from their experience of engagement in imaginary cultural experiences, during or afterwards. This process of mental 'abstraction' has been described differently, and can be seen as more or less constitutive of the experience itself. For Benson,[49] aesthetical experience, such as that involved in contemplating an artwork, demands two phases: one phase of absorption, in which the person 'looses' herself and surrenders to the semiotic guidance of the artefact – which may bring the experience of s*ubjective delocation*, the experience of an infinity of I positions – and a phase of reflection, when a person reflects on the experience and how it was actually realized. Tisseron, similarly, calls for a critical sense that enables the viewer to reflect upon how a cultural element – a film, an image – has moved or disturbed him.

Such critical reflection, enabled by *distancing* indications, can take two directions. One is oriented *towards the cultural element* itself: how that film was made to produce that effect, how a verse creates a sense of rhythm. The other direction is oriented *towards the self* – why was one so moved by seeing a child being abandoned by her mother in a film, or the hero coming back to his homeland? In that sense, the first critical stance is using various signs as tools to understand other signs – it is a *metasemiotic* reflection, like that of the art critic. The second stance uses various cues as *semiotic resources* – as mediators for self-reflection.[50] In many cases, the two stances are complementary. These forms of distancing can be trained – the first one is taught at school or in formal education, while the other is mostly developed informally, at home or with friends, when people

[48] Recently in France a fictionalized account was published of the life of Jan Karski, a member of the Polish resistance during the Second World War who tried – in vain – to call the world's attention to concentration camps (Haenel, 2009). It reactivated an older public debate in which Claude Lanzman, the director of *Shoah* (the major documentary about the Holocaust), who made Karski's testimony public in the 1980s, plays an important role. The central point is whether fiction is an appropriate means to transmit the memory of past tragedies (see Lanzmann, 2009, 2010a, 2010b, Haenel, 2010).

[49] Benson (2001). [50] Gillespie and Zittoun (2010b).

discuss how they felt about a film or a song. These two modes of distancing are part of the psychological means we have to create, maintain and modify boundaries between the real and the imaginary.[51]

### *Permeability*

However, and imaginary as they are, these cultural experiences obviously have an effect on our inner experiences and our social lives. Many authors have tried to qualify these (see above, Freud, Piaget, Vygotsky, Moreno, etc.). For some, the strength of these experiences is that while they are 'fictional', the emotional experience in which people engage is 'real'; hence crying at the end of a sad film (e.g. when the horse dies) is *really an experience of crying*, and thus it leaves us with the *actual* experience of relief that crying may bring (even if we have no attachment to horses whatsoever). Some call these experiences 'vicarious', in the sense that they enable us to have some of the benefits of experiences AS IF we had really had them, but without having to do so. What is important is not merely the distinction between the AS-IS and AS-IF worlds, but their constant 'move' into each other – crying when observing something in the AS-IF world (pretend domain) is real in the AS-IS world, and leads to a new move into the next aspect of the AS-IF world and so on.

However, having these experiences also has an effect upon other zones of experience, that is, on a person's understanding, or in her relationship to others and the world. First, through these experiences, people can create links between events located in different times and places. They can recall a past event, as when a picture reminds someone of a friend. They can open future pathways, as when interacting with art objects might enable a person to explore the options available to her and thus generate her own proximal zone of development,[52] or when a person watches films located in Asia before travelling there.[53] Second, they can have a *transformative* function: a person's emotional state can be transformed by the object, as when a person feel different before and after listening to a symphony.[54]

[51] However, the nature and status of these boundaries are evolving. Classically, the jump into fantasy was collectively staged (in carnival, in public theatre); with the vanishing of this collective handling of boundaries and the privatization of cultural experiences, people need to develop a greater awareness of specific cues and to develop reflective stances to identify real from imaginary experiences. In addition, it appears also more clearly that daily actions are infused with fiction and play-like dynamics. The question is whether we have the social knowledge needed to understand and handle these mixed experiences.

[52] Vygotsky (1933/1966). [53] Gillespie (2006). [54] Bollas (1993).

Possibly, people's representing abilities can also be transformed: in playing with pictures, or reading comic books, which are framed contents, people may reinforce their own *thinking abilities* to frame and contain experiences.[55] Third, when plays are shared, events that are negotiated 'in the game' may affect social relationships afterwards.[56] Also, people may realize that they have had the same cultural experience as others; these shared experiences can then participate in the shaping of collective identities – hence adults may feel they are part of the '*Star Wars*' generation, having spent time being a fan in their youth and finding affinities with former fans; or, readers of a specific text feel they are members of the same group as any unknown reader of the same text. In such examples, the 'effect' of the cultural experience, which is clearly 'imaginary', operates within the 'reality' – of one's inner life or of one's relationship to the socially shared reality.

A productive way to explain these effects is to argue that such imaginary cultural experiences *are actually made out of the same stuff as real experiences – they are enabled and guided by semiotic streams*. As such, they involve the same processes, and can affect our system of understanding in the same way as any other experience.[57] Hence, it is normal for imaginary experiences to affect human change and development. However, because they enable more freedom and exploration than other experiences, imaginary experiences are potentially catalysts for changes. And thus, it appears that many people actually use them as such.

### *Connecting play and fantasy: the function of cultural rituals*

One way by which human societies have acknowledged the special nature and the transformative functions of play and fantasy is through cultural rituals. Cultural rituals are usually events, isolated in time and space, under the responsibility of some sort of cultural specialist, in which people

[55] Tisseron (2013).

[56] The negotiation of roles and performance in role-play may bring children to reallocate positions in real social networks, as shown by Winther-Lindqvist (2009).

[57] Cultural experiences are enabled by a person's interaction with distinct, bounded cultural objects, made out of complex arrangements of signs, carrying meaning and likely to canalize experience as time unfolds and a person follows a story, listens to music, deciphers an image, etc. Cultural experiences are often multimodal: they function through the relationship between musical, visual and spatial semiotic arrangements. These can support each other (as when film music evolves consonantly with the scenario), or can be contradictory (as when a light melody is played at a dramatic moment). Yet, because they are semiotic, and thus canalize the very flow of our thinking, they affect not only current experience, but also the very nature of the processes themselves.

are invited to collectively cross a boundary between WHAT-IS in the socially shared reality, and WHAT-IF or WHAT COULD BE.

Traditional *initiation* rituals, such as those through which young men transit into adulthood within a given group, have been described as following a typical sequence. First the young men are taken apart from other children, their peers; they are then introduced to actions or stories that shake their understanding of the worlds and introduce them to the knowledge of adults; and they are reintroduced within the society, where they are now publicly acknowledged as 'adults'.[58] Specific narratives and symbolic actions guide each of these phases. In many cases, the liminal phase puts the young man in a state close to fantasy.

*Example: an initiation ritual*: in the Bille,[59] the preliminary phase creates such a state. In this phase young men to be circumcised are asked to follow the 'path of death' when they wake up and are still sleepy; then, men disguised as 'bushes' and hidden behind bushes jump at them, shout and make noises to scare them. Brought into a clearing, the young men are asked to wear a special hat as asign of humility, and clothes that remind them of the deceased. They are also threatened with death if they are frightened. This pre-liminal phase is meant to lead them to 'part from the mothers', who accompany their sons halfway, and cry as they escape from their world. After this follows the actual liminal phase, which lasts many days, during which time the actual initiation takes place. The post-liminal phase lasts two months, during which the young men recover from the circumcision before reintegrating in the group, where they will be treated like men.[60]

We can observe that the preliminary phase creates a dream-like state, in which facts can be one and their opposite: young men are scared to death, but at the same time they cannot be scared as they are dead, *because* they are alive, and alive because they are dead. The boundary is fused by assuming the fusion of the opposites – nothing is AS-IS anymore, and what might be a comedy (AS-IF men were bushes) becomes the new state of WHAT IS. Hence, traditional rituals are a complex staging of the boundaries between the real and the imaginary; they are social activities which are meant to shake and transform the individual. Of course, how much participants in such phenomena are 'really' taken in by the staging of a sacred space, or how much they participate AS-IF this was such a special event, is another question.

[58] Three steps described as pre-liminary, liminary and post-liminary by Van Gennep (1981) in his attempt to identify the commonalities in most of the rites of passage.

[59] A Kalabari-speaking Ijaw people in River State, Nigeria.

[60] Boe (1983).

For example, when asked about the moment at which children stopped believing in Santa Claus, parents' evaluations sometimes differ from those of their children – children tend to keep acting AS-IF they believed in Santa Claus – given the advantage this brings.[61] Once they clearly know that Santa Claus does not exist, they can act towards children younger than themselves AS-IF they believed that he existed, so that these younger children may enjoy the illusion.[62] In doing that they join the adults in creating yet another – purposeful – AS-IF world for the younger ones – believing (i.e. their own AS-IF) that the creation of such theatrical illusions is wanted by children and good for society. Advertisers invent ever new illusions assuming that it is the AS-IF world that triggers real purchases of advertised products in the AS-IS world.

## Summary: humans play and so they develop

The interest of melodies comes from their regularity, but also their capacity to surprise and play with conventions. If imagination is one of the core processes of the making of unique life trajectories, it is also what enables us to move through and beyond the boundaries of time and the social. And if so, it is because imagination is anchored in, and grows out of, our ability to play with life.

In search of the clear attributes of maturity and individuality, psychologists – as well as common sense – have tried to strongly distinguish children's play from adult experience, and the private realm of the mind from the hassle of the social world. However, after close examination, these distinctions fall. Classical reflections in anthroplogy and psychoanalysis – which were looking for general knowledge – show, first, that the processes engaged in children's play last life throughout, where they take more subtle forms – among which are the play of private fantasies, shared rituals and fictions. Second, they also remind us that, even in its most intimate forms, human fantasy is in essence social.

Play and creativity are present everywhere – in interpersonal processes, in social situations and even in people's understanding of culturally shared experiences – in their constant *bricolage* of meaning, people create disorder. We have thus seen that the boundaries between what is real and what is imaginary are both essential, and permanently permeable. At an

[61] The seven-year-old daughter of one of us (MG) even declared that she did not believe in Santa Claus any longer, but that she wanted to keep on with the ritual of receiving a gift overnight at Christmas AS-IF Santa still existed!

[62] Or so they declare to the interviewer... See Von Niedehäusern (2009), unpublished MA dissertation.

individual level, importing from the real to the imaginary and back is precisely the process by which one can move towards new experiences or elaborate past ones. Imagination is an inevitably productive process of our whole affective and cognitive system as it tries to grasp the not-yet-known immediate future.[63] At a collective level, playing with boundaries between what is and what could be is the tool of social change and innovation.

Playing and imagination are, however, not fully free. Not only is the most intimate social in nature but the social world also guides humans from the outside – the environment sets the stage for human playing. The on-going challenge is, for humans, to play with social constraints.

[63] The classic tradition of *Aktualgenese* (Friedrich Sander) and *microgenetic* processes (Heinz Werner) reveals the richness of 'intermediate gestalts' in the emergence of percepts and meanings (Abbey and Diriwächter, 2008).

# 10 Playing under the influence: activity contexts in their social functions

All play activities are embedded in a system of constraints – ecological and cultural. As we have shown above, adult activities of enquiry or entertainment are forms of play. Their embedding in the matrix of social constraints set up through cultural means is an arena for social regulation of power relations in a society.[1] We can discern different kinds of culturally organized settings – where human conduct is guided by constraints but *not scripted in exact detail.* The ornamented environment offers one form of peripheral guidance. Other settings are general blueprints that generally direct the ways in which experiencing might (or should) proceed. A person has the freedom – choice – to follow it by various ways of behaving – yet within the pre-set directions.[2] In fact, these settings – let us call them *acts* – are culturally guided in ways that the person performing that act chooses by her own will (yet following social suggestions – often very closely). Also, in their choice of fiction people eventually allow social discourse to enter their minds. Finally, it is through the redundancy of social discourse through various semiotic forms, and in different aspects of daily settings, that the constraints on – but also the conditions of – adult play are created.

## Environmental guidance – generated by a person at play

Human beings create fantasies both in their minds and in their immediate environments. The specific part of the environment that relates to the active organism becomes intertwined with it – it no longer has an external 'impact' upon the organism but becomes symbiotically related to it. The German term *Umwelt* allows us to characterize that organism-centred meaningful part of the environment.[3] Human beings reconstruct their

[1] The research programme of guided participation led by Barbara Rogoff (1990, 2003) provides many illustrations of how such embedding works.

[2] This is the elaboration of the general principle of bounded indeterminacy (Valsiner, 1997).

[3] See Chang (2009) for a contemporary set of elaborations of von Uexküll's *Umwelt* concept.

environments – as they become their *Umwelt* – and, in that way, guide the movement of the intra-psychological worlds.

*Material constraints – 'open' versus 'closed' materials for play:* All play is guided by a self-set task – and its constraints. Yet, aside from task constraints, it is the affordances of the very play objects that set up the range for possible novel actions with the given object. Thus a pile of sand – or plasticine – may be the materials for a builder or a sculptor to create something new. Less open are ready-made consumer products – iPods, MP3 players, etc. – which afford the reception of a similar (AS-IS) version of the same copy (listening to the same song *N* times) – yet do not allow for instrumental creation of an improvised (new) version of it – beyond a person's intramental imagery. In contrast, a musical instrument – a drum or a guitar – offers many improvisations – yet ones that are not repeatable in the form they first occurred.

Through the history of human sound-making – from giving meaning to thunder and lightning to inventing the first musical instrument – a drum or a string – we can see the creation of novel arenas of innovation. Likewise, the history of costume is linked to constructing meanings in relation to affordances. Dressing oneself up as a soldier, a policeman, or in school uniform sets up culturally prescribed material constraints for one's conduct (where the AS-IS version of imitation is privileged). Changing that uniform – taking it off, or exchanging it for frivolous evening garments[4] – is an act widening the AS-IF domain of imitation.

Social guidance is ephemeral, it is simultaneously everywhere – and nowhere. While making the claim that play and fantasy are socially guided we can immediately be challenged by examples like 'but my dream this past night was totally my own' or 'what I feel looking at this nice thing I might buy is my feeling and no one else's'. *The power of social guidance lies precisely in its camouflage.* It episodically and redundantly provides its input – in very many varied forms – to persons, and then leaves those persons to their own resources to consolidate and reassemble the received suggestions in their personal forms.

## *Need for variability*

Variability in nature and society is the resource for redundant control – the co-presence of different regulatory systems to make sure their object works reliably – and the main mechanism for organizing the life courses of open systems. Since open systems are not predictable from their initial

[4] Kennedy (1994).

context, and not controllable, what remains as a possibility for regulating them is the saturation of their environments by a variety of similarly orientating suggestions of very different forms. The target system will encounter similar suggestions in very different forms – wherever in its operational space it turns. It cannot escape the field – even though it can ignore many of the suggestions (but not all).

The main feature of the redundancy of human lives is the presence of cultural tools guiding people in directions similar to those suggested by the external social order and its internalized counterpart. Some suggestions are made externally – yet their function is supported through already internalized personal mechanisms. A characteristic example comes from the experience of a cross-cultural researcher who was worried about how twelve-year olds might respond to his administration of a group test:

> while negotiating to do some testing in a sample of American parochial schools, I mentioned to the director that, since it was a group test, we could handle several classes at once – providing of course that there would be no discipline problems. 'Professor Devereux', he said, 'you won't have any discipline problems in the parochial schools. *If anything happens, we will just have a sister come and stand in the door for a moment.*'[5]

The unity of internalized discipline and (if needed) adding to it the redundant semiotic marker ('we will just have a sister come and stand in the door *for a moment*') is an indicator of the episodic nature of explicated redundant control. The social rules in a parochial school – or in any other social context – are 'in the air' (so to say) of the participants who have constructed their social roles in the setting by internalization/externalization act (ordinarily) in the socially expected ways. Yet if there is a chance that the internalized version of self-control may be insufficient, the latent semiotic regulators of the external kinds are publicly displayed. Public signs that state the obvious, such as the warning recently observed in a shop 'Parents will be held responsible for any damage caused by their children' are an example of enhanced redundancy. While it is implicitly clear that parents regulate their children's relations with any environmental setting, here the owners of such a shop are bringing in the cultural notions of *responsible* and *damage*. Consider a similar sign put up at the entrance into a church or a temple for comparison. It is to be taken for granted that children will not be acting in ways that could damage church property, and that the parents will make sure that is the case. Yet at the church entrances one can observe signs for tourists ('shirts required' or 'you are entering into *a place of worship*') – other signs for redundant control.

[5] Devereux (1970, p. 105), emphasis added.

In the case of human development, the double patterning of life – environmental and intramental – is central. Patterns are constructed for a purpose – to guide the person encountering them towards some goal orientation. Most of these constructed cultural patterns are peripheral in their relation to our personal worlds – we live among them rarely noticing them in the background. We even consider them 'mere decorations' – or ornaments. Our lives are *ornamented* lives[6] – decorated by ourselves creating our home environments, the appearance of our cities or of our clothing – *yet in the decorating activity serious play is based on our fantasies that bring together the* AS-IS *of here and now with the* AS-IF *of 'there-where-and-when-I want to be'.*

### *The decorated world of the (self-) decorating person*

We surround ourselves with a myriad of seemingly useless things. Human beings create decorations – patterns – largely following patterning examples from nature that look beautiful to us – while for the species who use these patterns they are of utilitarian value. The colourful feather patterns of birds look beautiful to the human eye, while their functional value for the birds themselves may be in mating regulation or in merging with the environment to confuse predators. Birdsong can be a model for human music – but *music* is a pattern created with communicative functions for humans.

Cultural constructions differ from nature's patterns. While human-made ornaments may mimic nature, they are abstractions from natural patterns that guide human meaning-making. The whole enterprise of cultural organization of human lives entails the construction of ways of distancing oneself from the here-and-now settings while remaining within the settings. Ornaments lead to such abstracting generalization efforts – they are repetitive patterns of some abstracted aspects of reality rather than close to original 'copies' of the reality. They trigger further psychological generalization, which:

> consists in the subsequent naturalization of a pure ornament, i.e. an abstract form, and not in the subsequent stylization of the natural object. The crucial factor is contained in this antithesis. For it reveals that the primary element is not the natural model, but the law abstracted from it. It was therefore the artistic projection of the regularity of organic structure which, in consequence of the intimate organic connection of all living things, afforded the basis for the aesthetic experience of the spectator, and not concordance with the natural model.[7]

[6] Valsiner (2008b). [7] Wörringer (1963, p. 60).

## Setting the play: social acts

Sociological accounts of social settings often emphasize the determination of human action: hence, Goffman's theatrical model of the social stage of daily life turns people into mere puppets in powerful institutions. However, having put to the fore the importance of play and imagination, it appears in this book that even the seemingly limited areas of mundane activites are actually new settings for play – through social acts.[8] The quasi-existential question – do people feel free while they are *really* constrained, or are they *actually* free within the illusory constraints of the social – vanishes as it becomes one of the many variations of human play with boundaries.

### *Play on the human body: the dressing act*

The human body is a playground. In its 'natural' form it is naked – but the propensity for human cultural meaning-making transforms that form through culture. Human representation of the body:

> has the ability to render the naked as nude, as if 'nude' is another form or style of clothing, leaving behind 'naked' as the truly disrobed ... Although nakedness is most often performed during, with, or alongside practices of sexuality, it appears in frames that connote otherwise. In contemporary film, for example, nakedness has sometimes connoted vulnerability, humiliation, or comic transgression: almost compulsory in teenage comedies is a scene of male nudity in a public space for comic purposes.[9]

The *dressing act* is a form of play – and the mirrors needed for the player prior to any arrival in the public view indicate the centrality of such play for the self (primarily), for the others (secondarily) and *through* the others further for oneself (tertiarily). The dressing act begins at any moment of adornment of the body in private – with elaborate culturally constructed niches consisting of mirrors, dressing tables, holding cabinets for accessories, cosmetic and make-up tools, combs, hairdryers and many other small details in the scene of everyday life.

*Contexts and constructs in the dressing act:* the dressing act has a multitude of contextual versions that vary by society, social class, religious framing, interpersonal negotiations – to name just a few. It involves various layers of clothing – differentiation of underwear and overwear,

[8] Alex Gillespie (2006) has demonstrated that within the *touring act* British tourists visiting Ladakh insist upon their personal experiencing of precisely the kinds of scenes suggested to them by tourist guide books.

[9] Cover (2003, pp. 53–4).

considerations of ambient temperature and climatic conditions as these are viewed through the cultural prism.

The dressing act starts from purposefully modifying one's body surface itself – changing the body form or skin colour. It is a form of play – under the strict social guidance of public presentation rules. These rules are socially tied to suggested qualities of the self[10] – modesty, piousness, orderliness (in most cases) or rebelliousness and revolutionary intention (in others). Our contemporary urban environments are filled with tanning facilities where persons can darken their skin colour without encountering the rays of the sun. The history of the cosmetic industry in the United States provides examples – in the nineteenth century – of women (trying to look 'ladylike') whitening their skin with at times drastic means.[11] Similar moves – towards positively valued lighter skin (if a darker skin is locally frequent) or towards the opposite – competition on how dark one can get one's skin (without burning) – are documented all over the world.[12]

The social patterning of people's activities – linked with urbanization and work for hire – has led to an increased need for self-presentation play in a public setting:

> Women's rendezvous with modernity [in the early twentieth-century USA] brought them into the public realm that was not always welcoming. The changing status as workers, citizens, consumers, and pleasure seekers was acknowledged cosmetically: During the nineteenth century, the 'public woman' was a painted prostitute; by its end, women from all walks of life were 'going public': Women crowded onto trolleys, promenaded the streets, frequented the theatres, and shopped in the new palaces of consumption. They found jobs not only in the traditional work of domestic service, sewing, and farming, but also in offices, stores, and other urban occupations that required new kinds of face-to-face interactions. A new 'marriage market' substituted dating for courtship, and the dance hall for the front porch; a new sense of sexual freedom emerged.
>
> For women experiencing these social changes, the act of beautifying often became a lightening rod for larger conflicts over female autonomy and social roles. Among white women, for example, popular concern centred on the morality of the visible makeup – rouge, lipstick, mascara, and eye shadow. In the black

[10] Gordon (1992) demonstrates how nineteenth-century New England women acted in relation to dressing themselves (and others in their family), and managing the purchases and maintenance of clothes – as a major arena for development and maintenance of their selves. In terms of activity theory, if a particular person (or group of persons) is set up to be involved in an activity (dressing, undressing, preparing meals, repairing things, etc.) these activities become the objectified arenas for their self development over the life course.

[11] Peiss (1998, Chapter 1). [12] Ashikari (2005).

community, beauty culture was explicitly a political issue, long before the contemporary feminist movement made it so. Skin whiteners and hair straighteners were the tokens in a heated debate: Against charges of white emulation and self-loathing, many black women invoked their rights to social participation and cultural legitimacy precisely through their use of beauty aids.[13]

The social regulation of play is built on two power sources – consensus in peer relations, and relations with selected non-peer power holders (parents, grandparents, officials, etc.). It is in the arena of everyday mundane ways of conduct that the settings for enhanced and constricted openness to fantasy and its expression in play are set up. Overwhelmingly, human interaction is about 'small talk' rather than exchange of new information.[14] In that communication of nothing-new, the social censorship of play (and fantasy) becomes a regular daily pastime. Comments in nineteenth-century America between women about another woman – 'she paints' – were semiotic regulators for curbing the self-beautification efforts of the speakers themselves.

*The dressing act as arena for ideological disputes:* different parts of the dressing act are arenas for play – from head and the hair (hats, head-scarves, scarves) downwards to the mid-body arena of the waist and the buttocks (accentuated by belts, special devices for emphasizing the waist/buttocks contrasts like corsets, etc.), reaching the legs (stockings, boots) and to the end of the feet (shoes) – all constituting theatrical stages where the play of self-narcissism and other-seduction is set up by the person as her own 'theatre director.' In the history of societies the kinds of clothing – or fabrics from which clothes were made – were targets of social guidance and prohibition:

From the seventeenth to the eighteenth centuries, a high degree of artificiality and decorative exuberance in dress was required of upper-class men and women. A quarter of a century before the [French] Revolution, the philosophic critique denounced the general excesses of fashion and aristocratic consumption in the name of nature; it ended up imposing the artificiality of the natural, which was far from cheap.[15]

[13] Peiss (1998, pp. 6–7).

[14] Toda and Higuchi (1994) made a crucial point: most communication in our daily lives is between people who know one another well – hence communication does not bring much news. Yet its continuity can be a powerful self- and other-canalization device – by gossip or moral meta-communicative messages in the case of perceived excesses of play.

[15] Roche (1994, p. 46). In Japan (year 1648) the Tokugawa rulers prohibited persons of non-samurai classes from wearing silk clothes – to maintain social class distinctions. Social norms of what kind of fabric and clothes can be worn (and where) fit the 'privately public' arena of self-development in the case of the dressing act – the person can act AS-IF being of

Social class markers are written on body covers. In addition to the cultural selection of the arena within the exterior[16] of the body – where cultural meanings are constructed – we can observe at times escalating person-society conflicts around ideological issues projected onto the personal dressing act. The history of adolescent girls – of North African origin – wearing headscarves in French schools escalated to a society-level ideological and political drama.[17] The starting point of that drama lay in the individual dressing act of the girls. In September 1989, three girls of Moroccan and Tunisian origin – yet grown up in France and not well versed in Arabic or Islam – came to their middle school in Creil (near Paris) wearing headscarves. As objects of clothing, headscarves are just that – ways of covering and decorating the hair. Yet the timing of the girls' wearing of the scarves was different – the macro-social atmosphere was altered:

> At a different moment, the girls' appearance would likely have passed unnoticed. Girls had been showing up at this and other schools with scarves for years, and either attended the school with their scarves or agreed to remove them during class. Indeed an earlier class photo at the same school showed a girl in a headscarf as evidence of the middle school's openness to cultural diversity. But now international 'political Islam' appeared on magazine covers in the form of Iranian women in Islamic dress, adding a new dimension to scarves in French schools. The conjecture of domestic and foreign threats made the scarf-wearing into a national 'affair'.[18]

We can see that the arenas of human body selected for cultural negotiation are not politically neutral. Within that political suspicion focus (on 'political Islam') the self-beautifying dressing act carried out on the head zone led to local power conflict – the principal's demand that the girls take the scarves off, the girls' refusal, reprimands to the girls, publicity about the reprimands, all the different forces of the French political spectrum voicing their opinions and so on. A dressing act of the girls had become appropriated by French society as an arena for a *public focusing act* – the functions of which have nothing to do with the coverage of the human body.

*Public display of clothing – social direction of adults' play:* in order for any object of clothing to reach the personal-cultural domain of human

a different social class by wearing the kind of clothing of the desired kind. Since such wearing enters the public domain – of visibility to the others – it can lead to the resistance to and overcoming of the existing social boundaries (Ikegami, 2005, p. 256).

[16] In our current time, creation of such arenas for cultural combat also happens as projected into the inside of the body – different dieting programmes or surgical intervention culturally reorganizing internal body fat or size of the functional stomach.

[17] Bowen (2007). [18] Bowen (2007, p. 83).

everyday play, it has to be transferred from the creators of that object – designers, tailors – to their users. This is particularly so in our contemporary consumer society where almost nobody can or will make their own clothes.[19] The producers of different kinds of clothes need to bring these to the attention of a wide audience, and create channels for encounters to make these objects transferable to their consumers.

It is here that the social events of *fashion shows* enter as promoter signs to regulate the patterns of ordinary play through one's body. Fashion shows are installations of our contemporary world that are similar to fairytale-telling in the past – only they entail play-acting (by models) of different self-presentation modes of the often far-from-reality objects. As Georg Simmel pointed out:

> Two social tendencies are essential to the establishment of fashion, namely, the need of union on the one hand and the need for isolation on the other. Should one of these be absent, fashion will not be formed – its sway will abruptly end.[20]

Fashion lures individuals – as if they were unique – while it is made by collective similar actions. Acting in accordance with fashion is a differentiating step (myself from others) that unifies (myself with others, sharing the fashion).

The intermediate public encounter of the makers of body decoration devices and the people expected to consume them is located in places of commerce. Here the exterior (shop windows) and interior (of actual objects available in shops) create contrasts that operate as social guidance devices not only for potential consumers, but for the whole public so as to guide the meaning construction of particular objects. While the cultural look from the back is being promoted socially, the frontal (face-to-face) channel of communication occupies a central role in formal social

[19] For instance, a person knitting a sweater for himself maintains the roles of producer and consumer of a cultural object within the same person. The aesthetic patterns that a person knits into the object – ornaments, depictions of objects, etc. – are created by the person for himself. This unity of producer and consumer is altered once the same object is created for another person – an expectant mother knitting clothes for her soon-to-arrive child. Here it becomes an act of intergenerational communication through the symbolic value encoded in the constructed object, as it is filled with personal affective orientation – first of the mother-to-be towards her child, and then for the child towards his/her immediate family surroundings. This will change if the same object of child's clothing is brought in from the domain of high-volume mass production – even if the aesthetic form of the object is the same.

[20] Simmel (1959b, p. 301).

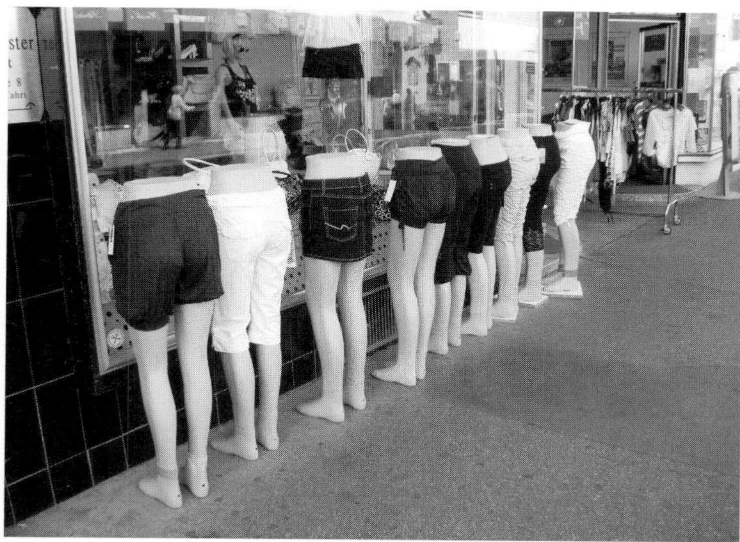

Figure 10.1 The special focus on the rear of the body in the making of jeans.

relationships. This is accentuated by the practice of portrait painting (and the display of portraits) in public spaces. The face

> accomplishes more completely than anything else the task of creating a maximum change of total expression by a minimum change of detail. The universal problem of art is to elucidate the formal elements of things by relating them to one another – to interpret the perceptible through its connection with the imperceptible.[21]

Aside from the perceptual information about the person as person, the front-to-front communication channel entails the potential dangers of 'casting an eye' or fight by gazes. Furthermore, the back view is further promoted in the making of different objects of clothing (Figure 10.1).

*Dressing for something:* the dressing act carries socially stratified directionality – we not only dress ourselves, but also dress 'up' – for specific symbolic settings – or reveal our bodies after they have been dressed in other theatrical settings (called strip-*tease*). The social suggestion of *dressing up* can occur on any basis – even in a context where normatively minimal body coverage is expected, such as on the beach. There, social guidance is active although it is contrary to the goals of the person to encounter the elements

[21] Simmel, (1959a, p. 280).

Figure 10.2 Dressing 'up' for minimal coverage of the body.

of sun and water. A person coming to the beach takes off overclothes (='dresses down') to encounter the desired impact of sun, sand and water – yet the person indeed 'dresses up' in the decision of what to wear for the gaze of the others in this minimalistic situation (Figure 10.2).

Further cultural construction of the socially presentable markers on the body – indexical signs – come from the public display of the evidence of having 'dressed up' for the beach – the white parts of skin left without sunburn under the cultural coverage of the minimal part of the body on the beach. Such indexical signs may be purposefully cultivated.[22]

*Culturally constructed bodies at play:* what we have described above is in theatrical terms merely setting up actors in their costumes – to enter the stage of play. The costumes are merely the basis for further play – which in the adult case takes the forms of many culturally established genres and scripts. Once the costumed body is ready to exit from the deeply private preparatory domain into the first quasi-public one (e.g. immediate family setting), and further to the completely public domain to be filled with social encounters, it is here that the diversity of playing begins.

[22] The crucial cultural invention of the negotiation of the meaning of skin colour (and patterning) is that of tanning studios and the paradoxes of their biological (burning the skin) and social (acquiring the desired dark skin color) relationships – see Vannini and McCright (2004).

Figure 10.3 The inviting pleasures of smoking.

*The smoking act*

The *act of smoking* is a good example of guided play in adulthood. First of all, smoking is a person-centred activity that can become addictive – hence repetitive by personal desire. That desire episodically calls for the personal need to 'smoke now', or to combine the experience of smoking with all kinds of other activities. It can provide a feeling of comfort, or be a crucial part of the establishment of self-identity. At the same time it is a social activity to which both positive and negative valuations can be added. Smoking a cigar can be part of the eating act – an after-meal pleasurable completion of the pleasure of eating (Figure 10.3.). Smoking has had relevant healing functions added to it in the history of Amerindian societies; in the history of Europe, it has been a part of gentlemanly conduct – up to having special classes at school on how to smoke in appropriate ways. Smoking in this sense has had a history of being considered a healthy (and healing) practice in some societies, sometimes – and being attacked as an undesirable practice in the same or other societies at other times.[23]

[23] Brewis and Grey (2008).

In the act of smoking, moments of personal-cultural play abound: the ways of holding a cigarette, pipe, or cigar, the ways of inhaling/exhaling, and the means of disposing of ashes (i.e. the cultural tool of ashtray) are all parts of personal play in the smoking act:

> Smoking as a social practice carries an immense and complex range of signifiers – danger, eroticism, freedom, intellectuality, youth, selfishness, foolishness, weakness, toughness, gullibility, individualism, bohemianism and much else besides ... Smoking, as with other forms of drug taking, has moreover been deplored and encouraged, regulated and deregulated, at different junctures ... The full history of the human use of tobacco goes back at least 18000 years ...and is particularly associated with South American cultures.[24]

Tobacco's arrival in Europe from the sixteenth century onwards set the stage for continuous ambivalence. The first anti-smoking Act in England can be located in early 1600s – within the same century in which 'healthy smoking' was an obligatory school lesson for aristocratic offspring.[25] The famous London restaurant *Rules*[26] includes the pleasures of a cigar among its offerings for gentlemen to finish their meals. That such a suggestion of the culinary pleasures of smoking is not a historical remnant of the risk-taking habits of the British higher classes is indicated by the inclusion of cigars among desserts on the menu of the Wiener Café in Frankfurt-am-Main's fashionable Goethestrasse area. Thus – even in our present day era of witchhunting for the few remaining smokers – we have indications of the opposite cultural promotion of smoking as part of nutritionial action.

The most recent anti-smoking wave of campaigns has taken shape since 1960s and has proliferated widely on the basis of social morality dramas.

Yet as is usual in cultural history, the opposites turn into each other – what was healthy becomes seen as unhealthy and vice versa. In our contemporary societies we can observe a gradually expanding social guidance towards eradicating smoking – first of all from public places. The meaning rationale used for this social guidance is the impact on 'the other' ('secondary smoking') – aside from the primary persuasive narratives on the dangers of smoking for one's health.

In the process of proliferating the new ideology of SMOKING IS UNHEALTHY a number of social segregation acts are introduced. The

[24] Brewis and Grey (2008, p. 968).

[25] Brewis and Grey (2008, p. 985 note 2): in the English public school Eton learning to smoke was a compulsory health measure – as it was viewed as prophylactic against the plague – and schoolboys were punished for *not* smoking.

[26] Rules was established by Thomas Rule in 1798 and is the oldest club of the kind in London. It serves traditional British food, specializing in classic game cookery, oysters, pies and puddings – as well as cigars (until the smoking ban), currently replaced by coffee and chocolates.

Figure 10.4 An outdoors symbolic 'smoking area'.

creation of 'smoker zones' can take different forms – they can be concentrated into enclosed spaces (with enhanced exposure to 'secondary smoking' – between the segregated in-group of 'smokers'), or – as in Figure 10.4, on a railway waiting platform in Germany – by symbolic marking of an outdoor 'smoking area'. It is obvious that marking an area for smokers by yellow lines on the platform does not delimit the impact of 'secondary smoke' for non-smoking passengers waiting for the train right beyond the yellow lines. The impact of the wind in the diluting of the smoke both inside and outside the marked areas reduces the 'health hazards' in the given context for all people on the platform.

This example demonstrates that behind the manifest content of 'health care' the symbolic guidance of the smoking act carries a secondary goal – that of separating one part of society from another, creating an ingroup/outgroup distinction, with an opposition built into it. Social institutions use such strategies – of divide and govern – widely, starting from gender segregation, age set making for separating persons into contrasting age groups or grade levels in schools, making ethnic boundaries through enforced marking of ethnicity and so on. The use of the smoking act for such purposes is thus only one example among many of the kind. Perhaps its specificity lies in its perfect masking – behind the manifest content of 'care for health'. In the setting depicted in Figure 10.4, the symbolic

Figure 10.5 A 'smoking zone' in Frankfurt airport funded by private business.

segregation of the 'outcast group' (smokers) from the 'ingroup' of non-smokers by yellow markers cannot be proven to benefit the health care of either. It only creates a symbolic display – a 'theatre scene' where the smokers are 'on stage' – to be evaluated by the audience (of non-smokers). Spatial symbolic segregation in public places is a perceptual ground for making distinctions of a further symbolic kind – the people involved in the smoking act who are confined in by the yellow markers are not expected to be viewed by the others as 'heroes' (Figure 10.5). The organization of public space according to such acts becomes part of the ornament of daily life; together, these organized spaces, which echo non-smoker discourse, posters and advertisements, create a redundant environment where it seems clear that 'smoking is bad' – yet also that smoking is something very special.

The example of the unity of contradictory messages about smoking within the same society at a given time is an excellent example of Serge Moscovici's (see Box 10.1) general claim about the unity of excitation and inhibition:

> Our society is an institution which inhibits what it stimulates. It both tempers and excites aggressive, epistemic, and sexual tendencies, increases or reduces the chances of satisfying them according to class distinctions, and invents prohibitions together with the means of transgressing them. Its sole purpose, to date, is self-

## Box 10.1 Serge Moscovici

Serge Moscovici (b. 1923) is the recognized central figure in contemporary research on social representations. The perspective continues the French intellectual tradition of *collective representations* (introduced by Emile Durkheim) but differs in Moscovici's focus on the *process of socially representing* the world in the ongoing flow of human personal lives.

Moscovici was born in Brăila, Romania into a Jewish family, the son of a merchant. During the Second World War, he was interned in Romania and placed in a forced labour camp. He arrived in France in 1948. Moscovici's doctoral thesis published in 1961 (*La psychanalyse, son image, son public* – in English 2006) introduced the social representations perspective through an analysis of the proliferation of psychoanalysis in France. In 1975 he established the European Laboratory of Social Psychology in Paris. In 1997, Moscovici authored an autobiographical essay titled *Chronique des années égarées* ('Chronicle of the Mislaid Years'). His other books include *L'expérience du mouvement. Jean-Baptiste Baliani, disciple et critique de Galilée* (1967); *Essai sur l'histoire humaine de la nature* (1968/1977); *La société contre nature* (1972/1994); *Hommes domestiques et hommes sauvages* (1974); *Social influence and social change* (1976); *Psychologie des minorités actives* (1979); *L'Age des foules. Un traité historique de psychologie des masses* (1981); *La Machine à faire les dieux* (1988); *Social Representations: Explorations in Social Psychology* (2000); *De la Nature. Pour penser l'écologie* (2002); *Réenchanter la nature. Entretiens avec Pascal Dibie* (2002); *The Making of Modern Social Psychology: The Hidden Story of How an International Social Science was Created* (2006, with I. Marková).

preservation, and it opposes change by means of laws and regulations. It functions on the basic assumption that it is unique, has nothing to learn, and cannot be improved. Hence its unambiguous dismissal of all that is foreign to it. Even its presumed artificiality, which might be considered a shortcoming, is taken, on the contrary, for a further sign of superiority, since it is an attribute of mankind.[27]

The social guidance of human play and development – through directing fantasies and restricting actions in social contexts – is inherently ambivalent. The suggestions 'you must not do X' trigger counter-action – together with other messages of 'you should do X'.[28] That creates the

[27] Moscovici (1976, p. 149).

[28] Consider the way in which female sexuality is socially guided in Mali:

> There are ingredients in the prevailing norms and practices with regard to both enhancing and hindering women's sexuality. The *magnonmakanw* are nuptial advisors whose role is to teach, promote, and sustain healthy and enjoyable sex among couples and adult members of the communities. At the same time there are bolokoli-kelau who are

ambiguity of the social world – where changes become possible thanks to such ambiguity. It is not complicated for cigarette manufacturers to include on the packages of their products different – verbal or graphic – warning statements about the 'killing features' of tobacco. Furthermore, the social segregation of smokers – into special open spaces (Figure 10.4) or closed ones (Figure 10.5 ) creates a captive audience for advertisements. The smoking places become supported as public advertising spots – and hence symbolically marked.

As the social space becomes saturated with discourse about a specific issue – here smoking – while its meanings and representations are inherently contradictory, it becomes an ambivalent semiotic field – and ultimately, it is rich in all possibilities. As social guidance proposes the one and the opposite, this maintains an arena for individual play.

## Play of destruction: the context of wartime

The inevitable even though sad fact is that human history is dominated by wars. The ease with which societies move from peace to war (and more tentatively – vice versa) is astounding. It is with a similar ease to 'dressing up' in our beach uniforms that in wartime warriors hide their personal humanity behind the symbolic powers of military uniforms – and act in ways very different from those of peacetime. The transition is set up through the unity of cultural guidance and situated activity – before entering the theatre of war the heroism and beauty of battle may be promoted among the civilian (still) peacetime public, especially for the young whose personal-cultural acceptance of the utopia of the war is the aim of such socialization. The leader of the Italian futurists Tommaso Marinetti – even though wounded in the First World War – would declare twenty years later:

> War is beautiful because it establishes man's dominion over the subjugated machinery by means of gas masks, terrifying megaphones, flame throwers and small tanks. War is beautiful because it initiates the dreamt-of metallization of the human body. War is beautiful because it enriches a flowering meadow with the fiery orchids of machine guns. War is beautiful because it combines the gunfire, the cannonades, the cease-fire, the scents, and the stench of putrefaction into a symphony. War is beautiful because it creates new architecture, like that of the big tanks, the geometrical formation flights, the smoke spirals from burning villages, and many others.[29]

traditional or modern practitioners entrusted with carrying out female circumcision for many reasons among which one is to diminish women's sensuality. [Diallo, 2004, p. 173]

[29] Tomlinson (2007, p. 56).

Once this social suggestion has arrived at its destination – tested by the lines of young people volunteering to go and 'defend' their 'motherland' (or whatever other mytho-poetic general social representation), they are uniformed and sent to the actual war zone. They are – by obeying the commands – put into a critical situation.[30] The aftermath of the warring act – for the survivors – has been known to be traumatic in the long term[31] (e.g. the 'shell shock' syndrome that followed the utopian fervour of young English gentlemen volunteering for duty in the First World War). Even now that war is in Britain referred to as *The Great War* – and the Second World War in Russia as the *Great Patriotic War*. The attribution of hyper-generalized affective meanings to acts of mass destruction is a way of making use of such destructive acts in the social construction of the present.

## Acts of a destructive kind: warring, hunting

The *warring act* can be seen as a transformation of the *hunting act*[32] and *retaliation act*[33] into a hypergeneralized meaning complex organized by social representations, or meaning fields, such as *enemy*, *defence*, *peace*, *honour*, *justice*, *progress*, etc. Most wars are claimed to be fought for positive values – *peace*, *honour* and *justice* – yet end up with destruction, and a continuation of the previous opposite social representations in a never-ending cycle. The warring act – when it happens – touches all persons of any age range. Aside from its centredness on destruction it is a form of play that is socially organized by way of culturally constructed meanings and social norms. Within these constraints, the participating agents become involved in active (and destructive) play – utilizing specific symbolic resources and destructive tools prepared for this phase in the given social order.

Furthermore, generic symbolic resources can be used for setting up the rules for the warring act. In the history of European society warfare has changed. From the collective ritualistic movement of brightly-uniformed

[30] People change their conduct in critical situations – in ways that deviate from the usual ones (Sherif and Sherif, 1956, Chapter 21).

[31] For short-term – and back-and-forth between frontline and home – adaptation see Macek (2000).

[32] The link with hunting has been described by Pandya (2000) in comparing Andaman islanders' conduct with that of hunted animals and killed enemies. An extension of the hunting act to humans can be seen in various versions of witch-hunting (Behrend, 2006). The construction of the meaning of another as a witch, followed by action against him/her, is one of the most serious forms of tragic play that human cultures have invented.

[33] A special version of the retaliation act is the *duelling act* (Elias, 1996, pp. 64–75) – ritualized contest of fight for symbolic causes (honour) among aristocratic social strata in European history (see also Frevert, 1995).

armies of contact combat weapons, marching towards one another as in the middle ages, European societies have arrived at the highly camouflaged military units of long-distance devastation tools. The social rules of non-involvement of the civilians have also changed over the course of the twentieth century. The development of military technology has turned the battlefield from a colourful and even musical[34] theatre stage into that of butchering ambushes linked with mass devastation. Norbert Elias has pointed out how the warring act has changed in its sociological structure – since the beginning of the twentieth century the previous 'aristocratic code' of warfare became 'bourgeoisified':

> In aristocratic circles, military values embodied in conceptual symbols such as courage, obedience, honor and discipline, responsibility and loyalty were usually part of a long family tradition. In accordance with their different social situation, middle class circles adopted the aristocratic code only in a certain version. In this way, it underwent a class-specific change in function: it lost the character of a tradition-bound and correspondingly little reflected upon pattern of behavior, and became expressed in an explicitly formulated doctrine hardened by reflection. What was for the aristocracy a more or less unquestioned tradition – a largely naïve high estimation of warlike values, a socially inherited understanding of the meaning of power potentials in the inter-state play of strength – was now cultivated much more consciously by the upper sectors of the middle classes as something newly obtained . . . the conclusion was drawn that war and violence were also good and splendid as political instruments.[35]

Elias's idea is supported by the proliferation of the romantic views of power (and brutality) in pre-1914 Europe, and the subsequent enthusiasm of ordinary citizens – young and old – to volunteer to 'fight for their country' – on both sides of the opponents – in the 'Great War'. Personal entrance into the warring act was supported by the internalized feeling of acting in a play that was something wonderful, glorious, and in which victory was a necessary outcome – rather than something that ended in the cemeteries of Verdun.

*Example: the peaceful war where only spirits do the killing:* the warring act in other societies can be organized culturally by a very different set-up. The war initiated by Alice Lakwena in Uganda – 'a war to eradicate war'[36] – was

[34] On the use of music in the history of warfare see Van Orden (2005).

[35] Elias (1996, pp. 180–1).

[36] For a full coverage, see Behrend (1999). A young Acholi (Uganda) tribeswoman Alice Auma, aged twenty-nine, converted from the Anglican to Catholic Church, had a 'calling' in 1985 of the spirit of Lakwena – an Italian captain who had died in the Second World War – and emerged first as a healing medium, and secondly as the commander of the Holy Spirit Movement and its army in a military action against war and violence that was commonplace in Uganda in 1986. The campaign ended in defeat in 1987, and the 'Lakwena spirit' left the medium.

deeply embedded in the syncretic religious worldviews of her tribe (and others). The call for 'war against war'[37] was successful as a religious appeal to a wide range of the populace – from children to the elderly – as a consolidated cultural construction to exit from the ongoing continuous devastations of the warring tribes. The religious call had the appeal to unify the fighters for peace – yet these were fighters ready for combat, and not peaceful demonstrators for the causes of peace. The actual soldiers were claimed to be joined by 140,000 spirits – invisible fighters – on the battlefield. These spirits were 'imported' from other places (Lakwena was Italian, others included actors like Dr Wrong Element from the USA, Ching Poh from China or Korea, Zairean, Lybian, Arab and other foreign spirits). The globalization of our present day world takes curious forms in the context of a syncretic religion on the battlefield. All the interested political powers currently active in Africa joined the 'regiment of spirits' of the Holy Spirit Movement. Of course such focus on the powerful invisible soldiers led Lakwena (a spirit commanding the army through Alice, the medium) to create special combat rules – the Holy Spirit tactics:

> the soldiers were forbidden to take cover when attacked. They were not to hide behind termite hills, trees, etc., for 'the Lord is your Cover and Shield'... They had to face the enemy standing erect and with naked torso. Nor were they to remain silent, but to sing church hymns for 10, 15, 30, or 45 minutes, as directed by the spirit.
>
> The Holy Spirit soldiers were forbidden to kill. Nor were they allowed to aim at the foe; it was the spirits who were to carry the bullets to the enemy and thus decide who among the enemies deserved death. The spirits would punish even the intent to kill with death or injury in the battle. With the spirits as killers, the Holy Spirit killing faded more and more into the background.[38]

The game rules for the warring act had here found an ingenious solution to reconciling the opposites – 'you shall not kill' (one of Lakwena's twenty moral commandments) and 'you shall liberate Uganda from evil' – by creating a redundant cultural meaning system that would explain every possible outcome on the battlefield. The actual soldiers never kill (as the spirits do it), and if they have been killed they must have 'sinned' against the moral code (as detected by spirits who killed them for it). Surprisingly (for outsiders) the military tactic of singing religious hymns on the

[37] Note that the sentence 'A war to end wars' seems to have been first used by US President T. W. Wilson in April 1918 to justify American participation in the First World War. It then became a widely used semiotic resource during that war. It was also used by young people during the Second World War (see Zittoun, Cornish, Gillespie and Aveling, 2008).

[38] Behrend (1999), pp. 57–8.

battlefield at times was successful – since the soldiers of the opponent (who also believed in spirits) ran away when approached by a hymn-singing column of half-naked soldiers who would open erratic indiscriminate automatic rifle fire. Battlefields can be grotesque.

## Playing with the social from within: using semiotic resources

In the constant play in which people are engaged, while creating their trajectories within the sets of constraints offered by social guidance, people use various signs and objects as semiotic resources. A semiotic resource is an object or a sign which is used by people, with some intention, to act on their own minds or those of others.[39] Using a semiotic resource often demands 'hi-jacking'[40] it – using it for a secondary function, not the obvious, or socially conventional one. Clothes, walls, words can be used as semiotic resources. Among possible resources, those coming from complex artefacts, such as books, films, artwork or music can be called 'complex' in the sense that they are explicitly (culturally) meant to carry meanings while enabling imaginary cultural experiences. Because of these, they demand a mobilization of personal experience and emotions, and are likely to substantially transform the self. Hence if any sign can become a *semiotic* resource, only these specific semiotic configurations that operate through the internalizing/externalizing personal culture of a person can become *symbolic* resources.

*Children as semiotic resources:* an extreme case of use of a semiotic resource is when people use as signs, things or entities which are primarily not meant to signify. In the adult presentation of children, the very real youngsters the adults take care of become in reality semiotic resources in the adults' own play. The use of children as a topic of interaction between adults, ranging from the proud showing–off of baby or child photos by parents and grandparents to captivated audiences often faking their superficial interest, to public discussions of what kinds of activities are 'educationally valuable' for children, to fussing about the incredible 'moral downfall' of the current young generation, turns children into signs – iconic (photos), indexical (recognizing and evaluating what

39 Gillespie and Zittoun (2010b).

40 Perriault (1989) used the expression 'hi-jacking' to describe how consumers use technical objects not as planned by their conceptors, with different intentions from the planned one and to achieve different goals. Many objects became 'famous' despite their inventors. Similarly, people who keep a novel mainly as-souvenir-of-a-friend use it for a secondary function with regard to the one planned by the author.

children have done) or symbolic (verbal banter about children). Using children as signs, however, turns people into parents. . .

*Using semiotic resources to reshape an identity trajectory:* while human lives are constantly on the move – there is no turning back in the irreversible flow of experiencing the world – at the self-regulatory level of psychological reflection about oneself human beings invent hypergeneralized meanings that act as flow stabilizers in the course of everyday living. The notion of identity is one of those – it is constructed (and cherished, defended against attacks, subjected to long processes of search if 'lost'). Almost every feature of the human life can be used to construct such a flow stabilizer – self-identity, family-identity, gender-identity, national identity are all constructs that fix the person's flow of personal experiences by way of a meta-semiotic frame. The crucial constructed feature is assumed stability.[41] That assumption is an effort to control the uncontrollable – personal flexibility of adaptation to new and imagined future circumstances. Because it demands the implication of imagination and feelings, use of complex artefacts has the power to maintain or transform this precious experience of 'identity' through ruptures.

*Films, music and novels as symbolic resources:* films, novels and songs – or most pieces of art – consist of 'frozen' meanings that have entered the public domain. They contain and carry around crystallized human experience. Often, films or novels become exemplary, inspirational and deeply transform the way in which one social group or a generation – or a civilization – understands their fate. More deeply than that, it has been convincingly shown that the very way in which we understand ourselves as humans depends on the shape of narratives circulating in the semiosphere: films and novels give us templates to think about our lives.[42] In that sense they constrain our imagination of ourselves. However, because of the process required to understand fiction – imagination, internalization and externalization – interpretation of artefacts is open ended. Thus people can make unique use of artefacts as symbolic resources.

As seen in the previous chapter, fictional artefacts enable cultural experiences that demand a certain degree of 'absorption', or acceptance of surrender to fantasy. However, we always have the possibility to step out of them, or to think back about them. In the following sequence, a young man, Gauthier Jurgensen, reflects on one of the many films that

[41] Even if (for example, talking about the 'identity' of deities in the Hindu religious system) we have to realize that the only specifiable constant in their identity is their change – transformation from one form into another – the new criterion of identity, instability, is itself formulated as stable (stability of instability).

[42] Bruner (2003); McAdams (1993).

were his 'brothers' during his childhood and youth – *The Graduate*, and on his proximity to the hero, Benjamin, played by Dustin Hoffman:

> Like the young Benjamin, I just finished my studies. My parents congratulated me many times. And, like him, I stay for hours sitting in my room. I look in the empty space and I wonder what I have to do to move to the next stage. All my life I thought it would be simple: kindergarten, school, college, university; study, get specialized, and work. No, it is not like that. There is a floating moment during which, like Benjamin, one stares at the empty space. What Mike Nichols made me feel, through the blurred gaze of Dustin Hoffman, is the silence of death that is in the head of the young graduate. Everything is so noisy around us: job offers, ambitious projects, parental expectations, the will to rest . . .[43]

In that sequence and what follows, Jurgensen makes a precise analysis of the feelings of a young man alienated from the world, prisoner of his internal silence, and needing a rupture from his parents. In order to do so, he clearly uses *The Graduate* and its multimodal construction (the image of Dustin Hoffman in a diving suit in the swimming pool, the music 'The sound of silence' used in the film) to reflect on his own emotional and existential situation. In a situation like this there is a different relationship to the artefact from the one that is created during the simple cultural experience. The person is not just having the experience, or describing the cultural artefact as such; rather, the cultural experience or the artefact is mentioned, or described, in relationship to something else, external to the fictional world. We can say that the cultural artefact has become a *symbolic resource* when it is thus intentionally related to something else, that belongs to one's inner life, or socially shared reality.[44] Hence, Jurgensen uses the film to reflect about himself – that is, to mediate interpersonal dialogue – and as social mediator when he writes that nobody can become his friend without having seen a film with him.

The use of cultural artefacts as symbolic resources makes it possible to distance one's experience from the here and now, to reflect on it, to explore alternatives and their consequences, to establish new links between events separated in time and to acknowledge diverse understanding. As such, artefacts and symbols can be powerful developmental catalysts: they can facilitate or trigger reconfigurations of people's understanding – as when after a rupture, such as someone's death, a poem helps to deal with the feeling of grief. Hence, a young woman found a verse of *The Prophet* by Khalil Gibran very important as she had to deal with the loss of a member of her family: 'The deeper the sorrow carves into your being, the more joy you can contain'. This poem offered a

[43] Jurgensen (2008, p. 14, our translation). [44] Zittoun (2006b, 2007b).

metaphor that enabled her to overcome her sadness, and that she then mobilized in other circumstances as a symbolic resource.[45]

Symbolic resources can also, in some cases, create ruptures in people's experiences, as when a novel or a piece of art is experienced as a turning point in one's experience. Here is one of these experiences described by a young man, as posted on a fan's blog:

My first Staind [a rock band] concert was at XYZ City in UK, I remember being so excited. Staind were really the first band I've felt so attached to. I listened to some really heavy music when I was little . . . but Staind had it all for me. I fell in love with the sound of honesty and Aaron's lyrics really helped me to . . . *wind down and mellow out, for the 3/4 minutes however long the song was on for I felt like I was layed on a beach somewhere far far away from any commotion that was going on around me.*

There was something unbelieveable about Staind that I could'nt quite get around, what have this band been through to get where they are. Where the hell does Mike's riffs come from? Why is Old Schools harmonised vocals giving me an orgasm? Why would I rather sit at home listening to Johns percussion fills than hang out with my friends and most of all why do Aarons lyrics seem so comforting. *I haven't been through nothing Aaron has so why do they help?* I know a lot of Staind fans say that Aarons lyrics help, I never understood why until my first Staind concert.

It was after school one Wednesday and I guess my Mum had got me and my partner tickets to see them. My partner . . . Sadie really enjoyed listening to them, she kinda had to . . . seen as though she liked spending time with me. I came home and sat in the living room whilst my Mum got ready and I had butterflies in my stomach. I was so nervous. We got in the car . . . I walked through the door and my Mum told me to text her let her know everything is okay, I text her the second I got in telling her all was all okay haha I was so nervous. . . . I stood there waiting impatiently, I was right it was suffocate, I was stood there mesmerized. Aaron didnt play guitar back then so he was moving around the stage slowly. Song after song I stood there and I took some photos and some videos, I remember they played 'Open Your Eyes' my favorite song off of Break The Cycle and in the second verse when Aarons starts singing louder and the lyrics change to talking about overpopulation, he looked straight in my eyes . . . I think. *Well it felt like it he did and It felt like he was talking to me, like he was staring at me and telling me to grow the fuck up and start doing things I had always felt never meant much to me. Really pursue my music, Care for my family, Stop drinking so much with friends that didnt no any better and try to introduce them to music. With that one line and stare I felt this rush of excitement and relief.* Who needs heroin or drugs when I have this feeling. They played loads of old songs at that concert which made my night, I mean I love Its Been A While, Outside, So Far Away, Zoe Jane, and the softer side but I loved it when they played Crawl, that chorus is just well to catchy. I was humming it all the way home . . . The concert ended and

[45] Zittoun (2006b).

Aaron ended the concert by telling the fans how much they mean to the band and that they will see us soon. That's all I thought about for about 3 weeks.[46]

In this sequence, the young fan describes his attachment to the songs and melodies of his band: when he listens to them in his room, they enable him to enter in a different time and space: '*I felt like I was layed on a beach somewhere far far away from any commotion that was going on around me.*' Although he knows he can get that effect with the music, he does not know why this band has this power on him. In that particular case, going to his first concert will be a turning point. In the narration, which has been shortened here, the description of the journey to the concert hall, his questions and doubts, create an impression of deep tension and stress. How much this narration – from the trip to the dramatic parting from the mother – echoes traditional initiation rituals is striking.[47] Once in that place, this goes on during the opening band – but when the band starts, the narrator is 'in' the experience again. Yet during the concert, the lyrics seem to be written for him – and they become immediately a highly significant experience, that tell him to grow up, do important things and stop doing other things. The songs become symbolic resources to reflect on his life, and to reorient it dramatically; they are powerful semiotic canalizing means and seem to catalyse changes. Hence, the whole set up, which creates a quasi 'sacred space', the anticipation, the admiration for the singer, the high emotional intensity of the experience, immediately turn them into symbolic resources. This experience has the power of an epiphany (as the title of the blog – 'my first Staind concert that changed my life' suggests), that is, a bifurcation point in his trajectory. The fact that the narrator has been thinking only about this experience for three months reveals his active use of all the components of that experience as a symbolic resource. It also turns the whole sequence into a form of 'self-initiation ritual'. Finally, the narrator turns this private experience of epiphany into a social act. Hence, by the very fact of sharing that event through a public narration on a blog, the narrator both stabilizes that experience – as externalization through language allows – and also renders it public. As such, he might both search for validation within a community of fans,

[46] My first Staind concert that changed my life. www.staind.com/profiles/blogs/my-first-staind-concert-that, retrieved 3 May 2009.

[47] See the Bille example in Chapter 9. One might wonder whether the 'ritual' type of narration has so much entered into our culture that this resemblance is an effect of the very fact of telling the experience. An alternative explanation is that such initiation rituals operate a basic psychological function (of ruptures and creations) and that when rituals are not organized collectively, people somehow manage to reinvent them through complex forms of personal *bricolage*.

that is, as a form of social recognition, and promote such experiences – as when people who have religious revelations feel the need to share them. One might even say that the young man is using an old cultural narrative genre[48] – sharing an epiphany – as a semiotic resource to organize his experience.

Very often, it is possible to follow people's trajectories by observing the artefacts that became symbolic resources for them, and how their uses brought about new changes, and new elements to be used as symbolic resources – trajectories of young artists, politically committed people,[49] converts to religious faiths – and turn even ordinary tools into centrally relevant symbolic resources in the middle of their activities. Thus, a twenty-year old young student (Ernst Haeckel) wrote home to his parents (in 1854):

> I would like this fervent wish . . . to come true, whose realization I dream of day and night, really a dream I have had since I was a child, namely, of a great trip into the tropics . . . to stay in some tropical land . . . where I can sit in some primeval forest *with my wife (that is, my inseparable microscope)* and, insofar as my bodily powers allow, to anatomize and microscopize animals and plants, to collect all sorts of zoological, botanical, and geographic knowledge, so that this material will allow me to accomplish something coherent . . .[50]

Uses of complex artefacts as symbolic resources may help people to confer sense on their experience to redefine their identities and to define new ways of acting or thinking (that is, learning) as means to overcome difficult ruptures of making choices in situations of bifurcation. They may also create new bifurcation points in a trajectory. In doing so, given their social nature, they participate in the creation of very personal and unique trajectories, within a given community and its semiosphere.

*Using symbolic resources to destroy:* Many of these transformations seem to be very generative and positive, and lead people to situations in which they open new opportunities for change. But can the use of symbolic resources be negative or destructive? Any developmental process includes construction and un-construction (of the previous forms), which can sometimes be viewed as destruction. The unity of the constructive and destructive sides of the human being is encoded in various myths – such as the Kali/Durga

48 Bruner (1990). 49 Zittoun (2006b, 2010).

50 Richards (2008, p. 83), emphasis added. Ernst Haeckel's life in science indeed resulted – yet later in his life – in the accomplishments of such trips. However, the personal tragedy of losing his real wife Anna – not the microscope – on his thirtieth birthday flavoured the rest of his life, leading to both further fury of discovery (e.g. discovery of a medusa species he named *Mitrocoma Annae* – Anna's headband (Richards 2008, p. 109), and a lifelong search for his female muse (which resulted in an extra-marital love story in his mid sixties with a young woman thirty years his junior (Richards 2008, pp. 413–19).

myth in the Hindu tradition. Any semiotic resource can be turned into a symbolic one if the intention is to destroy as opposed to construct. The core books of different religions have been used to legitimate both the killing of and loving of others.

*In themselves*, books, songs or images cannot be 'destructive' or 'cause' violence. However, books, songs and images are powerful when they give a person the 'words' or the melody that correspond to some unelaborated experience, unsolved problem or ambivalent feeling. Also, as people encounter books or films in certain historical times and social webs of networks, they may be constrained to give more attention to some artefacts than others. Hence, we may think that in times of great social insecurity, daily anxieties, uncertain causes of troubles, some artefacts name this anxiety and suggest possible solutions – as for instance a fictional text that suggests that a certain ethnic or religious group is responsible for all the misery and that the solution is to destroy its members. If many people at the same time use such a text as a symbolic resource to shape their feelings and actions in given situation – and if, at the same time, they can guide public opinion and prevent alternative meaning-making of the same situation – then their use of that symbolic resource may actually be seen as having destructive effects (think for example about of the Bible as resource for the Inquisition, or the *Protocols of Sion* as a resource for anti-Semitic policies).

*Private-public uses of semiotic resources:* each semiotic artefact is fitted in to some socially regulated context. In this sense our personal-cultural play is socially regulated. Consider the contexts for reading a book – it can happen in privacy (reading silently for oneself) or in a small group of friends (public reading sessions – reading aloud for others) or in the formal context of a famous writer reading his or her well-known book aloud to a live audience. Likewise, such reading contexts of books can be distanced into the private domain – listening to an actor's rendering of a book-on-tape in the privacy of one's car. Here the reading in public has become the act of listening in private – while doing something else. Likewise, attending live music performances (in public – being embedded in a crowd) versus listening to the same performances over the radio or from a recording in the privacy of one's room (or in the privacy-created-in-public through the modern technology of MP3 players and iPods). *Semiotically coded materials can be used (thus becoming semiotic resources) in very varied social contexts that differ in their ways of regulating the public<> private relationship of a person.* Some of these uses lead a person to participate in the public domain, while others turn the public exposure of a person into a private setting. A person walking in a crowded urban setting with complete immersion in music from an iPod is distanced from the public to the very private domain.

*The infinite uses of symbolic resources*: it is not only the frame of use of various resources that plays with the public–private boundary. To some extent, any use of a resource playing with internalization is illuminated at the contact of one's unique life experience; and any use of a symbolic resource, a deeply social artefact, may reshape a trajectory in a unique way. Consequently, people can make infinite use of existing resources. Novels and other artefacts are used to support processes of imagination – which, as we have seen, can connect people to their past and shape their future, bring them to AS IF experiences, and transform their understanding of the world, of people or of themselves. In the examples above, people anticipate, deal with, or provoke ruptures in what they perceive as their identities. From there, and through these uses of imaginary resources that enable distancing, people may learn, transform their self-narratives or gain self-reflection – and participate in their open-ended development.

## Summary: the social world as endless area of play

Melodies of life unfold in a space of constraints. In this chapter we have examined some of the many areas of play in adult life – for play to take place there must be a space for playing. Hence we have examined different modes of social guidance which are meant to canalize human trajectories. Each of them, we have proposed, offers new arenas of play, which have as many variations.

The social space – the street, the landscapes – as reshaped by humans, redundantly exposes people to shapes and signs which convey certain meanings, and eventually fosters certain modes of feeling or believing. Yet the wanderer, who may see his mood or general impressions reshaped by that environment, may also realize the absurd repetition of that environment and engage in imaginary – when not physical – explorations of that environment, which then becomes a major play arena.

Social life is then punctuated by specific subscenes – which are extremely codified in a historical and geographical environment. We have thus seen how the smoking act as well as the clothing act dictate their own standards and values, but also open free zones of exploration and play for adults. In addition, we have seen that, through the semiosphere, social acts are often associated with one meaning and its opposite – and the ambivalence inherent in many of these mini-stages of our daily lives eventually offers boundless freedom.

Finally, each of the objects, words or artefacts to which people are exposed, and which can be seen as guiding devices from the social world upon individuals, can also be understood as resources used by people to transform their very modes of thinking, feeling and imagining their life-course trajectory. Hence, melodies of life can be canalized, but they often develop precisely through the unique creative synthesis of the precise set of constraints in which they take place – all through life and until the last breath.

# 11 'Old age' as living forward

Human ageing has become one of the most prominent topics of public discussion and scientific discourse across various disciplines during the last thirty years. This is clearly due to the phenomenon generally described as demographic change, which involves continuing low fertility and reproduction on the one hand and continuous rises in expected life expectancy on the other. The phenomenon of over-ageing is currently most prominent in Japan as well as in Europe, where pronounced effects of population ageing on public expenditures, economy, employment, education, and health care – to name just the main criteria – will be expected by 2030.[1]

'Getting older' describes the individually and collectively shared experience of the ageing process, which in human history for a long time has been conceptualized as a unidirectional sequence leading to decline and death. Even though this still represents a significant part of the human life course and the 'human condition', several factors have now changed. People not only live longer but they also live longer in a much better physical condition than previously (i.e. the middle of the last century). Progress in medical research, an optimal health provision and a broad offer of care services in almost all Western societies has clearly led to a different way of ageing. Although ageing still indicates a unidirectional process towards death, our timespans have become much longer and are no longer best described by the general term of 'getting older'.

In the following we will give an overview of some models and theories elaborating the many facets of human ageing. We will put emphasis on two points that reflect a leitmotif in the theoretical discourse about ageing: the relationship between objective life conditions and subjective perception and evaluation of these, and the conceptualization of ageing as the

Dieter Ferring is deeply grateful to Anja Leist and Thomas Boll for their comments on this chapter.

[1] European Commission (2005).

result of individual lifespan development. In this sense, we will describe ageing as 'living forward'. In doing so, we will start with some basic conceptual differentiations of the ageing process.

## Third and fourth ages

The 'need' for age classification is clearly the result of a widening of the collective experience whereby ageing no longer fits into the frame of a single concept. A second and associated reason for this still global differentiation may be rooted in the need to change the negative stereotype still associated with human ageing.[2] Until the 1970s old age seemed to be a relatively short period of life whose predominant characteristic was decline in the physical and functional domains leading to death. This has changed now since one can clearly differentiate between the third age as a phase of comparatively fewer impairments and deficits, which may also be compensated, and the fourth age, where there is an increased probability of losses in learning potential and cognitive plasticity, and a heightened prevalence of neurodegenerative disorders and functional impairments in general. Paul Baltes and Jacqui Smith elaborate the dynamic differentiation between the third and the fourth ages:

> What specifically do we mean by the distinction between the Third and the Fourth Age? As an opening observation, we need to emphasize that, like most phenomena in human evolution and science, the idea of the Third and Fourth Age itself is undergoing change and strictly speaking is not tied to a specific age range. Rather, as phenotypic expressions, the Third and Fourth Age are dynamic and moving targets and are themselves subject to evolution and variation. A look at the difference in population ageing between developed and developing countries makes this point of historical-cultural contingency. In today's developing countries, ageing begins and ends earlier than in developed countries.[3]

In general, two ways to define the third and fourth age exist: a population-based and an individual-based definition and – according to Baltes and Smith:

> both modes are necessary to capture the essence of the distinction and to direct our interpretations and inquiries to directions that highlight the discontinuity and qualitative differences between the 'Ages' of old age.[4]

[2] The role of stereotypes is perhaps best described within the context of theories depicting the consequences of stereotypes for intergenerational communication. Speech accommodation theory (Coupland, Coupland, Giles and Henwood, 1988), the communication predicament model (Ryan, Giles, Bartolucci and Henwood, 1986) or the stereotype activation model (Hummert, 1994) all highlight the role of positive and negative stereotypes in influencing communicative behaviours to older adults.

[3] Baltes and Smith (2003, p. 5). [4] Baltes and Smith (2003, p. 5).

The population-based definition can follow two strategies. The first one puts the transition between the third and fourth ages at the age at which 50 per cent of the birth cohort is no longer alive, putting the transition in developed countries around seventy five to eighty years. The more differentiated second strategy considers the transition between the third and fourth age as the age at which 50 per cent of the people who reached age fifty or sixty have died. For developed countries – given longevity – this latter definitional strategy puts the beginning of the fourth age closer to eighty to eighty five years. The individual-based differentiation highlights that the transition between third and fourth ages could happen at different chronological ages given that the maximum individual life span may be up to 120 years.[5]

Besides individual examples of longevity, extreme longevity in families has also recently attracted research.[6] Here again a distinction is made between 'centenarians' and 'super-centenarians'. An evaluation of the third and the fourth age concerning physical and psychological indicators of individual functioning is clearly in favour of the third age being described as a period of relatively less impairment, which can, in most cases, be compensated. The fourth age is described by a high prevalence of physical, functional and psychological impairments – a *cascade of decline* that involves the systemic decline of all domains of functioning. This may lead to the question of whether longevity – as a generally highly valued goal – is still so attractive on closer examination.

On the other hand, findings based on population statistics describe (only) trends that do not necessarily have to correspond to the individual life. Also, there is considerable variability *within* the fourth age. Alice George, being one of the oldest illustrations of longevity as described in Box 11.1, certainly reached the fourth age by outliving her life expectancy several times, but it seems that she still showed remarkable functionality of senses and intelligence. Differing ways of physical and functional ageing may in general be explained by the interaction of biogenetic and sociocultural factors as well as individual life history, but this may not explain the subjectively experienced age at the individual level. 'When will I be old?' is thus a question that will always find an individual answer – irrespective of chronological age. 'Age' and 'old age' describe time periods associated with a reduction of physical and functional performances

[5] The person with the longest confirmed age span is still Jeanne Calment (France; birth 21 February 1875, death 4 August 1997) who lived 122 years and 164 days (Robine and Allard, 1999). For an overview and analysis of longevity see Jeune and Vaupel (1999) (retrieved in April 2010 at www.demogr.mpg.de/books/odense/6/index.htm).

[6] See Alpert, Desjardins, Vaupel and Perls (1999).

### Box 11.1 One of the first examples of longevity: Alice George in 1681

Peter Laslett highlights as one of the earliest descriptions of longevity Alice George who had 108 years as this was reported by John Locke in 1681:

This day I saw one Alice George, a woman as she said of 108 years old at Alhallontide last [1 November 1680]. She lived in St Giles parish in Oxford and hath lived in and about Oxford since she was a young woman. She was born at Saltwyche in Worcestershire, her maiden name was Alice Guise. Her father lived to 83, her mother to 96 and her mother's mother to 111. When she was young she was fair-haired and neither fat nor lean, but very slender in the waist, for her size she was to be reckoned rather amongst the tall than short women. Her condition was but mean, and her maintenance her labour, and she said she was able to have reaped as much in a day as any man, and had as much wages. She was married at 30, and had 15 children, *viz.* 10 sons and 5 daughters baptized, besides 3 miscarriages. She has 3 sons still alive, her eldest John living the next door to her, 77 years old the 25th of this month. She goes upright though with a staff in one hand, but yet I saw her stoop twice without resting upon anything, taking up once a pot and another time her glove from the ground.

Her hearing is very good and her smelling so quick that as soon as she came near me she said I smelt very sweet, I having a pair of new gloves on that were not strong scented. Her eyes she complains of as failing her, since her last sickness, which was an ague that seized her about 2 years since and held her about a year. And yet she made a shift to thread a needle before us, though she seemed not to see the end of the thread very perfectly. She has as comely a face as ever I saw any old woman and age hath neither made her deformed nor decrepit.

The greatest part of her food now is bread and cheese or bread and butter and ale. Sack [sherry] revives her when she can get it. For flesh she cannot now eat, unless it be roasting pig which she loves. She had, she said, in her youth a good stomach [appetite] and ate what came in her way, oftener wanting victuals than a stomach. Her memory and understanding are perfectly good and quick, and amongst a great deal of discourse we had with her and stories she told she spoke not one idle or impertinent [irrelevant] word. Before this last ague she used to go to church constantly on Sundays, Wednesdays and Saturdays. Since that she walks not beyond her little garden.

She has been ever since her being married troubled with vapours [either flatulence or depression] and so is still, but never took any physic but once about 40 years since, *viz.* one pennyworth of jalap [aperient], which the apothecary out of kindness making a large pennyworth wrought more than sufficiently. She said she was 16 in '88 [1588], and went then to Worcester to see Queen Elizabeth, but came an hour too late, which agrees with her account of her age.[7]

[7] Laslett (1996, pp. 137–8).

leading to different profiles of autonomy and dependence; and ageing always implies a loss of 'physical strength' and resilience.

This may be the logic that has led most European societies to choose the crude indicator of leaving 'work life' in its various forms as a starting point for ageing. No longer participating in 'active' working life thus represents the crucial marker when it comes to the social construction of ageing in most European countries. All member states of the European Union have a mandatory retirement age with only very few exceptions, for special positions such as the pope or monarch. Different traditions at transnational level on mandatory retirement may be illustrated by the following quotation from Lawrence:

> In the United States, older people do all kinds of jobs, some because they enjoy working, others because they need the money. The fundamental reason, however, is that unlike in Europe, all have the right by law to be considered for work, independent of age. Measures against age discrimination also operate in Australia and Canada. But in Europe and Japan, mandatory retirement policies condone and institutionalize discrimination.[8]

This view expresses a different perspective underlining the individual right to work independent of age against the background of a Protestant work ethic, whereas the European tradition may be read in the light of a paternalistic welfare ethic. Different views on mandatory retirement thus clearly reflect different values and traditions attached to participation in working life on the one hand but also different welfare state approaches and social security systems on the other.[9]

When coming to the psychological dimension of working life participation it becomes evident that the exit from working life represents a transition involving learning processes, identity changes and sense-making. The criterion 'participation in work life' as a marker of ageing is not necessarily reflected by the subjective experience of age. Being confronted with one's own ageing most people would certainly state that 'you are only as old as you feel', which underlines the subjective construction and evaluation of this universally shared experience.

Some examples will illustrate these genuine individual views and ways of ageing. First, we may refer to Jeanne Calment who allegedly said that 'age hasn't changed a thing about me'. She took up fencing at the age 85, she was still riding a bicycle at 100, and she appeared briefly in the 1990 film

8 Lawrence (2008, p. 588).

9 In many European countries, however, there is now a shift to postpone the onset of retirement age due to economic challenges: Germany has raised the retirement age from sixty-five to sixty-seven and France from sixty to sixty-two years; in the UK employers may terminate employment when a worker is older than sixty-five years.

production *Vincent and Me* as herself at the age of 114, which made her the oldest actress ever. Another example: the British band *The Zimmers* appeared in 2007 with their cover of the Who song 'My generation' which has had more than 5 million views worldwide on YouTube alone. The band comprised seventeen women and men with a mean age of seventy-eight – the lead singer was ninety years old, the oldest member a hundred.[10] Peter Oakley, another band member, and known as *geriatric1927*, has his own website 'the internet granddad' at YouTube where he presents himself as follows:

> I am a widower living alone in a county in the middle of England UK. My life has been very varied but my love of motorcycles has remained with me all of my life (no, I don't have piercings or tattoos). I am a bit of a recluse I suppose as partying and such do not appeal. I have a degree in fine art which I got at the age of 60+ so have interests there. Blues music is essential to my well being and have been addicted since a child. I have a background in mechanical engineering. I guess that's enough. Ask me if you want to know more . . .[11]

In 2006, *geriatric1927* was the most subscribed user on YouTube. A further example: in 2010, a book called *Nacktbadestrand* (Nude Beach) was published in which the author Elfriede Vavrik describes various sex encounters with differing partners, having been contacted by a lonely hearts ad at the age of seventy-nine.

In particular, this latter example shows a years-wise-old or very old person doing something associated with younger generations. This puts into perspective general trends and predictions about ageing during the third and the fourth ages. In the following we will try to set 'getting older' in the context of human development and thus delineate that ageing *per se* can only be reconstructed on the individual as well as on the collective level if one takes into account the normative and non-normative challenges underlying the human lifespan. Ageing is in this understanding 'living forward' – and we will start doing this by depicting early models of human development.

*On age classifications and human development*: Plato and Cicero as well as Aristotle and Seneca had already analysed and differently evaluated the individual chances and risks of ageing, and they arrived at different evaluations and recommendations for avoiding these risks in individual ageing. In '*De senectute*', Cicero made recommendations such as avoiding 'symposia', that is, gatherings where one ate and discussed. He also recommended training the memory. These recommendations are still

[10] The band's website is at www.thezimmersonline.com/Welcome.html.
[11] See www.youtube.com/user/geriatric1927.

found in today's guidelines for healthy ageing. Age classifications within the discourse of social sciences may be traced back to the beginning of the twentieth century. Here, the first models were published structuring the human lifespan in view of each life phase's predominant themes, tasks and crises and thus allowing for a differentiation of different life phases. All these models conceptualize human development across the life span as a bio-sociocultural co-construction comprising the influences of biogenetics, culture and personality dynamics on human behaviour.

Charlotte Bühler may be named first here. In 1933, she proposed five stages of the human lifespan and described these by the specific psychological processes underlying each phase as determined by the pursuit of life goals:

> Human life is seen as a process characterized by an intentionality, generated in the core-self system, and directed toward a fulfilment at the end. The intentionality materializes in phases of self-determination towards goals which in the ideal case bring the individual's best potentials to realization. The five phases are one in which self-determination is prepared and built up [childhood until fifteen years]; one in which life goals are set experimentally and programmatically [adolescence, fifteen to twenty-five years]; one in which life goals become specific and definite [adulthood, twenty-three to forty or fifty years]; one in which success and failure are being assessed [late adulthood; forty-five to fifty up to sixty to sixty-five]; and one in which rest or continuation of striving occur with a closure experience of fulfilment or unfulfilment, resignation, sometimes despair [sixty to sixty-five until the end of life].[12]

Bühler uses the term 'intentionality' to describe the 'inner coherence' and self-determination of human lives, which is put into effect by the pursuit of life goals. These comprise activities, personal relationships and self-development; overall fulfilment in these areas depends on how far one needs satisfaction, where creative expansion, self-limiting adaptation and upholding the internal order are realized with respect to any specific goal domain. Old age is, in such a conceptualization, the period where one may reap what one has sown: one can find fulfilment in having established important life goals or one may feel a lack of fulfilment if these could not be accomplished – a notion that will also be taken up in later models. The retrospective evaluation of one's life as it is described here also represents the crucial theme and psychosocial crisis within the model proposed by Erik Erikson.[13]

As already mentioned above, Erikson differentiates eight stages of the human lifespan by their underlying psychosocial crises. In this sequential model individual development depends on the solution to specific crises

12 Bühler (1968, p. 200). 13 Erikson (1963).

underlying the human life course from infancy to old age. Within Erikson's model, the task of old age starting at sixty-five years is described as the struggle to achieve a sense of ego integrity in resolving the conflict between 'integrity and despair'. The reflection of one's life and the evaluation of whether important life goals have been accomplished constitute the main tasks of this period and depending on the answers found, a sense of 'ego integrity' or fulfilment in Bühler's sense may be experienced. Otherwise despair about unaccomplished goals and thus developments that can no longer be changed may manifest themselves. Retrospection and the balancing evaluation of one's life thus represent the central tasks when people are getting older, according to Bühler and Erikson. This is also taken up by a third model that has been proposed by Robert Havighurst,[14] who differentiated between nine developmental phases across the human lifespan, describing them by their specific profile of developmental tasks.

Developmental tasks originate in Havighurst's view from the interplay of physical maturation, the constraints and demands of the society as well as the desires, aspirations and values of the individual. Given the interplay between individual and social factors, failure to accomplish developmental tasks may lead to disapproval by society as well as feelings of unhappiness and difficulties in accomplishing future tasks on the individual level. With respect to late life starting at the age of sixty years, Havighurst formulated six developmental tasks reflecting biological, social and individual processes of that life stage, namely:

1 adjusting to decreasing physical strength and health;
2 adjusting to retirement and reduced income;
3 adjusting to the death of a spouse;
4 establishing an explicit affiliation with one's age group;
5 adopting and adapting social roles in a flexible way;
6 establishing satisfactory physical living arrangements.

'Coping' with physical, social and material losses constitutes the main task of this life period due to the biology of ageing, whereas affiliating with one's age group as well as the adaptation to disengagement from social life and roles constitute the sociocultural background. Interestingly, neither the list enumerated by Havighurst in 1948, nor the Bühler and Erikson scenarios, contains a decline in cognitive performance or an indication of specific geriatric disorders, reflecting the different prevalence of these diseases in their times.

[14] Havighurst (1948).

Nevertheless, a common feature of these models is the accentuation of a *general deterioration* of biological, social and psychological factors as a common characteristic of age and old age, which surely reflects the objective social context of ageing at the lifetime of these authors. But on the other hand, all three models also give space to plasticity in ageing, since this may depend on intentionality or the solution to specific developmental crises or tasks. Ageing is in this view 'successful' if one achieves a sense of fulfilment or 'ego integrity' or if one adapts to the specifics of the changed life situation in old age. It is not surprising that Havighurst was one of the first authors who brought the concept of *successful ageing* into the scientific debate and thus started a series of theoretical models and empirical research on this issue.[15]

## Successful ageing and the many ways of defining success

In general, one can differ between the idiographic and the nomothetic approach chosen for the description and explication of human ageing – one may delineate the idiosyncracy and the multitude of phenomena of individual ageing in context or one may try to identify regularities and universal laws of human ageing. These two approaches are also implied in the following quotation of Rowe and Kahn,[16] who stated that *ageing is a universal but by no means a uniform process*, thus accentuating universal regularities on the one side and considerable inter-individual differences in ageing on the other. The statement also underlines the eminent difficulty in defining 'success' when it comes to ageing (and other domains as well).

Ageing represents a developmental phenomenon to be described on multiple dimensions and out of several scientific perspectives. Depending on the perspective and dimension under consideration, differential descriptive profiles and subsequent 'normative' evaluations of ageing are considered successful or not may emerge. Ageing becomes in this view a balancing of gains and losses – and this applies to both the scientific perspective as well as the individual perspective. Furthermore, the qualification 'successful' also depends on the given sociocultural and historical context. It goes without saying that living as a fisherman on a tropical island will require different adaptive efforts from being a pensioner in a Western European country.

Successful ageing as it is defined by Rowe and Kahn[17] describes the ability to maintain three relative and interrelated key elements or characteristics: (1) low probability of disease and disease-related disability;

[15] Havighurst (1961). [16] Rowe and Kahn (1998). [17] Rowe and Kahn (1998).

(2) high cognitive and physical functional capacity; and (3) high engagement with life (i.e. activity). Ageing is further differentiated with respect to non-pathological and pathological ageing; the first category is further differentiated as regards *usual* or *average* ageing and *successful* ageing. Usual ageing is defined as ageing, in which extrinsic factors heighten the effects of intrinsic ageing processes (i.e. normal functional decrements due to the genetic programme), whereas successful ageing refers to ageing in which extrinsic factors (e.g. nutrition, activity, lifestyle) counteract intrinsic ageing processes or play a neutral role so that there is little or no functional loss at all.[18] The authors recommend that theory and research should focus on the group of successfully ageing individuals in order to identify those processes that underlie an optimal ageing process.

The Rowe and Kahn definition describes a special form of ageing in which a person of sound mind actively participates in social life and is not debilitated by diseases and/or functional impairments. This does not represent a descriptive but rather a prescriptive statement and thus implies a normative value judgement. The qualification conveys that there are more or less clear-cut 'success' criteria and that – depending on these – one may or may not age successfully. Such a normative evaluation of ageing is implicit (and not explicit) in all approaches using this term. Such an implicit meaning is also transported by other concepts such as 'productive ageing'[19] or 'conscious ageing'[20] that accentuate specific key elements, which should be predominant in evaluating the ageing process.

The step from a descriptive to a prescriptive statement clearly carries the risk of overgeneralization and a reduction of individual phenomena to consensually agreed upon criteria. Within this context, one may highlight – as a further point – that the definition of success can in general be realized from three different perspectives: (1) one may use more or less objective criteria (e.g. lifetime in years; the incidence and prevalence of medically diagnosed diseases and illnesses, functional impairments); (2) one may rely on predominant theories and models of ageing and derive verifiable standards, which may be described by their interindividual validity (e.g. 'productivity'; activity); (3) one may choose subjective self-ratings as the defining criteria. All three approaches are used and all of them have their shortcomings. Especially when it comes to the comparison between 'objective' and theoretically derived criteria on the one hand and 'subjective' criteria of functioning on the other hand, a convergence is not necessarily to be expected – this phenomenon is valid across all life

[18] Rowe and Kahn (1987). [19] Baltes and Montada (1996). [20] Moody (2002).

periods and it has especially and repeatedly been illustrated in social indicators and psycho-gerontological research.[21]

Strawbridge, Wallhagen and Cohen[22] demonstrated the divergence between objective and subjective indicators of ageing in a sample of 857 subjects aged between sixty-five and ninety-nine years. The authors identified in a first step persons who were successfully ageing by using the objective criteria proposed by Rowe and Kahn as indicators (namely the absence of disease, disability and risk factors; maintaining physical and mental functioning, and active life engagement). Besides this, they also asked participants to rate the way they were ageing by responding to the question 'I am ageing successfully (or ageing well)' with 'agree strongly', 'agree somewhat', 'disagree somewhat' or 'disagree strongly'. When applying this subjective criterion they identified 50.3 per cent of the sample who rated their ageing as successful compared to 18.8 per cent who were classified as ageing successfully according to Rowe and Kahn's criteria. The authors point out that although the absence of chronic conditions and maintaining functioning were positively associated with successful ageing for both definitions, many participants with chronic conditions and with functional difficulties still rated themselves as ageing successfully, which illustrates that it is not the objective life situation but rather the subjective perception and construction of one's life situation that constitutes individual reality. This ability to surpass 'objective' conditions, reconstructing them and creating new meanings (see above the creation of AS-IF realities) is as much central in old age as it is throughout life, as we have tried to show in these pages.

*The transformation of objective into subjective reality*: within psycho-gerontological research, there is a (self-evident) emphasis on subjective criteria when it comes to the evaluation of the life situation in old age. Besides retaining personal autonomy, the balance of positive and negative affect, especially life satisfaction, represents one of the most popular criterion variables here. The concept has been described as the cognitive component of subjective well-being implying a judgemental process, in which the present life situation – the 'is', AS IS – is compared and weighed towards a desired life situation – the 'ought',[23] enabled by imagination and that we have called WHAT COULD BE. Interestingly, few differences have been observed when cross-sectional comparisons of life satisfaction ratings were performed between younger and older age groups. The overall result pattern that emerges here can be described as inconsistent

[21] Zapf (1984); see also Filipp and Ferring (1991); Staudinger, (2000).
[22] Strawbridge, Wallhagen and Cohen (2002).
[23] See Diener (1984); Ferring & Filipp (1997).

and slightly in favour of results indicating comparable levels of life satisfaction across different age groups.[24] Our recent report shows that most longitudinal studies found a rather slight, sometimes even non-significant average decline in life satisfaction from middle to old age (up to about seventy or eighty-five years).[25] Studies which also included a sufficiently large number of individuals beyond eighty-five up to a hundred plus years found a more pronounced decline in very old age compared to the earlier phases of old age.[26]

Basically, one may contrast the possible divergences between the objective and the subjectively experienced life situation as follows.[27] If the life situations that may be described with respect to objective criteria as 'good' or 'bad' do correspond with the subjective judgements, their convergence may be described as 'actual well-being' and 'deprivation' respectively. The case in which an objectively 'good' life situation is judged as bad may be circumscribed as 'dilemma of discontent'. The phenomenon that a 'bad' life situation is judged as good is described here as 'satisfaction paradox'. Thus, satisfaction in the face of age-related losses and impairments indicates the effective use of adaptive processes in old age that allow for a regulation of subjective well-being. Life satisfaction in old age may be dynamically shaped by reducing discrepancies between the 'is' and the 'ought'. This may involve changing the evaluation of the present life situation by using new evaluation criteria, or changing the evaluation of the desired life situation by changing one's aspirations and expectations.[28]

This principle is described in Aesop's fable 'The Fox and the Grapes', where the fox devalues what he cannot get – the grapes. The principle is also founded in Leon Festinger's concept of *cognitive dissonance*[29] where a person copes with contradictory ideas and behaviour by adjusting his evaluation criteria. A smoker, for instance, changes or denies the perceived risk of smoking for her life expectancy. A person who has been proud of his physical fitness and experiences significant losses of physical capacity may redefine the importance of physical fitness for his well-being. We will come back to these manoeuvres below.

The identification of indicators of successful ageing and the divergence between the objective standards and the subjectively perceived situation may also serve as a leitmotif to describe predominant models of ageing in the aftermath of and inspired by Erikson's and Havighurst's models.

[24] E.g., Diener and Suh (1998). [25] Ferring and Boll (2010).

[26] Gerstorf, Ram, Röcke, Lindenberger and Smith (2008); Gerstorf, Ram, Eastabrook, Schupp, Wagner and Lindenberger (2008).

[27] Zapf (1984). [28] Ferring and Boll (2010). [29] Festinger (1957).

*Models of ageing (well)*: core pieces of the early definition of 'successful ageing' by Havighurst have been 'adding life to the years' and 'getting satisfaction from life', thus combining objective and subjective criteria which have been used in many other approaches. How one may obtain satisfaction from life in old age has been controversially discussed; two sociological approaches – both rooted in symbolic interactionism and thus underlining the importance of social roles and statuses – will be presented here.

In framing the ageing process, *disengagement theory*[30] puts the emphasis on reduced individual capabilities and diminished interest on the one hand and societal disincentives for participation on the other, and thus expects that individuals will gradually withdraw or disengage from social roles in the process of ageing. Ageing is in this view characterized by voluntary retirement from work or family life, and the pursuit of solitary, passive activities as preparation for death. Leaving aside that the theory's premises have been criticized ever since it was first published, the socio-cultural background for the theory would constitute a society with a shorter life expectancy, an earlier onset of disability, physically demanding work roles and few organized activities and participation for older adults; this is certainly (no longer) valid in current Western societies. Learning to accept, that is, making sense of the experience, that one's capacities diminish, and that certain roles can no longer be fulfilled, represent a developmental task of getting old, but certainly constitute only one of several tasks. Within this line of reasoning, one may also hold that the theory excludes the subjective view on disengagement. Thus, what is missing is that disengagement from specific activities may have different meanings for different individuals: retirement may be a long desired positive experience for one person, and for another it may represent a critical life event.

*Activity theory* marks the contra-position to disengagement theory[31] and active participation in daily and social activities is described here as a prerequisite for successful ageing. The theory holds that self-esteem and life satisfaction largely depend on the importance that is assigned to a person's social roles; individuals in old age who remain actively engaged in desired activities should therefore be more satisfied than those who can no longer participate. This theoretical approach can also be linked to increasing offers of social participation as a predominant feature of the 1960s and 1970s in Western countries. The active participation of older individuals in social and daily activities was clearly desired and thus

[30] Cumming and Henry (1961). [31] Lemon, Bengtson and Petersen (1972).

became one of the core domains in evaluating the ageing process as successful. The theory does not specify, however, whether all activities can be considered as beneficial, or whether certain activities should be avoided due to impairments in physical strength. An older lady of ninety-five years who still cleans all the windows in her house is active but she remains so at a certain risk for her health. Having to work in old age to earn one's living is certainly also an activity but will pose a strain to one's health. Comparable to disengagement theory, activity theory does not elaborate the subjective view and specific individual meaning that may underlie specific activities. Doing sports may in this view be the satisfying continuation of a lifetime habit for one person while it may put another person under stress.

Nevertheless, the concept of 'active ageing' has a positive connotation and it is used nowadays within the context of models that deal with the effects of demographic change in Europe. Walker,[32] for instance, pointed out that active ageing will represent the central concept to deal with an increasingly ageing society in Europe. He uses the concept in the 'classical' meaning referring to both an increase of older workers in the labour force and the promotion of productive activities in the retirement phase.

Both activity and disengagement theory – as sociological theories – focus on the social status and roles of a person and they derive a more or less uniform prescription about the way people should age within society. Without further evaluation of their different theoretical and practical value, the prescriptive statement underlying both approaches implies that certain lifestyles will guarantee successful ageing. In the case of these two theories, the recommended lifestyles are diametrically opposed since one recommendation is to accept disengagement and withdraw from social life and roles whereas the other believes in an active role and participation in social life. However, such unidimensional descriptions of ageing lack power when it comes to describing and explaining ageing at the individual level together with the various inter- and intra-individual differences in dealing with the diverse tasks of ageing observed here. The concept of differential ageing conceptualizes this phenomenon and it will be described in the following.

*Differential ageing*: the Bonn Longitudinal Study on Ageing (BOLSA) represents the first longitudinal study on the process of ageing in Europe and results from this study set the frame for a cognitive theory of ageing that has been developed by Hans Thomae, who was also the initiator of this milestone study. Thomae not only emphasized the objective

[32] Walker (2002).

incidence but also the interpretation and evaluation of age-correlated impairments and losses as the crucial factor in determining a person's life satisfaction in old age. In his view, human ageing is always 'differential ageing' since the interpretation of age-related changes depends on the one hand on the needs, motives and aspirations of the elderly and on the other hand on the present socially shared stereotypes of old age in a given society. The essential feature for life satisfaction in this line of reasoning is the balance between individual needs and *perceived* reality. Three postulates describe the cognitive theory of ageing: (1) perception of change rather than objective change is related to behavioural change; (2) any change in the situation of the individual is perceived in terms of the dominant concerns and expectations of the individual; (3) adjustment to ageing is a balance between the cognitive and motivational structure of the individual.[33]

With these postulates, Thomae underlines the subjective construction of reality and he questions normative approaches formulating inter-individually accepted adjustment criteria. Referring to adjustment to ageing consisting of the balance between the cognitive and motivational structure in his third postulate, he thus wrote:

> This postulate stems from the fact that neither 'disengagement theory' nor any of its derivates can offer sufficient criteria for 'successful ageing'. It is in agreement with those approaches which tried to define life styles as intervening variables between the life situation of the aged and adjustment ... However no kind of classifying different ways of ageing meets the great variety of interindividual differences. Defining adjustment to ageing by the principle of balance between situations as it is perceived on the one hand and motivational state or structure on the other hand, we neither have to superimpose an 'ideal' or 'normal' pattern of ageing nor a classificatory system on the different varieties.[34]

In discussing findings of the BOLSA, Thomae differentiated between 'ageing styles' (*Alternstile*) and 'ageing drama' (*Altersschicksale*), both accentuating an active and non-deficit view of the elderly: 'ageing styles' are described as an individual's active attempts to shape his or her development; *Altersschicksale* describe the individual coming to terms with predetermined normative age related events which cannot be prevented or avoided (i.e. losses and functional impairments). Thomae always emphasized interindividual variability and differentiation of ageing at the individual level, thus underlining the uniqueness of the individual biography. In doing so, he underlined the role of individual and social factors without neglecting the biological factors underlying ageing. He

[33] See Thomae (1970). [34] Thomae (1970, p. 8).

considered these as important explanatory factors that cannot be changed in the short run, whereas 'better knowledge of the psychodynamics of ageing . . . might help some aged person already today and tomorrow'.[35]

The implementation of longitudinal studies finally emphasized the conceptualization of the ageing process as a developmental phenomenon; in this view development covers the whole lifespan and does not stop in early adolescence.[36] When discussing the problems of the elderly in adjusting to their social situation after retirement, disengagement from social roles as well as the reduction of life time, Thomae – like Charlotte Bühler – points out:

> many observations point to the fact that adjustment problems related to the ageing process start early in adult life. Many studies on individual awareness of ageing of their own personality conducted for the last forty years show that the earliest age at which for the first time the awareness of age becomes a problem is in the middle twenties. Experimental studies on psychomotor performance and learning, or studies on adjustment of different age groups on traffic conditions show the same tendency, the trend toward a certain decline is observable in early adulthood or at least in middle age. Therefore, it seems justified not to restrict the term ageing psychologically to a rather limited stage of life (e.g. beyond the 70's) and to include the whole life span between early adulthood and old age in research on ageing . . . Very often adjustment problems of the aged person are a variation of those of the middle-aged. However more important is the fact that the way in which the individual copes with these problems in early or middle adulthood is decisive for the degree to which the major problems of life in old age are met.[37]

In this view, ageing is a result of the prior individual lifespan development – with respect to the available personal coping resources as well as with respect to perceived adjustment – and this can be best understood by taking a biographical view. Against the background of longitudinal studies on responses to stress, Thomae further emphasized the plasticity of the human person. Ageing is in such a view not a unidirectional process but it may lead to several possible outcomes depending on the subjective representation and associated ageing styles and/or ageing struggles.[38] Lifespan development and differential ageing are also part of the theoretical perspective added by Atchley,[39] who conceptualized ageing within the context of an individual's lifelong development by accentuating continuity. He summarizes his approach as follows:

> continuity theory is a social psychological theory of continuous adult development . . . It uses feedback systems theory to create a view of adults as dynamic, self-aware entities who use patterns of thought created over their

[35] Thomae (1970, p. 13). [36] Baltes (1987). [37] Thomae (1963, p. 366).
[38] See Lehr and Thomae (1993). [39] Atchley (1972).

lifetimes to describe, analyze, evaluate, decide, act, pursue goals, and interpret input and feedback. Although social processes such as socialization and social control have input to the person's internal system, the conscious being who interprets the input also creates the resulting personal constructs, including personal construction of the life course, life events, life stages, age norms, and age grading.[40]

Within this approach to ageing, development across the lifespan is focused with respect to continuity. The fundamental proposition is immediately and intuitively evident: a person who has had an introverted youth will retain this behaviour and certainly not become an outgoing extrovert in old age. There are also several and evident examples for preserving a certain lifestyle in the music business, if one thinks about the Rolling Stones whose oldest member is sixty-nine, or Ringo Starr, former member of the Beatles, aged seventy. The above cited *geriatric1927* holds that he always had a love of motorcycles. Continuity theory also forecloses theories of the self which focus on those occasions of getting older when continuity is challenged, that is, if one's representation of the self and the world have to be changed – this may happen if we are confronted with irreversible losses such as losing a loved person or when losing a competence or capacity that is crucial to oneself.

What one has acquired during life as cognitive styles of describing, analysing, evaluating and deciding will thus be preserved.[41] This makes even more sense from an evolutionary perspective since an organism will only memorize those learning experiences that have been proved to be functional, that is, serving an adaptation goal. The theory also hints – in the same way as Thomae argues – that individual ageing is determined by events and decisions already taken during earlier periods of the lifespan.

In the view of continuity theory, subjective reality has priority over objective reality; moreover, ageing is not a distinct period of time but it represents the continuity of development since one 'lives forward' using what one has gained across life.[42] In such a view, (successful) ageing implies the voluntary preservation of habits, lifestyles and relationships from early to mid- and late life. Parallel to the shift of paradigm within developmental psychology, which accentuated the plasticity and variability of developmental processes over the life course, ageing has thus been reconstructed as part of individual development, which may be described as the continuity or discontinuity of individual development.

[40] Atchley (2006, p. 266).
[41] This is what we have thematized in this book as *Melodies of Living*.
[42] Similar ideas are expressed with the notions of *epigenesis* (Chapter 1) and self-narrative (Chapter 6).

Both Thomae's cognitive theory and continuity theory mark a shift in the theoretical focus on ageing, since the individual perception and 'construction' of ageing have henceforward been considered predominant compared to objective criteria when describing the ageing process as 'successful'.[43] As a consequence of this paradigm shift, regulatory processes have been brought into focus and the adaptive nature of the ageing individual has been highlighted. Within psycho-gerontology and lifespan developmental psychology focus has been put on the individual within its socio-ecological and biographical context. Here, a paradigmatic definition of the quality of ageing is avoided since multiple – sometimes mutually exclusive – criteria are specified by which ageing may be described, thus accounting for the inter-individual variance that can be observed in the ageing process.

*Ageing and cognitive regulation*: Paul Baltes and Margaret Baltes[44] took up several prior conceptions in specifying those processes which may contribute to successful or optimal ageing, and which are explicated within the framework of the theory of selective optimization with compensation (SOC). Successful ageing is defined here as the attainment or maximization of positive outcomes and goals and the avoidance or minimization of negative outcomes and goals. In order to achieve this hedonistic principle, the components of selection, compensation and optimization are used. *Selection* implies the selection and concentration on goals and desired outcomes that can be achieved in old age; *compensation* implies the use of compensatory means to adapt to capacities that are no longer intact, and *optimization*, finally, implies the best use of still intact capacities. The differential use of these manoeuvres should represent the explanatory moment of differences in objective and subjective indicators of ageing within this model. Baltes and Baltes[45] delineate that the nature of what constitutes gains and losses or desired outcomes and goals is conditioned by cultural and personal factors as well as by the position in the lifespan of an individual. The model thus represents a meta-model, which can be applied to study the whole developmental process and it integrates social and cultural as well as individual factors. Such a characterization of gains and losses underlines at the same time the interplay between objective (i.e. socioculturally agreed upon) and individually defined gains, underlining that the two may not necessarily converge.

43 As already illustrated above, Thomae refrained from using this term and he always was careful not to superimpose meanings or classifications on human ageing (see also Thomae, 2002).

44 Baltes and Baltes (1990).

45 Baltes and Baltes (1990).

If the SOC model is applied to explain individual forms of ageing, the three regulatory processes may to a certain degree be characterized by the use of two different processes, which may be described as 'changing the world' and 'changing the self'. This dichotomy was first proposed by Rothbaum, Weisz and Snyder[46] and has influenced much subsequent reasoning and many models on coping in old age. Starting from the premise that the preservation and experience of control is an essential human need, the authors differentiate in their two-process model of perceived control between primary (i.e. 'changing the world') and secondary control ('changing the self'). *Primary control* comprises active behavioural endeavours to change one's environment in order to achieve one's goals and to preserve personal autonomy; *secondary control* involves the manipulation and accommodation of one's internal cognitive and affective states (i.e. changing one's goals and aspirations) in order to reduce the impact of events that are not controllable by primary control endeavours. The authors state that 'secondary control ... is particularly likely in cases of prolonged failure to obtain highly desired and important incentives, or cases in which the inability is perceived as permanent',[47] and thus outline the scenario justifying the suitability of this theory for the description of coping in old age.

The dichotomy described here is also to be found within the two-process model proposed by Brandtstädter and co-workers.[48] Here, successful ageing is seen as a dynamic process of balancing assimilative, accommodative and immunizing strategies in order to maintain a realistic sense of self. While *assimilative* activities represent behavioural endeavours to prevent or reduce losses in domains that are central to the self, *accommodative* processes comprise the cognitive regulation of aspirations and goals (such as disengagement from blocked goals or lowering of aspirations). *Immunizing* strategies imply the selective and self-serving filtering and processing of information, which may be a threat to the self-esteem (e.g. by selective comparisons). Heckhausen and collaborators[49] also emphasize these processes in their model. They propose a lifespan theory of primary and secondary control in close conceptual relation to the theory proposed by Rothbaum,[50] and predict that secondary control strategies are more frequently used at a higher age in order to

46 Rothbaum, Weisz and Snyder (1982).
47 Rothbaum, Weisz and Snyder (1982, p. 29).
48 See for instance Brandstädter and Greve (1994).
49 Heckhausen and Schulz (1995) and Schulz and Heckhausen (1996).
50 Rothbaum, Weisz and Snyder (1982).

preserve self-esteem and self-efficacy, since external restrictions increase with increasing age.

Summing up, one may hold that theory and research on the concept of successful ageing have increasingly emphasized the role of individual cognitive processes in adapting to the changed life situation in old age. In such a view, there has been a shift from more or less objective criteria to more subjective criteria when evaluating the quality of ageing. Furthermore, all of the models listed up till now imply a certain '*Zweckrationalität*' ('rationality of goal orientation') of the ageing individual – the underlying motivation being to achieve the best adaptive outcome in a given situation.

## Summary: the experience of ageing as individual construction

Delineating the divergence between what is objectively true or real and what is subjectively true or real, it becomes obvious that the experience of ageing and its associated phenomena represent individual constructions: constructions that are developed throughout life when confronted with approaching ageing. One does certainly not start thinking about ageing when reaching retirement age. Each birthday marks a step further towards what may be described as age and old age. Furthermore, people around us are getting older – this includes loved ones, significant others and all those persons that catch our attention for diverse motives and reasons. Fathers and mothers die and often confront us with the first and irrevocable 'normative' losses of the human lifespan. Losses concerning our mental functioning that are in general associated with old age already occur early in life – minor declines in fluid intelligence, and in particular speed of information processing being one of them. Eyesight and hearing represent two further domains in which one may already early in life be confronted with deterioration. Even though these are due to biological processes that also underlie human ageing, interestingly, no one would start describing themselves as old when using glasses – hearing aids may make a difference here because these are more clearly associated with the image of ageing. Furthermore, most changes in our functioning appear continuously and they evolve gradually rather than appearing abruptly.

This quality may be true for the process of ageing as well – age is *a polite man that knocks on your door* – as Goethe[51] has put it – but no one opens the door until the man enters without being asked for. If we become (a

[51] Goethe (1814/2008, p. 225).

posteriori) aware that we have changed in a way that is associated with our representation of ageing, we may see ourselves as getting old. Although the signs may already be there, they may not attract our attention, perception, and interpretation – and this process starts already at the middle of the life span, or even earlier as Thomae put it. Even if we become aware of changes, these may be interpreted in a more self-serving way. This is convincingly illustrated by subjective age estimates: asking people how old they feel with respect to a certain domain will almost always result in underestimations of age. This is moderated by the domain under consideration though: evaluating one's physical functioning will leave less interpretative space than, for instance, mental fitness where criteria may be defined individually and idiosyncratically. Furthermore, underestimations of one's age decrease with increasing age, which may indicate that one is coming to terms with one's age. Subjective age estimates demonstrate again what has been described within cognitive models of adaptation – persons shape 'objective' reality into a subjective reality by relying on subjective criteria.

Experiencing that one is 'getting older' may thus be characterized as a process during which one successively processes information that may be linked with the individual representation of getting older. The Piagetian differentiation between assimilation and accommodation may be used here to describe this type of information processing. People develop representations about ageing across the lifespan, and these are fed by individual and collectively shared signs and symbols. These categories are subject to assimilation and accommodation. Asking a three-year-old child when one will be old may result in rather concrete ascriptions of the type 'when your hair is grey', 'when you have children'. At the age of ten, children may actively refer to already more elaborated representations of old persons and deduce attributes and characteristics of elderly persons they know.[52] During adolescence and young adulthood, age *per se* is certainly not a threat, though one may learn in multiple ways during emerging adulthood that ageing implies a heightened probability of meeting threatening losses. Intergenerational relations within families in general and especially loss experiences represent ways of getting to know the risks associated with ageing. Furthermore, ageing and ageing persons are becoming more and more prominent in public discourse, be it social policy, be it the media offering information about the process of ageing. Diagnostic information about ageing is thus available, but will it be integrated in one's view of the self? Developing a representation of oneself

[52] See Newman, Faux and Larimer (1996).

as ageing may therefore be best understood with reference to the dynamics underlying the development of the representation of the self and here one may refer to Bühler, Thomae, Atchley and Brandstädter.

According to them, the constitution and preservation of the self represents a lifespan task described by three underlying motives:

1 Developing a sense of continuity is a central task of self construction. Ageing is involved in this task insofar as it implies the construction of temporal continuity across the life span with the result of being still the same person.[53]
2 Establishing distinctiveness and discrimination constitutes a further need underlying the construction of the self. Identifying characteristics indicating that one is different from others serves the motive of preserving uniqueness.[54]
3 Biographical relevance of individual characteristics also becomes an integral part of one's self-view since we only integrate those characteristics as central parts of our self which are 'important', that is, which have an adaptive value within our life. Developing a representation of ageing will happen within the context of these dynamics.

When we grow older, we are bombarded with stimulation from a flow of events and situations but only some of these enter our perception. This is in part due to the limited capacity of human information processing which leads us to focus on those specific aspects of our experiences that are related to specific needs or motives in a specific situation. Furthermore, objective reality is sometimes very ambiguous and complex, but individuals have considerable power to define and shape reality through their constructions and appraisals.[55] The 'paradox of denial'[56] is one illustration of this phenomenon. Sometimes, we are selectively *in*attentive to certain aspects of a threatening situation and this implies, by definition, that a person must have some awareness of such threatening information in order to know where *not* to look.

Besides, what is happening to the individual is due to biogenetic programme and socio-ecological context; the individual also seeks experiences that are congruent with his or her self representation, and specific experiences are then integrated or assimilated. If experiences are discrepant with our representation of the 'person-we-are', we may start a process of successively integrating this 'bad news' by accommodation, that is, changing our representation. Learning to know that one's physical fitness

[53] This also represents the central motive underlying temporal comparisons (Albert, 1977).

[54] See also Ferring and Hoffmann (2007).

[55] See Ferring and Filipp (2000).

[56] See Breznitz (1986).

has decreased, learning to adapt to changes in one's physical appearance constitute examples of such typical tasks. Continuity of the self – in the sense of biographical orientation – may still represent one of the crucial motives in doing so since the self is conservative, and integrating discrepant information about oneself may be achieved by several self-serving strategies that still allow for a sense of continuity. Several models elaborate that the self-concept shows considerable stability across the lifespan, which is explained by the functioning of self-stabilizing mechanisms.[57] In this view, it becomes evident that the fact of ageing – becoming an 'old person' – may, step by step, be integrated within one's representation of the self. The following quotation underlines the necessity of 'becoming constituted in time' and coming to terms with changes:

> How is becoming oneself constituted in time? It is not completed on reaching adulthood. On the contrary, this is when the complex processes of protecting and testing identity begins. We experience ourselves as identical essentially during and after decisive and impressionable experiences of change. The form of our life preserves its unmistakable quality because we experience profound changes in ourselves and must react to these transformations.
>
> One look at the natural structure of our life in childhood and youth, adolescence and adulthood, ageing, and the end of life makes this clear. These changes of a meaningful and enduring life are bound up with changes in our way of seeing the world. The point is that the unique totality of life represents a continuous task of interpretation; it develops, on the one hand, in accordance with the existential dialectic of the concrete individual situation and the concrete action. On the other hand, it progresses in accordance with the perspective of the totality of our existence, through the changes of life.
>
> In growing up and maturing, one's perspective changes in a meaningfully experienced life. Human beings are not just to be understood as meaningful projects in themselves, but rather as beings capable of fundamental changes in perspective. They must be capable of this too, for the unique totality of life says that everything fundamental happens only once: only once is everyone a child, a young person, an adult, only once is there an entry into later life. These all occur without a chance to rehearse: life is a continuous premiere. Every new opportunity in life is simultaneously a loss; every loss, a gain. Therefore, Kierkegaard (1946) says life can be understood backwards; living, however, must be done forwards.[58]

The 'unique totality of life' thus represents a 'permanent task of interpretation', and 'everything fundamental happens only once'. When putting it like this each of the fundamental changes one encounters is a 'premiere' – though some 'premieres' in the play of life may be more similar to one another than others. It is in this life-play analogy that it also gets quite

[57] See Brandtstädter (1999). [58] Rentsch (1997 p. 264ff.)

evident that it is always *the same player* on the stage, even if he or she plays many parts, as Shakespeare has described it in the seven ages of man:

> All the world's a stage,
> And all the men and women merely players,
> They have their exits and entrances,
> And one man in his time plays many parts,
> His acts being seven ages . . .[59]

Shakespeare spins the wheel from the 'infant mewling and puking in the nurse's arms' to the 'Last scene of all, that ends this strange eventful history Is second childishness and mere oblivion Sans teeth, sans eyes, sans taste, sans everything.' The eventful story is thus ended in age.

*Life must be lived forwards* but can only be understood backwards. Getting older is thus 'living forward', and old age is continuity throughout the individual's life history in terms of lifestyles and habits, likes and dislikes but it is also a continuous, never-ceasing stream of experiences that are losses and gains at the same time.

[59] From Shakespeare's *As You Like It*, 1600 (Shakespeare, 2008).

# 12 Epilogue: the course of life as a melody

*Human Development in the Life Course: Melodies of Living* has the ambition of offering a framework that captures the time-dependent psychological processes by which people develop all through their lives. Our theoretical orientations have brought us to see human life from a dynamic perspective and to examine people's evolving sense of their own lives – how they imagine what was, and what could be; how they experience ruptures in their trajectories; and how they perceive and are sensitive to the meaning-saturated environments in which they live. Beyond what we think are general processes of meaning-making, we have also emphasized the unique 'melody' by which a person confers sense on her life – and the richness of variations of a person's 'style' across time and space. This metaphor – borrowed from Wilhelm Dilthey – allowed us to capture both the affective nature (melody is not a noise) of the emerging life course and the active role of the maker of that course. Human beings are the composers of their lives.

In this epilogue, we wish, first, to reflect on the methodological choices made in this book, second, on the theoretical innovations we made, and altogether, on what we hope this book will enable others to do.

## What we didn't do

We are obviously not the first to propose a psychology of the life course. Our predecessors had various ambitions: some of them were principally interested in seeing the evolutions of psychological capacities through maturation and decline;[1] others tried to characterize typical phases of a life;[2] a few attempted to identify psychological processes that play a central role in people's orientation in their daily lives.[3]

*No large-scale longitudinal studies*: These past studies were also based on a wide variety of data. The most impressive studies are the longitudinal

[1] Baltes (1997); Baltes and Mayer (1999). [2] Levinson (1978). [3] Erikson (1959b).

ones: studies during which teams of researchers regularly gathered data from a large group of people over ten, twenty or fifty[4] years. Such studies are on the one hand extremely interesting, yet – on the other hand, even though it seems paradoxical – very limited. In the case of the large samples that are so deeply appreciated by funding agencies and peer reviewers, the actual gathering of information inevitably needs to be very systematic and manageable. As a consequence, most such studies are based on standardized methods that generate limited data, based on the state of theorizing of the researchers who were the initiators of the project. The generation of researchers who took over the follow-up task from the initiators may already have developed new perspectives – yet the standard routine of data gathering prescribes the following of the initial script.[5] There has been intense scholarly discussion about the methodologies used in such studies, in terms of the comparison between longitudinal and cross-sectional data.[6] Some of the main limitations, which some scholars have tried to address, are first, that they almost never capture a person's perspective on her life; and second, that when they follow a person's change through time (e.g. her score on self-esteem scales over the years) they do not document in a systematic way the evolution of the environment in which the person lives, and therefore, they cannot explain the sociocultural dynamics by which these changes actually occurred.[7]

A major reason for the limited value of such large-sample based longitudinal investigations is the borrowing of our contemporary social imperative in psychology of the 'belief in large numbers'[8] – the large number of research participants is expected to allow scientists to discover the generalized patterns that are true for all human beings. Yet this strategy is becoming non-productive both in practice and in theory. In practice, the sustainability of large-sample-based research is undermined by the ever-uncertain funding policies of grant-giving institutions as well as by the self-selected discontinuation in the studies by the participants. Or – in our globally dynamic world – the participants may move around in ways no longer accessible by the resources-limited researcher.

However, a more important limitation of the large-sample-based and long-term longitudinal studies is theoretical – psychology as a whole has been misguided about the appropriation of the statistical modes of generalization[9] that hides the richness of the individual cases. For example, in

[4] As in the Wisconsin longitudinal study (Hauser, 2009).
[5] Although data collection sometimes evolves with time.
[6] Baltes, Reese and Nesselroade (1988); Giele and Elder (1998).
[7] We thank Roger Säljö for suggesting this point. See also Elder (2002).
[8] Gigerenzer *et al.* (1989). [9] Toomela and Valsiner (2010).

most existing longitudinal studies the connections between different data acquisition points (sequence of developmental states) is made through correlation or regression analysis tools that are *applied to the whole sample*, looking for changes in average results over time. This procedure, based on the ergodicity principle,[10] completely obscures any possibility of looking at individual life-course trajectories over the same time frame – despite the availability of the longitudinal data. Longitudinally collected data are *de facto* treated as if they were ordinary comparisons of any groups – only here designated by age.

*No extraordinary people*: yet there are new developments in sight. We see a return to a single-case based methodological tradition under the growing focus on idiographic science[11] – what is generalized to be true for all is based on the high interindividual variety of very different – unique – intraindividual developmental paths. Of course this idiographic look is not new in life-course psychology. The seminal work of Charlotte Bühler (1893–1974) – first in Vienna and after 1938 in the United States – was built on the careful charting of individual life courses. It is also worth remembering that one of the most quoted authors in lifespan psychology is Erik H. Erikson,[12] who was actually interested in people's active role in their own lives – yet seen as resulting from complex social, biological and psychological processes. He is well known for his descriptions of crises and their resolution across the lifespan. It is interesting to note that his theoretical attempt was based, on the one side, on clinical cases (young people having psychotherapy with him), and on the other hand, on the analyses of biographical material, as in his analyses of Gandhi, Martin Luther King, etc. Although Erikson started by using such materials in order to highlight general developmental principles, his later analysis rather aims at 'explaining' the biographies of famous men.[13] Normally, a psychologist would claim that no matter how interesting these celebrated cases were, it would be very difficult to build a general psychology on the basis of the lives or such exceptional characters. Yet the 'exceptional nature' of these people is our *post factum* narrative reconstruction of their life courses – *after* they have become socially marked as 'famous'. During their own emerging personal lives these people were as ordinary as any other – it is very doubtful whether the everyday lives of Gandhi, Martin Luther King or any other celebrated person who – *for us by now* – has become a fictional character similar to Karamazov, Madame Bovary

[10] As discussed in Chapter 1.

[11] Molenaar (2004), Lamiell (1998, 2003, 2009), Salvatore, Valsiner, Strout-Yagodzinski and Clegg (2009).

[12] Erikson (1959b, 1968). [13] Erikson (1993a, 1993b.)

or Steven Daedalus, differed drastically in their ways of sleeping, waking, eating, running around and doing all the ordinary everyday tasks human beings do. The power of narrative reconstruction of the past not only creates our future but also gives ordinary human beings a symbolic status that is made official by the label 'celebrity' or 'historically important person'.

*A new methodological perspective and old problem–narrative psychology*: over the past two decades, with the narrative turn, narrative accounts have become a very important source of scholarly activity. However, narratives about the past – such as life reviews, or autobiographical accounts[14] – reflect complex reconstructive processes, which always reorder or rearrange past events in the light of the present or the future. However interesting such accounts may be, they nevertheless mostly flatten the actual processes of change, partly because of the canonical demands of narration, because of the social settings in which these narration are recalled and, finally, because of the work of memory and self-construction itself. One is here reminded of James Mark Baldwin's claim about development:

> ...that series of events is truly genetic [developmental] which cannot be constructed before it has happened, and which cannot be exhausted backwards, after it has happened.[15]

This statement – called 'positive postulate' by Baldwin himself – emphasizes focusing the study of development on that of *unfolding novel processes*, rather than their prediction or retrospective explanation. Narrative accounting of what has happened in the past cannot reveal how the narrated developmental process occurred in that past. Likewise, a study of the schematic patterns for the future – cognitive scripts or stage accounts of development – cannot pre-establish the actual emerging life course. Human beings are not only composers – they improvise in the making of their own life courses.

## Literature, diaries and photography and secondary analysis in psychology

In this book, we first attempted to document how people, at different times of their life course, experience the situations they are involved in, reconstruct the past or imagine their futures. For this we needed sufficiently good evidence that would give us accounts from such first person perspectives. Thus, we were attentive to public sources of first person

[14] See for instance Disch (1989) on life reviews, McAdams (2001) on narratives, Pasupathi, Mansour and Brubaker (2007) on autobiography.

[15] Baldwin (1906, p. 21).

perspective data. We discovered that there was much evidence to build such a reflection, and also that psychologists have no exclusivity in gathering relevant data about human lives. Very often, fiction writers surpass psychologists in their feeling into relevant human life complexities. Along similar lines, persons themselves who entrust their experiences to their diaries and make them public in autobiographies have privileged access to their personal lives, while taking their look from 'outside in'. Hence, we used diverse materials in our book: on-line diaries, oral history accounts, quasi-autobiographical novels, research interviews, therapeutic interviews. We chose this material for its 'richness' and its ability to enable the reader to 'experience' some of the aspects of others' experiences.[16] This combination of the sources of evidence reflects the width of coverage of the authors. We chose data that are open to interpretation, and we proposed interpretations based on the theoretical framework we are developing.

Such material is, to various extents, 'authentic' or, on the other hand, fictionalized. The boundary between fact and fiction is very difficult to draw: when a teenager writes a diary online, he is at the same time expressing or working through something which really matters to him, and playing with the fact that he is creating an extremely public message; when a psychologist-novelist writes a scene depicting the despair of a five-year-old, he is probably convoking his own past experience and the experiences of many young patients, and his skills as a writer to convey that experience to the reader. But similarly, when we propose a secondary analysis of data collected and published by a colleague, we also 'trust' the discourse constructed in an interaction, edited and analysed for a particular public. Even more so, as we have shown, a psychotherapeutic setting can itself be seen as enabling people to transform the narratives they have of their lives. So we have to face a methodological basic issue – *all psychological phenomena are fictional extensions* beyond what has actually happened in a person's life. This follows from the dynamic systems look at the emergence of new meaning based on the previous state of affairs – moving towards the anticipated future.

This apparent relativism raises interesting questions, which are at the heart of various debates – we will mention them although we cannot resolve them here. Mainly, once it is assumed that any historical (or objective) account demands some form of narrativization and interpretation of facts, and once it becomes clear that many fictions are more or less hidden real stories, boundaries between fact and fiction become blurred. Of course, in

[16] See Bradley (2005, p. 166) for a defence of a 'psychography' on the same basis as ethnography's 'thick description'.

our usual scheme of dividing knowledge, history (or psychology) and fiction belong to different enterprises, communities, sets of activities; they are regulated by different rules, and have different methodological principles by which insiders may assess the quality of the work produced.[17]

The problem is, however, at the level of the text produced: what is it meant to convey to the reader or the audience? And how do readers and audience interpret these texts or representations, as the rules of the professional communities that produced them are not necessarily accessible? If after all, the goal is for readers to 'experience' being a Nazi officer, is it a problem that a published diary is in fact a fiction written by a young man?[18] On the other hand, if the goal is to inform the reader of the 'actual facts', is it allowed to a psychologist to present the more 'juicy bits' of fictionalized truth?[19] In addition, can we not say that fiction is also in itself a sort of psychological or sociological enquiry about life – whether its authors consider themselves as 'experimentalists' of life,[20] or whether scientists consider them as revealing important issues about humans in their social worlds?[21] Without entering into this debate, we must, however, emphasize that such issues concern psychological writing, as 'empirical examples' are, on the one hand, the basis on which theory is founded, but also have the rhetorical function of enabling the reader to have 'a sense of what we are talking about'.

In psychology, we are not the first to base some analysis on, or illustrate theories by, combined sources of evidence. Some psychological authors use theories to analyse fictions (which has often been called 'applied psychology'), aiming at revealing the 'truth' of fiction or of its authors.[22] In other cases, psychological theories are applied to well-known fictions in order to make theories more easily accessible to a general public.[23] However, our goal is different: we wanted data that gave us trustable access to how people make sense of the environment, at various points in their lives, and in diverse settings. How, therefore, to identify 'trustable' data, or data that are legitimate for such an enterprise?

First of all, we chose data for their similarity to biographical accounts.[24] When data may be fictionalized, we confront different data sources that

[17] Bruner (2003). [18] For instance Littell (2009). [19] Binet (2010).

[20] For example, Zola (1890). [21] Barrère and Martuccelli (2009); Brinkmann (2009).

[22] See for instance Freud on Da Vinci (1910/2001), Michelangelo (1914/2001), E. T. A. Hoffman (1919/2001).

[23] Mulholland (2008); Niemiec and Wedding (2008).

[24] Not only did we not produce *ad hoc* data, we even scarcely chose it: we used available data as they came along. For instance, when we started working with online diaries, we simply chose the first data that gave enough information to start an analysis. We were not looking for the most interesting or most representative ones. As these databases are of public access, any sceptical reader can go and check them.

present occurrences of the phenomena we are interested in, so that some commonalities may appear across data sources – diaries, fictions, recordings of daily conversation. Second, we never give these examples *per se*, or to fascinate or capture the reader; rather, we present these data as *exempli*, or typical materials, on the basis of which we propose our theoretical analyses. Our theoretical propositions are as transparent as possible as regards their goal, their purpose and their possible implications. Third, using data that are publicly available we take a specific epistemological stance. Indeed, we consider that it is by confronting our models and theoretical elaboration with concrete examples that we can examine whether they are robust or subtle enough to account for the diversity of human experience. Here, using public data is an invitation to the reader to critically examine our theoretical propositions. There was a fourth option, which we did not use here, and which may be worth recalling. Online diaries or oral histories recall events or people's experiences in specific times and spaces. Even when these frames are not made explicit, it is nowadays most of the time possible to gather information about these places. Hence, it is possible to work on biographical material (diaries, letters, pictures, papers) – externalizations allowing access to a person's subjective experiences – while also documenting the actual environments in which these experiences objectively took place, especially if the person in question is famous, or took part in major historical events.[25]

We used here a second type of unusual data for a psychological book. In effect, we wanted to document the sociocultural world in which people live. We were thus sensitive to the sort of messages present in the organization of our environments, and that people often internalize without being aware of them. Theorizing such phenomena at the fringe of the consciousness, one of us (JV)[26] proposed many pictures of street scenes that enable us to illustrate and support our arguments.

Yet there are a number of good reasons to be cautious. One of them is that the material we used, with the exception of these images, consists of mostly verbal accounts, and even more, written ones. An authentic developmental psychology should be able to capture and analyse other forms of externalization. Second, we did not use 'really developmental data' – in the sense that we did not use material obtained from one given person over the years; only such material (as in diaries or in letters) enables the capturing of changes in a person's understanding of her environment and her life as time passes by. However, we hope that the current theoretical propositions may invite such analysis in the future. And third, we

[25] Gillespie (2005); Gillespie and Zittoun (2010a); Zittoun and Gillespie (2012).
[26] Valsiner (2006).

could not bring together both the street scenes that we found interesting together with what people actually think of them – and here we lack a real first-person perspective. In the contemporary sociology of urban living new methods for bringing such perspectives in – the 'go-along' kind of interviewing[27] – help to bring that perspective to our science.

## The idiographic/nomothetic 'controversy': a misunderstood story

The problem of 'first' versus 'third' person perspective intersects with how general knowledge is – and can be – constructed. Psychology is a discipline on the border of two main domains of knowledge – that about nature as it is 'out there', and that about the mind as it is 'in me'. The partition that sciences inherited from the nineteenth century – of *Naturwissenschaften* (natural sciences) and *Geisteswissenschaften*[28] (literally 'spiritual sciences', usually translated as humanities) – has haunted psychology ever since it gained autonomy from philosophy and physiology.

It was Wilhelm Windelband who, in his rectoral inauguration speech in the University of Strasbourg in 1894, took it on himself to sort out the mindscape of sciences, and to locate psychology in that landscape. Psychology, as the study of the soul (*Seele*), was ambiguous – this was particularly visible in the efforts to label the discipline.[29] Psychology in the nineteenth century dealt with complex ephemeral phenomena. In contrast to history's records of 'real things and events' – rulers, wars, and their one-off material

[27] Kusenbach (2003).

[28] Already in the untranslatability of this contrast from German ('natural' versus 'soul'-sciences) into English ('natural sciences' and 'humanities') we can see the problem of artificial separation of the two sides. 'Humanities' does not fit *Geisteswissenschaften* – the Ango-Saxon tradition eliminates the nuances of the 'soul' from treating phenomena of a subjective kind.

[29] As 'spiritual natural science' – *geistige Naturwissenschaft* – cf. Windelband (1904, p. 10). More precisely – in the case of psychology:

> ihrem Gegenstand nach ist sie nur als Geisteswissenschaft und in gewissem Sinne als die Grundlage aller übrigen zu characterisieren; ihr ganzes Verfahren aber, ihr metodisches Gebahren is vom Anfang bis zum Ende dasjenige der Naturwissenschaften. Daher sie denn es sich hat gefallen lassen müssen, gelegentlich als die 'Naturwissenschaft des innere Sinnes' oder gar als 'geistige Naturwissenschaft' bezeichnet zu werden' (Windelband, 1904, pp. 9–10):
>
> > to judge by its subject, it can only be characterized as a humanity, and in a certain sense as the foundation to all others; but its entire procedure, its methodological arsenal, is from beginning to end that of the natural sciences. For this reason, psychology has had to allow itself to be characterized at times as the 'natural science of inner sense' or even as 'the natural science of the mental' [Windelband, 1998, p. 11].

results – ruins, captured territories and handicapped soldiers – psychology dealt with the complex internal perception of the world by the rulers and by the ruled. While history's objects of analysis could be preserved directly – as they are encoded in ruins, archaeological findings, and chronicles – psychology's phenomena died with their authors.

*A misleading neologism: idiographic and nomothetic perspectives*: Windelband introduced the contrast between knowledge that emphasizes the *general* (*nomothetic*) and knowledge focused on the *particular* (*idiographic*).[30] The context in which he introduced these terms is informative about the confusions that have raged in psychology around the issues of the reality[31] of the phenomena observed in a single case:

> the empirical sciences [*Erfahrungswissenchaften*] seek in the knowledge of reality either the general in the form of natural law or the particular in the historically determined form [*geschichtlich bestimmten Gestalt*]. They consider in one part the ever-enduring form, in the other part the one-time [*einmalige*] content [*Inhalt*], determined within itself, of an actual happening. The one comprises sciences of law [*Gesetzwissenschaften*], the other sciences of events [*Ereigniswissenschaften*]; the former teaches what always is [*was immer ist*], the latter what once was [*was einmal war*]. If one may resort to neologisms [*neue Kunstausdrücke*], it can be said that the scientific thought is in one case nomothetic, in the other idiographic.[32]

Windelband's contrast was built on classical philosophical grounds – as Plato focused on the general immutable character of phenomena, Aristotle sought the same – generality – in the purposefully developing individual being. Thus both nomothetic and idiographic perspectives – in their different ways – strive towards the gaining of generalized knowledge.

Furthermore – remembering the inevitability that anything that happens to an individual organism, human or other, is a singular phenomenon (as it unfolds for the organism in irreversible time) – the basis of all knowledge in life sciences is inevitably idiographic, that is, based on the uniqueness of the individual situation. On the basis of such uniqueness, it is our mental systems that create knowledge either by ongoing comparison of another unique situation with the previous one (retaining the time parameter), or by accumulating such unique situations into collections

[30] Windelband (1904, p. 12; 1998, p. 13).

[31] Interestingly, this necessary primacy of the unique-to-be-made general was missed by Windelband, who perhaps unwillingly – as his 1894 speech was meant to bring peace to warring ideologies of disciplines – fed further into the fight between materialist (identified by *Naturwissenschaften*) and idealist (assumed to belong to *Geisteswissenschaften*) camps. The notion of nomothetic became synonymous with the former, that of idiographic – with the latter. This has led psychologists to the need to take sides on one or the other side of the divide.

[32] Windelband (1998, p. 13), inserts from Windelband (1904, p. 12).

of similarly classified situations (losing the time parameter). Thus, all life science is idiographic as it strives towards generalization about its phenomena through time. The latter limit makes it inevitable that any new phenomenon to be explained is discovered first in its singular form. Each re-observation of these forms – or 'sampling' – is in effect finding other uniquely singular forms in their contexts that belong to the same category. The result of such enquiry can become nomothetic, in the sense of generalization based on evidence that 'once was' and 'another time was as well', and – given that – 'may be on the next occasion'. Yet the 'may be' need not necessarily mean 'will be' – except in the cases of non-developmental phenomena (because they do not develop, they last). The possibility of the emergence of a new form maintains the tension of all nomothetic knowledge as it faces new – idiographic – encounters with the phenomena.

While Windelband's distinction aimed at giving a place to psychology as science of the mind (*Seelenwissenchaft*) we have here pointed out that the singularity of the phenomenon is not limited to human experience. It follows from the principle of *epigenesis*, and has as consequence that the *ergodicity principle* does not hold for any life phenomenon. Nevertheless, the semiotic function adds considerable complexity to human experiences, as opposed to alleged experiences in other forms of life. The version of the epigenetic landscape metaphor presented in these pages is an attempt to depict the complexity of the human life course, and throughout the book we have discussed the influence of meaning-making on the present situation. At any moment for a human being, meaning-making will be the vehicle for past experiences and projections into the future. Through our different understandings of past experiences and our different plans for the future we will have an exponential increase in complexity and variety of our, specifically human, life courses.

*Words and their contexts*: The controversy between *Naturwissenschaften* and *Geisteswissenchaften* further escalated when the distinction between nomothetic and ideographic knowledge was paralleled in the context of Anglo-Saxon philosophy and academic debate.[33] There, the latter (*Geisteswissenschaften*) was replaced by the notion of 'the humanities' in the rendering into English – with complete loss of any implication of general knowledge or science.[34]

[33] The nomothetic<>idiographic contrast appeared in English in 1898 (Münsterberg, 1898). It was actively utilized by Gordon Allport later – albeit without success – to bring psychology in North America to a reasonable look at this contrast, not to speak of its use.

[34] In fact, this translation leads to not only non-scientific but a positively anti-scientific surplus meaning (Lamiell, 1998, p. 27, 2009). No surprise that the notion of

In the Anglo-Saxon context the concept of science was reserved for either mathematical logic or 'objective' empirical research, while the study of human experiences – in their complexity – was considered unscientific and relegated to being art, rather than science. In the German language, sciences were separated in two domains of knowing – about nature (*Naturwissenschaften*) and about the spirit (*Geisteswissenschaften*). The contrast between the opposites in the two languages was not the same – the English opposition inscribed an exclusive separation between the terms (if X is 'science' it cannot be 'art' (and vice versa), while the German one maintained an inclusive separation where the *Geist* could give flavour to the approach to the *Natur*, based on the inclinations of the thinker.

Yet, in both cases the whole – the unity of knowing – became lost. Unlike the beginning of the nineteenth century where poetry could be part of human enquiry, by two centuries later it is not assumed that a poem could enlighten physicists – or even psychologists – to create an innovative hypothesis in their research fields. The arts and humanities may be fascinating – yet not 'serious enough' – for the enterprise of science. At best they can provide some anecdotal evidence – but no penetrating understanding of the micro-, macro-, or psycho-cosmos. Yet the creator of the meaning – a knowledge-making scientist – is one in thinking and feeling. She or he unites the art of science with the pleasures of its logic – and suffers from the increasing avalanche of administrative bureaucratic management techniques.

*Experience – what is it?* Throughout our book we have brought in various examples of the ways in which human beings – young and old – reflect upon their own relating with their worlds – *semiospheres*. Their worlds are made by them – through the use of signs – humanized and turned into unique moments of the melodies of their *living onwards* – within their person-centred and personally assembled subjective feelings that are possible through the *immersion-within-this* world. We can sense the smell of freshly baked croissants reaching us from the bakery through the open window. It does not change our life course in any major way – yet is a momentary chord in the music of our waking up to live another day in this wondrous world. We will not, however, be able to smell the flowers in our own funeral processions – nor hear the sobbing and speeches of the friends whom we have left behind in this world. Our social worlds are centred upon our subjective relating to it – that subjectivity of relating is the unique process of experiencing that world. We rely upon others to create the *bricolage* of our own subjective worlds – ranging from momentary tastes,

idiographic – and the use of single cases – has been absent or ridiculed as 'soft' in twentieth-century psychology as it has moved to the dominance zone of the English language (Toomela, 2007).

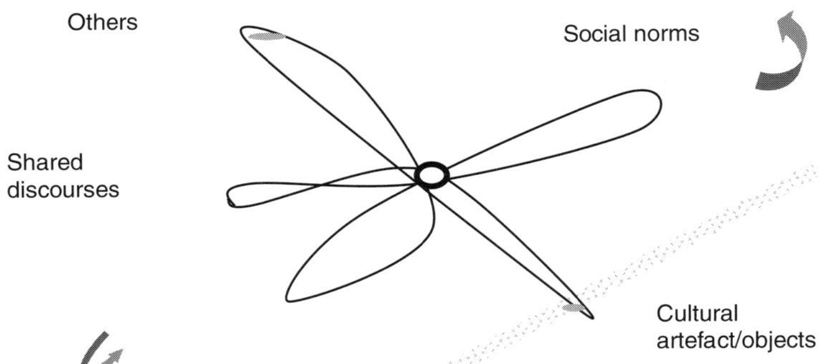


Figure 12.1 Emergence of the subject.

smells, or words to personal philosophies of living – that are possible through the immediate relating with our semiospheres.

But how can even such new sensual experiences, how can our unique subjective worlds, find a place in a world saturated with discourses and norms, buzzing with streams of endless narratives and reports, replete with other people's experience materialized in urban arrangements, architecture, books and blogs?

Our proposition is that the uniqueness of our melodies precisely emerges there where we experience the world, and where we step out of it to reflect on it. One way to represent this emergence is to consider that it occurs precisely at the meeting point of the many semiotic streams in which we are immersed (see Figure 12.1).[35] In effect, at each instant, we are in semiotic loops – social norms, shared discourses, various forms of knowledge, the presence of real and imaginary others – which all have canalizing functions, and are also mutually dependent.

Our subjectivity emerges at the core of this crossing, where who we are enables us to carve out an unique space – a room of our own,[36] a thinking space.[37] Processes such as distancing, learning from experience, i-moments and reflexivity, creative synthesis and overall, imagination, are the processes by which we can be extracted from social constraint and constitute this internal space – internal breathing.

As this unfolds as we move through our social and temporal space, and this ever-new respiration becomes a unique melody. Thus, the core and continuous process of emergence, within a person and through the fields of constraints in which she is located, constitutes the creation of one's

[35] Zittoun (2012b). [36] Woolf (1989). [37] Perret-Clermont (2004).

melody of living. And a unique life melody is also the trace the person leaves in the space she traverses over the time of a life course.

## What still needs to be done

In this book, we have outlined a rather ambitious project of an authentic life-course psychology. If the material we have used so far has enabled us to deepen and enrich our understanding of specific moments of the life course, and highlight the central importance of meaning-making and especially imagination in people's making of their trajectories, we have not actually yet achieved a developmental psychology that fully integrates time. However, this book is programmatic, and has tried to bring together the main elements required for such a project: a plausible metatheoretical frame, relevant methodologies – yet much still needs to be done.

First, we have outlined a theoretical stance for the study of human life courses. With roots in mathematics and sciences on non-living material (physics and chemistry), dynamic systems approaches – among which is DST – have an ever increasing impact on life sciences in general, although still limited in psychology.[38] Using DST to describe psychological development, we have shown its shortcomings, notably in failing to account for the complexity of human life courses given the richness of human experiences over time, and notably the meaning-making of past experiences (and future possibilities) that can impact on the present situation at any time. Therefore we have complemented DST with an epigenetic view, mainly inspired by the work of Gilbert Gottlieb, which gives a better account of the time dimension, important to the understanding of a human life course. The epigenetic landscape metaphor has been an effort to synthesize trajectories of human life courses and their different influences. Yet our effort to apply it to the human life course as a whole is only a first step in a direction that should be very productive for the human sciences.

The most important point of a life-course psychology should be to give insight to the developmental trajectory of a life. The challenge is to bind together episodes and microgenetic developmental courses, that is, the development of particular skills, relationships and daily life routines, into a whole that covers the development of the individual as such over a

[38] The reader is invited to visit the webpages of the Society for Chaos Theory in Psychology and Life Sciences (www.societyforchaostheory.org/) to witness efforts to have DST accepted and implemented in psychology. Here, through the work of Alan Fogel, we have used DST metaphorically to explicate the core change processes of human development as not, in principle, different from other change processes in the world, whether of the life sciences or of the sciences studying non-organic matter and processes.

lifetime (ontogenesis). As if microgenetic studies were not difficult enough, to see the network of micro-developmental paths under a whole seems an insurmountable task. It quickly becomes clear that conventional scientific methods will not be able to undertake such an endeavour.

Second, methods that would enable the capture of data corresponding to the nesting of developmental processes of a different scale have been identified. Hence, *actual microgenetic studies* (such as the study of regular recordings of mother–infant interaction[39] in the same setting, or of a series of psychotherapeutic sessions) makes it possible to study a given frame – a motive – and its evolution; *studies of transitions*[40] highlight the moves between frames and the changes required; and studies which capture longer life trajectories enable us to capture how these segments combine in a unique melody. Studying through a focus on microgenesis is a methodological imperative. Any science of human development needs to focus on the study of *transitions* in order to grasp the detailed change processes underlying microgenesis, and, by consequence, also ontogenesis and human development at large. This focus has been usually overlooked by the tendency of psychologists to create descriptive accounts of outcomes of development through determining some kinds of stages of development. From our viewpoint such stage models are static depictions of the forms that have already emerged in the course of development. They are categories – distinguished from one another ('stage B' is different from 'stage A') that are ordered within time. From the description of such forms we cannot go back to studying the processes of their emergence – yet it is precisely the latter that developmental science needs to accomplish. In our book here we have repeated that claim in many ways – yet its importance in general needs to be highlighted once more. Human lives cannot be studied without a consistently developmental theoretical focus and its matching methodologies.

Nevertheless, the difficulty of producing data to be authentically developmental is immense. That difficulty is rooted in the axiomatically non-developmental nature of psychology's methodology where the 'real' and the 'imaginary' are treated as irreconcilable opposites. The 'real' is automatically assumed to 'be valid' – in contrast to 'the imaginary' that is not – because it does not 'exist' (as 'the real'). In our book we have re-united the two – using the irreversible time focus that does not allow these two to be exclusively separated. Today's 'real' in the dynamic melody of my living anticipates my 'imaginary' as I face tomorrow, and when it becomes 'real', with yet another imaginary anticipation of the day after tomorrow, and so

[39] Vedeler and Garvey (2009).
[40] Zittoun (2009) for a methodological reflection on the study of transitions.

on. The notion of melody as a metaphor for living fits such unity – it reflects the integration of the past (i.e. tones in a sequence that we feel as a melody) that runs into the future – we anticipate *the next tone* in the melody of our living. Melodies emerge as gestalts based on irreversible time, unifying the past with the future.

Time – irreversible, as it flows from the past infinity towards the future – is the key in any developmental investigation. Over recent years researchers have produced increasingly substantive thinking in identifiying methodologies that enable the capture of time in psychology seen as a development science.[41] The key process under scrutiny needs to be the process of emergence – something that was not (before) comes into existence. Yet – how can we know the 'nothing-that was before'? Social science methodologies have been ill prepared to conceptualize 'nothingness' of this kind. Furthermore – the unity of structural levels of organization – microgenesis, mesogenesis, macrogenesis (of personal life course, and of cultural history) carries a substantive challenge of how to combine these data of different scales – and this is where models such as the epigenetic model and DST models may support such integration.[42]

## What we have learned

*Human Development in the Life Course: Melodies of Living* has enabled us to bring together the ingredients of a life-course enquiry still to be done. But doing so, it has also brought together important insights from different fields of psychology usually separated. This in itself is an important step for the identification of general developmental process. Here are some of the lessons learned.

[41] For recent methodological innovations see Abbey and Surgan (2012); Toomela and Valsiner (2010); Valsiner, Molenaar, Lyra and Chaudhary (2009).

[42] Even in this programmatic book, the tension between the imperative to render the time dimension and to outline different parts of the epigenetic landscape in a more static way is always present. When the reader feels herself lost in the lack of a time dimension, it will be useful to keep in mind that time is important to the whole team of authors, while it has been a difficult challenge to write in such a way that the time dimension clearly appears in the text. There may, however, be rarer cases, more difficult to understand for the reader, where the topography of the epigenetic landscape becomes diffuse, due to its continuous changes over time (instead of a steady hillside, imagine a (physically impossible) tilted sea surface, agitated by the wind, where long waves created over a long ocean distance, like the waves of the Pacific, are intercepted by a strong wind blowing in a direction perpendicular to the deep wave). In such cases, the reader is lost as to where any particular factor (≈wave top and valley) has what influence when. Most empirical sources, be they narratives, microgenetic descriptions or fiction, will sacrifice the time dimension to the benefit of the factors of interest, which, then, will tend to be described in static, generalized terms.

Again, the meta-model taken from DST, complemented with epigenetics, has shown how different types of change in a life course – emerging from within, or through interactions with people and the world – bring about new adjustments within the person or in her location or capacities to act in the world. Of all the changes people live, special attention needs to be given to intransitive changes (level 2, leading to level 3 changes) – those that break routine adjustments. Specifically, such intransitive changes are also those that are candidates for being experienced as important changes by people. Hence, the study of ruptures in the life course – as perceived by people – is a very good entry into psychological development in the life-course.

At the level of the overall trajectory, ruptures are potential points of bifurcation – this is where the broom of time has to be fully deployed and explored. At the level of psychological processes, ruptures involve processes of identity transformation, learning and further meaning-making. Having a closer look at these processes, usually described by different research streams, we observed that, first of all, all of them are of a semiotic nature and therefore involve processes of differentiation, organization and hierarchization. Heinz Werner's and Jean Piaget's theoretical legacies from the twentieth century – which followed the poetic insights of Johann Wolfgang Goethe – would acquire new relevance in our developmental science of the twenty-first century. No longer can we accept unidimensional reduction of the melodies of living to either the 'behaviour' and 'the genes', or upwards – to 'social power' or 'text' identifications of living human beings. Our theoretical system requires a look at human agency *within* its context – overcoming the exclusive separation of the person and the immediate world.

We have also observed the importance of key processes: in terms of identity narratives, a key development process seems to be reconceptualization – which demands leaving old positions, distancing from self, envisaging alternatives, the creation of continuity between an old and new positions and, finally, some form of social recognition. In psychotherapy, these processes appear in the very specific semiotic mode that is self-narration, which has also certain implicit, culturally defined rules. Learning implies that a person abandons an inadequate way of doing or understanding, explores alternatives in an exploratory zone, and eventually understands divergences of perspectives and conflictual positions, before integrating new ways of doing, thinking or conceptualizing with previous ones, in a socially acknowledged manner. Yet this may take place in everyday situations as well as in formal institutions. Especially in the second case, these processes of distancing and reorganizing modes of representing need to go along the specific semiotic system of the discipline at hand – learning maths demands the mastery of a socially stabilized formal system – and knowledge in that discipline demands mastering both the specific contents and the language for describing them. In informal learning, learning necessarily gets organized, probably through cultural guidance, but knowledge as such does not include a formal way of describing that organization; rather, life experience is progressively generalized in personal life philosophies which may take a more or less conventional form. Finally, in terms of sense-making, the same basic grammar has been observed – of distancing and exploration, and the emergence of a creative synthesis, which may lead to the reorganization of one's whole mode of understanding. The less theorized sense-making is nevertheless highly 'cultivated' through social guidance – and so these moves may bring people to be more or less defined in the terms of values pre-existing in their environment, or more or less participating in social innovation.

Hence, learning, identity reorganization and sense-making demand the same key processes – although they have been crystallized, both in the social world in people's understanding, under different headings. Because these modes of thinking-learning are embedded in different frames, which have developed idioloects and traditions, they are further differentiated by the logic of the semiotic mode which dominates them. Through human history, the actual operations required by mathematical reasoning became different from these required for weaving a carpet – partly because of their specific framing which became insitutionalized.

Nevertheless, the motor of the process of change in all three activities is the same: imagination and the use of resources, we have shown, are the means by which people can explore alternatives, overcome limits and boundaries, transform existing realities, in minds and in reality. As people move through time and space, their capacities to imagine, supported by knowledge and experience, semiotic resources and social guidance, evolve and are transformed – and a challenge would be to describe how.

Finally, what we have called a person's 'style' of playing the melody of her life has probably to do with her mode of playing, the types of exploration in which she engages and her preferred types of resource. It also probably has to do with how – in specific tasks as well as in major life bifurcations – she chooses or creates pathways, which may be more or less consonant or dissonant with cultural guidance and choices made by people who share her life. It is also about how the person deals with the permanent ambivalence and plurivocity of the world. A unique life-course eventually emerges out of the infinite numbers of possibilities offered to a person – and so one's melody of living.

## Future prospects

*Human Development and the Life Course – Melodies of Living* is an invitation for further enquiries, in form, in content and in style. First, we hope that our theoretical proposals can be an impetus for future integrative work on developmental issues. Indeed, one of the main issues in current research is the great fragmentation of data, models and notions. We have tried here to bring many perspectives and theoretical views by grounding them in a more general theoretical work, which required us to render explicit abstract theoretical assumptions (e.g. on time and space). We hope to have offered a stable ground for further enrichment and elaborations. Second, we have proposed a set of theoretical tools that may be useful to analyse life-course data or to guide further researches. Third, we have proposed a way to articulate theory and data that is unusual in a 'serious' scientific book. We hope to have demonstrated the usefulness of such ways of proceeding, liberating us from the economic and technical issues associated with new data collection, and preferring to use and analyse existing data, available to all. Fourth, we have demonstrated the interest in authentic collaborative scientific writing. We hope that this will encourage others to engage in such experiences – while provoking and disturbing, still potentially creative.

# References


Abbey, E. A. (2007). Perpetual uncertainty of cultural life: becoming reality. In J. Valsiner and A. Rosa (eds.), *Cambridge Handbook of Sociocultural Psychology* (pp. 362–72). New York: Cambridge University Press.

Abbey, E. A. and Diriwächter, R. (eds.) (2008). *Innovating Genesis*. Charlotte, NC: Information Age Publishers.

Abbey, E. A. and Surgan, S. (eds.) (2012). *Developing Methods in Psychology*, series History and Theory of Psychology. New Brunswick, NJ: Transaction Publishers.

Abbey, E. A. and Valsiner, J. (2004). Emergence of meanings through ambivalence [58 paragraphs]. *Forum Qualitative Sozialforschung / Forum: Qualitative Social Research* (online journal), 6(1), (1), Art. 23. Available at: www.qualitative-research.net/fqs-texte/1-05/05-1-23-e.htm (date of access: 10 January 2006).

Albert, S. (1977). Temporal comparison theory. *Psychological Review*, 84, 485–503.

Alléon, A.-M., Morvan, O. and Lebovici, S. (1990). *Devenir 'adulte'?* Paris: Presses universitaires de France.

Allport, G. W. and Odbert, H. S. (1936). Trait-names: a psycho-lexical study. *Psychological Monographs*, 47(211), 1.

Almås, A. and Hajduk, J. H. *et al.* (2003). *Epigenetisk landskap: illustrasjon av utviklingen i mentale landskap*. Trondheim, Norway: Norwegian University of Science and Technology (NTNU).

Alpert, L., Desjardins, B., Vaupel, J. W. and Perls, T. T. (1999). Extreme longevity in a family: a report of multiple centenarians within a single generation. In B. Jeune and J. W. Vaupel (eds.), *Validation of Exceptional Longevity*. Monographs on Population Aging 6 (pp. 225–34). Odense University Press.

Anisov, A. (2001). Svoistva vremeni [Features of time]. *Logical Studies*, 6, 1–22.

(2005). Time as a computation process. In A. N. Pavlenko (ed.), *Zamysel Boga v teoriakh fiziki kosmologii. Vremia* (pp. 72–88). Saint Petersburg: MetaNexus.

Anony. (last modified 2009). 'entry "Open systems".' Wikipedia. Retrieved 15 September 2009, from http://en.wikipedia.org/wiki/Open_system_(systems_theory).

Apuleius (1993). The tale of Cupid and Psyche. In *The Golden Ass*, trans. P. G. Walsh (pp. 75–113). Oxford University Press.

Arkovitz, H. and Engle, D. (2007). Understanding and working with resistant ambivalence in psychotherapy. In S. G. Hofmann and J. Weinberg (eds.), *The Art and Science of Psychotherapy* (pp. 171–90). New York: Routledge.

Ashikari, M. (2005). Cultivating Japanese whiteness. *Journal of Material Culture*, 10(1), 73–91.

Atchley, R. C. (1972). *The Social Forces in Later Life: An Introduction to Social Gerontology*. Belmont, CA: Wadsworth.

(2006). Continuity theory. In R. Schulz, Linda S.Noelker, K. Rockwood and R. Sprott (eds.), *The Encyclopedia of Aging: A Comprehensive Resource in Gerontology* (pp. 266–8). New York: Springer.

Audi, R. (2002). *Epistemology: A Contemporary Introduction to the Theory of Knowledge* (2nd edn). London: Routledge.

Audigier, F., Crahay, M. and Dolz, J. (eds.) (2006). *Curriculum, enseignement et pilotage*. Brussels: De Boeck Université.

Aumont, B. and Mesnier, P. (2005). *L'acte d'apprendre* (3rd edn). Paris: Editions L'Harmattan.

Auslander, L. (2000). Bavarian crucifixes and French headscarves. *Cultural Dynamics*, 12(3), 283–309.

Auster, P. (2008). *Man in the Dark*. London: Faber and Faber.

Baillargeon, R. and De Vos, J. (1991). Object permanence in young infants: further evidence. *Child Development*, 62(2), 1227–46.

Baillargeon, R., Spelke, E. S. and Wasserman, S. (1985). Object permanence in five-month-old infants. *Cognition*, 20(3), 191–208.

Bakhtin, M. M. (1934/1975). Slovo v romane [Discourse in the novel]. In M. Bakhtin, *Voprosy literatury i estetiki* (pp. 73–232). Moscow: Khudozhestvennaya Literatura.

(1979/1996). *Speech Genres and Other Late Essays*. University of Texas Press.

(1981). *The Dialogic Imagination*. University of Texas Press.

(1984). *Rabelais and His World*, trans. H. Iswolsky (new edn). Bloomington, IN: Indiana University Press.

Baldwin, J. M. (1892). Origin of volition in childhood. *Science*, 20 (511), 286–7.

(1906). *Thought and Things: A Study of the Development and Meaning of Thought, or Genetic Logic*. Vol. I: *Functional Logic, or Genetic Theory of Knowledge*. London: Swan Sonnenschein & Co.

(1908). *Thought and Things: A Study of the Development and Meaning of Thought, or Genetic Logic*. Vol. II: *Experimental Logic, or Genetic Theory of Thought*. London: Swan Sonnenschein & Co.

(1911). *Thought and Things: A Study of the Development and Meaning of Thought, or Genetic Logic*. Vol. III: *Interest and Art Being Real Logic*. London: Swan Sonnenschein & Co.

(1915/2009). *Genetic Theory of Reality* (2nd edn). New Brunswick, NJ: Transaction Publishers.

Baltes, M. M. and Montada, L. (1996). *Produktives Leben im Alter*. Frankfurt a.M., D: Campus.

Baltes, P. B. (1987). Theoretical propositions of life-span developmental psychology: on the dynamics between growth and decline. *Developmental Psychology*, 23(5), 611–26.

(1997). On the incomplete architecture of human ontogeny. Selection, optimization and compensation of developmental psychology. *American Psychologist*, 52(4), 266–380.

Baltes, P. B. and Baltes, M. M. (1990). Psychological perspectives on successful aging: the model of selective optimization with compensation. In P. B. Baltes and M. M. Baltes (eds.), *Successful Aging: Perspectives from the Behavioral Sciences* (pp. 1–34). New York: Cambridge University Press.

Baltes, P. B. and Kunzmann, U. (2004). The two faces of wisdom: wisdom as a general theory of knowledge and judgment about excellence in mind and virtue vs. wisdom as everyday realization in people and products. *Human Development*, 47(5), 290–9.

Baltes, P. B. and Mayer, K. U. (eds.) (1999). *The Berlin Aging Study: Aging from 70 to 100*. Cambridge University Press.

Baltes, P. B. and Smith, J. (2003). New frontiers in the future of aging: from successful aging of the young old to the dilemmas of the fourth age. *Gerontology*, 49(2), 123–35.

Baltes, P. B., Reese, H. W. and Nesselroade, J. R. (1988). *Life-span Developmental Psychology: Introduction to Research Methods* (reprint from 1977 edn). Hillsdale, NJ: Lawrence Erlbaum.

Baltes, P. B., Staudinger, U. M. and Lindenberger, U. (1999). Lifespan psychology: theory and appplication to intellectual functioning. *Annual Review of Psychology*, 50, 471–507.

Barrère, A. and Martuccelli, D. (2009). *Le roman comme laboratoire. De la connaissance littéraire à l'imagination sociologique*. Villeneuve d'Asq: Presses universitaires du Septentrion.

Barth, F. (1969). *Ethnic Groups and Boundaries: The Social Organisation of Culture Difference*. Boston: Little, Brown & Company.

Bartlett, F. (1932). *Remembering*. Cambridge University Press.

Bateson, G. (1972/1999). *Steps to an Ecology of Mind*. The University of Chicago Press.

Bauman, Z. (2000). *Liquid Modernity*. Cambridge: Polity Press.

Baumeister, R. F. (1987). How the self became a problem: a psychological review of historical research. *Journal of Personality and Social Psychology*, 52(1), 163–76.

Beach, K. (1999). Consequential transitions: a sociocultural expedition beyond transfer in education. *Review of Research in Education*, 24, 124–49.

Beck, A. T., Steer, R. A., Ball, R. and Ranieri, W. (1996). Comparison of Beck Depression Inventories -IA and -II in psychiatric outpatients. *Journal of Personality Assessment*, 67, 588–97.

Beck, U. (2007). *World at Risk*. Cambridge: Polity Press.

Becker, H. (2008). Twenty three thoughts about youth. In M. O. Gonseth, Y. Laville and G. Mayor (eds.), *La marque jeune* (pp. 258–61). Neuchâtel: MEN.

Beckett, S. (1952/2010). *Waiting for Godot*. London: Faber and Faber.

Behrend, H. (1999). *Alice Lakwena and the Holy Spirits*. Oxford: James Curry.

(2006). Witchcraft, evidence and the localization of the Roman Catholic Church in Western Uganda. In R. Rottenburg, B. Schnepel and S. Shimada (eds.), *The Making and Unmaking of Differences* (pp. 43–59). Bielefeld: transcript.

Benson, C. (2001). *The Cultural Psychology of Self: Place, Morality and Art in Human Worlds*. London: Routledge.

Benthan, J. (1789). *The Panopticon Writings*, ed. Miran Bozovic (pp. 29–95). London: Verso. Available on line at http://cartome.org/panopticon1.htm.

Benussi, V. (1913/2002). Psychologie der Zeitauffassung. In M. Antonelli (ed.), *Psychologische Schriften Vittorio Benussi. The rules of art. Genesis and structure of the literary field*. Amsterdam: Rodopi.

Bergman, L. R. and El-Khouri, B. M. (2003). A person-oriented approach: methods for today and methods for tomorrow. *New Directions for Child and Adolescent Development*, 101, 25–38.

Bergson, H. (1888/1970). *Essai sur les données immédiates de conscience* (144[th] edn). Paris: Presses universitaires de France.

(1910). *Time and Free Will: An Essay on the Immediate Data of Consciousness*. London: Allen & Unwin.

(1946/2007). *The Creative Mind: An Introduction to Metaphysics*. New York: Citadel Press/Dover publications.

(1972). La perception du changement. In H. Bergson, *Mélanges* (pp. 888–914). Paris: Presses universitaires de France.

Berntsen, D. (2009). *Involuntary Autobiographical Memories: An Introduction to the Unbidden Past*. Cambridge University Press.

Bertalanffy, L. v. (1968). *General System Theory*. New York: George Braziller.

Besnard, P. (1995). The study of social taste through first names: comment on Lieberson and Bell. *American Journal of Sociology*, 100(25), 1313–17.

Billett, S. (2008). Learning throughout working life: a relational interdependence between personal and social agency. *British Journal of Educational Studies*, 56(1), 39–58.

(2009). Conceptualizing learning experiences: contributions and mediations of the social, personal and brute. *Mind, Culture and Activity*, 16(1), 32–47.

Binet, L. (2010). *HHhH (Himmler's Hirn heisst Heydrich)*. Paris: Grasset and Fasquelle.

Bion, W. R. (1984). *Learning from Experience*. London: Karnac Books.

Bjørgen, I. A. (1993). The truncated and the intact concept of learning. *Revista Portuguesa de Educação*, 6(2), 23–54.

Bluck, S. and Habermas, T. (2001). Extending the study of autobiographical memory: thinking back about life across the life span. *Review of General Psychology*, 5, 135–47.

Boe, P. (1983). Circumcision – the rites of manhood in the Bille Tribe. In E. A. A. de Adegbola (ed.), *Traditional Religion in West Africa* (pp. 73–89). Nairobi and Kampala: Uzima Press.

Boesch, E. A. (1991). *Symbolic Action Theory and Cultural Psychology*. Berlin: Springer.

(1993). The sound of the violin. *Schweizerische Zeitschrift für Psychologie*, 52(2), 70–81.

(2000). *Das lauende chaos*. Bern: Hans Huber.

Bollas, C. (2003). *Being a Character: Psychoanalysis and Self Experience*. New York: Routledge.

Borgatti, S. P., Mehra, A., Brass, D. J. and Labianca, G. (2009). Network analysis in the social sciences. *Science*, 323(5916), 892–5.

Borges, R. and Gonçalves, M. (2009). Os momentos de inovação na terapia narrative. Análise das inovações centradas no problema e centradas na mudança [Innovative moments in narrative therapy: Analysis of innovations centred in the problem and centred in the change]. Manuscript in preparation.

Bosworth, B. (2007). *Lifelong Learning: New Strategies for the Education of Working Adults*. Washington, DC: The Center for American Progress. Retrieved 30 September 2009, from www.americanprogress.org/issues/2007/12/pdf/nes_lifelong_learning.pdf.

Boud, D. and Garrick, J. (eds.) (1999). *Understanding Learning at Work*. London: Routledge.

Bourdieu, P. (1992/1996). *Rules of Art: Genesis and Structure of the Literary Field*, trans. S. Emanuel. Stanford University Press.

Bouška, T. and Pinerová, K. (2009). *Czechoslovak Political Prisoners: Life Stories of 5 Male and 5 Female Victims of Stalinism*. Europe of Citizen programme: Education and Culture Programme.

Bowen, J. R. (2007). *Why the French do not Like Headscarves*. Princeton University Press.

Bradley, B. S. (2005). *Psychology and Experience*. Cambridge University Press.

Branaman, A. (1997). Goffman's social theory. In C. Lemert and A. Branaman (eds.). *The Goffman Reader* (pp. xiv–lxxxii). Malden, MA: Blackwell.

Brandtstädter, J. (1999). Sources of resilience in the aging self: toward integrating perspectives. In T. M. Hess and F. Blanchard-Fields (eds.), *Social Cognition and Aging* (pp. 123–41). San Diego, CA: Academic Press.

Brandtstädter, J. and Greve, W. (1994). The aging self: stabilizing and protective processes. *Developmental Review*, 14, 52–80.

Bransford, J. D., *et al.* (2006). Foundations and opportunities for an interdisciplinary science of learning. In R. Sawyer (ed.), *The Cambridge Handbook of the Learning Sciences* (pp. 19–34). Cambridge University Press.

Brewis, J. and Grey, C. (2008). The regulation of smoking at work. *Human Relations*, 61(7), 965–87.

Breznitz, S. (1986). Are there coping strategies? In S. McHugh and T. M. Vallis (eds.), *Illness Behavior: A Multidisciplinary Model* (pp. 325–9). New York: Plenum Press.

Brinegar, M. G., Salvi, L. M., Stiles, W. B. and Greenberg, L. S. (2006). Building a meaning bridge: therapeutic progress from problem formulation to understanding. *Journal of Counselling Psychology*, 53, 165–80.

Brinkmann, S. (2006). Mental life in the space of reasons. *Journal for the Theory of Social Behaviour*, 36(1), 1–16.

(2009). Literature as qualitative inquiry: The novelist as researcher. *Qualitative Inquiry*, 15(8), 1376–94.

(2010). Guilt in a fluid culture. *Culture and Psychology*, 16(2), 253–66.

Bronfenbrenner, U. (1979). *The Ecology of Human Development*. Cambridge, MA: Harvard University Press.

Brossard, M. (2004). *Vygotski. Lectures et perspectives de recherches en éducation*. Villeneuve d'Asq: Presses universitaires du Septentrion.

Brousseau, G. (1983). Les obstacles épistémologiques et les problèmes en mathématiques. *Recherches en Didactique des Mathématiques*, 4(2), 165–98.

Bruner, J. S. (1986). *Actual Minds, Possible Worlds*. Cambridge, MA: Harvard University Press.

(1990). *Acts of Meaning*. London: Harvard University Press.
(1991). The narrative construction of reality. *Critical Inquiry*, 18(1), 1–21.
(2003). *Making Stories: Law, Literature, Life*. Harvard University Press.
Bühler, C. (1933). *Der menschliche Lebenslauf als psychologisches Problem* [The course of human life as a psychological problem]. Göttingen: Verlag für Psychologie.
(1968). The course of human life as a psychological problem. *Human Development*, 11, 184–200.
Bühler, K. (1934/1965). *Sprachtheorie*. Jena-Stuttgart: Gustav Fischer.
(1990). *Theory of Language: The Representational Function of Language*. Amsterdam: John Benjamins.
Bullough, E. (1912). 'Psychical distance' as a factor in art and an aesthetic principle. *Journal of Psychology*, 5(2), 87–118.
Buten, H. (1981/2000). *When I Was Five I Killed Myself*. New York: Washington Square Press.
Čapek, K. (1936/1991). *Entretiens avec Masaryk*, trans. M. David. La tour d'Aigues: Editions de l'Aube.
Carolina Consortium on Human Development (1996). Developmental science: a collaborative statement. In R. B. Cairns, G. Elder and E. J. Costello (eds.), *Developmental Science* (pp. 1–6). New York: Cambridge University Press.
Carpendale, J. I. M. and Müller, U. (2004). *Social Interaction and the Development of Knowledge*. Mahwah, NJ: Lawrence Erlbaum Associates.
Carstensen, L. L. (1991). Socioemotional selectivity theory: social activity in life-span context. *Annual Review of Gerontology and Geriatrics*, 11, 195–217.
Caspi, A., McClay, J. *et al.* (2002). Role of genotype in the cycle of violence in maltreated children. *Science*, 297(5582), 851–4.
Caspi, A., Sugden, K. *et al.* (2003). Influence of life stress on depression: moderation by a polymorphism in the 5-HTT gene. *Science*, 301(5631), 386–9.
Cesari Lusso, V. (2004). *Il mestiere di... nonna e nonno. Gioie e conflitti nell'incontro fra tre generazioni*. Trento: Erickson.
Cesari Lusso, V. and Muller, N. (2001). Quelle est la place de l'expérience dans l'apprentissage à l'âge adulte? Qu'est-ce qui se construit? Qu'est-ce qui se co-construit? Qu'est-ce qui se déconstruit? In J. J. Ducret (ed.), *Actes du colloque 'Constructivismes: Usages et perspectives en éducation'* (pp. 574–82). Geneva: SRED (Service de la recherche en éducation).
Chang, R. S. (ed.) (2009). *Relating to Environments*. Charlotte, NC: Information Age Publishers.
Chombart de Lauwe, M. (1979). *Un Monde autre, l'enfance. De ses représentations à son mythe* (2nd edn). Paris: Payot.
Clot, Y. (2002). *La fonction psychologique du travail* (3rd edn). Paris: Presses universitaires de France.
Cole, M. (1992). Context, modularity, and the cultural constitution of development. In L. T. Winegar and J. Valsiner (eds.), *Children's Development Within Social Context*. Vol. II*: Research and Methodology* (pp. 5–31). Hillsdale, NJ: Erlbaum.
(1995). Culture and cognitive development: from cross-cultural research to creating systems of cultural mediation. *Culture & Psychology*, 1(1), 25–54.

Cole, M. and Engeström, Y. (2007). Cultural-historical approaches to designing for development. In J. Valsiner and A. Rosa (eds.), *Handbook of Sociocultural Psychology* (pp. 484–507). Cambridge University Press.

Cooper, M. (2004). Encountering self-otherness: 'I-I' and 'I-Me' modes of self relating. In H. J. M. Hermans and G. Dimaggio (eds.), *The Dialogical Self in Psychotherapy* (pp. 60–73). New York: Brunner-Routledge.

Cornish, F., Zittoun, T. and Gillespie, A. (2007). A cultural psychological reflection on collaborative research. Conference Essay: ESF Exploratory Workshop on Collaborative Case Studies for a European Cultural Psychology [37 paragraphs]. *Forum Qualitative Sozialforschung / Forum: Qualitative Social Research*, 8(3), Art. 21, http://nbn-resolving.de/urn:nbn:de:0114-fqs0703217.

Coupland, N., Coupland, J., Giles, H. and Henwood, K. (1988). Accommodating the elderly: invoking and extending a theory. *Language and Society*, 17, 1–41.

Cover, R. (2003). The naked subject: nudity, context and sexualization in contemporary culture. *Body and Society*, 9(3), 53–72.

Crites, F. (1986). Story time: recollecting the past and projecting the future. In T. R. Sarbin (ed.), *Narrative Psychology: The Storied Nature of Conduct* (pp. 152–73). New York: Praeger.

Cruz, G. and Gonçalves, M. M. (2009). Momentos inovativos e mudança espontânea: Um estudo exploratório [Innovative moments and spontaneous change: An exploratory study]. Manuscript submitted for publication.

Cumming, E. and Henry, W. E. (1961). *Growing Old: The Process of Disengagement*. New York: Basic Books.

Cunha, C. (2007a). Constructing organization through multiplicity: a microgenetic analysis of self-organization in the dialogical self. *International Journal of Dialogical Science*, 2, 287–316.

(2007b). Processos dialógicos de auto-organização e mudança: Um estudo microgenético [Dialogical processes of self-organization and change: A microgenetic study]. Unpublished masters' dissertation, Universidade do Minho, Portugal.

Cunha, C. and Ribeiro, A. (2009). Rehearsing renewal of identity: reconceptualization on the move. In M. M. Gonçalves and J. Salgado (eds.), *Processes of Innovation: Studying Change in Psychotherapy and Everyday Life*. Manuscript in preparation.

Cunha, C., Gonçalves, M. M, Valsiner, J., Mendes, I. and Ribeiro, A. P. (in press). Rehearsing renewal of identity: reconceptualization on the move. In M. C. Bertau, M. M. Gonçalves and P. Raggatt (eds.), *The Development of the Dialogical Self*. Charlotte, NC: InfoAge Publishing.

Daniels, H. (2001). *Vygotsky and Pedagogy*. London: Routledge.

(2007). Pedagogy. In H. Daniels, M. Cole and J. V. Wertsch (eds.), *The Cambridge Companion to Vygotsky* (pp. 307–31). New York: Cambridge University Press.

Danziger, K. (1990). *Constructing the Subject: Historical Origins of Psychological Research*. New York: Cambridge University Press.

Danziger, K. (2008). *Marking the Mind: A History of Memory*. Cambridge University Press.

de Saint-Georges, I. & Filliettaz, L. (2008). Situated trajectories of learning in vocational training interactions. *European Journal of Psychology of Education*, 23(2), 213–33.

De Saussure, F. (1916/2005). *Cours de linguistique générale*, ed. T. de Mauro. Paris: Payot.

de Shazer, S. (1991). *Putting Difference to Work*. New York: Norton.

Deely, J. (2010). *Semiotic Animal*. South Bend, In: St Augustine's Press.

Del Río, P. (2002). The external brain: eco-cultural roots of distancing and mediation. *Culture & Psychology*, 8(2), 233–65.

Del Río, P. and Alvarez, A. (2007). Prayer and the kingdom of heaven. In J. Valsiner and A. Rosa (eds.), *Cambridge Handbook of Sociocultural Psychology*. New York: Cambridge University Press.

Detert, N. E., Llewelyn, S. P., Hardy, G. E., Barkham, M. and Stiles, W. B. (2006). Assimilation in good- and poor-outcome cases of very brief psychotherapy for mild depression: an initial comparison. *Psychotherapy Research*, 16, 408–21.

Devereux, E. C. (1970). Socialization in cross-cultural perspective: comparative study of England, Germany and the United States. In R. Hill and R. König (eds.), *Families in East and West: Socialization Processes and Kinship Ties* (pp. 73–110). Paris: Mouton.

Dewey, J. (1916). *Démocratie et éducation*. Paris: L'Age d'Homme.

Diallo, A. (2004). Paradoxes of female sexuality in Mali. In S. Arnfred (ed.), *Rethinking Sexualities in Africa* (pp. 173–89). Stockholm: Nordiska Afrikainstitutet.

Dickinson, E. (1890/2004). *Poems: Three Series, Complete*. EBook #12242. Retrieved at: www.gutenberg.org/files/12242/12242-h/12242-h.htm.

Diener, E. (1984). Subjective well-being. *Psychological Bulletin*, 95, 542–75.

Diener, E. and Suh, E. M. (1998). Subjective well-being and age: An international analysis. In K. W. Shaie, M. P. Lawton and M. Powell (eds.), *Annual Review of Gerontology and Geriatrics: Focus on Motion and Adult Development*, vol. XVII (pp. 304–423). New York: Springer.

Dimaggio, G. (2006). Disorganized narratives in clinical practice. *Journal of Constructivist Psychology*, 19, 103–8.

Dimaggio, G., Salvatore, G., Azzara, C. and Catania, D. (2003). Rewriting self-narratives: the therapeutic process. *Journal of Constructivist Psychology*, 16, 155–81.

Disch, R. (1989). *Twenty Five Years of the Life Review: Theoretical and Practical Considerations*. New York/London: The Haworth Press.

Dominicé, P. (2007). *La formation biographique*. Paris: L'Harmattan.

Draaisma, D. (2004). *Why Life Speeds up as you get Older: How Memory Shapes our Past*. Cambridge University Press.

Driesch, H. (1899). Die Lokalisation morphogenetischer Vorgänge. *Archiv für Entwickelungsmechanik der Organismen*, 8, 36–111.

Ducret, J.-J. and Céllerier, G. (2007). *L'équilibration. Concept central de la conception piagétienne de l'épistémogenèse*. Fondation Jean Piaget pour recherches psychologiques et épistémologiques. Available on-line at www.fondationjeanpiaget.ch/fjp/site/textes/VE/JJD_GC_equilibration.pdf, retrieved 8 August, 2010.

Dümmler, K., Dahinden, J. and Moret, J. (2010). Gender as 'Cultural stuff' ethnic boundary making in a classroom in Switzerland. *Diversities*, 12(1), 19–37.

Dupriez, B. (1980). *Gradus. Les procédés littéraires (Dictionnaire)*. Paris: 10/18.

Durkheim, E. (1894). *Les règles de la méthode sociologique*. Available on line at: http://classiques.uqac.ca/classiques/Durkheim_emile/regles_methode/durkheim_regles_methode.pdf, retrieved 23 February 2009.

Duveen, G. (2007). Culture and social representations. In J. Valsiner and A. Rosa (eds.), *Handbook of Sociocultural Psychology* (pp. 543–59). Cambridge University Press.

Duveen, G. and Lloyd, B. (eds.) (1990). *Social Representations and the Development of Knowledge*: Cambridge University Press.

Eckensberger, L. H. (2011). Culture inclusive action theory: action theory in dialectics and dialectics in action theory. In J. Valsiner (ed.), *The Oxford Handbook of Psychology and Culture*. New York: Oxford University Press.

Eco, U. (2009). On the ontology of fictional characters: a semiotic approach. *Sign System Studies*, 37 (1/2), 82–98.

Edensor, T. (2006). Reconsidering national temporalities: institutional times, everyday routines, serial spaces and synchronicities. *European Journal of Social Theory*, 9(4), 525–45.

Elder, G. H. J. (2002). The Life Course and Aging. Conference presented at the Gerontological Society of America, Boston, MA. Retrieved from www.unc.edu/~elder/presentations/Life_Course_and_Aging.html.

Elder, G. H. J. and Giele, J. Z. (eds.) (2009). *The Craft of Life Course Research*. New York/London: Guilford Press.

Elder, G. H. J., Kirkpatrick Johnson, M. and Crosnoe, R. (2004). The emergence and development of life course theory. In J. T. Mortimer and M. J. Shanahan (eds.), *Handbook of the Life Course* (pp. 23–50). New York: Springer.

Elias, N. (1996). *The Germans*. New York: Columbia University Press.

Engeström, Y. (1999). Activity theory and individual and social transformation. In Y. Engeström, R. Miettinen and R.-L. Punamaki (eds.), *Perspectives on Activity Theory*. Cambridge University Press.

(2005). *Developmental Work Research: Expanding Activity Theory in Practice*. Berlin: Lehmanns Media.

Eppler, E.(2002). *Vom gewaltmonopol zum gewaltmarkt? Die Privatisierung und Kommerzialisierung der gewalt* (5th edn). Frankfurt am Main: Suhrkamp Verlag.

Erikson, E. H. (1959a). Author's preface. In *Identity and the life cycle. Selected papers* (1959 edn, pp. 1–3). New York: International Universities Press. Retrieved 4 August 2009, from www.archive.org/details/identityandtheli011578mbp.

(1959b). *Identity and the Life Cycle. Selected papers* (1959 edn). New York: International Universities Press. Retrieved from http://www.archive.org/details/identityandtheli011578mbp.

(1963). *Childhood and Society*. New York: Norton.

(1968). *Identity: Youth and Crisis*. London: Faber and Faber.

(1993a). *Gandhi's Truth: On the Origins of Militant Nonviolence*. New York: W. W. Norton and Company.

(1993b). *Young Man Luther: A Study in Psychoanalysis and History*. New York: W. W. Norton and Company.

European Commission (2005). *Green Paper Confronting demographic change: a new solidarity between the generations*. Retrieved July 2010, from http://ec.europa.eu/social/main.jsp?catId=89&langId=en.

(2006). *Adult Learning: It is Never too Late to Learn*. Brussels: Commission of the European Communities. Retrieved 30 September 2009, from http://eur-lex.europa.eu/LexUriServ/site/en/com/2006/com2006_0614en01.pdf.

EzEldin, M. (2007). *Maryam's Maza*. American University of Cairo Press.

Fadiga, L., Craighero, L. and Olivier, E. (2005). Human motor cortex excitability during the perception of others' action. *Current Opinion in Neurobiology*, 15, 213–18.

Ferreira, T., Salgado, J. and Cunha, C (2006). Ambiguity and the dialogical self: in search of a dialogical psychology. *Estudios de Psicologia*, 27, 19–32.

Ferring, D. (2008). Von 'Disengagement' zu 'Successful Aging'. Modellvorstellungen über das (gute) Altern. In D. Ferring, M. Haller, H. Meyer-Wolters and T. Michels (eds.), *Sozio-kulturelle Konstruktion des Alters. Transdisziplinäre Perspektiven* [Sociocultural construction of aging: transdisciplinary perspectives] (pp. 257–72). Würzburg: Könighausen & Neumann.

Ferring, D. and Boll, T. (2010). Subjective well-being in old age. In L. Bovenberg, A. van Soest and A. Zaid (eds.), *Aging, Health, and Pensions in Europe* (pp. 173–205). Houndmills, Basingstoke, Hampshire: Palgrave Macmillan.

Ferring, D. & Filipp, S.-H. (1997). Subjektives Wohlbefinden im Alter. Struktur- und Stabilitätsanalysen [Subjective well-being in old age: Analyses of structure and stability]. *Psychologische Beiträge*, 39, 236–58.

(2000). Coping as a 'reality construction': on the role of attentive, comparative, and interpretative processes in coping with cancer. In J. Harvey and E. Miller (eds.), *Loss and Trauma: General and Close Relationship Perspectives* (pp. 146–65). Philadelphia, PA: Brunner/Mazel.

Ferring, D. and Hoffmann, M. (2007). 'Still the same and better off than others?' Social and temporal comparisons in old age. *European Journal of Aging*, 4, 23–34.

Festinger, L. (1957). *A Theory of Cognitive Dissonance*. Stanford University Press.

Festinger, L., Riecken, H. W. and Schachter, S. (1956/1964). *When Prophecy Fails: A Social and Psychological Study of a Modern Group that Predicted the Destruction of the World* (2nd edn). New York: Harper & Row.

Fields, J. (1999). 'Fighting the corsetless evil': shaping corsets and culture, 1900–1930. *Journal of Social History*, Winter, 355–84.

Filipp, S.-H. and Ferring, D.(1991). Zur inhaltlichen Bestimmung und Erfassung von Lebensqualität im Umfeld schwerer körperlicher Erkrankungen [Conceptualization and assessment of quality of life in the context of physical illness]. *Praxis der Klinischen Verhaltensmedizin und Rehabilitation*, 16, 274–83.

Fischer, K. (1997). Locating frames in the discursive universe, *Sociological Research Online*, 2(3), www.socresonline.org.uk/socresonline/2/3/4.html, accessed 15 February 2009.

Fivush, R. (2009). Sociocultural perspectives on autobiographical memories. In M. L. Courage and N. Cowan (eds.), *The Development of Memory in Infancy and Childhood* (pp. 283–301). Hove and New York: The Psychology Press.

Foa, E. B. and Kozak, M. J. (1986). Emotional processing of fear: exposure to corrective information. *Psychological Bulletin*, 99, 20–35.

Fogel, A. (1993a). *Developing through Relationships*. London: Harvester Wheatsheaf and University of Chicago Press.

(1993b). Two principles of communication: co-regulation and framing. In J. Nadel and L. Camaioni (eds.), *New Perspectives in Early Communicative Development* (pp. 9–22). London: Routledge.

(1995). Development and relationships: A dynamic model of communication. In J. B. Slater (ed.), *Advances in the Study of Behavior*, vol. XXIV (pp. 259–290). New York: Academic Press.

(1997). Information, creativity, and culture. In C. Dent-Read and P. Zukow-Goldring (eds.), *Evolving Explanations of Development, Ecological Approaches to Organism-Environment Systems* (pp. 413–43). Washington, DC: APA Publications.

(2006). Dynamic systems research on interindividual communication: the transformation of meaning-making. *Journal of developmental processes*, 1(1), 7–30.

Fogel, A. and Garvey, A. (2007). Alive communication. *Infant Behavior and Development*, 30(2), 251–7.

Fogel, A., de Koeyer, I., Bellagamba, F.and Bell, H.(2002). The dialogical self the first two years of life: embarking on a journey of discovery. *Theory and Psychology*, 12(2), 191–205.

Fogel, A., Garvey, A., Hsu, H. C. and West-Stroming, D. (2006). *Change Processes in Relationships: A Relational-historical Approach*. Cambridge/New York: Cambridge University Press.

Fonagy, P., Gergely, G., Jurist, E. and Target, M. (2005). *Affect Regulation, Mentalization and the Development of the Self* (new edition). London: Other Press LLC.

Forman, E. A., Minick, M. and Stone, C. A. (eds.) (1993). *Contexts for Learning: Sociocultural Dynamics in Children's Development*. Oxford University Press.

Foucault, M. (1975). *Surveiller et punir. Naissance de la prison*. Paris: Gallimard.

(1986/2006). Of other places. In J. Morra and M. Smith, (eds.) (2006). *Visual Culture: Spaces of Visual Culture*, trans. J. Miskoniec (pp. 93–101). London: Routledge.

Freud, A. (1927/1974). The methods of child analysis. In *The Writings of Anna Freud*. New York: International Universities Press.

Freud, S. (1899/2001). Screen memories. In J. Strachey (ed.), *The Standard Edition of the Complete Psychological Works of Sigmund Freud*, vol. III (pp. 301–22). London: Vintage/The Hogarth Press.

(1900/1953). The interpretation of dreams. In J. Strachey (ed. and trans.), *The Standard Edition of the Complete Psychological Works of Sigmund Freud*, vols. IV–V). London: The Hogarth Press and the Institute of Psycho-analysis.

(1908/1959). Creative writers and day-dreaming. In J. Strachey (ed. and trans.), *The Standard Edition of the Complete Psychological Works of Sigmund Freud*, vol. IX (pp. 141–53). London: The Hogarth Press and the Institute of Psycho-analysis.

(1910/2001). Leonardo Da Vinci and a memory of his childhood. In J. Strachey (ed.), *The Standard Edition of the Complete Psychological Works of Sigmund Freud* vol. XIII (pp. 57–138). London: Vintage/The Hogarth Press.

(1914/2001). The Moses of Michelangelo. In J. Strachey (ed.), *The Standard Edition of the Complete Psychological Works of Sigmund Freud*, vol. XI (pp. 209–238). London: Vintage/The Hogarth Press

(1919/2001). The 'Uncanny'. In J. Strachey (ed.), *The Standard Edition of the Complete Psychological Works of Sigmund Freud*, vol. XVII (pp. 217–56). London: Vintage/The Hogarth Press.

(1927/1961). The future of an illusion. In J. Strachey (ed. and trans.), *The Standard Edition of the Complete Psychological Works of Sigmund Freud*, vol. XIII (pp. 1–56). London: The Hogarth Press and the Institute of Psycho-analysis.

Frevert, U. (1995). *Men of Honour: A Social and Cultural History of the Duel*. Cambridge: Polity Press.

Gallese, V. (2003). A neuroscientific grasp of concepts: from control to representation. *Philosophical Transactions of the Royal Society*, B, 358, 1231–40.

Gallese, V., Fadiga, L., Fogassi, L. and Rizzolatti, G. (1996). Action recognition in the premotor cortex, *Brain*, 119, 593–609.

Garvey, A. and Fogel, A. (2007). Dialogical change processes, emotions, and the early emergence of self. *International Journal for Dialogical Science*, 2(1), 51–76.

Gell, A. (1992). *Anthropology of Time*. Oxford: Berg.

Gelso, C. J. and Harbin, J. (2007). Insight, action, and the therapeutic relationship. In L. G. Castonguay and C. E. Hill (eds.), *Insight in Psychotherapy* (pp. 293–312). Washington, DC: American Psychological Association.

Georgaca, E. (2001). Voices of the self in psychotherapy: a qualitative analysis. *British Journal of Medical Psychology*, 74, 223–36.

Gergen, K. J. and Gergen, M. M.(1988). Narrative and self as a relationship. In L. Berkowitz (ed.), *Advances in Experimental Social Psychology*, vol. XXI. San Diego: Academic Press.

Gerstorf, D., Ram, N., Estabrook, R., Schupp, J., Wagner, G. G. and Lindenberger, U. (2008). Life satisfaction shows terminal decline in old age: longitudinal evidence from the German Socio-Economic Panel Study (SOEP). *Developmental Psychology*, 44, 1148–59.

Gerstorf, D., Ram, N., Röcke, C., Lindenberger, U. and Smith, J. (2008). Decline in life-satisfaction in old age: longitudinal evidence for links to distance to death. *Psychology and Aging*, 23, 154–68.

Gibson, J. J. (1986). *The Ecological Approach to Visual Perception*. Hillsdale, NJ: Lawrence Erlbaum Associates.

Giele, J. Z. and Elder, G. H. J. (1998). Life course research: development of a field. In J. Z. Giele and G. H. J. Elder (eds.), *Methods of Life Course Research: Qualitative and Quantitative Approaches* (pp. 5–27). Thousand Oaks, CA: London: Sage.

Giele, J. Z. and Elder, G. H. (eds.) (1998). *Methods of Life Course Research. Qualitative and Quantitative Approaches*. Thousand Oaks, CA/London: Sage.

Gigerenzer, G., Swijtink, Z., Porter, T., Daston, L., Beatty, J. and Krüger, L. (1989). *The Empire of Chance*. Cambridge University Press.

Gillespie, A. (2005). Malcolm X and his autobiography: identity development and self-narration. *Culture & Psychology*, 11(1), 77–88.

(2006). *Becoming Other: From Social Interaction to Self-reflection*. Greenwich, CT: Information Age Publishers.

Gillespie, A. and Zittoun, T. (2010a). Studying the movement of thought. In A. Toomela and J. Valsiner (eds.), *Methodological Thinking in Psychology: 60 years Gone Astray?* (pp. 69–88). Charlotte, NC: Information Age Publishers.

(2010b). Using resources: Conceptualising the mediation and reflective use of tools and signs, *Culture and Psychology*, 16(1), 37–62.

Gillespie, A., Cornish, F., Aveling, E. and Zittoun, T. (2008). Living with war: community resources, self-dialogues and psychological adaptation to World War II. *Journal of Community Psychology*, 36(1), 35–52.

Gilliéron, E. (1992). Cadre et processus thérapeutiques. In M. Grossen and A.-N. Perret-Clermont (eds.), *L'espace thérapeutique. Cadres et contextes* (pp. 121–36). Lausanne: Delachaux et Niestlé.

Glaveanu, V. (2010). Principles for a cultural psychology of creativity. *Culture & Psychology*, 16(2), 147–63.

Goethe, J. W. von. (1814/2008). *The Poems of Goethe*. Rockville, MD: Wildside Press LLC.

Goffman, E. (1961a). *Asylums: Essays on the Social Situation of Mental Patients and Other Inmates*. New York: Anchor books.

(1961b/1997). Social life as game. In C. Lemert and A. Branaman (eds.), *The Goffman Reader* (pp. 129–46). Malden, MA/Oxford/Victoria: Blackwell.

(1974). *Frame Analysis: An Essay on the Organization of Experience*. New York: Harper and Row.

Goldstein, J. (1999). Emergence as a Construct: History and Issues. *Emergence: A Journal of Complexity Issues in Organizations and Management*, 1(1), 49–72.

Goldstein, K. (1934/2000). *The Organism*. New York: Zone Books.

Gonçalves, M. M. and Salgado, J. (2006). Narrative therapies, psychology and the nature of empirical research. *Studia Psychologica*, 6, 171–88.

Gonçalves, M.M., Matos, M. and Santos, A. (2009). Narrative therapy and the nature of 'innovative moments' in the construction of change. *Journal of Constructivist Psychology*, 22, 1–23.

Gonçalves, M. M., Matos, M., Salgado, J., Santos, A., Mendes, I., Ribeiro, A., Cunha, C. and Gonçalves, J. (2010). Innovations in psychotherapy: tracking the narrative construction of change. In J. D. Raskin, S. K. Bridges and R. Neimeyer (eds.), *Studies in Meaning 4: Constructivist Perspectives on Theory, Practice, and Social Justice* (pp. 29–64). New York: Pace University Press.

Gonçalves, M. M., Ribeiro, A., Matos, M., Santos, A. and Mendes, I.(2010). The Innovative Moments Coding System: a new coding procedure for tracking changes in psychotherapy. In S. Salvatore, J. Valsiner, S. Strout and J. Clegg (eds.), *YIS: Yearbook of Idiographic Science 2009 – Volume II*. Rome: Fireira Publishing Group.

Gonçalves, M. M., Ribeiro, A., Conde, T., Matos, M., Martins, C. and Stiles, W. (2009). *How Bypassing Innovative Moments in Psychotherapy Contributes to Therapeutic Failure: The Role of Mutual in-feeding*. Manuscript in preparation.

Gonseth, O.Laville, Y. and Mayor, G. (eds.) (2008). *La marque jeune*. Neuchâtel: MEN.

Gordon, B. (1992). Meanings of mid-nineteenth century dress: images from New England women's writings. *Clothing and Textiles Research Journal*, 10(3), 44–52.

Gottlieb, G. (1971). *Development of Species Identification in Birds*. University of Chicago Press.

(1999). Probabilistic epigenesis and evolution. In Heinz Werner Lecture Series, 23. Worcester, MA: Clark University Press.

(2002). *Individual Development and Evolution: The Genesis of Novel Behavior*. Mahwah, NJ: Lawrence Erlbaum.

(2003). Probabilistic epigenesis of development. In J. Valsiner and K. J. Connolly (eds.), *Handbook of Developmental Psychology* (pp. 3–17). London: Sage.

(2007). Probabilistic epigenesis. *Developmental Science*, 10(1), 1–11.

Granott, N. (1998). We learn, therefore we develop: learning versus development – or developing learning? In M. C. Smith and T. Pourchot (eds.), *Adult Learning and Development: Perspectives from Educational Psychology* (pp. 15–34). Philadelphia: Lawrence Erlbaum Associates.

Grass, G. (2007). *Peeling the Onion: A Memoir*. Orlando, FL: Harcourt.

Griffin, N. and Jacquette, D. (eds.) (2009). *Russell vs. Meinong: The Legacy of 'On Denoting'*. London: Routledge.

Groos, K. (1908). *The Play of Man*. New York: D. Appleton.

Grossen, M. (1998). *La construction de l'intersubjectivité en situation de test*. Cousset (Fribourg): DelVal.

(2001). La notion de contexte: quelle définition pour quelle psychologie? Un essai de mise au point. In J. P. Bernié (ed.), *Apprentissage, développement et significations* (pp. 59–76). Bordeaux: Presses universitaires de Bordeaux.

(2010). Interaction analysis and psychology: a dialogical perspective. *Integrative Psychological and Behavioral Science*, 44(1), 1–22.

Grossen, M. and Perret-Clermont, A.-N. (eds.) (1992). *L'espace thérapeutique. Cadres et contextes*. Lausanne: Delachaux et Niestlé.

Grossen, M. and Salazar Orvig, A. (2011). Dialogism and dialogicality in the study of the self. *Culture and Psychology*, 17(4), 491–509.

Grossen, M., Zittoun, T. and Ros, J. (2012). Boundary crossing events and potential appropriation space in philosophy, literature and general knowledge. In E. Hjörne, G. van der Aalsvoort and G. de Abreu (eds.), *Learning, Social Interaction and Diversity: Exploring School Practices* (pp. 15–33). Rotterdam/Boston/Taipei: Sense Publishers.

Grossmann, R. (1974). *Meinong*. London: Routledge and Kegan Paul.

Habermas, T. (1996). *Geliebte Objekte. Symbole und Instrumente der Identitätsbildung*. Berlin/New York: Walter de Gruyter.

Habermas, T. and Bluck, S. (2000). Getting a life: the emergence of the life story in adolescence. *Psychological Bulletin*, 126, 748–69.

Hacking, I. (1999). *The Social Construction of What?* Cambridge, MA: Harvard University Press.

Haenel, Y. (2009). *Jan Karski*. Paris: Editions Gallimard.

(2010). Le recours à la fiction n'est pas seulement un droit, il est nécessaire. *Le Monde*, 26 January 2010, p. 19.

Hagestad, G. O. (1986). The transition to grandparenthood: unexplored issues. *Journal of Family Studies*, 7(2), 115–30.

Hale, H. C. (2008). The development of British military masculinities through symbolic resources. *Culture & Psychology*, 14(3), 305–32.

Halfmann, R. and Lindquist, S.(2010). Epigenetics in the extreme: prions and the inheritance of environmentally acquired traits. *Science*, 330, 629–32.

Hall, G. S. (1897). A study of fears. *American Journal of Psychology*, 8, 141–50.

(1922). *Senescence: The Last Half of Life*. London/New York: D. Appleton and Co.

Hanna, J. L. (1988). *Dance, Sex, and Gender: Signs of Identity, Dominance, Defiance, and Desire*. University of Chicago Press.

Hare, A. P. and Hare, J. R. (1996). *J. L. Moreno*. London/Thousand Oaks, CA: Sage.

Harré, R. and Gillett, G. (1994). *The Discursive Mind*. London: Sage.

Harré, R., Moghaddam, F. M., Cairnie, T. P., Rothbart, D. and Sabat, S. R. (2009). Recent advances in positioning theory. *Theory and Psychology*, 19, 5–31.

Harris, P. L. (2000). *The work of the imagination*. Oxford/Malden, MA: Wiley-Blackwell.

Hauser, R. M. (2009). The Wisconsin longitudinal study: designing a study on the life course. In G. H. J. Elder and J. Z. Giele (eds.), *The Craft of Life Course Research* (pp. 29–50). New York/London: Guilford Press.

Havighurst, R.J. (1948). *Developmental Tasks and Education*. New York: David Mc Kay.

(1961). Successful aging. *The Gerontologist*, 1(1), 8–13.

Hayes, J. A., and Cruz, J. M. (2006). On leading the horses to water: therapists, insight, countertransference and client insight. In L. G. Castonguay and C. E. Hill (eds.), *Insight in Psychotherapy* (pp. 279–92). Washington, DC: American Psychological Association.

Hecht, T. (1998). *At Home in the Street: Street Children of Northeast Brazil*. Cambridge University Press.

Heckhausen, J. and Schulz, R. (1995). A life-span theory of control. *Psychological Review*, 102, 284–304.

Hedegaard, M. and Chaiklin, S. (2005). *Radical-local teaching and learning*. Aarhus: University Press.

Hegel, G. W. (1986). *The Jena System, 1804–5: Logic and metaphysics*. Kingston: McGill-Queen's University Press.

(2001). *Vorlesungen über die Logik*. Hamburg: Felix Meiner Verlag.

(2006). Planet orbits. Translation of the 1801 dissertation by David Healan. www.hegel.net/en/v2133healan.htm.

(2008). *Lectures on logic*. Bloomington, IN: Indiana University Press.

Herbst, D.P. (1995) What happens when we make a distinction: an elementary introduction to co-genetic logic. In T. A. Kindermans and J. Valsiner (eds.), *Development of Person–Context Relations* (pp. 67–70). Hillsdale, NJ: Lawrence Erlbaum.

Hermans, H. J. M. (1996). Voicing the self: from information processing to dialogical interchange. *Psychological Bulletin*, 119, 31–50.

(2001). The dialogical self: toward a theory of personal and cultural positioning. *Culture & Psychology*, 7(3), 243–81.

(2003). The construction and reconstruction of a dialogical self. *Journal of Constructivist Psychology*, 16, 89–130.

(2004). The dialogical self: between exchange and power. In H. J. M. Hermans and G. Dimaggio (eds.), *The dialogical self in psychotherapy* (pp. 13–28). Hove and New York: Brunner-Routledge.

Hermans, H. J. M. and Hermans-Jansen, E. (1995). *Self-narratives: The Construction of Meaning in Psychotherapy*. New York: Guilford.

Hermans, H. J. M. and Hermans-Konopka, A. (2010). *Dialogical Self Theory: Positioning and Counter–Positioning in a Globalizing Society*. Cambridge University Press.

Hermans, H. J. M. and Kempen, H. J. (1993). *The Dialogical Self: Meaning as Movement*. San Diego, CA: Academic Press.

Hill, C., Castonguay, L. G., Angus, L., Arnkoff, D. B., Barber, J. B., Bohart, A. C. *et al.* (2007). Insight in psychotherapy: definitions, processes, consequences, and future directions. In L. G. Castonguay and C. E. Hill (eds.), *Insight in Psychotherapy* (pp. 441–54). Washington, DC: American Psychological Association.

Hinde, R., Perret-Clermont, A.-N. and Stevenson-Hinde, J. (eds.) (1985). *Social Relationships and Cognitive Development*. Oxford University Press.

Hodges, M. I. (2008). Rethinking time's arrow. *Anthropological Theory*, 8(4), 399–429.

Holm, C. (2006). *Amor und Psyche. Der Erfindung eines Mythos in Kunst, Wissenschaft und Alltagskultur (1765–1840)*. Munich: Deutscher Kunstverlag.

Honos-Webb, L. and Stiles, W. B. (1998). Reformulation of assimilation analysis in terms of voices. *Psychotherapy*, 35, 23–33.

Hoodfar, H. (1997). *Between Marriage and the Market: Intimate Politics and Survival in Cairo*. Berkeley, CA: University of California Press.

Houellebecq, M. (2001). *Atomised* (new edn). London: Vintage.

Houssaye, J. (2000). *Le triangle pédagogique* (3rd edn). Berne: Peter Lang.

Howe, M. L., Courage, M. L. and Rooksby, M. (2009). The genesis and development of autobiographical memory. In M. L. Courage and N. Cowan (eds.), *The Development of Memory in Infancy and Childhood* (pp. 177–96). Hove and New York: The Psychology Press.

Hummert, M. L. (1994). Stereotypes of the elderly and patronizing speech. In M. L. Hummert, J. M. Wiemann and J. F. Nussbaum (eds.), *Interpersonal Communication in Older Adulthood* (pp. 162–84). Thousand Oaks, CA: Sage.

Hundeide, K. (1991). Cultural limitations on cognitive enrichment. In *Helping Disavantaged Children* (pp. 102–117). London: Jessica Kingsley.

(2005). Socio-cultural tracks of development, opportunity situations and access skills. *Culture & Psychology*, 11(2), 241–61.

Hviid, P. (2008). 'Next year we are small, right?' Different times in children's development. *European Journal of Psychology of Education*, 2(23), 183–98.

Iacoboni, M., Molnar-Szakacs, I., Gallese, V., Buccino, G., Mazziotta, J. C. and Rizzolatti, G. (2005). Grasping the intentions of others with one's own mirror neuron system. *PLoS Biology*, 3(3), e79.

Ikegami, E. (2005). *Bonds of Civility: Aesthetic Networks and the Political Origins of Japanese Culture*. New York: Cambridge University Press.

Illeris, K. (ed.) (2009). *Contemporary Theories of Learning: Learning Theorists... in their own Words*. Routledge.

Jablonka, E. and Lamb, M. (1995). *Epigenetic Inheritance and Evolution: The Lamarckian Dimension*. New York: Oxford University Press.

Jacob, F. (1981). *Le jeu des possibles. Essai sur la diversité du vivant*. Paris: Fayard.

James, W.(1890/2007). *The principles of Psychology*, vol. II. New York: Cosimo Classic.

Jensen, T. K. (2005). The interpretation of signs of child sexual abuse. *Culture & Psychology*, 11(4), 469–98.

Jeune, B. and Vaupel, J. W. (eds.) (1999). *Validation of Exceptional Longevity*. Monographs on Populations Aging 6, Odense University Press.

Johnston, T. D. and Edwards, L. (2002). Genes, interactions, and the development of behavior. *Psychological Review*, 109(1), 26–34.

Jones, T. H. (1925). *Education in East Africa*. New York: Phelps-Stokes Foundation.

Jöreskog, K. G. and Goldberger, A. (1975). Estimation of a model with multiple indicators and multiple causes of a single latent variable, *Journal of the American Statistical Association*, 70, 631–9.

Josephs, I. E. (1998). Constructing one's self in the city of the silent: dialogue, symbols, and the role of 'as if' in self development. *Human Development*, 41, 180–95.

Josephs, I. and Valsiner, J. (1998). How does autodialogue work? Miracles of meaning maintenance and circumvention strategies. *Social Psychology Quarterly*, 61, 68–83.

Josephs, I., Valsiner, J. and Surgan, S. E. (1999). The process of meaning construction – dissecting the flow of semiotic activity. In J. Brandstadter and R. M. Lerner (eds.), *Action and Development: Theory and Research through the Life Span*. London: Sage Publications.

Joyce, J. (1964). *A Portrait of the Artist as a Young Man*. New York: Viking.

Jurgensen. G. (2008). *J'ai grandi dans les salles obscures*. Paris: JCLattès.

Jurgrau, T. (ed.) (1991). *Story of My Life: The Autobiography of George Sand*. Albany, New York: SUNY Press.

Kanogo, T. (2005). *African Womanhood in Colonial Kenya 1900–50*. Oxford: James Currey.

Kauffman, S. A. (1993). *The Origins of Order: Self-Organization and Selection in Evolution*. New York: Oxford University Press.

(2000). *Investigations*. Oxford University Press.

Kennedy, D. (1994). *Sexy Dressing Inc*. Cambridge, MA: Harvard University Press.

Klein, M. (1932/1975). *The Psycho-analysis of Children*. New York: Delacorte.

Klemp, N. *et al*. (2008). Plans, takes, and *mis*-takes. *Outlines: Critical Social Studies*, 10(1), 4–21.

Knowledge *noun*, in *The Oxford Dictionary of English* (rev. edn). Oxford University Press. Available online from *Oxford Reference Online* www.oxfordreference.com/views/ENTRY.html?subview=Main&entry=t140.e41822, retrieved 30 September 2009.

Kohler, A. (in preparation), Raisonnements qualitatifs en physique au carrefour des technologies, des expérimentations et des interactions sociales. PhD dissertation, Neuchâtel, University of Neuchâtel.

Komatsu, K. (2010). Emergence of young children's presentational self in daily conversation and its semiotic function. *Human Development*, 53, 208–28.

Koop, V. (2007). *Dem Führer ein Kind Schenken. Die SS-Organisation Lebensborn e. V.* Köln: Böhlau.

Kopping, K. P.(1997). *The Games of Gods and Man: Essays in Play and Performance*. Hamburg: LIT Verlag.

Korteweg, A. and Yudakul, G.(2009). Islam, gender and immigrant integration: boundary drawing in discourses on honor killing in the Netherlands and Germany. *Ethnic and Racial Studies*, 32(2), 218–38.

Koslofsky, C. (2002). From presence to remembrance: the transformation of memory in the German Reformation. In A. Confino and P. Fritzsche (eds.), *The Work of Memory* (pp. 25–38). Urbana, IL: University of Illinois Press.

Kovalevskaya, S. (1978). *A Russian Childhood*. New York: Springer.

Kuehling, S. (2005). *Dobu: Ethics of Exchange on a Massim Island, Papua New Guinea*. Honolulu, HI: University of Hawaii Press.

Kusenbach, M. (2003). Street phenomenology: the Go-Along as ethnographic research tool. *Ethnography*, 4(3), 455–85.

Lakoff, G. and Johnson, M. (1980). *Metaphors we Live by*. University of Chicago Press.

Lamarck, J. (1809). *Philosophie Zoologique*. Paris: De l'Impremerie Dumenil-Leseur.

Lamiell, J. T. (1998). 'Nomothetic' and 'idiographic': contrasting Windelband's understanding with contemporary usage. *Theory and Psychology*, 8 (1), 23–38.

(2003). *Beyond Individual and Group Differences*. Thousand Oaks, CA: Sage.

(2009). Reviving person-centered inquiry in psychology: why its erstwhile dormancy? In J. Valsiner, P. Molenaar, M. Lyra and N. Chaudhary (eds.), *Dynamic Process Methodology in the Social and Developmental Sciences* (pp. 31–43). New York: Springer.

Lanzmann, C. (2009). *Le lièvre de Patagonie*. Paris: Editions Gallimard.

(2010a). 'Jan Karski' de Yannick Haenel. Un faux roman. *Marianne*, 23 January 2010. Retrieved 31 January, 2010, from www.marianne2.fr/Jan-Karski-de-Yannick-Haenel-un-faux-roman_a184324.html.

(2010b). Non, Monsieur Haenel, je n'ai en rien censuré le témoignage de Jan Karski. *Le Monde*, 31 January – 1 February, 2010, p. 16.

Larkin, P. (1953/2003). 'Continuing to live', in Larkin, P. (2003). *Collected Poems*, ed. A. Thwaite. London: Faber and Faber.

LaRossa, R. and LaRossa, M. M. (1981). *Transition to Parenthood*. Beverly Hills: Sage Publications.

Laslett, P. (1996). *A Fresh Map of Life* (2nd edn). London: Weidenfeld.

(1999) The bewildering history of the history of longevity. In B. Jeune and J. W. Vaupel (eds.), *Validation of Exceptional Longevity*. Monographs on Populations Aging 6. Odense University Press.

Latour, B. and Woolgar, S. (1986). *Laboratory Life* (2nd edn). Princeton University Press.

Lave, J. and Wenger, E. (1991). *Situated Learning: Legitimate peripheral participation*. Cambridge University Press.

Lawrence, J. A. and Valsiner, J. (1993). Conceptual roots of *internalization*: from transmission to transformation. *Human Development*, 36, 150–67.

Lawrence, P. A. (2008). Retiring retirement. *Nature*, 453, 588–590 (28 May 2008). Retrieved July 2010, from www.nature.com/nature/journal/v453/n7195/full/453588a.html.

Lazarus, R. S. (1993). From psychological stress to the emotions: a history of changing outlooks. *Annual Review of Psychology*, 44(1), 1–22.

Lehr, U. and Thomae, H. (1993). Coping in longitudinal perspective. In G. L. Van Heck, P. Bonaiuto, I. J. Deary and W. Nowack (eds.), *Personality Psychology in Europe*, vol. IV. (pp. 367–87). Tilburg University Press.

Leiman, M. (2002). Toward semiotic dialogism: the role of sign mediation in the dialogical self. *Theory and Psychology*, 12, 221–35.

Leiman, M. and Stiles, W. B. (2001). Dialogical sequence analysis and the zone of proximal development as conceptual enhancements to the assimilation model: the case of Jan revisited. *Psychotherapy Research*, 11, 311–30.

Lembo, R. (2000). *Thinking through Television*. Cambridge University Press.

Lemon, B. W., Bengtson, V. L. and Petersen, J. A. (1972). An exploration of the activity theory of aging: activity types and life expectation among in-movers to a retirement community. *Journal of Gerontology*, 27(4), 511–23.

Leontiev, A. N. (1975). *Deiatel'nost, soznanie, lichnost'*. Moscow: Politizdat.

Levinson, D. J. (1978). *The Seasons of a Man's Life*. New York: Ballantine Books.

Lévi-Strauss, C. (1962/1966). *The Savage Mind*, trans Weidenfeld and Nicolson Ltd. The University of Chicago Press.

Levy, R., Ghisletta, P., Le Goff, J., Spini, D. and Widmer, E. (eds.) (2005). *Towards an Interdisciplinary Perspective on the Life Course*. Amsterdam: Elsevier.

Lewes, G. H. (1875). *Problems of Life and Mind*. London, Trübner.

Lewin, K. (1926/1951). Intention, Will, and Need, trans. D. Rapaport. In D. Rapaport (ed.), *Organization and Pathology of Thought* (pp. 95–153). New York: Columbia University Press.

(1936). *Principles of Topological Psychology*. New York and London: McGraw Hill.

(1939). Field theory and experiment in social psychology: concepts and methods. *American Journal of Sociology*, 44, 868–96.

(1942). Field theory and learning. In N. B. Henry (ed.), *The Forty-First Yearbook of the National Society for the Study of Education*. Part II: *The Psychology of Learning* (pp. 215–42). Bloomington, IN: Public School Publishing Co.

(1943). Defining the field at a given time. *Psychological Review*, 50, 292–310.

(1951). *Field Theory in the Social Sciences*. New York: Harper and Brothers.

Lickliter, R. (in press). Biological development: theoretical approaches, techniques, and key findings. In P. Zelazo (ed.), *Oxford Handbook of Developmental Psychology*. New York: Oxford University Press.

Lickliter, R. and Honeycutt, H. (2010). Rethinking epigenesis and evolution in light of developmental science. In M. S. Blumberg, J. H. Freeman and S. R. Robinson (eds.), *Oxford Handbook of Developmental Behavioral Neuroscience* (pp. 30–47). New York: Oxford University Press.

Lightfoot, C. (1997). *The Culture of Adolescent Risk-taking*. New York: Guilford Press.

Linell, P. (2009). *Rethinking Language, Mind, and World Dialogically: Interactional and Contextual Theories of Human Sense-Making*. Charlotte, NC: Information Age Publishers.

Littell, J. (2009). *The Kindly Ones*. London: Chatto and Windus.

Little, D. (1995). Learning as dialogue: the dependence of learner autonomy on teacher autonomy. *System*, 23(2), 175–81.

Lobato, J. (2006). Alternative perspectives on the transfer of learning: history, issues, and challenges for future research. *Journal of the Learning Sciences*, 15(4), 431–49.

Lotman, J. (2005). On the semiosphere. *Sign System Studies*, 33(1), 205–29.

Lotman, J. M. (1984). *O semiosfere. Trudy po Znakovym Systemam* (Tartu), 17, 5–23. [Also in J. M. Lotman, *Izbrannye stati*. vol. I (pp. 11–24). Tallinn: Aleksandra, 1992.]

(1993). Kul'tura kak subject I sama-sebe object. In J. M. Lotman, *Izbrannye stati*, vol. III (pp. 368–75). Tallinn: Aleksandra.

(2000). *Universe of the Mind: A Semiotic Theory of Culture* trans. A. Shukman. Bloomington and Indianapolis: Indiana University Press.

Lotze, H. (1864). *Mikrokosmus. Ideen zur Naturgeschichte und Geschichte der Menschheit*, vol. III Leipzig: S. Hirzel.

Luria, A. R. (1976). *Cognitive Development*. Cambridge, MA: Harvard University Press.

(1987). *The Mind of a Mnemonist: A Little Book About a Vast Memory*. Cambridge, MA: Harvard University Press.

Lysaker, P. H. and Lysaker, J. T. (2006). A typology of narrative impoverishment in schizophrenia: implications for understanding the process of establishing and sustaining dialogue in individual psychotherapy. *Counseling Psychology Quarterly*, 18, 57–68.

Macek, I. (2000). War within: everyday life in Sarajevo under siege. *Acta Universitatis Upsaliensus, Uppsala Studies in Cultural Anthropology*, 29, 1–313.

Magnusson, D., Bergman, L. R., Rudinger, G. and Torestad, B. (eds.) (1994). *Problems and Methods in Longitudinal Research: Stability and Change*. Cambridge/New York: Cambridge University Press.

Mainardi, P. (2003). *Husbands, Wives, and Lovers: Marriage and its Discontents in Nineteenth-century France*. New Haven, CT: Yale University Press.

Mandler, J. (1984). *Stories, Scripts, and Scenes: Aspects of Schema Theory*. Hillsdale, NJ: Erlbaum.

Mann, T. (1929/2000). Mario and the Magician. In *Mario and the Magician and other stories*, trans. H. T. Lower-Porter (pp. 113–57). London: Vintage.

Marková, I. (2005). *Dialogicality and Social Representations: The Dynamics of Mind*. Cambridge University Press.

(2006). On the 'inner alter' in dialogue. *International Journal for Dialogical Science*, 1(1), 125–47.

Marková, I., Linell, P., Grossen, M. and Salazar Orvig, A. (2007). *Dialogue in Focus Groups: Exploring Socially Shared Knowledge*. London/Oakville: Equinox.

Markus, H. and Nurius, P. (1986). Possible selves. *American Psychologist*, 41, 954–69.

Marquez, G. G. (2003). *Viver para contá-la*. Lisbon: D. Quixote.

Marsico, G., Komatsu, K. and Iannaccone, A. (2011). *Crossing Boundaries: Intercontextual Dynamics between Family and School.* Charlotte, NC: Information Age Publishers.

Märtsin, M. (2010). Identity in dialogue. *Theory and Psychology*, 20(3), 436–50.

Matos, M., Santos, A., Gonçalves, M. M. and Martins, C. (2009). Innovative moments and change in narrative therapy. *Psychotherapy Research*, 19, 68–80.

Maturana, H. R. and Varela, F. C. (1987). *The Tree of Knowledge: The Biological Roots of Human Understanding.* Boston, MA: Shambhala.

Mayer, K. U. (2009). New directions in life course research. *American Review of Sociology*, 35, 413–33.

Mbembe, A. (2003). Necropolitics. *Public Culture*, 15(1), 11–40.

McAdams, D. P. (1993). *The Stories we Live by: Personal Myths and the Making of the Self.* New York: William Morrow.

(2001). The psychology of life stories. *Review of General Psychology*, 5(2), 100–22.

(2005). *The Person: A New Introduction to Personality Psychology* (4th edn). New York: John Wiley and Son.

McTaggart, J. E. (1908). The unreality of time. *Mind*, New Series, 17(68), 457–74.

Mead, G. H. (1934/1967). *Mind, Self and Society, from the standpoint of a Social Behaviorist.* University of Chicago Press.

Mehan, H., Hertweck, A. and Meihls, J.L. (1986). *Handicapping the Handicapped: Decision Making in Students' Educational Careers.* Stanford University Press.

Meinong, A. (1904). *Untersuchungen zur Gegenstandstheorie und Psychologie.* Leipzig: J. A. Barth.

Meira, L., Gonçalves, M., Salgado, J. and Cunha, C. (2009). Everyday life change: contribution to the understanding of daily human change. In M. Todman (ed.), *Self-Regulation and Social Competence: Psychological Studies in Identity, Achievement and Work–family Dynamics* (pp. 145–54). Athens: ATINER.

Mellor, D. H. (1981). *Real Time.* Cambridge University Press.

Menon, U. and Shweder, R. A. (1994). Kali's tongue: cultural psychology and the power of 'shame' in Orissa. In S. Kitayama and H. Markus (eds.), *Emotion and Culture* (pp. 237–80). Washington, DC: American Psychological Association.

Mercer, N. and Littleton, K. (2007). *Dialogue and the Development of Children's thinking.* Oxon/New York: Routledge.

Messer, S. B. and McWilliams, N. (2007). Insight in psychodynamic therapy: theory and assessment. In L. G. Castonguay and C. E. Hill (eds.), *Insight in Psychotherapy* (pp. 9–30). Washington, DC: American Psychological Association.

Mildenberger, F. (2007). *Umwelt als Vision: Leben und Werk Jakob von Uexkülls (1864–1944).* Stuttgart: Franz Steiner Verlag.

Miller, G. A., Galanter, E. and Pribram, K. H. (1960). *Plans and the Structure of Behavior.* New York: Holt, Rinehart, and Winston.

Milnor, J. (1985). On the concept of attractor. *Communications of Mathematical Physics*, 99, 177–95.

Molenaar, P. C. M. (2004), A manifesto on psychology as idiographic science: bringing the person back into scientific psychology, this time forever, *Measurement: Interdisciplinary research and perspectives*, 2, 201–18.

Molenaar, P. C. M., Huizinga, H. M. and Nesselroade, J. R. (2003). The relationship between the structure of inter-individual and intra-individual variability. In U. Staudinger and U. Lindenberger (eds.), *Understanding Human Development* (pp. 339–60). Dordrecht: Kluwer.

Monk, G. and Gehart, D. R. (2003). Sociopolitical activist or conversational partner? Distinguishing the position of the therapist in narrative and collaborative therapies. *Family Process*, 42, 19–30.

Moody, H. R. (2002). Conscious aging: a strategy for positive development in later life. In J. Ronch and J. Goldfield (eds.), *Mental Wellness in Aging: Strength-based Approaches*. New York: Human Services Press.

Moreno, J. L. (1947). Sociometry and the social psychology of G. H. Mead. *Sociometry*, 10, 350–3.

(1953). *Who Shall Survive: Foundations of Sociometry, Group Psychotherapy and Sociodrama* (2nd edn). Beacon, NY: Beacon House.

Mortimer, J. T. and Shanahan, M. J. (eds.) (2004). *Handbook of the Life Course*. New York: Springer.

Moscovici, S. (1961/2008). *Psychoanalysis: Its Image and Its Public*. ed. G. Duveen, trans. D. Macey. Cambridge: Polity Press.

(1976). *Society against Nature: The Emergence of Human Societies*. Atlantic Highlands, NJ: Humanities Press.

(1984). Introduction. Le domaine de la psychologie sociale. In S. Moscovici (ed.), *Psychologie sociale* (pp. 5–22). Paris: Presses universitaires de France.

(1985). Innovation and minority influence. In S. Moscovici, G. Mugny and E. van Avermaet (eds.), *Perspectives on Minority Influence* (pp. 9–51). Paris/Cambridge: Maison des sciences de l'homme/Cambridge University Press.

Moshenska, G. (2008). A hard rain: children's shrapnel collections in the Second World War. *Journal of Material Culture*, 13(1), 107–25.

Mulholland, N. (ed.) (2008). *The Psychology of Harry Potter: An Unauthorized Examination of the Boy who Lived*. Dallas, TX: Benbella Books.

Muller Mirza, N. (2001). *Apprendre dans les Réseaux d'échanges de savoirs. Analyses au sein du réseau de Strasbourg*. Dossiers de psychologie, 51. Université de Neuchâtel.

Muller Mirza, N. and Perret-Clermont, A.-N. (1999). Negotiating identities and meanings in the transmission of knowledge: analysis of interactions in the context of a Knowledge Exchange Network. In J. Bliss, R. Säljö and P. Light (eds.), *Learning Sites, Social and Technological Resources for Learning* (pp. 47–60). Amsterdam: Pergamon.

(2009). *Argumentation and Education: Theoretical Foundations and Practices*. Dordrecht: Springer.

Münsterberg, H. (1898). Psychology and history. *Psychological Review*, 6(1), 1–31.

Neimeyer, R. A., Herrero, O. and Botella, L. (2006). Chaos to coherence: psychotherapeutic integration of traumatic loss. *Journal of Constructivist Psychology*, 19, 127–46.

Nelson, K. (2007). *Young Minds in Social Worlds: Experience, Meaning, and Memory*. Cambridge, MA/London: Harvard University Press.

Nelson, K. (ed.) (2006). *Narratives from the Crib* (2nd edn). Cambridge, MA: Harvard University Press.

Newman, S., Faux, R. and Larimer, B. (1996). Children's views on aging: their attitudes and values. *The Gerontologist*, 37, 412–17.

Nicolet, M. (1995). *Dynamiques relationnelles et processus cognitifs: Étude du marquage social chez des enfants de 5 à 9 ans*. Lausanne, Paris: Delachaux et Niestlé.

Niemiec, R. M. and Wedding, D. (2008). *Positive Psychology at the Movies: Using Films to Build Virtues and Character Strengths*. Cambridge, MA: Hogrefe and Huber.

O'Hanlon, B. (1998). Possibility therapy: an inclusive, collaborative, solution-based model of therapy. In M. F. Hoyt (ed.), *The Handbook of Constructive Therapies: Innovative Approaches from Leading Practitioners* (pp. 137–58). San Francisco: Jossey-Bass.

Ohnuki-Tierney, E. (2006). *Kamikaze Diaries*. University of Chicago Press.

Omer, H. and Alon, N. (1997). *Constructing Therapeutic Narratives*. Northvale, NJ: Jason Aronson.

Oppenheimer, P. (ed. and trans.). (1995). *Till Eulenspiegel: His Adventures*. Oxford: Oxford Paperbacks.

Osatuke, K. and Stiles, W. B. (2006). Problematic internal voices in clients with borderline features: an elaboration of the assimilation model. *Journal of Constructivist Psychology*, 19, 287–319.

Osatuke, K., Glick, M. J., Gray, M. A., Reynolds, D. J., Humpreys, C. L., Salvi, L. M. and Stiles, W. B. (2004). Assimilation and narrative. Stories as meaning bridges. In L. E. Angus and J. McLeod (eds.), *The Handbook of Narrative Psychotherapy: Practice, Theory, and Research* (pp. 193–210). London: Sage.

Ouspensky, P. D. (1949/2001). *In Search of the Miraculous: The Definitive Exploration of G.I. Gurdjieff's Mystical Thought and Universal View*. New York: Harvester Books.

Overton, W. E. (2002). Development across the lifespan. In R. M. Lerner, M. A. Easterbrooks, J. Mistry and I. B. Weiner (eds.), *Handbook of Psychology* (vol. VI, pp. 13–42). New York: John Wiley and Sons.

Pandya, V. (2000). Making the other: vignettes of violence in Andamanese culture. *Critique of Anthropology*, 20(4), 359–91.

Panksepp, J. (1998). *Affective Neuroscience*. New York: Oxford University Press.

Pasupathi, M., Mansour, E. and Brubaker, J. R. (2007). Developing a life story: constructing relations between self and experience in autobiographical narratives. *Human Development*, 50, 85–110.

Peirce, C. S. (1892). The law of mind. *The Monist*, 2(4), 533.

(1901/1958). 'On the logic of drawing history from ancient documents especially from testimonies', in *Collected Papers* (pp. 89–153). Cambridge, MA: Harvard University Press.

Peiss, K. (1998). *Hope in a Jar: The Making of America's Beauty Culture*. New York: Holt.

Pereira, S. and Diriwächter, R. (2008). Morpheus awakened: Microgenesis in daydreams. In E. Abbey and R. Diriwächter (eds.), *Innovative Genesis: Microgenesis and the Constructive Mind in Action* (pp. 157–83). Charlotte, NC: Information Age Publishers.

Perkins, N. and Salomon, G. (1990). *The Science and Art of Transfer. Transfer at risk*. Retrieved 30 September 2009, from http://learnweb.harvard.edu/alps/thinking/docs/trancost.htm.

(1994). Transfer of learning. In T. Husen and T. Postelwhite (eds.), *International Handbook of Educational Research* (2nd edn, vol. XI, pp. 6452–7). Oxford: Pergamon Press.

Perret-Clermont, A.-N. (1980). *Social Interaction and Cognitive Development in Children*. London: Academic Press.

(2004). The thinking spaces of the young. In A.-N. Perret-Clermont, C. Pontecorvo, L. Resnick, T. Zittoun and B. Burge (eds.), *Joining Society: Social Interactions and Learning in Adolescence and Youth* (pp. 3–10). New York/Cambridge: Cambridge University Press.

Perret-Clermont, A.-N., and Barrelet, J. (eds.) (2008). *Jean Piaget and Neuchâtel: The Learner and the Scholar*. Hove/New York: Psychology Press.

Perret-Clermont, A.-N., Carugati, F. and Oates, J. (2004). A socio-cognitive perspective on learning and cognitive development. In J. Oates and A. Grayson (eds.), *Cognitive and Language Development in Children* (pp. 305–32). Oxford: The Open University, Blackwell Publishing.

Perret-Clermont, A.-N, Pontecorvo, C., Resnick, L., Zittoun, T. and Burge, B. (eds.) (2004). *Joining Society: Learning and Development in Adolescence and Youth*. Cambridge/New York: Cambridge University Press.

Perriault, J. (1989). *La logique de l'usage. Essai sur les machines à communiquer*. Paris: Flammarion.

Piaget, J. (1937/1955). *The Child's Construction of Reality*, trans. M. Cook. London: Routledge and Kegan Paul.

(1945/1951). *Play, Dreams, and Imitation in Childhood*. New York, Norton.

(1945/1976). *La formation du symbole chez l'enfant. Imitation, jeu et rêve, image et représentation* (6th edn). Neuchâtel, Delachaux et Niestlé.

(1952). *The Origins of Intelligence in Children*, trans. M. Cook. New York: International University Press.

(1974/1980). *Adaptation and Intelligence: Organic Selection and Phenocopy*. London: University of Chicago Press.

Pieterse, J. N. (2009). Globalization and human integration: We are all migrants. In *Globalization and Culture: Global Mélange*. Lanham, MD and Plymouth, UK: Rowman and Littlefield.

Pike, K. L. (ed.) (1967). *Language in Relation to a Unified Theory of Structure of Human Behavior* (2nd edn.). The Hague: Mouton.

Pizzarroso, N. and Valsiner, J. (2009). Why developmental psychology is not developmental: Moving towards abductive methodology. Paper presented at the Conference of the Society of Research in Child Development. Denver, CO.

Popper, K. (1972). *Conjectures and Refutations*. London: Routledge and Kegan Paul.

Prediger, S. (2008). The relevance of didactic categories for analysing obstacles in conceptual change: revisiting the case of multiplication of fractions. *Learning and Instruction*, 18(1), 3–17.

Prigogine, I. and Stengers, I. (1984). *Order out of Chaos: Man's New Dialogue with Nature*. New York: Bantam.

Psaltis, C. and Duveen, G. (2006). Social relations and cognitive development: the influence of conversation type and representations of gender. *European Journal of Social Psychology*, 36, 407–30.

Psaltis, C., Duveen, G. and Perret-Clermont, A.-N. (2009). The social and the psychological: structure and context in intellectual development. *Human Development*, 52(5), 291–312.

Ramanujan, A. K. (1991). Toward a counter-system: women's tales. In A. Appadurai, F. J. Korom and M. A. Mills (eds.), *Gender, Genre, and Power in South Asian Expressive Traditions* (pp. 33–55). Philadelphia: University of Pennsylvania Press.

Ramanujan, A. K., Rao, V. N. and Shulman, D. (1994). *When God is a Customer: Telugu Courtesan Songs by Ksetrayya and Others*. Berkeley, CA: University of California Press.

Raudsepp, M. (2005). Why is it so difficult to understand the theory of social representations? *Culture & Psychology*, 11(4), 455–68.

Rentsch, T. (1997). Aging as becoming oneself: a philosophical ethics of late life. *Journal of Aging Studies*, 11, 263–71.

Ribeiro, A. P. and Gonçalves, M. M. (2011). Maintenance and transformation of problematic self-narratives: a semiotic-dialogical approach. *Integrative Psychological and Behavioral Science*, 45, 281–303.

Richards, R. J. (2008). *The Tragic Sense of Life: Ernst Haeckel and the Struggle over Evolutionary Thought*. University of Chicago Press.

Richardson, K. (2008). How dynamic systems have changed our minds. In A. Fogel, B. J. King, and S. G. Shanker (eds.), *Human Development in the Twenty-First Century* (pp. 25–40). Cambridge University Press.

Rizzolatti, G. and Sinigaglia, C. (2008). *Mirrors in the Brain: How our Minds Share Actions and Emotions*. New York: Oxford University Press.

Roberts, K. (2008). *Youth in Transition: Eastern Europe and the West*. London: Palgrave Macmillan.

Robine, J.-M. and Allard, M. (1999). Jeanne Calment: validation of the duration of her life. In B. Jeune and J. W. Vaupel (eds.), *Validation of Exceptional Longevity*. Monographs on Populations Aging 6. Odense University Press.

Roche, D. (1994). *The Culture of Clothing*. Cambridge University Press.

Rochex, J.-Y. (1998). *Le sens de l'expérience scolaire*. Paris: Presses universitaires de France.

(2004). La notion de rapport au savoir. Convergences et débats théoriques. *Pratiques Psychologiques*, 10, 93–106.

Rogoff, B. (1990). *Apprenticeship in Thinking*. New York: Oxford University Press.

(2003). *The Cultural Nature of Human Development*. New York: Oxford University Press.

Rönnqvist, L. and von Hofsten, C. (1994). Neonatal finger and arm movments as determined by a social and an object context. *Early Development and Parenting*, 3(2), 81–94.

Rosa, A. (2007). Acts of Psyche: actuations as synthesis of semiosis and action. In J. Valsiner and A. Rosa (eds.), *The Cambridge Handbook of Sociocultural Psychology* (pp. 205–37). Cambridge University Press.

Rossi, S., De Capua *et al.* (2008). Distinct olfactory cross-modal effects on the human motor system. *PLoS*, 3(2), e1702 www.plosonline.org.

Rothbaum, F., Weisz, J. R. and Snyder, S. (1982). Changing the world and changing the self: a two-process model of perceived control. *Journal of Personality and Social Psychology*, 42, 5–37.

Rotter, J. (1966). Generalized expectancies for internal versus external control of reinforcements. *Psychological Monographs*, 80, 609.

Rowe, J. W. and Kahn, R. L. (1987). Human aging: usual and successful. *Science*, 237, 143–9.

(1998). *Successful aging*. New York: Pantheon Books.

Rudolph, L. (2006). The fullness of time. *Culture & Psychology*, 12(2), 169–204.

Ryan E. B., Giles H., Bartolucci G. and Henwood, K. (1986). Psycholinguistic and social psychological components of communication by and with the elderly. *Language and Communication*, 6, 1–24.

Salazar-Sutil, N. (2008). Maradona Inc: Performance politics off the pitch. *International Journal of Cultural Studies*, 11(4), 441–58.

Salgado, J. and Cunha, C. (2012). Positioning microanalysis: The development of a dialogical-based method for idiographic psychology. In S. Salvatore, A. Gennaro and J. Valsiner (eds.), *Making Sense: Generating Uniqueness*. Yearbook of Idiographic Science, vol. IV. Charlotte, NC: Information Age Publishers.

Salgado, J. and Ferreira, T. (2005). Dialogical relationships as triads: implications for the dialogical self theory. In P. K. Oles and H. J. M. Hermans (eds.), *The Dialogical Self: Theory and Research*. Lublin, Poland: Wydawnictwo KUL.

Salgado, J. and Gonçalves, M. (2007). The dialogical self: social, personal, and (un) conscious. In A. Rosa and J. Valsiner (eds.), *The Cambridge Handbook of Sociocultural Psychology*. Cambridge University Press.

Salgado, J. and Hermans, H. J. M. (2005). The return of subjectivity: from a multiplicity of selves to the dialogical self. *E-Journal of Applied Psychology*, 1, 3–13.

Salgado, J. and Valsiner, J. (2010). Dialogism and the eternal movement within communication. In. C. Grant (ed.), *Beyond Universal Pragmatics* (pp. 101–22). Bern: Peter Lang Publishing.

Säljö, R. (2003). Epilogue: from transfer to boundary-crossing. In T. Tuomi-Gröhn and Y. Engeström (eds), *Between School and Work: New Perspectives on Transfer and Boundary-crossing* (pp. 311–21). Amsterdam: Pergamon.

Salomon, G. (1997). No distribution without individuals' Cognition: a dynamic interactional view. In G. Salomon (ed.), *Distributed Cognitions: Psychological and Educational Considerations* (pp. 111–38). Cambridge/New York: Cambridge University Press.

Salvatore, S., Valsiner, J., Strout-Yagodzinski, S. and Clegg, J. (eds.), (2008). *YIS: The Yearbook of Idiographic Science*, vol. I. Rome: Fireira Publishing.

Sarbin, T. R. (1986). The narrative and the root metaphor for psychology. In T. R. Sarbin (ed.), *Narrative Psychology: The Storied Nature of Human Conduct* (pp. 3–21). New York: Praeger.

Sartre, J.-P. (1936/1989). *L'imagination* (3rd edn). Paris: Presses universitaires de France.

Sato, T., Hidaka, T. and Fukuda, M. (2009). Depicting the dynamics of living the life: the trajectory equifinality model. In J. Valsiner, P. Molenaar, M. Lyra and N. Chaudhary (eds.), *Dynamic Methodologies in the Social Sciences* (pp. 217–40). New York: Springer.

Sato, T., Hidaka, T., Kido, A., Nishida, M. and Akasaka, M. (2011). The authentic culture of living well: pathways to psychological well-being. In J. Valsiner (ed.), *The Oxford Handbook of Psychology and Culture*. New York: Oxford University Press.

Sato, T., Yasuda, Y., Kido, A., Takada, S. and Valsiner, J. (2006). The discovery of the trajectory equifinality Model. *Qualitative Research in Psychology*, 5, 255–75 (in Japanese).

Sato, T., Yasuda, Y., Kido, A., Arakawa, A., Mizoguchi, H. and Valsiner, J. (2007). Sampling reconsidered: idiographic science and the analyses of personal life trajectories. In J. Valsiner and A. Rosa (eds.), *Cambridge Handbook of Sociocultural Psychology* (pp. 82–106). New York: Cambridge University Press.

Schachter, D. L., Eich, J. E. and Tulving, E. (1978). Richard Semon's theory of memory. *Journal of Verbal Learning and Verbal Behavior*, 17, 721–43.

Schiff, B. (2006). The promise (and challenge) of an innovative narrative psychology. *Narrative Inquiry*, 16, 19–27.

Schiffauer, W. (1999). *Islamism in the Diaspora: The Fascination of Political Islam among Second Generation German Turks*. Working Paper. Oxford: Transnational Communities Program.

Schulz, R. and Heckhausen, J. (1996). A life-span model of successful aging. *American Psychologist*, 51, 702–14.

Schunk, D. H. (2003). *Learning Theories: An Educational Perspective* (4th edn.). Upper Saddle River, NJ/Columbus, Ohio: Prentice Hall.

Schütz, A. (1944/1964). The stranger: an essay in social psychology. In *Collected Papers*. Vol. II: *Studies in Social Theory* (pp. 91–105). The Hague: Martinus Nijhoff.

Schütz, A. and Luckmann, T. (1973). *The Structures of the Life-world*. Evanson, IL: Northwestern University Press.

Schwarz, M. (2009). Is psychology based on a methodological error? *IPBS: Integrative Psychological and Behavioral Science*, 43(2), 185–213.

Scribner, S. and Cole, M. (1981/1986). *Psychology of Literacy*. Cambridge, MA: Harvard University Press.

Segal, H. (1991). *Dream, Phantasy and Art*. London: Routledge.

Semerari, A., Carcione, A., Dimaggio, G., Nicolò, G. and Procacci, M. (2004). A dialogical approach to patients with personality disorders. In H. J. M. Hermans and G. Dimaggio (eds.), *The Dialogical Self in Psychotherapy* (pp. 220–34). Hove and New York: Brunner-Routledge.

Sewertzoff, A. N. (1929). Direction of evolution. *Acta zoologica*, 10, 59–141.

Shakespeare, W. (2008). *The Oxford Shakespeare: As You Like It*, ed. A. Brissenden. Oxford: Oxford Paperbacks.

Shanahan, M. J. and S. M. Hofer (2005). Social context in gene-environment interactions: retrospect and prospect. *Journals of Gerontology Series B – Psychological Sciences and Social Sciences*, 60, 65–76.

Shanahan, M. J. and Porfelli, E. (2002). Integrating the life course and life-span: formulating research questions with dual points of entry. *Journal of Vocational Behavior*, 61, 398–406.

Sherif, M. and Sherif, C. W. (1956). *An Outline of Social Psychology*. New York: Harper and Brothers.

(1901/1959a). The aesthetic significance of the face. In K. H. Wolff (ed.), *Georg Simmel, 1858–1918* (pp. 276–81). Columbus, OH: The Ohio State University Press.

Simmel, G. (1904/1959b). Fashion. In K. H. Wolff (ed.), *Georg Simmel, 1858–1918* (p. 294–319). Columbus, OH: The Ohio State University Press.

(1908). Vom Wesen der Kultur. *Österreichische Rundschau*, 15, 36–42.

Simmel, G. (1908/1971a). Subjective culture. In G. Simmel, *Individuality and Social Forms*. University of Chicago Press.

(1911/1971b). The adventurer. In G. Simmel, *Individuality and Social Forms*. University of Chicago Press.

Simon, H. A. (1990). Invariants of human behavior. *Annual Review of Psychology*, 41, 1–19.

Singer, D. G. and Singer, J. L. (2005). *Imagination and Play in the Electronic Age*. Cambridge, MA and London: Harvard University Press.

Sluzki, C. (1992). Transformations: a blueprint for narrative changes in therapy. *Family Process*, 31, 217–30.

Smedslund, J. (1995). Psychologic: common sense and the pseudoempirical. In J. A. Smith., R. Harré and L. van Langenhove (eds.), *Rethinking Psychology* (pp. 196–206). London: Sage.

Smith, B. (1988). Gestalt theory: an essay in philosophy. In B. Smith (ed.), *Foundations of Gestalt Theory* (pp. 11–81). Munich: Philosophia Verlag.

(1999). Truth and the visual field. In J. Petitot, F. J. Varela, B. Pachoud and J. M. Roy (eds.), *Naturalizing Phenomenology* (pp. 317–29). Stanford, CA: Stanford University Press.

Smith, L. B., Thelen, E., Titzer, R. and McLin, D. (1999). Knowing in the context of acting: the task dynamics of the A-not-B error. *Psychological Review*, 106, 235–60.

Smythe, W. E. (2005). On the psychology of 'As If'. *Theory and Psychology*, 15, 3, 283–303.

Soanes, C. and Stevenson, A. (eds.). (2005). *The Oxford Dictionary of English* (rev. edn). Oxford University Press.

Sokol Chang, R. (ed.) (2009). *Relating to Environments: A New Look at Umwelt*. Charlotte, NC: Information Age Publishers.

Sovran, T. (1992). Between similarity and sameness. *Journal of Pragmatics*, 18, 4, 329–44.

Special Section in *Science*, 2010, vol. 330, pp. 611–630 (29 October).

Star, S. L. and Griesemer, J. R. (1989). Institutional ecology, 'translations' and boundary objects: amateurs and professionals in Berkeley's Museum of Vertebrate Zoology, 1907–39. *Social Studies of Science*, 19(3), 387– 420.

Staudinger, U.(2000). Viele Gründe sprechen dagegen, und totzdem geht es vielen Menschen gut. Das Paradox des subjektiven Wohlbefindens. [Many reasons speak against it, yet many people feel good: the paradox of subjective well-being]. *Psychologische Rundschau*, 51, 185–97.

Stephen, M. (1982). 'Dreaming is another power!': The social significance of dreams among the Mekeo of Papua New Guinea. *Oceania*, 53(2), 106–22.

Stern, D. N. (1985). *The Interpersonal World of the Infant: A View from Psychoanalysis and Developmental Psychology*. New York: Basic Books.

(2004). *The Present Moment in Psychotherapy and Everyday Life*. New York: W. W. Norton and Co.

Stiles, W. B. (1999). Signs and voices in psychotherapy. *Psychotherapy Research*, 9, 1–21.

Stiles, W. B., Elliot, R. *et al.* (1990). Assimilation of problematic experiences by clients in psychotherapy. *Psychotherapy*, 27, 411–20.

Strauss, C. and Quinn, N. (1997). A *Cognitive Theory of Cultural Meaning*. Cambridge University Press.

Strawbridge, W. J., Wallhagen, M. I. and Cohen, R. D. (2002). Successful aging and well-being: Self-report compared with Rowe and Kahn. *Gerontologist*, 42, 727–33.

Sullivan, H. S. (1953). *The Interpersonal Theory of Psychiatry*. New York: Norton.

Sully, J. (1896). *Studies of Childhood*. New York: D. Appleton.

Sundarasaradula, D. and Hasan, H. (2005). A unified open systems model for explaining organisational change. In D. Hart and S. Gregor (eds.), *Information System Foundations: Constructing and Criticising*. Canberra: ANUE Press.

Sutherland, P. and Crowther, J. (eds.) (2006). *Lifelong Learning: Concepts and Contexts*. Oxford/New York: Routledge.

Szasz, T. (1965/1988). *The Ethics of Psychoanalysis: The Theory and Method of Autonomous Psychotherapy* (3rd edn). New York: Syracuse University Press.

Takiura, S. (1978). Is time real? In Y. Nitta and H. Tatematsu (eds.), *Japanese Phenomenology* (pp. 79–88). Dordrecht: D. Reidel.

Tanggaard, L. (2008). Learning at school and work: boundary crossing, strangeness and legitimacy in apprentices' everyday life. In V. Aarkrog and C. Helms Jorgensen (eds.), *Divergence and Convergence in Education and Work* (pp. 219–37). Bern: Peter Lang.

Thelen, E. and Smith, L. B. (1994). *A Dynamic Systems Approach to the Development of Cognition and Action*. Cambridge, MA: MIT Press.

Thomae, H. (1963). Ageing and problems of adjustment. *International Social Science Journal*, 15(3), 366–76.

(1968). *Das Individuum und seine Welt*. Göttingen: Hogrefe-Verlag.

(1970). Theory of aging and cognitive theory of personality. *Human Development*, 13, 1–16. [In German: Thomae, H. (1971). Die Bedeutung einer kognitiven Persönlichkeitstheorie für die Theorie des Alterns. *Zeitschrift für Gerontologie*, 4, 8–18.]

(1983). *Alternsstile und Alternsschicksale. Ein Beitrag zur Differentiellen Gerontologie*. Bern: Huber.

(2002). Psychologische Modelle und Theorien des Lebenslaufs [Psychologcial models and theories of the life span]. In G. Jüttemann and H. Thomae (eds.),

*Persönlichkeit und Entwicklung* (p. 12–45) [Personality and development]. Weinheim: Beltz.

Thomas, W. I. (1923). *The Unadjusted Girl*. Boston: Little, Brown and Co.

Thompson, N. S. and Valsiner, J. (2002). Doesn't a dance require dancers? *Behavioral and Brain Sciences*, 25(5), 641–2.

Thorson, J. A. and Davis, R. E. (2000). Relocation of the institutionalized aged. *Journal of Clinical Psychology*, 56(1), 131–8.

Tiberghien, A. (2003). Des connaissances naïves aux savoirs scientifiques. In M. Kail and M. Fayol (eds.), *Les sciences cognitives et l'école* (pp. 353–413). Paris: Presses universitaires de France.

Tisseron, S. (2003). *Comment Hitchcock m'a sauvé la vie*. Paris: Armand Colin.

(2005). La vérité de l'expérience de fiction, *L'Homme*, 3–4 (175–6), 131–45.

(2006). *La Honte. Psychanalyse d'un lien social* (2nd edn). Paris: Dunod.

(2013). The reality of experience of fiction. In A. Kohn(ed.), *Little Madnesses: Winnicott, Transitional Phenomenon and Cultural Experience* (pp. 121–342). London: Towris.

Toda, M. and Higuchi, K. (1994). Common sense, emotion, and chatting and their roles in interpersonal interaction. In J. Siegfried (ed.), *The Status of Common Sense in Psychology* (pp. 208–44). Norwood, NJ: Ablex.

Tomlinson, J. (2007). *The Culture of Speed*. London: Sage.

Toomela, A. (2007). Culture of science: strange history of the methodological thinking in psychology. *IPBS: Integrative Psychological and Behavioral Science*, 41(1), 6–20.

(2008). Variables in psychology: a critique of quantitative Psychology. *IPBS: Integrative Psychological and Behavioral Science*, 42(3), 245–65.

(2009). How methodology became a toolbox – and how it escapes from that box. In J. Valsiner, P. Molenaar, M. Lyra and N. Chaudhary (eds.), *Dynamic Process Methodology in the Social and Developmental Sciences* (pp. 45–66). New York: Springer.

(2011). Travel into a fairy land: a critique of modern qualitative and mixed methods psychologies. *Integrative Psychological and Behavioral Science*, 45(1), 21–47.

Toomela, A. and Valsiner, J. (eds.) (2010). *Methodological Thinking in Psychology: Have 60 Years Gone Astray?* Charlotte, NC: Information Age Publishers.

Toulmin, S. (1990). *Cosmopolis: The Hidden Agenda of Modernity*. University of Chicago Press.

Trevarthen, C. (1977). Descriptive analyses of infant communicative behavior. In H. R. Schaffer (ed.), *Studies in Mother–Infant Interaction* (pp. 227–70). London: Academic Press.

Trevarthen, C. and Hubley, P. (1978). Secondary intersubjectivity: confidence, confiding, and acts of meaning in the first year. In A. Lock (ed.), *Action, Gesture, and Symbol: The Emergence of Language* (pp. 183–229). London: Academic Press.

Tsuji, Y. (2006). Railway time and rubber time. *Time & Society*, 15(2–3), 177–95.

Tulving, E. (1972). Episodic and semantic memory. In E. Tulving and W. Donaldson (eds.), *Organization of Memory* (pp. 381–403). New York: Academic Press.

Tulviste, P. (1991). *The cultural-historical development of verbal thinking*. Commack, NY: Nova Science Publishers.

Tuomi-Gröhn, T., Engeström, Y. and Young, M. (2003). From transfer to boundary-crossing between school and work as a tool for developing vocational education: an Introduction. In T. Tuomi-Gröhn and Y. Engeström (eds.), *Between School and Work: New Perspectives on Transfer and Boundary-crossing* (pp. 1–17). Oxford: Elsevier.

Turner, V. (1969/1995). *The Ritual Process: Structure and Anti-structure*. New York: Aldine de Gruyter.

(1973). The center out there: pilgrim's goal. *History of Religions*, 12, 191–230.

(1982). *From Ritual to Theatre: the Human Seriousness of Play*. New York: PAJ Publications.

Usher, J. and Neisser, U. (1993). Childhood amnesia and the beginnings of memory for four early life events. *Journal of Experimental Psychology: General*, 122, 155–65.

Vaihinger, H. (1911/1922). *Die Philosophie des als ob. System der Theoretischen, Praktischen und Religiosen Fiktionen der Menschheit auf Grund Eines Idealistischen Positivismus, mit einem Anhang uber Kant und Nietzsche*. Leipzig: Felix Meiner.

(1911/1935). *The philosophy of 'as if'. A system of the theoretical, practical and religious fictions of mankind*, trans. C. K. Ogden. London: Kegan Paul.

Valsiner, J. (1987). *Culture and the Development of Children's Action: A Cultural-Historical Theory of Developmental Psychology*. New York: John Wiley & Sons.

(1997). *Culture and the Development of Children's Action: A Theory of Human Development* (2nd edn.). Chichester: Wiley.

(1998). *The Guided Mind: A Sociogenetic Approach to Personality*. Cambridge, MA: Harvard University Press.

(1999). I create you to control me: a glimpse into basic processes of semiotic mediation. *Human Development*, 42(1), 26–30.

(2000). *Culture and Human Development*. London: Sage.

(2001). Process structure of semiotic mediation in human development. *Human Development*, 44, 84–97.

(2002). Forms of dialogical relations and semiotic autoregulation within the self. *Theory and Psychology*, 12, 251–65.

(2003). Sensuality and sense: cultural construction of the human nature. *Human Affairs* (Bratislava), 13, 151–62.

(2005). Affektive Entwicklung im kulturellen Kontext. In J. B. Asendorpf (ed.), *Enzyklopädie der Psychologie.* Vol. III*: Soziale, emotionale und Persönlichkeitsentwicklung* (pp. 677–728). Göttingen: Hogrefe.

(2006). The street. *Khora II*, 5, 69–84 [Escuela Técnica Superior de Arquitectura de Barcelona].

(2007a). Human development as migration: striving towards the unknown. In L. M. Simao and J. Valsiner (eds), *Otherness in Question: Labyrinths of the Self* (pp. 349–78). Charlotte, NC: Information Age Publishers.

(2007b). *Culture in Minds and Societies*. New Delhi: Sage.

(2007c). Constructing the internal infinity: dialogic structure of the internalization/externalization process. *International Journal of Dialogical Science*, 2, 1, 207–21.

(2008a). Constraining one's self within the fluid social worlds. Paper presented at the 20th Biennial ISSBD meeting, Würzburg.

(2008b). Ornamented worlds and textures of feeling: the power of abundance. *Outlines: Critical Social Studies*, 10(1), 67–78.

(2009a). Integrating psychology within the globalizing world. *IPBS: Integrative Psychological and Behavioral Science*, 43(1), 1–16.

(2009b). A persistent innovator: James Mark Baldwin rediscovered. In J. Valsiner (ed.), *James Mark Baldwin's Genetic Theory of Reality*. New Brunswick, NJ: Transaction Publishers.

(2009c). Baldwin's quest: a universal logic of development. In J. W. Clegg (ed.), *The Observation of Human Systems: Lessons from the History of Anti-reductionistic Empirical Psychology* (pp. 45–82). New Brunswick, NJ: Transaction Publishers.

(2011). Constructing the vanishing present between the future and the past / Construyendo el desvanecimiento del presente entre el futuro y el pasado. *Infancia y Aprendizaje*, 34(2), 141–50.

Valsiner, J. and Cabell, K. (2011). Self making through synthesis. In H. Hermans and T. Gieser (eds.), *Handbook of Dialogical Self Theory*. Amsterdam: John Benjamin.

Valsiner, J. and Han, G. (2008). Where is culture within the dialogical perspectives on the self? *International Journal for Dialogical Science*, 3, 1–8.

Valsiner, J. and Rosa, A.(eds.) (2007). *The Cambridge Handbook of Sociocultural Psychology*. Cambridge/New York: Cambridge University Press.

Valsiner, J. and van der Veer, R. (2000). *The Social Mind*. New York: Cambridge University Press.

Valsiner, J., Molenaar, P. C., Lyra, M. C. and Chaudhary, N. (2009). *Dynamic Process Methodology in the Social and Developmental Sciences*. New York: Springer Verlag.

Van der Veer, R. and Valsiner, J. (1993). *Understanding Vygotsky: A Quest for Synthesis*. London: Wiley-Blackwell.

Van Geert, P. (2003). Dynamic systems approaches and modeling of developmental processes. In J. Valsiner and K. J. Connolly (eds.), *Handbook of Developmental Psychology* (pp. 640–72). London: Sage Publications.

Van Gennep, A. (1981). *Les rites de passage. Etude systématique des rites de la porte et du seuil, de l'hospitalité et de l'adoption, de la grossesse et de l'accouchement, de la naissance, de l'enfance, de la puberté, de l'initiation, de l'ordination, du couronnement, des fiançailles et du mariage, des funérailles, des saisons, etc.* Paris: Editions A. and J. Piccard.

Van Orden, K. (2005). *Music, Discipline, and Arms in Early Modern France*. University of Chicago Press.

Vannini, P. and McCright, A. (2004). To die for: the semiotic seductive power of the tanned body. *Symbolic Interaction*, 27(3), 309–32.

Vavrik, E. (2010). *Nacktbadestrand*. Vienna: edition a.

Vedeler, D. and Garvey, A. (2009). Dynamic methodology in infancy research. In J. Valsiner, C. M. Molenaar, C. D. P. Lyra and N. Chaudhary (eds.),

*Dynamic Process Methodology in the Social and Developmental Sciences* (pp. 431–53). New York: Springer.

Vergnaud, G. (2009). The theory of conceptual fields. *Human Development*, 52(2), 83–94.

Vermersch, P. (2006). *L'entretien d'explicitation* (5th edn). Paris: ESF Editeur.

Von Foerster, H. (1984). On constructing a reality. In P. Watzlawick, (ed.). *The Invented Reality* (pp. 41–62). New York: W. W. Norton.

Von Niedehäusern, S. (2009). La manière dont le Père Noël vit et disparaît pour les enfants. Unpublished MA dissertation, Institute of Psychology and Education, University of Neuchâtel.

Von Uexküll, J. J., and Kriszat, G. (1934). *Streifzüge durch die Umwelten von Tieren und Menschen*. Berlin: Julius Springer.

Vygotsky, L. S. (1933/1966). Play and its role in the mental development of the child. *Soviet Psychology*, 12(6), 62–76.

(1934/1986). *Thought and Language*. Cambridge, MA: MIT Press.

(1971). *The Psychology of Art*. Cambridge, MA and London: MIT Press.

(1978/1997). Interaction between learning and development. In M. Gauvain and M. Cole (eds.), *Readings on the Development of Children* (2nd edn, pp. 29–36). New York: W. H. Freeman and company.

Waddington, C. H. (1975). *The Evolution of an Evolutionist*. Ithaca, NY: Cornell University Press.

Wagner, G. P. (2004). The embryo of a dialogue. *Science*, 305, 1405–6.

Wagoner, B. (2008). Narrative form and content of remembering. *IPBS: Integrative Psychological and Behavioral Science*, 42(3), 315–23.

(2011). Culture in constructive remembering. In J. Valsiner (ed.), *The Oxford Handbook of Psychology and Culture*. New York: Oxford University Press.

Walker, A. C. (2002). A strategy for active ageing. *International Social Security Review*, 55, 121–39.

Watzlawick, P., Weakland, J. and Fisch, R. (1974). *Change: Principles of Problem Formation and Problem Resolution*. New York: Norton.

Weisstein, E. W. (2010). From MathWorld – A Wolfram Web Resource.

Wells, C. G. (1999). *Dialogic inquiry*. Cambridge University Press.

Werner, H. (1957). The concept of development from a comparative and organismic point of view. In D. B. Harris (ed.), *The Concept of Development* (pp. 125–48). Minneapolis: University of Minnesota Press.

Werquin, P. (2007). *Terms, Concepts and Models for Analysing the Value of Recognition Programs*. Vienna: OECD Organisation for Economic Co-operation and Development. Retrieved 21 September 2009, from www.oecd.org/dataoecd/33/58/41834711.pdf.

(2010). *Recognising non-formal and informal learning: Islands of good practice*, Paris: OECD. Retrieved 1 March 2011, from www.oecd.org/dataoecd/22/12/44600408.pdf.

West, L., Alheit, P., Andersen, A. S. and Merrill, B. (eds.) (2007). *Using Biographical and Life History Approaches in the Study of Adult and Lifelong Learning: European Perspectives*. Bern: Peter Lang.

White, M. (2007). *Maps of Narrative Practice*. New York: Norton.

White, M. and Epston, D. (1990). *Narrative Means to Therapeutic Ends*. New York: Norton.

Wickner, W. and Scheckman, R. (2005). Protein translocation across biological membranes. *Science*, 310, 1452–5.

Wiener, C., Strauss, A., Fageraugh, S. and Suczek, B. (1979). Trajectories, biographies, and evolving medical technology science. Labor and delivery and the intensive care nursery. In A. Strauss and J. Corbin (eds.) (1997). *Grounded Theory in Practice* (pp. 229–50). Thousand Oaks CA: Sage.

Wikipedia contributors, (2010). 'Chaos theory'. Page Version ID: 365736253. Retrieved 3 June 2010, from http://en.wikipedia.org/w/index.php?title=Chaos_theory&oldid=365736253.

Windelband, W. (1904). *Geschichte und Naturwissenschaft*. Strasbourg: Heitz and Mündel.

(1904/1998). History and natural science. *Theory & Psychology*, 8(1), 5–22.

Winnicott, D. W. (1958/1990). The capacity to be alone. In D. W. Winnicott, *The Maturational Processes and the Facilitating Environment* (reprints, pp. 29–36). London: Karnac Books.

(1967/1986). The concept of a healthy individual. In D. W. Winnicott, *Home is Where we Start from: Essays by a Psychoanalyst* (pp. 21–38). London: Penguin Books.

(1971/1991). *Playing and Reality*. London: Routledge.

(1989). *Psychoanalytic Explorations*. London: Karnac Book.

Winther-Lindqvist, D. (2009). Children's Development of Social identity in Transitions. Unpublished PhD Thesis, University of Copehnagen.

Witasek, S. (1901). Zur psychologischen Analyse der ästhetischer Einfühlung. *Zeitschrift für Psychologie und Physiologie der Sinnesorgane*, 25, 1–49.

Wong, P. T. P. and Watt, L. M. (1991). What types of reminiscence are associated with successful aging. *Psychology and Aging*, 6, 272–9.

Woolf, V. (1929/1989). *A Room of One's Own*. San Diego/New York/London: A HarvestBook. Harcourt, Inc.

Wörringer, W.(1963). *Abstraction and Empathy: A Contribution to the Psychology of Style*. New York: International Universities Press.

Wortham, S. (2001). *Narratives in Action: A Strategy for Research and Analysis*. New York: Teachers College Press.

Yamamoto, T. and Takahashi, N. (2007). Money as a cultural tool mediating personal relationships. In J. Valsiner and A. Rosa (eds.), *Cambridge Handbook of Sociocultural Psychology* (pp. 508–23). New York: Cambridge University Press.

Yamada, Y. and Kato, Y. (2006). Images of circular time and spiral repetition: the generative life cycle model. *Culture & Psychology*, 12(2), 143–60.

Yang, N. D. (1998). Exploring a new role for teachers: promoting learner autonomy. *System*, 26(1), 127–35.

Zapf, W. (1984). Individuelle Wohlfahrt: Lebensbedingungen und wahrgenommene Lebensqualität. In W. Glatzer and W. Zapf (eds.), *Lebensqualität in der Bundesrepublik. Objektive Lebensbedingungen und subjektives Wohlbefinden* [Quality of life in the Federal Republic of Germany: Objective living conditions and subjective well-being] (pp. 13–26). Frankfurt am Main: Campus Verlag.

Zittoun, T. (2004a). Preapprenticeship as a transitional space. In A. -N. Perret-Clermont, C. Pontecorvo, L. Resnick, T. Zittoun and B. Burge (eds.) *Joining Society: Social Interaction and Learning in Adolescence and Youth* (pp. 153–76). Cambridge/New York: Cambridge University Press.

(2004b). Symbolic competencies for developmental transitions: The case of the choice of first names. *Culture & Psychology*, 10(2), 131–61.

(2004c). Memorials and semiotic dynamics. *Culture & Psychology*, 10(4), 477–95.

(2005). *Donner la vie, choisir un nom. Engendrements symboliques* [Giving life, choosing a name. Symbolic begetting]. Paris: L'Harmattan.

(2006a). *Insertions. A quinze ans, entre échecs et apprentissage* [Insertions. Being fifteen, from failure to apprenticeship]. Bern: Peter Lang.

(2006b). *Transitions: Development through symbolic resources*. Coll. Advances in Cultural Psychology: Constructing Development. Greenwich (CT): InfoAge.

(2006c). Difficult secularity: Talmud as symbolic resource. *Outlines: Critical social studies*, 8(2), 59–75.

(2007a). Dynamics of interiority. In L. Simão and J. Valsiner (eds.), *Otherness in Question: Development of the Self, Advances in Cultural Psychology: Constructing Development* (pp. 187–214). Greenwich (CT): InfoAge.

(2007b). The role of symbolic resources in human lives. In J. Valsiner and A. Rosa (eds.), *Cambridge Handbook of Socio-Cultural Psychology* (pp. 343–61). Cambridge University Press.

(2008a). Development through transitions. *European Journal of Psychology of Education*, 23(2), 165–82.

(2008b). Janet's emotions in the whole of human conduct. In R. Diriwaechter and J. Valsiner (eds.), *Striving for the Whole: Creating Theoretical Synthesis* (pp. 192–228). Piscataway: Transaction Publishers.

(2008c). La musique pour changer la vie. Usages de connaissances, dynamiques de reconnaissance. *Education and Sociétés*, 22(2), 43–55.

(2008d). Sign the gap: dialogical self in disrupted times. *Studia Psychologica*, 6 (8), 73–89.

(2009). Dynamics of life-course transitions: a methodological reflection. In J. Valsiner, P. Molenaar, M. Lyra and N. Chaudhary (eds.), *Dynamic process methodology in the social and developmental sciences* (pp. 405–30). New York: Springer.

(2010). How does an object become symbolic? Rooting semiotic artefacts in dynamic shared experiences. In B. Wagoner (ed.), *Symbolic Transformations: The Mind in Movement through Culture and Society* (pp. 173–92). London: Routledge.

(2012a). Life course. In J. Valsiner (ed.), *Handbook of Culture and Psychology* (pp. 513–35). Oxford University Press.

(2012b). On the emergence of the subject. *Integrative Psychological and Behavioral Science*, 46(3) 259–73.

Zittoun, T. (in press). Trusting for learning. In P. Linell and I. Marková (eds.), *Trust and language*. Charlotte, NC: Information Age Publishers.

Zittoun, T. and Gillespie, A. (2012). Using diaries and self-writings as data in psychological research. In E. Abbey and S. Surgan (eds.), *Developing Methods in Psychology*, series 'History and Theory of Psychology' (pp. 1–26). New Brunswick, NJ/London, UK: Transaction Publishers.

Zittoun, T., Baucal, A., Cornish, F. and Gillespie, A. (2007). Collaborative research, knowledge and emergence. *Integrative Psychological and Behavioral Science*, 41(2), 208–17.

Zittoun, T., Cornish, F., Gillespie, A. and Aveling, E.-L. (2008). Using social knowledge: a case study of a diarist's meaning making during World War II. In W. Wagner, T. Sugiman and K. Gergen (eds.), *Meaning in Action: Constructions, Narratives and Representations* (pp. 163–79). New York: Springer.

Zittoun, T., Duveen, G., Gillespie, A., Ivinson, G. and Psaltis, C. (2003). The uses of symbolic resources in transitions. *Culture & Psychology*, 9(4), 415–48.

Zola, E. (1890). *Le roman expérimental.* Paris: Charpentier. Available online for instance http://lettres.tice.ac-orleans-tours.fr/php5//coin_prof/realisme/roman-experimental.htm, accessed 26 May 2010.

# Index